READINGS IN TRIAL ADVOCACY AND THE SOCIAL SCIENCES

A Four-Volume Anthology of Scholarly Articles

Series Editor

ROBERT M. KRIVOSHEY

Ohio State University College of Law

Series Contents

VOLUME

4

INSTRUCTIONS, VERDICTS, AND JUDICIAL BEHAVIOR

Edited with introductions by

ROBERT M. KRIVOSHEY

Routledge
Taylor & Francis Group
New York London

First published 1994 by Garland Publishing, Inc.

This edition published 2013 by Routledge
711 Third Avenue, New York, NY 10017, USA
2 Park Square, Milton Park, Abingdon, Oxon OX14 4RN

Routledge is an imprint of the Taylor & Francis Group, an informa business

Library of Congress Cataloging-in-Publication Data

Instructions, verdicts, and judicial behavior / edited with an introduction by Robert M. Krivoshey.
p. cm. — (Readings in trial advocacy and the social sciences ; v. 4)
ISBN 0-8153-1422-1 (alk. paper)
1. Instructions to juries—United States. 2. Verdicts—United States. 3. Judicial process—United States. 4. Nonverbal communication (Psychology)—United States. I. Krivoshey, Robert M. (Robert Martin), 1942– . II. Series.
KF8984.A75I57 1994
347.73'758—dc20
[347.307758] 93-32631
CIP

To the Memory of My Father
Max Krivoshey

CONTENTS

Series Introduction

"... Therefore, a competent number of sensible and upright jurymen, chosen by lot from among those of the middle rank, will be found the best investigators of truth, and the surest guardians of public justice."

Blackstone, Commentaries on the Common Law

"In all criminal prosecutions, the accused shall enjoy the right to a speedy and public trial, by an impartial jury of the State and district wherein the crime shall have been committed, which district shall have been previously ascertained by law. . . ."

Sixth Amendment to the United States Constitution

"In Suits at common law, where the value in controversy shall exceed twenty dollars, the right of trial by jury shall be preserved, and no fact tried by a jury, shall be otherwise re-examined in any Court of the United States, than according to the rules of the common law."

Seventh Amendment to the United States Constitution

The origin of the right to trial by jury is shrouded in the historical past. Some historians trace its origin to Saxon or Norman practice; others to early Scandinavian tribunals or even Germanic custom. Whatever its origin in England, however, the reception of the common law by the American colonists insured that it would become an essential feature of American views of their own liberties. The trial of John Peter Zenger for libel in 1734 demonstrated the power of colonial juries to defy what they considered the tyranny of the Crown and its Governors. Ultimately, the First Continental Congress in 1774 declared it "a great and inestimable privilege" and ended up condemning the King in the Declaration of Independence for depriving Americans of that benefit. In order to guarantee that trial by jury would be a bulwark against arbitrary governmental power, it was embedded in the Bill of Rights to the United States Constitution. Although its meaning and application have been the subject of countless cases since its adoption, there can hardly be any doubt that it will remain the primary vehicle for the settlement of disputes in the foreseeable future.

It is only recently, however, that jury trials have been the subject of systematic study. Within the past twenty-five years, psychologists, sociologists, and speech communication experts have applied the basic techniques of the social sciences to the study of jury trials and their outcomes. Some of these studies have cast doubt on many long-cherished notions of the practicing bar, while others have enhanced our knowledge and understanding of the most effective means of persuasion and communication. These studies have been published in a vast array of publications, ranging from the Journal of Applied Psychology to the Southern Speech Communication Journal, hence making access difficult for scholars, students, attorneys, and others interested in how the social sciences have modified our views of the jury trial process.

Recently, books for practicing attorneys or for sociology and criminal justice courses have synthesized new research, and called attention to its implications for the jury trial process. However, these books' citations do not meet the immediate needs of the scholar interested in examining the original study. This series offers sourcebooks containing over one hundred of the most significant articles from over fifty journals, to increase our understanding of courtroom dynamics.

The volumes in this series match the phases of a jury trial. The first volume on the formation and behavior of juries, includes articles covering such issues as jury research, jury decision making, juror bias, jury selection, and extrinsic factors influencing jury verdicts. The second volume covers issues as diverse as nonverbal communication, the use of language, and the effects of the opening statement on mock juror verdicts. The third volume focuses on presentation of evidence and includes articles on the impact of the physical appearance of attorneys and witnesses, special issues involved in rape cases and the use of child witnesses, eyewitness identification, expert testimony, and the effects of different types of evidence. The final volume raises issues ranging from ability of jurors to understand judicial instructions to the ability of attorneys to predict the outcome of pending litigation.

The series was made possible through the help of many people, most notably Professor Philip Sorensen of the Socio-Legal Center of the Ohio State University College of Law and Joseph Murray, my research assistant. Professor David Goldberger, director of the clinical programs, was always generous with his time and Professor Barbara Snyder provided crucial encouragement. Professor Michael Saks of the University of Iowa made invaluable recommendations. Finally, Professor Goldie Shabad, my wife and the editor's editor, provided the one gift without which this could never have been completed; time.

Introduction

Jurors make the determination as to what facts can be ascertained. It is for the judge to instruct them as to the law that they are to apply to the facts. Obviously, since jurors are not lawyers, the instructions provided by the court must be comprehensible in order for them to apply the law competently. Lawyers, trained in the power of words, have long believed that those used to explain the law can be crucial to the outcome. They will often submit specific instructions to be read by the court to the jury and appellate courts will frequently reverse jury verdicts if the instructions are not accurate statements of the law. It is thus assumed by all that the precise wording of the instructions can be determinative of the outcome. This assumption is borne out by at least one study indicating that the number of guilty verdicts may significantly increase if a lax definition of reasonable doubt is given. The questions raised by social scientists concern the extent of the efficacy and importance of jury instructions and whether jurors actually understand the instructions read to them. In addition, issues such as whether limiting instructions have the desired effect or whether particular instructions on a specific issue in the trial make a difference have been raised by psychologists and communication experts. For example, will a specific instruction outlining the dangers inherent in eyewitness testimony increase juror skepticism concerning that testimony?

Jury instructions, however, are only one of the issues examined in this volume. Articles are also included that explore problems related to specific types of trials and verdicts. These include those inherent in severed or joined trials, the biases involved in multiple offense cases, a systematic examination of mock jury deliberations in the award of damages as well as an examination of the influence of expert testimony in determining damages.

Finally, an article is included on the ability of attorneys to predict their success at trial. One of the great changes in the legal profession in the past fifteen years has been the growing success of Alternative Dispute Resolution or Mediation. Inundated by cases, the court system has been looking for ways to alleviate its case load and resolve disputes short of jury trial. The increase in mediation attempts has largely been successful and will no doubt grow in the future. While this series has been concerned with issues involved in trial advocacy, this article on lawyers' ability to predict their success has been included because such prediction has an impact on the decision of the trial attorney to settle, mediate or litigate the case.

The last section concerns judicial behavior. If it is true that a majority of human communication is nonverbal and that the most respected and authoritative person in the courtroom is the judge, it should not come as a surprise that the judge's nonverbal communication may indicate to the jury his evaluation of the evidence. His body posture, gesticulations and eye contact will be sending cues to the jury even though it is essential that the trial judge appear impartial. Although the articles chosen here provide an outstanding introduction to the issue, it is recognized that more research in this area needs to be done.

This volume is organized in the following manner:

A. Jury Instructions (6 articles)

B. Verdicts (6 articles)

C. Judicial Behavior (2 articles)

Journal of Personality and Social Psychology
1979, Vol. 37, No. 10, 1877–1887

On the Requirements of Proof: The Timing of Judicial Instruction and Mock Juror Verdicts

Saul M. Kassin and Lawrence S. Wrightsman
University of Kansas

At the close of a trial, the judge instructs the jury that the defendant is presumed innocent, that the burden of proof is on the prosecution, and that guilt must be established beyond a reasonable doubt. In view of criticisms that the judge's charge has no effect on jury decisions, the present study examined whether the timing of judicial instruction mediates its efficacy. One hundred seven mock jurors watched a 1-hour videotape of a trial and were instructed by the judge either before the evidence, after the evidence, or not at all. Results for posttrial measures indicated that although the timing manipulation had no significant effect on the standards of reasonable doubt adopted by subjects, those who were instructed before the evidence viewed the defendant as less likely to have committed the crime and demonstrated a lower conviction rate than subjects in the instructions-after and no-instructions groups. Results for a series of mid-trial judgments of 54 subjects further indicated that preinstructed subjects were less likely to convict throughout the trial. These findings are discussed, and their implications for procedural reform in the courtroom are noted.

In trials by jury, the judge is obligated to instruct jurors in both general and case-specific matters of law. These instructions serve a number of functions: The judge orients jurors in their task, outlines the undisputed facts and issues of the case, explains the relevant law, and informs jurors about procedural matters (McBride, 1969). From the defendant's perspective, perhaps the most crucial of the mandatory instructions is that concerning the "requirements of proof" (LaBuy, 1963). Specifically, the accused is entitled to the instruction that he or she is presumed innocent, that the burden of proof is on the prosecution, and that all elements of the crime must be proven to a constitutional standard of "beyond a reasonable doubt."

Although the potential importance of the judge's charge is widely recognized (McCart, 1964), its actual effectiveness is a subject of controversy. On the one hand, the courts assume that jurors understand their instructions, use them in making decisions, and are acutely sensitive to even minor variations in wording. Thus, attorneys often request specific instructions, appellate courts have occasionally reversed verdicts on the basis of an improperly worded instruction, and many states currently favor the practice of having judges recite a preapproved pattern instruction in order to ensure standardization. Experimental support for the effect of variations in instructional content has recently been obtained. Kerr et al. (1976) presented mock jurors with one of three definitions of reasonable doubt: one that described a lax criterion of reasonableness (i.e., "you need not be absolutely sure that the defendant is guilty to find him guilty," p. 286), one that described an extremely stringent criterion (i.e., "if you are not sure and certain of his guilt, you must

This research was conducted while the first author was on a postdoctoral fellowship at the University of Kansas and was supported in full by Faculty Research Grant 3401 to the second author. We would also like to thank Martin F. Kaplan and two anonymous reviewers for their helpful comments on the manuscript.

Requests for reprints should be addressed to Saul M. Kassin, who is now at the Department of Psychological Sciences, Purdue University, West Lafayette, Indiana 47907.

find him not guilty," p. 286), and one in which reasonable doubt was not defined. As it turned out, these varying definitions significantly influenced both individual and group verdicts—a lax criterion resulted in a high conviction rate, whereas a stringent one produced a low rate of conviction. Subjects for whom reasonable doubt was not explicated fell between these extremes. This study thus demonstrated that verdicts are indeed influenced by the reasonable doubt element of the requirements-of-proof instruction.

On the other hand, it has been suggested by legal scholars (Frank, 1949) and researchers (Sealy & Cornish, 1973) that these instructions have little effect on jurors' verdicts. One common criticism is that because they are written in statutory language, the instructions are often confusing to laypersons untrained in the law (Elwork, Sales, & Alfini, 1977). In fact, one study revealed that 40% of 375 sampled jurors reported that they did not understand their judge's instruction (Hervey, 1947). A second criticism is aimed at the timing of the judge's charge. Although the procedure is not fixed by law, the jury is typically instructed at the close of the trial presentation, that is, after the evidence has been presented. Although it is possible that this sequence increases the salience of the instruction and its availability for recall during deliberation,[1] a number of sources (e.g., McBride, 1969) have questioned the utility of an instruction that is given at a stage where jurors might have already decided on a verdict. Kalven and Zeisel (1966) noted that jurors often form very definite opinions about a defendant's guilt or innocence before the close of the trial. Accordingly, Judge E. Barrett Prettyman (1960) argued the following:

> It makes no sense to have a juror listen to days of testimony only then to be told that he and his conferees are the sole judges of the facts, that the accused is presumed to be innocent, that the government must prove guilt beyond a reasonable doubt, etc. What manner of mind can go back over a stream of conflicting statements and alleged facts, recall the intonations, the demeanor, or even the existence of the witnesses, and retrospectively fit all these recollections into a pattern of evaluation and judgment given him for the first time after the events; the human mind cannot do so. . . . Why should not the judge, when the jury is sworn, then and there tell them the rules of the game. (p. 1066)

In view of the flexibility in courtroom procedure and the potential importance of a judge's charge to the jury, the absence of research on temporal factors associated with the instructions is surprising (Elwork, Sales, & Alfini, 1977, is an exception). After all, order effects in the perception of unfolding behavior sequences have repeatedly been noted in both person perception (Jones et al., 1968) and jury contexts (Walker, Thibaut, & Andreoli, 1972). In the latter study, Walker et al. (1972) varied the order in which the prosecution and defense presented their cases but did not address the issue of judicial instruction.

The present study was designed to investigate the relationship between the timing of a judge's instructions and mock juror verdicts for a criminal case. In particular, the aims of the research were twofold. First, we sought to determine whether or not a prototypical, ecologically valid instruction on the requirements of proof influences jurors' decisions and whether the timing of that instruction mediates its efficacy. In order to achieve these goals, requirements-of-proof instructions were gleaned from those currently employed (DeVitt & Blackmar, 1977; LaBuy, 1963; McBride, 1969) and were introduced to subjects before testimony, after testimony, or not at all. At the conclusion of the trial presentation, subjects rendered their individual verdicts and answered a number of other case-related questions. Since the requirements of proof are defendant oriented, their effectiveness should be manifested in a lowered rate of conviction. Based on jurors' tendencies to make early decisions about guilt or innocence and Judge Prettyman's (1960) reasoning that instructions can have their intended effects only when they are delivered before jurors have made up their minds, a kind of primacy or inoculation effect was predicted. That is, the present instructions should produce fewer guilty verdicts when presented before the evidence than when presented after it.

The second general aim of the present study was to explore the mechanism or cog-

[1] Jones and Goethals (1971) have termed this the "recall readiness" hypothesis for recency effects.

nitive process that underlies the proposed order effect. Requirements-of-proof instructions may operate either by decreasing the belief that the defendant committed the crime (i.e., a lowered probability-of-commission estimate) or by increasing the standard or threshold to which that likelihood is compared (i.e., a stringent interpretation of reasonable doubt). Consequently, both were assessed. A collateral issue addressed here was whether or not subjects who are instructed prior to the presentation of evidence evaluate evidentiary information differently as it unfolds from those who do not receive prior instruction. Accordingly, half the subjects in each instruction group made judgments of guilt–innocence at various points during the trial. It was hypothesized that instructed subjects would set a higher standard by which to evaluate the case against the defendant and would therefore be less influenced by the prosecutor's case throughout the trial.

Method

Subjects and Design

A total of 107 introductory psychology students (47 male, 60 female) participated in the study. The experiment was conducted in 25 small groups ranging in size from 3 to 7 and took 1 hour and 20 minutes to complete. Each group was randomly assigned to one of six cells produced by the 3 (Judge's Instructions Before Evidence, Instructions After Evidence, No Instructions) × 2 (Multiple Judgments vs. Single Judgment Only) factorial design.

Procedure

Upon entering, subjects were told that they would observe a videotaped trial simulation, after which they would be asked to render a verdict. They were further instructed that as jurors they should be attentive but should not take notes and should not converse while the trial presentation was in progress.

All subjects were then told that in order to get the entire trial presentation on one reel of tape, a few pauses and meaningless exchanges had been deleted, but that all the testimony remained intact. Those groups who were to receive the judge's instruction, however, were informed that this instruction had inadvertently been deleted but would be read to them at the appropriate time from the original transcript. Finally, subjects in the multiple-judgment cells were informed of the fact that at certain points the tape would be stopped and their judgments would be assessed. The trial was then presented.

The Trial

The stimulus trial was one that had previously been employed (Juhnke et al., 1979). Stylistically, the simulation was presented on a 1-hour (black and white) videotape in which a number of law students retried a case in a realistic courtroom setting. It was filmed from a juror's perspective: the judge, attorneys, and witness stand were all in view.

Substantively, the trial was based on an actual criminal case in which the defendant, Ronald Oliver, was charged with stealing a car and with transporting it across state lines.[2] Though continuously presented, the trial consisted of the following three distinct phases: (a) opening statements by prosecutor and defense; (b) direct examination, cross-examination, and redirect examination of two prosecution witnesses (the salesman from whom the vehicle was stolen and the arresting officer) and one defense witness (the defendant); and (c) closing arguments of counsel (prosecution, defense, prosecution). The judge's instructions on the requirements of proof represented a fourth phase whose presence–absence and timing were varied.

In one condition, these instructions appeared prior to the introduction of evidence (i.e., between the first and second phases). In a second condition, they appeared after the closing arguments (i.e., after the third phase). In a third condition, no instruction was given. The specific instruction employed was neither strong nor weak. Rather, it was patterned after the approved instructions designed to convey each element of the requirements of proof: presumption of innocence, burden of proof, and reasonable doubt (see DeVitt & Blackmar, 1977; McBride, 1969). The instruction read as follows:

> Ladies and gentlemen of the jury—at this point I want to emphasize that the law presumes the defendant, Ronald Oliver, to be innocent unless proven otherwise. A defendant begins the trial with a "clean slate" with no evidence against him.
>
> This presumption places the burden ***not*** upon the defendant to prove his innocence but, on the contrary, the burden is on the prosecution to convince you beyond any reasonable doubt that the defendant, Ronald Oliver, committed the crime. That burden never shifts at any stage of the proceeding to the defendant. Ronald Oliver has no obligations of any kind to go forward and prove that he is innocent.
>
> You have now heard the term "reasonable doubt."

[2] A transcript taken verbatim from the videotape and a summary of the trial are available upon request.

Table 1
Pattern of Final Verdicts in Each of the Six Cells

Instruction and verdict	Multiple judgments		Single judgments	
	No.	%	No.	%
Before				
Guilty	7	39	6	35
Not guilty	11	61	11	65
After				
Guilty	12	63	10	56
Not guilty	7	37	8	44
None				
Guilty	12	71	10	56
Not guilty	5	29	8	44

What is it? It is a doubt based upon reason and common sense—the kind of doubt that would make a reasonable person hesitate to act in important matters. To summarize, the defendant is presumed innocent, so the prosecution must prove to your satisfaction beyond any reasonable doubt that Ronald Oliver is guilty. If two conclusions can reasonably be drawn from the evidence—one of innocence and one of guilt—the jury should adopt the one of innocence.

Dependent Measures

At the close of the trial, all subjects responded individually and without deliberation to a two-page questionnaire in which they first rendered a dichotomous judgment (guilty–not guilty) and indicated their confidence in that verdict on a 0–8-point scale. They then rated the strength of the evidence as well as their interest and involvement in the case (all on 0–8-point scales).

Since verdicts are a function of the perceived probability that the defendant committed the crime and of the standard of proof deemed necessary for conviction, both of these variables were also assessed. All subjects were thus asked, "What is the likelihood that the defendant committed the crime?" to which they responded by circling a number from 0 to 100 (in multiples of 5), and "A defendant should be found guilty if there is at least a ________% chance that he committed the crime." Finally, subjects answered 16 short-answer recall questions that pertained to the major facts of the case (e.g., "On what highway was Ron Oliver stopped?"). The total number of correctly recalled items served as a measure of fact recall.

In addition to providing these outcome data, half the subjects indicated their judgments (guilty–not guilty), confidence values, and probability-of-commission estimates at six distinct points during the trial—after both the direct examination and cross-examination of each witness. Specifically, they were asked, "If the trial ended now, would you vote that the defendant is *guilty* or *not guilty*?" "How confident are you in this judgment?" (0–8) "What is the likelihood that the defendant committed the crime?" (0–100). It was thus possible to trace beliefs as the trial unfolded and to examine whether subjects who were already instructed on the requirements of proof (instructions before) evaluated the evidence differently from those who had not yet been instructed (instructions after and no instructions). Previous research employing these multiple judgments (e.g., Weld & Danzig, 1940) has been criticized on the ground that such a procedure may bias final verdicts (Davis, Bray, & Holt, 1977). For that reason, only half the subjects in the present study made these on-line responses. A comparison of their posttrial responses with those of single-judgment subjects thus provided a test for the (non)reactivity of the procedure.

Results

Outcome Measures

Overall, 53% of the subjects voted guilty and 47% voted not guilty. The pattern of verdicts in each cell appears in Table 1.

In order to test for all main and interaction effects and to determine which model best fits these categorical data, these dichotomous judgments were analyzed with a likelihood ratio (goodness of fit) chi-square (Fienberg, 1977). Results indicated that the simplest model that described the observed frequencies was the two-way interaction between instructional set and verdicts, $\chi^2(6) = 1.21$, $p > .97$. None of the more complicated models (i.e., those involving the multiple vs. single judgments factor) contributed any explanatory power to this Instructional Set × Verdict model. Put another way, the pattern of verdicts was accounted for by the main effect for timing of instruction. Table 1 shows that the instructions-before condition produced 37% guilty verdicts, compared to 59% in the instructions-after and 63% in the no-instructions conditions.

A scalar variable was defined by combining subjects' verdicts with their confidence ratings (confidence itself was unaffected by the independent variables). Specifically, positive confidence values were assigned to guilty verdicts and negative values to verdicts of not guilty. Scores could thus range from −8 (maximum confidence in not-guilty verdict) to 8 (maximum confidence in guilty verdict). A 2 × 3 analysis of variance on this measure revealed one marginally significant effect for timing of instruction, $F(2, 101) = 2.90$, $p < .06$. Duncan's multiple-range test further indicated that subjects in the instructions-before condition were less likely ($p < .05$) to convict the defendant than were noninstructed subjects (means of −.94 and 2.35, respectively). Instructions-after ($M = 1.79$) and noninstructed conditions did not so differ. An analysis of variance on the probability-of-commission estimates yielded results that closely paralleled those for the verdict–confidence measure—the only significant effect was for timing of the judge's instruction, $F(2, 101) = 2.92$, $p < .06$. Only subjects who received instructions before the evidence viewed the defendant as less likely to have committed the crime ($p < .05$) than did the noninstructed subjects (mean percentage estimates of 64% and 77.6%, respectively); those who were instructed after the reception of evidence ($M = 73.1\%$) did not lower their probability-of-commission estimates.

Contrary to predictions, no significant differences were obtained on evaluations of evidence strength, interpretations of reasonable doubt, or self-ratings of interest and involvement. Interestingly, a close look at the reasonable-doubt data indicates that the overall estimate of reasonable doubt ($M = 86.07$) was almost identical to that previously reported for college students (Simon & Mahan, 1971, obtained a general estimate of 87% and an estimate of 85% when the crime was auto theft). Subjects thus believed that there should be at least an 86% chance that the defendant committed the crime in order to vote for conviction.

Finally, subjects demonstrated a moderately high level of recall, averaging 12.15 correctly recalled items from a total of 16.[3] Further analysis indicated that a main effect was obtained for timing of instruction on the number of case-related facts recalled, $F(2, 101) = 3.26$, $p < .05$. Surprisingly, subjects in the instructions-after condition recalled fewer items ($M = 11.30$) than those in either the instructions-before ($M = 12.51$) or noninstructed ($M = 12.69$) conditions. The presence of the instruction between the evidence and response assessment apparently inhibited recall.

Table 2
Pattern of Mid-Trial Verdicts for the Three Instruction Groups at Each of the Six Decision Points

Instruction and verdict	Decision point 1	2	3	4	5	6
Before						
Guilty	8	8	8	7	5	8
Not guilty	10	10	10	11	13	10
After						
Guilty	16	16	17	16	13	15
Not guilty	3	3	2	3	6	4
None						
Guilty	15	14	15	14	14	12
Not guilty	2	3	2	3	3	5

Note. Decision points 1–6 immediately follow the direct examination and cross-examination of the prosecution's two witnesses and the defendant.

In sum, the mere timing of instructions had an impact on jurors' final judgments. Results for the verdict–confidence measure tended to support the major hypothesis that instructions on the requirements of proof would reduce subjects' tendencies to convict (i.e., relative to no instructions) only when delivered prior to the introduction of testimony. Although the timing variable had no significant effect on interpretations of reasonable doubt, preinstructed subjects actually viewed the defendant as less likely to have committed the crime than either the instructions-after or no-instructions subjects. Those who received instructions at the end of the trial did not respond differently on the verdict and probability-of-commission measures from those who were never instructed. In fact, they even recalled fewer of the case-related

[3] Only the major facts in the case were tested. Moreover, these facts were typically repeated throughout the trial proceedings (e.g., the highway on which Ron Oliver was stopped was first mentioned during the prosecutor's opening statement and was reiterated during the examination of both the arresting officer and the defendant and during the closing arguments). As a result, the facts tested could not be classified for further analysis as proprosecution or prodefense, nor could they be located at a single point in the trial.

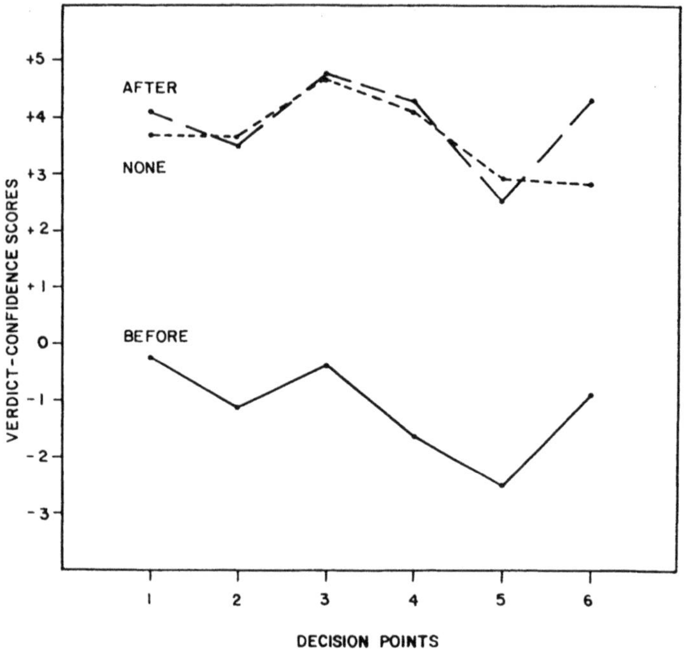

Figure 1. The pattern of verdict–confidence scores for the three groups at each of six decision points. (Higher scores indicate confidence in guilt.)

facts than all other subjects did. Finally, whether or not subjects made mid-trial judgments did not affect any of the above variables. The nonreactive nature of this multiple-judgment procedure was thus confirmed.

Process (Mid-Trial) Measures

Overall, 68% of the mid-trial responses were guilty verdicts. For the 54 subjects who made these judgments, the pattern of verdicts is presented in Table 2. As with the outcome data, these verdicts were analyzed with a likelihood ratio goodness-of-fit chi-square. Again, the simplest model that explained the observed frequencies was the two-way interaction between instructional set and verdicts, $\chi^2(30) = 6.50$, $p = 1.0$. Although a higher order model comprised of both Instruction × Verdict and Decision Point × Verdict interactions also fits the data, $\chi^2(20) = 3.13$, $p = 1.0$, it did not contribute significantly to the predictions made by the simpler model. Mid-trial verdicts were thus accounted for by the effect for instructional set. Table 2 shows that across all decision points the instructions-before group yielded 41% guilty verdicts, compared to 82% in both the instructions-after and no-instructions groups.

A verdict–confidence measure was again created and was this time submitted to a 3 (Instructions) × 6 (Decision Point) analysis of variance. Figure 1 illustrates the strong main effect for the instruction factor, $F(2, 51) = 10.15$, $p < .001$, on these verdict scores. As before, this analysis clearly indicated that subjects who were instructed before the evidence ($M = -1.14$) were consistently less likely to convict the accused ($p < .001$) than were either the instructions-after or noninstructed subjects (Ms = 3.91 and 3.65, respectively). These latter groups did not differ. An additional main effect for the decision point factor, $F(5, 255) = 4.26$, $p < .001$, indicated, as expected, that verdict scores fluctuated widely as the trial pro-

Table 3
Correlation Coefficients of Mid-Trial and Final Verdict–Confidence Scores in Each Group and Across All Groups

Group	Verdict–confidence score 1	2	3	4	5	6
Before	.14	.42	.57**	.46**	.42	.54*
After	.22	.22	.18	.15	−.03	−.15
None	.31	.30	.37	.42	.45	.86***
Overall	.28*	.41**	.47***	.44**	.36**	.52***

Note. Correlations are based on *ns* of 18, 19, and 17 ($N = 54$).
* $p < .05$. ** $p < .01$. *** $p < .001$.

gressed. As might be anticipated, the conviction rate was highest at the third point—right after the prosecutor examined his second witness ($p < .01$), and lowest at the fifth point—right after the direct examination of the defendant ($p < .01$). The interaction between instructional set and decision point did not approach significance ($F < .1$).

On the question of whether jurors' early impressions were predictive of their final pre-deliberation verdicts, Table 3 presents the correlations between subjects' mid-trial and final verdict–confidence scores. It can be seen that over all multiple-judgment groups the average correlation between mid-trial and posttrial verdict scores was .44 ($p < .01$). In fact, the average correlation between the verdict scores rendered at even the first decision point and those given at the end of the trial was .28 ($p < .05$). To some extent, then, subjects' decisions were substantially formed very early in the trial presentation.

Results for the repeated probability-of-commission measures followed a similar pattern (see Figure 2). A main effect for timing of instruction, $F(2, 5) = 6.58$, $p < .005$, re-

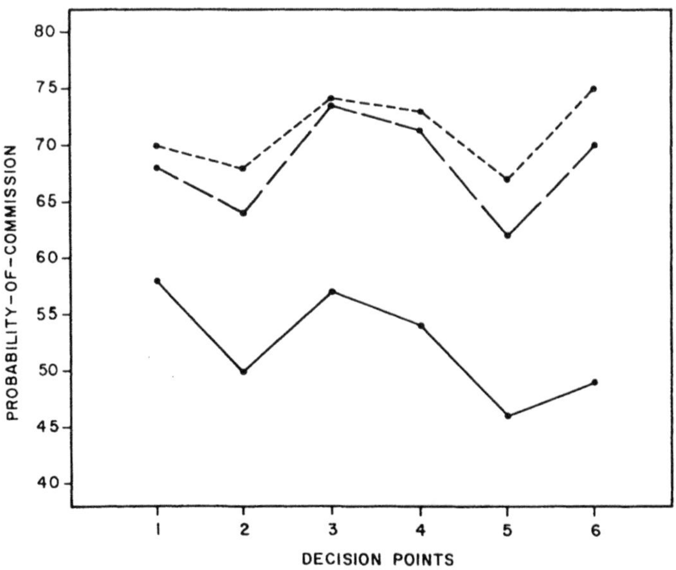

Figure 2. The pattern of probability-of-commission estimates for the three groups at each of six decision points.

vealed that during the trial, the instructions-before group ($M = 52.5\%$) viewed the defendant as less likely to have committed the crime ($p < .01$) than either the instructions-after or no-instructions groups (68.16% and 71.67%, respectively), who again did not differ from each other. Moreover, a main effect for the decision point factor, $F(5, 255) = 3.08$, $p < .01$, indicated that the perceived probability of commission was lowest at the fifth point—right after the defendant testified in his own behalf.

In sum, subjects' mid-trial judgments fluctuated in the predicted directions (i.e., guilty judgments after the prosecutor's examination and not-guilty judgments after the defense's examination). More important, these judgments were influenced largely by whether or not subjects had been instructed on the requirements of proof. That is, although instructional set and decision point did not interact (i.e., their curves were almost perfectly parallel, thereby indicating that pre-instructed subjects were neither less influenced by the prosecutor's testimony nor more influenced by the defendant's testimony), subjects who had been instructed before the evidence immediately and continually viewed the defendant as less likely to have committed the crime.

Discussion

The present study demonstrated what might be described as a primacy effect. A judge's instruction to the jury was effective when delivered prior to but not after the presentation of evidence. That is, mock jurors who were instructed on the presumption of innocence, burden of proof, and reasonable doubt before observing the testimony were ultimately less likely to vote for conviction. It was noted earlier that verdicts are a function of the perceived likelihood that the defendant committed the crime and of the standard or threshold to which that likelihood is compared. In the present experiment, variations in the timing of the instruction affected estimates of the probability of commission but not interpretations of reasonable doubt. Subjects who received the instructions before the evidence thus demonstrated a low rate of conviction because they actually viewed the defendant as less likely to have committed the crime.

Although the present experiment was not theoretically guided, it now appears that an information integration model of juror judgments (Kaplan & Kemmerick, 1974) might well describe the results. Briefly, each piece of evidentiary and nonevidentiary information possesses some scale value along a dimension of guilt–innocence and a weight that determines the importance of that information. A trial judgment is then formed on the basis of a weighted-average combination of stimulus components. In the context of the present study, subjects received two global categories of information: the trial presentation and judicial instruction. From the probability-of-commission responses of noninstructed subjects, the scale value of the trial information may be estimated at .78 (i.e., .78 is the marginal mean for noninstructed subjects). Although the scale value of the requirements of proof instruction was not assessed in the present study, it should—by legal ideal—have implied a scale value or initial probability of commission of 0 (Ostrom, Werner, & Saks, 1978). On the assumption that the scale values of the instruction and trial presentation remained constant (these assumptions are supported indirectly by the lack of a timing effect on interpretations of reasonable doubt and ratings of evidence strength, respectively), to what do we attribute the effects for the timing manipulation? Within an impression formation paradigm, Anderson (1965) found that later adjectives keep a fixed scale value but decrease in their weight. This mechanism describes the present results—the prodefendant instruction received a greater weight when delivered before than when delivered after the evidence.[4]

What *process* underlies these findings? At least two plausible mechanisms are worth evaluating. It was hypothesized that pre-instructed subjects would demand a greater burden of proof when evaluating the strength

[4] Note that although the present analysis treats judges' instructions as information that has a scale

of the prosecutor's case as it unfolds during the trial. This critical, evaluative "schema" was expected to manifest itself in different fluctuating patterns in the responses of the instructed (instructions-before) and noninstructed (instructions after and no instructions) mid-trial judgment groups. However, the absence of an Instruction × Decision Point interaction on verdicts and probability-of-commission ratings ruled out this hypothesis. In fact, the three instruction groups demonstrated remarkably similar mid-trial shifts in judgment (see Figure 1). Those who had been instructed were neither more influenced by the defense nor less influenced by the prosecutor than the others were. Instructed subjects thus did not reject or distort the prosecutor's evidence to fit an initial impression or presumption of innocence. And why should they? Luchins (1957) has demonstrated that by forewarning observers of the imminence of additional information, the proactive effects of early information on subsequent information are suppressed. Subjects in the present study and jurors in general *expect* to be confronted with inconsistent information. Early information in this setting (i.e., judicial instruction) is thus unlikely to produce the strong bias that would stimulate the processes of discounting or assimilation.

The process that did appear to operate was considerably less complex. Subjects who were instructed before the evidence were more likely than the others were to vote for acquittal and indicated a lower probability of commission *even from the first decision point*. Although they responded similarly to testimony that followed, their initial leanings resulted in fewer guilty verdicts at the conclusion of the trial. The impact of this initial reaction is reflected in the significant correlation between first and final verdict scores. Simply put, most preinstructed subjects "presumed innocent," whereas the others "presumed guilty."

The *practical* implications of the present study are straightforward. Mandatory code provisions do not forbid or discourage judges from using their discretion in instructing the jury before the trial. A number of states (e.g., Indiana, 1966), individual judges (e.g., Prettyman, 1960), and legal scholars (e.g., McBride, 1969) have thus adopted or advocated delivery of preliminary instructions prior to the presentation of evidence. In Missouri (1964), for example, the Supreme Court Committee on Jury Instructions recommended that "the jury be instructed before the trial begins. . . . The committee believes that it is better to draw the jury's attention to these matters before the trial rather than waiting until after the jurors may have reached a decision" (quoted in McBride, 1969, p. 62). This latter example is unfortunately an exception rather than the rule, which is that preliminary instructions are vastly underutilized (DeVitt & Blackmar, 1977). Viewed in this context, the present study provides firm support for proponents of procedural reform in the courtroom. The Anglo-American system of justice has traditionally favored the accused on the philosophy that acquitting a truly guilty person is better than convicting a truly innocent one (Ploscowe, 1935). Yet the present results suggest that the accused may not benefit from this protective instruction unless it is delivered to jurors *before* the trial. In this regard, perhaps the requirements of proof might well be included in the currently popular "juror handbooks" that are distributed to jurors as part of a pretrial orientation (National Institute of Law Enforcement and Criminal Justice, 1975) and might perhaps be presented at both the beginning and the end of the proceedings (Elwork et al., 1977).

From a methodological standpoint, the multiple-judgment procedure initially employed by Weld and Danzig (1940) merits increased consideration in future research. The present study confirmed that it does not bias jurors' ultimate verdicts or any other posttrial measures (also see Pyszczynski, Note

---

value and weight, Kaplan and his colleagues are quick to point out that strictly speaking, because instructions do not pertain to the specific defendant or crime, they do not relate to information scale value (S_i). Instead, instructions should affect an initial impression of the defendant that exists prior to jurors' receiving information about him or her (S_o), that is, the impression of defendants in general (see Kaplan & Miller, 1978).

1). Moreover, it appears to be valuable for examining jurors' reactions to the trial as it unfolds. Questions concerning the relative impact of different trial phases (e.g., opening statements and closing arguments, direct examination vs. cross-examination) and different kinds of evidence (e.g., tangible exhibits, expert or eyewitness testimony) may be fruitfully investigated through the mid-trial assessment of verdicts.

Finally, some of the limitations of the present results deserve mention. As with other nonevidentiary factors, the timing of an instruction cannot be expected to influence the outcome of a one-sided case (i.e., an extremely strong or weak case against the defendant). Rather, the effects should be considered limited to close, ambiguous cases. Note also that the present experiment assessed the verdicts of nondeliberating jurors. Whether or not deliberation provides enough of a corrective strategy to erase the timing effect upon juries remains open to question. Finally, the trial used in the present study was much shorter than the average criminal case. Whether or not the timing manipulation would affect jurors' responses in realistically longer trials remains to be seen.

Reference Note

1. Pyszczynski, T. A. *The effects of opening statements on liability judgments at various points in a simulated jury trial.* Unpublished master's thesis, University of Kansas, 1978.

References

Anderson, N. H. Primacy effects in personality impression formation using a generalized order effect paradigm. *Journal of Personality and Social Psychology,* 1965, *2,* 1–9.

Davis, J. H., Bray, R. M., & Holt, R. W. The empirical study of decision processes in juries: A critical review. In J. L. Tapp & F. J. Levine (Eds.), *Law, justice, and the individual in society: Psychological and legal issues.* New York: Holt, Rinehart & Winston, 1977.

DeVitt, E. J., & Blackmar, C. B. *Federal jury practice and instructions* (Vols. 1–3). St. Paul, Minn.: West Publishing, 1977.

Elwork, A., Sales, B. D., & Alfini, J. J. Juridic decisions: In ignorance of the law or in light of it? *Law and Human Behavior,* 1977, *1,* 163–189.

Fienberg, S. E. *The analysis of cross-classified data.* Cambridge, Mass.: MIT Press, 1977.

Frank, J. *Courts on trial: Myth and reality in American justice.* Princeton, N.J.: Princeton University Press, 1949.

Hervey, J. C. Jurors look at our judges. *Oklahoma Bar Association Journal,* 1947, *25,* 1508–1513.

Indiana pattern jury instructions. Indianapolis, Ind.: Bobbs-Merrill, 1966.

Jones, E. E., & Goethals, G. R. *Order effects in impression formation: Attribution context and the nature of the entity.* Morristown, N.J.: General Learning Press, 1971.

Jones, E. E., Rock, L., Shaver, K. G., Goethals, G. R., & Ward, L. M. Pattern of performance and ability attribution: An unexpected primacy effect. *Journal of Personality and Social Psychology,* 1968, *10,* 317–340.

Juhnke, R., Vought, C., Pyszczynski, T. A., Dane, F. C., Losure, B. D., & Wrightsman, L. S. Effects of presentation mode upon mock jurors' reactions to a trial. *Personality and Social Psychology Bulletin,* 1979, *5,* 36–39.

Kalven, H., & Zeisel, H. *The American jury.* Boston: Little, Brown, 1966.

Kaplan, M. F., & Kemmerick, E. D. Juror judgment as information integration: Combining evidential and nonevidential information. *Journal of Personality and Social Psychology,* 1974, *30,* 493–499.

Kaplan, M. F., & Miller, L. E. Reducing the effects of juror bias. *Journal of Personality and Social Psychology,* 1978, *36,* 1443–1455.

Kerr, N. L., Atkin, R. S., Stasser, G., Meek, D., Holt, R. W., & Davis, J. H. Guilt beyond a reasonable doubt: Effects of concept definition and assigned decision rule on the judgments of mock jurors. *Journal of Personality and Social Psychology,* 1976, *34,* 282–294.

LaBuy, W. J. *Jury instructions in federal criminal cases.* St. Paul, Minn.: West Publishing, 1963.

Luchins, A. S. Primacy-recency in impression formation. In C. I. Hovland (Ed.), *The order of presentation and persuasion.* New Haven, Conn.: Yale University Press, 1957.

McBride, R. L. *The art of instructing the jury.* Cincinnati, Ohio: W. H. Anderson, 1969.

McCart, S. W. *Trial by jury.* Philadelphia: Chilton Books, 1964.

Missouri Supreme Court Committee on Jury Instructions. *Missouri approved jury instructions.* New York: Vernon Law Book Company, 1964.

National Institute of Law Enforcement and Criminal Justice. *A guide to jury system management.* Washington, D.C.: U.S. Department of Justice, 1975.

Ostrom, T. M., Werner, C., & Saks, M. J. An integration theory analysis of jurors' presumptions of guilt or innocence. *Journal of Personality and Social Psychology,* 1978, *36,* 436–450.

Ploscowe, M. The development of present-day criminal procedures in Europe and America. *Harvard Law Review,* 1935, *48,* 433–473.

Prettyman, E. B. Jury instructions—First or last? *American Bar Association Journal,* 1960, *46,* 1066.
Sealy, A. P., & Cornish, W. R. Juries and the rules of evidence. *Criminal Law Review,* April 1973, 208–223.
Simon, R. J., & Mahan, L. Quantifying burdens of proof: A view from the bench, the jury, and the classroom. *Law and Society Review,* February 1971, 319–330.
Walker, L., Thibaut, J., & Andreoli, V. Order of presentation at trial. *Yale Law Review,* 1972, *82,* 216–226.
Weld, H. P., & Danzig, E. R. A study of the way in which a verdict is reached by a jury. *American Journal of Psychology,* 1940, *53,* 518–536.

Received December 11, 1978 ■

0091-4169/83/7501-198
THE JOURNAL OF CRIMINAL LAW & CRIMINOLOGY Vol. 75, No. 1

Printed in U.S.A.

CRIMINOLOGY

TOWARD CRIMINAL JURY INSTRUCTIONS THAT JURORS CAN UNDERSTAND*

LAURENCE J. SEVERANCE**
EDITH GREENE***
ELIZABETH F. LOFTUS****

I. INTRODUCTION

In April 1982, a Guatemalan busboy named Luis Marin went to trial, accused of intentionally starting a fire that killed twenty-six people at a Harrison, New York conference center. The evidence against defendant Marin was purely circumstantial. The prosecution argued to the jury that Marin was about to be fired for working under an assumed name, and that he intended to set a small fire in order to emerge as a hero and win back his job. Although the police did not find Marin with any incriminating evidence, the prosecution introduced testimony from co-workers to the effect that moments before the fire began Marin had disappeared, and suggested in argument that he used gasoline from his car to start the fire.[1]

The jury deliberated extensively. At one point during the deliberations, they asked the judge to clarify whether "intent includes state of

* This research was supported by grant 80-12333 from the National Science Foundation to Elizabeth Loftus and Laurence Severance. We gratefully acknowledge the assistance of Carla Iafrate, Wade Moberg, Kari Seeger, Barbara Johnson, Tim Seckel, and Debbie Pearce in collecting data reported herein. We also acknowledge the help of Jane Goodman in providing psycholinguistic analyses of protocol data reported herein.

** Attorney in private practice, Seattle. J.D., University of Washington, 1980; Ph.D., Duke University, 1974; B.A., University of California, Riverside, 1968.

*** Postdoctoral Research Associate, University of Washington. Ph.D., University of Washington, 1983; M.A., University of Colorado, 1977; B.A., Stanford University, 1975.

**** Professor of Psychology, University of Washington. Ph.D., Stanford University, 1970; B.A., U.C.L.A., 1966.

[1] Newsweek, Apr. 26, 1982, at 59.

mind, or what the accused was thinking" at the time.[2] The jury eventually found Marin guilty beyond a reasonable doubt. Four days after the conviction, however, the judge overturned the jury's verdict, reasoning that because the prosecution's case failed to negate other explanations for the crime, the circumstantial evidence was insufficient to support a verdict of guilty beyond a reasonable doubt.[3]

The Marin case illustrates the importance in criminal trials of the jury's understanding legal instructions from the judge on concepts such as "criminal intent" and "reasonable doubt." Where the jurors' understanding of these concepts differed from the judge's, opposite verdicts were reached with obviously profound consequences for the defendant.

From a legal perspective, the judge's instructions are crucial information intended to provide the jury with proper legal standards for reaching a verdict. As one court stated:

> The chief purpose of a charge is to aid the jury in clearly understanding the case and in arriving at a correct verdict. If this is not done, there can be no assurance that the verdict represents a finding by the jury under the law and upon the evidence presented.[4]

This Article begins with an analysis of some of the problems resulting from the necessary process of instructing jurors on the laws they should apply to facts in reaching a verdict. We document a need for jury instructions that are both understandable to lay people and legally accurate. We then present the results of research aimed at improving jurors' understanding of several key criminal jury instructions. The instructions on which we focused describe the concepts of reasonable doubt, criminal intent, and the limited use of evidence of prior convictions. We report a set of new instructions that were tested empirically and found to be psychologically sound. These linguistically simplified instructions and the existing pattern instructions on which they are based were presented to a nationwide sample of trial judges for purposes of comparison and assessment of their legal adequacy. We conclude the Article with a discussion of the judges' reactions to the different versions of each instruction.

A. THE CONCERN FOR LEGAL ACCURACY IN JURY INSTRUCTIONS

In formulating jury instructions, considerable controversy may arise as to what constitutes an accurate statement of the law. Seemingly minor changes in wording have been the basis of successful appeals. For example, in *People v. Garcia*,[5] a state appellate court cited a half dozen

---

2 N.Y. Times, Apr. 7, 1982, at 11.

3 *Id.*

4 Warren v. Parks, 31 N.C. App. 609, 612, 230 S.E.2d 684, 687 (1976) (citation omitted).

5 54 Cal. App. 3d 61, 126 Cal. Rptr. 275, *cert. denied*, 426 U.S. 911 (1976).

erroneous variations in jury instructions on the concept of "proof beyond a reasonable doubt" in reversing a defendant's conviction of second degree murder on the ground of jury misinstruction. The court in *Garcia* noted that "well intentioned efforts to 'clarify' and 'explain' reasonable doubt criteria have had the result of creating confusion and uncertainty, and have repeatedly been struck down by the courts of review . . . ."[6] Because appeals based on alleged error in instructing the jury are common,[7] judges are often reluctant to deviate from language approved by higher courts, even where that language is difficult for the jurors to understand.

In most jurisdictions, an important response to the problem of inaccurate jury instructions has been the development of pattern instructions. Pattern jury instructions are statements of the law designed by committees of judges and lawyers for presentation to jurors; depending on the requirements of each individual trial, the court selects particular pattern instructions for use.[8] There is some evidence that pattern instructions reduce the number of reversals based on claims that the law was incorrectly stated;[9] however, a reliable effect of pattern instructions in reducing the overall number of appeals has not been demonstrated.[10]

B. THE CONCERN FOR JUROR MISUNDERSTANDING OF JURY INSTRUCTIONS

A second problem with jury instructions arises where instructions that are technically accurate statements of the law are ambiguous or misinterpreted by jurors. Misunderstanding can arise from the syntax of the instructions,[11] the manner of presentation, or the general unfamiliarity of lay people with legal terminology.

A recent case illustrates the point. Defendant was driving a car, in which his girlfriend was a passenger, when he ran into a parked car. The two fled the scene on foot and were stopped within a few blocks by the police. Defendant was charged with knowingly driving a stolen car. At trial, his girlfriend testified that he did not know the car was stolen until she told him at the time of the accident. The defendant testified

---

6 *Id.* at 63, 126 Cal. Rptr. at 276.

7 *See* Nieland, *Assessing the Impact of Pattern Jury Instructions*, 62 JUDICATURE 185, 188 (1978).

8 *E.g.*, WASHINGTON PATTERN JURY INSTRUCTIONS—CRIMINAL (WPIC) (West 1977) [hereinafter cited as WASHINGTON PATTERN JURY INSTRUCTIONS—CRIMINAL]; CALIFORNIA JURY INSTRUCTIONS—CIVIL: BOOK OF APPROVED JURY INSTRUCTIONS (BAJI) (P. Richards rev. 6th ed. 1977).

9 Nieland, *supra* note 7, at 194.

10 *Id.* at 190.

11 Syntax generally refers to sentence structure or the arrangement of words to show their mutual relations in a sentence.

that he was sick and too sleepy to notice details that would have indicated that the car was stolen. The jury was instructed on the definition of knowledge in statutory language:

> Knowledge. A person knows or acts knowingly or with knowledge when: (i) he is aware of a fact, facts, or circumstances or result described by a statute defining an offense; or (ii) he has information which would lead a reasonable man in the same situation to believe that facts exist which facts are described by a statute defining an offense.[12]

The jury convicted the defendant. He appealed, alleging that part (ii) of the definition of knowledge was ambiguous because it could have led the jury to conclude erroneously (a) that it might presume knowledge if it found that a reasonable person would have known the car was stolen, or (b) that the statute redefined knowledge to include the case where an ordinary person in the defendant's situation would have known the car was stolen. The Washington State Supreme Court agreed with the defendant and reversed the conviction on the ground that both of these interpretations of "knowledge" were incorrect; thus, the statute was sufficiently ambiguous to "seriously infringe on the rights of the defendant, if a juror used the wrong interpretation . . . ."[13] Thus, pattern instructions that have been drafted to be legally accurate may fail to convey a correct understanding of the law to jurors.

Pattern instructions also have been criticized for being too abstract. Because they are written generally to apply in all cases, it can be argued that they do not apply effectively to the facts of any case in particular. In addition, the language of pattern instructions is often derived from statutory language and case law definitions; thus, many pattern instructions still embody obvious linguistic difficulties.

Ideally, jury instructions should be both legally accurate and understandable to the jurors who hear them. The trend, however, has been to emphasize legal accuracy rather than clarity. Consider for example, the early position taken by the drafters of California's pattern instructions for criminal jury trials: "The one thing an instruction must do above all else is correctly state the law. This is true regardless of who is capable of understanding it."[14] One appellate court actually discouraged a trial judge from presenting legal concepts to the jury in simplified language, although the simplified language was held not to misstate the law.[15] Other appellate courts, however, have acknowledged the importance of clear language. For example, in *People v. Wilson*,[16] an appel-

---

12 WASH. REV. CODE ANN. § 9A.08.010(1)(b) (1983).

13 State v. Shipp, 93 Wash. 2d 510, 515, 610 P.2d 1322, 1325 (1980).

14 CALIFORNIA JURY INSTRUCTIONS—CRIMINAL: BOOK OF APPROVED JURY INSTRUCTIONS (BAJI) 44 (1950).

15 *See* Davis v. State, 373 So. 2d 382 (Fla. Dist. Ct. App. 1979).

16 258 Cal. App. 2d 578, 65 Cal. Rptr. 839 (1968).

late court reversed a trial jury's decision where the judge had given pattern instructions instead of using "concrete and direct language defining the rather simple issues of fact which the case presented."[17] The court stated further:

> Form [pattern] instructions . . . can be of great value to the judge in preparing his charge to the jury, but it is a misuse of these resources to read to the jury a lengthy and confusing incantation made up of form instructions submitted by the parties.[18]

C. EMPIRICAL STUDIES OF LINGUISTIC DIFFICULTIES FOR JURORS

Recent social science research suggests that jurors' difficulties in understanding instructions on the law are considerable and widespread. Strawn and Buchanan assessed juror comprehension of oral criminal pattern instructions used in Florida by comparing the understanding of subject-jurors who received instructions to that of a comparable group of subjects that did not receive instructions.[19] They found that although the instructions helped to some extent,[20] the instructed jurors still missed 27% of the test items and failed to show any improved comprehension for four of nine crucial content areas addressed by the instructions.[21] Elwork, Sales, and Alfini studied Michigan civil pattern instructions on the law of negligence and found no reliable differences between a group receiving no instructions and a group receiving the pattern instructions.[22] More recently, on the basis of further extensive testing, these researchers concluded that prior to deliberating on a defendant's guilt or innocence, the average juror may understand only about half of the legal instructions presented by the judge.[23] From this they concluded that many verdicts in criminal jury trials reflect misunderstandings of the juror's role in the process and of what the law requires.

These data corroborate the subjective impressions of the judges and commentators. One Oregon trial judge stated, for example, "When I read instructions to the jury, I hope that I will see a light go on in the

---

17 *Id.* at 585, 65 Cal. Rptr. at 844.

18 *Id.*

19 Strawn & Buchanan, *Jury Confusion: A Threat to Justice*, 59 JUDICATURE 478 (1976).

20 For example, 77% of instructed jurors understood that the effect of a not guilty plea is to require the state to prove the charges against the defendant, *id.* at 481; and 66% of instructed jurors knew that a statement made by a defendant could not be considered as evidence against him unless it was freely and voluntarily made, *id.*

21 *Id.* at 482. Instructed jurors failed to comprehend the meaning of "reasonable doubt," "information," "material allegation," and "breaking and entering" any better than the control group of jurors that had received no instructions. *Id.*

22 Elwork, Sales & Alfini, *Juridic Decisions: In Ignorance of the Law or in Light of It?* 1 LAW & HUM. BEHAV. 163, 163 (1977).

23 J. ALFINI, B. SALES & A. ELWORK, MAKING JURY INSTRUCTIONS UNDERSTANDABLE 12 (1982).

jurors' eyes, but I never do."[24]

D. IDENTIFYING SPECIFIC INSTRUCTIONS IN NEED OF REFINEMENT

1. *Archival Data*

Evidence confirming the difficulties jurors have understanding judges' instructions has been derived from a systematic analysis of the questions jurors asked of judges during the course of their deliberations.[25] In an earlier study,[26] we reviewed court records of jury trials in nineteen superior courts in the State of Washington, noting all instances where the jury, during the course of its deliberation, sent written messages to the judge and the judge responded. Such questions and answers were included in the trial court's record and thus were accessible as public records. From the records of 405 jury trials, including both civil and criminal actions, we found that about one quarter of these juries submitted written questions. In many instances, jurors who had received the recommended pattern instructions sought further clarification. For example, one submitted item stated, "We are 11-1, one person feels they need a better definition of intent." Other juries had questions about "reasonable doubt": "We request further clarification of 'reasonable doubt' as it pertains to credibility of the witnesses," and "Can reasonable doubt apply to the jury as a whole and not just to individual jurors?" Invariably, the judges refused to paraphrase or offer an alternative explanation for the problematic instructions. In nearly all instances, judges simply referred the jurors back to the problematic instructions for rereading.[27]

Not all sources of misunderstanding can be identified by analyzing the questions juries ask because jurors sometimes think they have understood instructions when in fact they have not.[28] Nevertheless, our earlier research into the patterns of questions asked by jurors[29] has identified certain criminal jury instructions that, regardless of their legal importance and virtually universal application, are difficult for jurors to comprehend.

First, jurors had difficulty understanding instructions on "reasonable doubt" and the closely linked concept of "presumption of inno-

---

24 Personal oral communication to L. Severance (Oct. 3, 1980).

25 An implicit assumption here is that jurors' questions correspond to their lack of understanding about a certain legal issue.

26 Severance & Loftus, *Improving the Ability of Jurors to Comprehend and Apply Criminal Jury Instructions*, 17 LAW & SOC'Y REV. 153 (1982).

27 *Id.* at 172.

28 *See* O'Mara & von Eckartsberg, *Proposed Standard Jury Instructions—Evaluation of Usage and Understanding*, 48 PA. BAR A.Q. 542, 550 (1977).

29 Severence & Loftus, *supra* note 26.

cence." Second, deliberating juries were left with questions about the meaning of "intent" even after receiving a pattern instruction defining the concept.[30] For many crimes, "intent" is a mental state that must be proven to find guilt: a person is not found guilty of a crime unless the admitted acts were committed with the requisite intent, i.e., the intent to accomplish an illegal result.[31] The obvious difficulties with this concept made instructions concerning "intent" a natural choice for closer examination.

The third problem on which we chose to focus arises when jurors hear evidence in court and then are instructed to limit their consideration of that evidence to a certain purpose. For example, a frequently used limiting instruction concerns evidence of prior convictions. Where a defendant's prior convictions are admitted into evidence, the jury normally is instructed to consider the prior convictions solely to evaluate the credibility of the defendant as a witness and not as evidence of a propensity to commit crimes such as the one charged. The Federal Rules of Evidence, along with many state jurisdictions, permit evidence of prior convictions to be admitted under certain circumstances.[32] Based in part on the questions asked by jurors on this issue, we selected limiting instructions on the use of prior convictions for further study.

---

[30] *Id.* at 170-71. For example, the Washington pattern instruction given to juries when "intent" is an element of an alleged crime states: "A person acts with intent or intentionally when acting with the objective or purpose to accomplish a result which constitutes a crime." WASHINGTON PATTERN JURY INSTRUCTIONS—CRIMINAL, *supra* note 8, at 10.01. *See* Table 1 *infra*.

[31] For example, Washington Pattern Jury Instruction 35.02 listing the elements of first degree assault reads in part:

> To convict the defendant of the crime of assault in the first degree, each of the following elements of the crime must be proved beyond a reasonable doubt:
>
> (1) That on or about the ____ day of ________, 19__, the defendant assaulted ________________;
>
> (2) That the assault was committed [with a firearm] [or] [with a deadly weapon] [or] [by a force or means likely to produce death];
>
> (3) That the defendant acted with intent [to kill a human being] [or] [to commit ____________ upon the [person] [or] [property] of the person assaulted, or another]; and
>
> (4) That the acts occurred in ________________ County, Washington.

WASHINGTON PATTERN JURY INSTRUCTIONS—CRIMINAL, *supra* note 8, at 35.02 (bracketed material in original).

[32] Federal Rule of Evidence 609 provides in part:

> For the purpose of attacking the credibility of a witness, evidence that he has been convicted of a crime shall be admitted if elicited from him or established by public record during cross-examination but only if the crime (1) was punishable by death or imprisonment in excess of one year under the law under which he was convicted, and the court determines that the probative value of admitting this evidence outweighs its prejudicial effect to the defendant, or (2) involved dishonesty or false statement, regardless of the punishment.

FED. R. EVID. 609(a).

2. *Experimental Analysis of Specific Pattern Instructions*

The pioneering work of Strawn and Buchanan[33] and Elwork, Sales, and Alfini[34] suggested that an empirical approach could be used effectively to pinpoint comprehension difficulties in specific jury instructions. Building on this earlier work, in our previous study we presented an hour-long videotaped burglary trial to a group of college students who were eligible for jury duty.[35] The tape was followed by either (a) no instructions, (b) general pattern instructions concerning the jury's duties,[36] but excluding any specific instructions, or (c) general pattern instructions plus three additional specific pattern instructions pertaining to "reasonable doubt," "intent," and restrictions on the use of evidence concerning prior convictions.[37]

The videotaped trial was an enactment, filmed in an actual courtroom with a real judge and credible actors as witnesses. The facts were intentionally balanced so that the defendant's guilt or innocence was unclear. The defendant had one prior conviction to which he admitted during cross-examination.[38]

After observing the videotaped trial and hearing one of the sets of instructions, half of the participants were instructed to deliberate for up to thirty minutes; the others were not. Thereafter, each subject answered a questionnaire designed to measure comprehension and ability to apply the legal concepts embodied in the instructions.

a. The questionnaire

The subjects were asked to give a verdict of "guilty" or "not guilty" and then indicate how certain they were that their verdict was correct. We employed two different measures of jurors' understanding. First, we examined their ability to comprehend the meaning of instructions through the use of multiple choice questions that required the respondent to distinguish between correct and incorrect expressions of an instruction's meaning. There were separate sets of items probing the "reasonable doubt/presumption of innocence" instruction, the "intent"

33 Strawn & Buchanan, *supra* note 19.

34 Elwork, Sales & Alfini, *supra* note 22.

35 Severance & Loftus, *supra* note 26.

36 Instructions on the three critical legal concepts obviously are not given in isolation. Judges invariably instruct juries on their general duties and they often refer back to those general instructions when trying to clarify deliberating jurors' confusion. *See supra* note 27 and accompanying text.

37 Pattern instructions were those developed for jurors in criminal trials in the State of Washington. *See* WASHINGTON PATTERN JURY INSTRUCTIONS—CRIMINAL, *supra* note 8.

38 Thanks are extended to Dr. Barbara Hart, of the University of Texas, who made the videotape available for our research.

instruction, the limiting instruction, and the general instructions.[39]

Second, we assessed the subjects' abilities to apply jury instructions correctly to novel fact patterns. Subjects were presented with a series of single paragraph descriptions of factual situations.[40] They responded to each paragraph by indicating on a scale ranging from -3 (Strongly Disagree) to +3 (Strongly Agree) whether they concurred with a proposed solution at the end of the factual situation. Each example tested their abilities to apply concepts embodied in the pattern instructions correctly in order to reach a legally accurate decision.

b. Findings

For the "comprehension" measures, subjects who received no instructions erred 35.6% of the time; subjects with general pattern instructions erred 34.7% of the time; and subjects with general plus specific pattern instructions erred 29.6% of the time.[41] "Reasonable doubt/presumption of innocence" was the only concept for which a specific pattern instruction was helpful. For this instruction, there was a comprehension error rate of 32.1% with no instructions, 34% with the general instruction only, but 26.2% with general plus specific instructions.[42]

---

[39] An example of a comprehension measure for "intent" is the following: Intent to commit a crime:

(a) cannot be proved without the testimony of a psychologist;
(b) cannot be proved since it rests within a person's mind;
(c) is assumed whenever a crime is committed;
(d) can be proved when a person acts with a clear purpose.

In the example, (d) is the correct answer.

[40] An example of an "application" test item for reasonable doubt/presumption of innocence is the following:

> A used car dealer claims that the accused hot wired one of his cars and drove it to the ocean 200 miles away, where it was found the next day. The accused has the burden of proving beyond a reasonable doubt that he was not in the vicinity at the time of the alleged crime, nor ever in the stolen car.

[41] $F(2,210) = 5.04$, $p < .007$. Throughout this Article, reference will be made to the notion of "statistical significance." Statistical significance is a term that implies that the likelihood that two measurements differ by chance is less than some acceptable level. In most social science research the minimum acceptable level is .05, represented as $p < .05$. This figure means that the probability that the statistical event being measured (for example, an improvement in comprehension) occurred by chance is less than 1 in 20 (5/100). Thus, $p < .007$ means that the probability that these comprehension scores could have resulted by chance and were not due to our experimental manipulations is less than 7 in 1000. For an explanation of the various basic methods of computing statistical significance, see A. EDWARDS, STATISTICAL ANALYSIS 132-35 (3d ed. 1969). The F test or Fisher ratio is used to determine whether two or more samples differ significantly: the larger the F ratio, the larger the level of significance. The number within the parentheses indicate the number of "degrees of freedom" associated with the Fisher ratio. For an explanation of the concept of degrees of freedom, see A. EDWARDS, *supra*, at 142.

[42] $F(2,210) = 4.03$, $p < .02$.

For the "application" measures, subjects tended to agree with the correct applications of the law more strongly when specific instructions had been given than when they had not.[43] When the effects of individual specific instructions were analyzed separately, however, the specific instruction on "intent" actually diminished agreement with the correct application of the law, relative to no instructions and to the general pattern instruction only.[44] The specific instruction concerning reasonable doubt/presumption of innocence had no significant effect on subjects' application abilities.[45] In fact, the limiting instruction was the only specific instruction that seemed to aid subjects in correctly applying the law.[46]

Taken together, these results demonstrated that people without legal training have difficulty comprehending and applying pattern instructions. Even with those instructions, the overall error rate for the comprehension measures was 29.6%, and the overall level of agreement with correct applications of the instructions was not significantly different from the level of agreement given no instructions at all. None of the results were affected reliably by the presence or absence of deliberation prior to subjects' answering the questionnaire.

II. Improving the Clarity of Criminal Jury Instructions

From a psychological perspective, the work of Elwork, Sales, and Alfini[47] and Charrow and Charrow[48] has suggested that specific psycholinguistic principles can be applied to jury instructions to eliminate problematic language, simplify meaning, and present instructions in a clear, logical way. From a legal perspective, however, the large number of verdicts that are reversed for error because of incorrect jury instructions suggests the potential folly of altering existing pattern instructions too dramatically.

In rewriting existing pattern instructions to improve juror understanding,[49] we applied a range of specific principles that had been tested with success in other contexts.[50] We tried to eliminate legal jargon and uncommon words on the assumption that people have more difficulty

---

43 $F(2,210) = 4.01$, $p < .02$.

44 $F(2,210) = 2.99$, $p < .05$.

45 $F(2,210) = 0.85$, n.s.

46 $F(2,210) = 5.77$, $p < .004$.

47 Elwork, Sales & Alfini, *supra* note 22, at 176; J. Alfini, B. Sales & A. Elwork, *supra* note 23, at 171.

48 Charrow & Charrow, *Making Legal Language Understandable: A Psycholinguistic Study of Jury Instructions*, 79 Colum. L. Rev. 1306, 1307-08 (1979).

49 *See* Severance & Loftus, *supra* note 26.

50 *See supra* notes 22-23, 47-48 and accompanying text. Charrow and Charrow's influential research suggested that jurors' ability to correctly paraphrase their instructions was en-

perceiving, remembering, and comprehending unfamiliar words. We also replaced abstract words with more concrete ones and avoided using homonyms (similar sounding words with more than one meaning). We made changes in grammar to avoid compound sentences[51] and awkward, passive constructions.[52]

To insure a logical structuring of the paragraphs, we used both hierarchical and algorithmic organizing principles. In a hierarchical structure, high-level concepts are broken down into their lower-level components and then integrated. According to the algorithmic method of structuring, ideas are presented so that an understanding of any particular idea follows from the understanding of previous ideas.

Some of the revisions we made were directly responsive to our analysis of subjects' errors in comprehending the pattern instructions. For example, with regard to "intent," many subjects (29%) indicated doubts that a mental state such as intent could ever be proven beyond a reasonable doubt, even though the law clearly requires this finding for conviction. We made certain changes in order to reduce this type of apparent confusion.

We next submitted the rewritten instructions to legal scholars in order to validate the legality of the revised instructions.[53] Further changes were made to satisfy their concerns. The results of our efforts, instructions with improvements that were still legally sound according to our legal experts, became the focus of empirical investigation. These

---

hanced considerably when certain linguistic features that impede comprehension were eliminated. The major psycholinguistic principles they applied included:

(1) substituting active voice for passive voice, Charrow & Charrow, *supra* note 48, at 1325-26;

(2) inserting "whiz" phrases ("which is . . ." or "that is . . .") where needed, *id*. at 1323-24;

(3) eliminating multiple negatives, *id*. at 1324-25;

(4) reorganizing sentences to properly locate misplaced phrases and eliminate complicated embedding, *id*. at 1323, 1327-28;

(5) reducing item lists and strings to no more than two, where possible, *id*. at 1326;

(6) using directives such as "must," "should," and permissives such as "may" to help focus the jurors' attention, *id*. at 1324;

(7) replacing uncommon words with ones that are more common in the language, *id*. at 1324; and

(8) rearranging existing instructions into a more logical organization, *id*. at 1326-27.

[51] For example, the sentence, "Such evidence may be considered by you in deciding what weight or credibility should be given to the testimony of the defendant and for no other purpose," was broken into two parts: "You may not use this evidence in deciding whether he or she is guilty or innocent. You may use evidence of prior convictions only to decide whether to believe the defendant's testimony and how much weight to give it." *See infra* Table 1.

[52] For example, the phrase "you have an abiding belief in the truth of the charge . . ." was replaced by "you believe in the truth of the charge . . . ." *See infra* Table 1.

[53] Professor John Junker and former Superior Court Judge and Professor Charles Z. Smith, both of the University of Washington School of Law, provided legal insight in developing revised instructions.

instructions appear in Table 1, side by side with pattern jury instructions.

TABLE 1

EXAMPLES OF PATTERN INSTRUCTIONS AND THEIR REVISED COUNTERPARTS

Topic	Pattern Instruction	Revised Instruction
Use of Prior Conviction to Impeach a Defendant	Evidence that the defendant has previously been convicted of a crime is not evidence of the defendant's guilt. Such evidence may be considered by you in deciding what weight or credibility should be given to the testimony of the defendant and for no other purpose.	Evidence that the defendant has previously been convicted of a crime is not evidence of the defendant's guilt in this case. You may not use this evidence in deciding whether he or she is guilty or innocent. You may use evidence of prior convictions only to decide whether to believe the defendant's testimony and how much weight to give it.
Intent	A person acts with intent or intentionally when acting with the objective or purpose to accomplish a result which constitutes a crime.	A person acts with intent or intentionally when he or she acts with the objective or purpose to accomplish a result that is a crime. It is possible to prove intent beyond a reasonable doubt by either direct or circumstantial evidence.
Burden of Proof; Presumption of Innocence; Reasonable Doubt	The defendant has entered a plea of not guilty. That plea puts in issue every element of the crime charged. The plaintiff has the burden of proving each element of the crime beyond a reasonable doubt. A defendant is presumed innocent. This presumption continues throughout the entire trial unless you find it has been overcome by the evidence beyond a reasonable doubt.	The defendant has entered a plea of not guilty. That plea puts in issue every element of the crime charged. The defendant is presumed to be innocent and is not required to prove his or her innocence or any fact. This presumption of innocence is present at the beginning of the trial and continues unless you decide after hearing all the evidence that there is proof beyond a reason-

[a] In State v. Walker, 19 Wash. App. 881, 884, 578 P.2d 83, 85 (1978), additional language in the pattern instruction stating, "You are not to consider doubts that are unreasonable or which are unsupported by evidence or lack of evidence," was found by the court there to be unnecessarily confusing, although the language was not held to be erroneous.

TABLE 1—Continued

Topic	Pattern Instruction	Revised Instruction
Burden of Proof; Presumption of Innocence; Reasonable Doubt (continued)	A reasonable doubt is one for which a reason exists.[a] A reasonable doubt is such a doubt as would exist in the mind of a reasonable person after fully, fairly and carefully considering all of the evidence or lack of evidence. If, after such consideration, you have an abiding belief in the truth of the charge, you are satisfied beyond a reasonable doubt.	able doubt that the defendant is guilty. The state has the burden of proving each element of the crime beyond a reasonable doubt. A reasonable doubt about guilt is not a vague or speculative doubt but is a doubt for which a reason exists. A reasonable doubt is a doubt that would exist in the mind of a reasonable person after that person has fully, fairly and carefully considered all of the evidence or lack of evidence. If, after such thorough consideration, you believe in the truth of the charge, you are satisfied beyond a reasonable doubt. If you are satisfied beyond a reasonable doubt that all elements of the charge have been proved, then you must find the defendant guilty. However; if you are left with a reasonable doubt about the proof of any element, then you must find the defendant not guilty.
General Introductory Instruction	It is your duty to determine the facts in this case from the evidence produced in court. It is also your duty to accept the law from the court, regardless of what you personally believe the law is or ought to be. You are to apply the law to the facts and in this way decide the case. The order in which these instructions are given has no significance as to their relative importance. The attorneys may properly discuss any specific instructions they think are particularly significant. You	As jurors in this case, you have several duties: First, it is your duty to determine the facts in this case from the evidence produced in court; Second, it is your duty to accept the law as I will instruct you, regardless of what you personally believe the law is or ought to be; Third, to reach a verdict, you are to apply the law to the facts and in this way decide the case. With regard to your duty to determine the facts in this case, the evidence you are to consider consists of the testimony of

TABLE 1—Continued

Topic	Pattern Instruction	Revised Instruction
General Introductory Instruction (continued)	should consider the instructions as a whole and should not place undue emphasis on any particular instruction or part thereof. The information in this case is only an accusation against the defendant which informs the defendant of the charge. You are not to consider the filing of the information or its contents as proof of the matters charged. The evidence you are to consider consists of the testimony of the witnesses and the exhibits admitted into evidence. It has been my duty to rule on the admissibility of evidence. You must not concern yourselves with the reasons for these rulings. You will disregard any evidence which either was not admitted or which was stricken by the court. In determining whether any proposition has been proved, you should consider all of the evidence introduced by all parties bearing on the question. Every party is entitled to the benefit of the evidence whether produced by that party or by another party. You are the sole judges of the credibility of the witnesses and of what weight is to be given the testimony of each. In considering the testimony of any witness, you may take into account the opportunity and ability of the witness to observe, the witness' memory and manner while testifying, any interest, bias, or prejudice the witness may have, the reasonableness of the testimony of the	the witnesses and exhibits which I have admitted into evidence. You must not concern yourselves with the reasons for these rulings. You will disregard any evidence which either was not admitted or which was stricken by me. In determining what facts have been proved, you should consider all of the admitted evidence. Every party is entitled to the benefit of all the evidence, whether produced by that party or by another party. The law does not permit me to express my views about the facts or evidence in any way and I have not intentionally done so. The law also does not permit me to try to influence your judgment as to the believability or credibility of witnesses. You are the sole judges of the credibility of the witnesses and of what weight is to be given to the testimony of each. In evaluating the testimony of any witness, you may take into account the following factors: the opportunity and ability of the witness to observe the facts; the accuracy of the witness' memory; the witness' manner while testifying; any interest in the case or bias or prejudice the witness may have shown; the reasonableness of the witness' testimony considered in light of all the evidence; and any other factors that bear on believability and weight. If it appears to you that I have expressed my opinion concerning the evidence or the witnesses at any time, you must disregard

TABLE 1—Continued

Topic	Pattern Instruction	Revised Instruction
General Introductory Instruction (continued)	witness considered in light of all the evidence, and any other factors that bear on believability and weight. Counsel's remarks, statements and arguments are intended to help you understand the evidence and apply the law. They are not evidence, however, and you should disregard any remark, statement or argument which is not supported by the evidence or the law as given to you by the court. The lawyers have the right and the duty to make any objections which they deem appropriate. Such objections should not influence you, and you should make no presumption because of objections by counsel. The law does not permit me to comment on the evidence in any way, and I have not intentionally done so. If it appears to you that I have so commented, during either the trial or the giving of these instructions, you must disregard such comment entirely. You have nothing whatever to do with the punishment to be inflicted in case of a violation of law. The fact that punishment may follow conviction cannot be considered by you except insofar as it may tend to make you careful. You are officers of the court and must act impartially and with an earnest desire to determine and declare the proper verdict. Throughout your deliberations you will permit neither sympathy nor	such opinion entirely. With regard to your duty to accept the law as I will instruct you, you should consider the instructions as a whole and should not place undue emphasis on any particular instruction or part of an instruction. The order in which the instructions are given has no significance as to their relative importance. The lawyers may properly discuss any specific instructions they think are particularly significant. With regard to your duty to apply the law, the fact that the defendant has been charged is only an accusation. You are not to consider the filing of a written charge or its contents as proof of the matters charged. The lawyer's remarks, statement and arguments are intended to help you understand the evidence and apply the law. They are not evidence, however, and you should disregard any remark, statement or argument that is not supported by the evidence or by my instructions on the law. The lawyers have the right and the duty to make any objections which they think are appropriate. Such objections should not influence you, and you should make no presumption because of objections by the lawyers. You have nothing whatever to do with the punishment in case of a violation of law. The fact that punishment may follow conviction cannot be considered by you except that it

TABLE 1—Continued

Topic	Pattern Instruction	Revised Instruction
General Introductory Instruction (continued)	prejudice to influence you.	may tend to make you careful. Throughout your deliberations you will permit neither sympathy nor prejudice to influence you. You are officers of the court and must act impartially and with an earnest desire to determine and declare the proper verdict. To reach a verdict, your decision must be unanimous.

Our first test of the new instructions compared the responses of subjects who viewed the videotaped trial used in our previous study and then received either no instructions, general plus specific pattern instructions, or revised versions of those same instructions. The same questionnaire measures were taken as in the prior study.

The results showed consistently more accurate responses with the revised instructions. Most importantly, we found that revised instructions led subjects to endorse more strongly the correct applications of the targeted legal concepts than did pattern instructions or no instructions.[54] Comprehension was also improved, with subjects who received revised instructions averaging 20.3% errors in comparison to 29.3% with no instructions and 24.3% with pattern instructions.[55] Although the overall difference between revised and pattern instructions did not reach statistical significance for the multiple choice comprehension measures, the pattern of results for each of the individual concepts was consistent in showing lowest error rates with revised instructions.[56]

The experimental studies described above were conducted in a university setting with students who were registered voters, and thus eligible for jury duty, serving as subjects. In order to demonstrate the utility of these revisions for actual jurors, the next step was to move our research into a more generalizable setting.

III. Testing the Advantages of Revised Language on Actual Jurors

To obtain a test population more representative of real juries, we

54 $F(2,210) = 8.15, p < .001$.
55 $F(2,210) = 8.65, p < .001$.
56 *See* Severance & Loftus, *supra* note 26, at 190, Table 6.

approached the Washington state court system for assistance.[57] After reviewing the procedures we had used in testing student subjects, the court administrator and judges of the superior courts for the State of Washington allowed us to test two important populations: persons who had been selected and who had reported for jury duty in the past, and persons who were currently serving as jurors and awaiting assignment to courtrooms of the King County Superior Courts in Seattle, Washington.[58]

A. OVERVIEW OF METHODOLOGY

Persons who had served previously as jurors (ex-jurors) and persons who were currently on jury duty (current jurors) were shown the same videotaped burglary trial that we used in the earlier studies with college students. They then heard either (a) pattern instructions pertaining to reasonable doubt, intent, restrictions on use of evidence of prior convictions, and general instructions outlining the jurors' duties, or (b) our revised versions of these same instructions (see Table 1). These were the same variations we tested previously with college students. Since actual jurors are always given instructions at the close of trial, the no instruction condition was not included in this experimental design. After watching the trial and hearing the instructions, half of the participants deliberated to reach a verdict and the other half gave individual verdicts. All subjects completed questionnaires designed to measure their

---

57 We are particularly indebted to the Honorable Francis E. Holman and to King County Superior Court Administrator Robert Cannon and Assistant Court Administrator Michael Cason for their cooperation and assistance in implementing this research.

58 Ex-jurors in our study were randomly selected from lists of jurors who had served on jury duty in King County, Washington between February and September 1981. In all, 445 ex-jurors were contacted by mail and asked to participate in a study of jury behavior. Two hundred fifty-seven (64%) of those contacted agreed to participate. Ex-jurors' reluctance to participate appeared to be closely tied to the distance they were asked to travel to our testing location at the University of Washington. Those ex-jurors who actually participated may have had a higher degree of interest in jury duty than those who chose not to participate.

One hundred sixty-two ex-jurors were contacted by telephone and actually participated in the research. These subjects participated in groups of three or more, but in all cases there were six persons on each deliberating jury. A total of 72 ex-jurors deliberated (36 heard pattern instructions; 36 heard revised instructions). Ninety did not deliberate (40 heard pattern instructions; 50 heard revised instructions).

Among current jurors, there was a much higher rate of participation. Jurors in King County serve for a two-week period and during this time, they may or may not be selected for actual juries. Therefore, a considerable amount of time is spent awaiting assignment to a courtroom. These persons seemed interested in participating in our research rather than just waiting. We solicited subjects from those waiting and had 100% participation. In all, 144 current jurors participated in our research. Thirty-six persons participated in each of the four conditions (receiving either pattern or revised jury instructions, then either deliberating or not deliberating). All current jurors observed the videotaped trial while sitting in the jury box of an actual courtroom. Those who deliberated retired to the adjacent jury room to deliberate.

comprehension of the instructions and ability to apply the concepts embodied therein. Each of the four possible combinations (pattern or revised instructions and deliberation or no deliberation) was presented both to ex-jurors and to current jurors.

B. PROCEDURE

All participants in the study were told that they would be viewing a videotaped trial from another jurisdiction, after which they would hear instructions from a judge and then would be asked to reach a verdict. They were told further that we would be comparing their reactions to those of the jurors at the actual trial in order to evaluate the use of videotaped trial materials. This procedure was intended to encourage all participants to behave as actual jurors and take their roles seriously.

At the close of the trial and after the judge's instructions, participants were randomly divided into two groups. Each group was independently assigned to deliberate or not. Those in the deliberating groups were escorted to a conference room (ex-jurors) or jury room (current jurors), asked to choose a foreperson, given one written set of the judge's instructions they had heard,[59] and asked to notify the experimenter when a verdict had been reached. They were left to deliberate for up to thirty minutes. After reaching a verdict, each participant was given a questionnaire to complete. Participants in the no deliberation group were given the questionnaire immediately following the videotaped trial and judge's instructions. These people were not provided with a written set of the judge's instructions.

C. QUESTIONNAIRE

The questionnaire first elicited a verdict of "guilty" or "not guilty" and then asked subjects to indicate how certain they were that their verdict was correct. Next, thirty multiple choice questions measured comprehension of the targeted concepts embodied in the instructions, and ten items measured jurors' ability to apply those concepts to novel fact situations. These questions were identical to those used in the earlier work testing college students. All jurors were also asked to give their subjective impressions of the judge's instructions, i.e., how effective the instructions were in helping them to understand the law. Jurors who deliberated were asked several questions about the deliberation process: how much they had participated in the discussion; how they would rate the overall quality of the deliberation; how much discussion of the

[59] The standard practice in the State of Washington is for attorneys to submit two copies of their proffered instructions to the judge. One copy, containing citations, is for the judge's perusal; the second copy is routinely sent into the jury room.

judge's instructions they would have preferred. All jurors were given the additional task of defining in their own words the legal concepts of "reasonable doubt" and "intent," and were asked to indicate the legally proper way to use evidence of prior convictions. Finally, demographic information (i.e., age, ethnicity, and amount of jury experience) was obtained for all jurors.

D. RESULTS

1. Comparison of Ex-jurors and Current Jurors

The responses of ex-juror subjects and current juror subjects differed in several ways that affected our interpretation of the other results. First, the ex-jurors who participated in our research were significantly more experienced with jury duty than were current juror subjects. As indicated in Table 2, our ex-juror sample had been called to jury duty, had been assigned to a courtroom for the jury selection process, and had actually served on juries more than had our current jurors. While it is possible that the experience of the Current jurors would have been more similar to ex-jurors by the time their jury duty was completed, at the time that they participated in our research there were significant differences in the degree of experience between the two samples.

TABLE 2

DEMOGRAPHIC FEATURES AND EXPERIENCE OF EX-JUROR AND COURTHOUSE JUROR PARTICIPATION IN THE RESEARCH

	Subject Sample		
Individual Characteristic	Ex-Jurors (n = 162)	Current Jurors (n = 144)	Statistical Significance
Age	48.7 yrs.	43.3 yrs.	p = .004
Years of education	14.6 yrs.	13.8 yrs.	p = .006
Number of times on jury duty	2.00	1.46	p = .001
Number of times assigned to a courtroom for the jury selection process	3.25	1.95	p = .001
Number of civil trials actually served on	0.53	0.60	p = .462
Number of criminal trials actually served on	1.49	0.58	p = .001

Second, ex-jurors were significantly older and more educated than Current jurors. These differences, also summarized in Table 2, support the idea that those ex-jurors who agreed to take the time to participate in our research were to some degree self-selected in terms of their interest in juries and jury duty. Current jurors and ex-jurors did not differ in overall ethnic composition.

Although the experiments took place in an actual court setting for one group (current jurors) and in a university conference room for the others (ex-jurors), all subjects seemed to take the procedure seriously. Thus, we believe that differences between the two groups' responses are due largely to experiential and demographic factors rather than setting.

2. *Verdicts*

Overall, 35.5% of our subjects found the defendant guilty and 64.5% found him not guilty. The effects on verdicts of instructions, opportunity to deliberate, and setting are summarized in Table 3. These results demonstrate two significant effects. First, the Current jurors were more lenient than Ex- jurors, with only 28.5% of the former voting to convict as compared to 41.3% of the latter.[60] Second, those jurors who deliberated were less likely to find the defendant guilty than were the jurors who did not have an opportunity to deliberate, as 28.4% of those

TABLE 3

PERCENT OF JURORS WHO FOUND DEFENDANT GUILTY
(X = 35.5)

	Pattern Instruction	Revised Instruction
Ex-Jurors (X = 41.3%)		
No Deliberation	46	35
Deliberation	44	40
Current Jurors X = 28.5%)		
No Deliberation	40	44
Deliberation	22[a]	08[b]

Note: Row values with different superscripts differ at .05 level of significance.

[60] $Z = 2.37$, $p < .02$. The Z-test is a statistical test for determining whether the difference between two proportions is statistically significant. For an explanation of the Z-test, see J. BRUNING & B. KINTZ, COMPUTATIONAL HANDBOOK OF STATISTICS 199-201 (1968).

who deliberated voted to convict as compared to 41.3% of those who did not deliberate.[61] Variations in the instructions did not affect verdicts significantly.

All jurors were asked to indicate how certain they were of their verdicts on a scale from 1 to 7 where 1 = Extremely uncertain, and 7 = Extremely certain. Only one variable seemed important here: current jurors were significantly more certain of their verdicts (x = 4.91) than were ex-jurors (x = 3.09).[62]

3. *Comprehension Measures*

On the thirty multiple choice questions designed to assess jurors' understanding of the law as defined in the instructions, ex-jurors demonstrated better comprehension (21.4% errors over all thirty questions) than current jurors (26.1%).[63] For two of the individual instructions, the distinction between current and ex-jurors was also significant. For questions dealing specifically with the intent instruction, there were 33% errors for ex-jurors, and 39% errors for current jurors.[64] For questions that concerned jurors' general duties, the error rate for ex-jurors was 6%, and for jurors tested during jury duty, 11%.[65] All of these differences may be due to the different demographic characteristics and jury experience of our two samples.

Based on our earlier work with college students, we anticipated that regardless of whether or not jurors deliberated, the revised instructions would enhance comprehension relative to the pattern instructions. The relevant data appear in Table 4 for each instruction. In three out of four cases—questions pertaining to reasonable doubt are the exception—jurors who heard the revised instructions tended to make fewer errors than jurors who heard pattern instructions, although statistical significance was achieved only for questions about the limiting instruction.[66] The results indicated, however, that deliberating jurors who heard revised instructions achieved slightly higher comprehension (20.8% errors over all thirty questions) than did deliberating jurors who heard pattern instructions (25.4% errors).[67] This same pattern was statistically significant for questions pertaining to the limiting instruction

61 $Z = 2.39$, $p < .02$.
62 $F(1,296) = 127.45$, $p < .001$.
63 $F(1,297) = 9.80$, $p = .002$.
64 $F(1,297) = 6.07$, $p = .014$.
65 $F(1,297) = 12.61$, $p < .001$.
66 $F(1,297) = 4.32$, $p = .039$.
67 $F(1,297) = 3.27$, $p = .072$.

TABLE 4

MEAN PERCENT ERRORS ON COMPREHENSION QUESTIONS FOR SUBJECTS HEARING PATTERN AND REVISED INSTRUCTIONS

Instruction	Pattern Instruction	Revised Instruction
Intent	36.6	35.1
Limiting instruction	44.5[a]	36.3[b]
Reasonable doubt	23.5	25.2
Jurors' general duties	8.6	7.4
Overall	24.3	22.8

Note: Row means with different superscripts differ at .05 level of significance.

when it was analyzed separately.[68] Thus, overall, the revised instructions did improve comprehension, especially when those instructions were accompanied by an opportunity to deliberate.

4. Ability to Apply Instructions

With regard to the ten questions measuring jurors' abilities to apply the instructions to novel fact patterns, we predicted that the revised versions of the instructions would lead to more accurate applications of the

TABLE 5

MEAN LEVEL OF AGREEMENT WITH CORRECT APPLICATION OF THE LAW

Instruction	Pattern Instruction	Revised Instruction
Intent	0.59	0.59
Limiting instruction	1.15[a]	1.46[b]
Reasonable doubt	1.68	1.81
Overall	1.07	1.22

Note: Higher numbers indicate more correct responding; row means with different superscripts differ at .05 level of significance.

68 $F(1,297) = 4.08$, $p = .044$.

law. Data on the mean level of agreement with the correct application of these instructions are shown in Table 5, with responses coded so that the closer a number is to +3, the greater the agreement with the correct application of the law. Our findings demonstrate that jurors who heard revised instructions tended to apply the instructions more accurately than jurors who heard pattern instructions. Despite the consistent trend, however, the only statistically significant effect for type of instruction was for the questions regarding the limiting instruction.[69]

As with our previous findings, jury sample (ex-jurors vs. current jurors) and the opportunity to deliberate were important variables. For example, ex-jurors agreed more often with correct applications of "reasonable doubt" than current jurors.[70] Across all ten scenarios, however, this pattern held only for those jurors who did not deliberate; the mean level of agreement for non-deliberating ex-jurors was 1.31, and for non-deliberating current jurors, .97.[71] Where jurors had been given an opportunity to deliberate, there was no difference in ex-jurors' and current jurors' abilities to apply the law correctly. The impact of experiential and educational differences between ex-jurors and current jurors thus seemed to be reduced by the deliberation process.

5. Jurors' Subjective Impressions of the Judge's Instructions

A key objective in attempting to make jury instructions understandable is to ensure that the proper legal standards are applied consistently to defendants in different trials. If instructions are not understandable, verdicts will tend to be based on idiosyncratic features of the trial or personal attitudes of the jurors rather than on the proper legal standards.[72] We asked jurors to indicate how effective the judge's instructions were in helping them to understand the law on a scale that ranged from 1 (Not at all effective) to 5 (Extremely effective).

Current jurors who received revised instructions and then deliberated perceived those instructions to be significantly more effective than jurors in any of the other conditions.[73] Since current jurors were less experienced and less well educated than ex-jurors, it appears likely that

---

69 $F(1,297) = 4.81$, $p = .029$.

70 Ex-jurors' mean = 1.90; current jurors' mean = 1.56. $F(1,292) = 5.74$, $p = .017$.

71 $p < .05$ by Newman-Keuls test. Overall jury sample × opportunity to deliberate interaction: $F(1,288) = 4.84$, $p = .029$. The Newman-Keuls test is a systematic procedure for comparing all possible pairs of group means. For an explanation of the method of constructing such tests, see B. WINER, STATISTICAL PRINCIPLES IN EXPERIMENTAL DESIGN 191-96 (2d ed. 1971).

72 Strawn & Buchanan, *supra* note 19, at 478.

73 Mean response with revised instructions and deliberation = 3.84; with pattern instructions and deliberation, 3.34. Overall interaction: $F(1,285) = 8.43$, $p = .004$.

current jurors were especially in need of simple and clear instructions in order to understand the law, and, as a result, the revised instructions were more effective for them than were the pattern instructions. Ex-jurors, who were somewhat better educated and more experienced, apparently benefited less from the simplified language of the revised instructions than did current jurors, with the result that there were no significant differences between their perceived effectiveness of revised and pattern instructions.

6. *Deliberating Jurors' Subjective Impressions of Deliberations*

For jurors who deliberated, variations in the instructions (revised and pattern) and subject population (ex-jurors and current jurors) did not affect either the extent to which jurors felt they had participated in the deliberations, or ratings of the overall quality of the group deliberations.

All groups indicated that they thought they had had about the right amount of discussion concerning the instructions: on a scale ranging from 1 (Preference for a lot less discussion of the instructions) to 3 (Preference for the same amount of discussion) to 5 (Preference for a lot more discussion), the overall mean response was 3.36. None of the experimental manipulations caused reliable variation from this mean.

7. *Jurors' Paraphrases of Specific Jury Instructions*

In our final series of questions, we attempted to evaluate our jurors' understanding of the judge's instructions by asking them to paraphrase some of the concepts central to the instructions that they had heard at the close of the trial.[74] Each juror was asked to write an explanation of the legal concepts "reasonable doubt" and "intent," and of the restricted use of evidence of prior convictions. We then analyzed the written responses to each term.[75]

As a basis for evaluating the jurors' understanding, the content of each instruction was divided into units of meaning to provide a convenient list of essential legal components to which the paraphrase could be compared. Although pattern and revised instructions were analyzed separately, the content units for each were virtually identical. This similarity was attributable to the fact that most of the revisions were syntactical rather than semantic. Table 6 summarizes the component units of meaning for each instruction. Each juror's paraphrases were compared

[74] This idea sprang from the work of Charrow & Charrow, *supra* note 48.

[75] Special thanks are extended to Ms. Jane Goodman for her assistance in performing this analysis.

with the component units of meaning of the given instructions and categorized as (a) essentially correct, (b) erroneous, or (c) ambiguous.

TABLE 6

COMPONENT UNITS OF MEANING FOR THREE TARGETED LEGAL CONCEPTS, PRESENTED BY CONCEPT

Reasonable Doubt	Intent
presumption of innocence	act
doubt for reason	purpose/objective
doubt in mind	crime
reasonable person	
consider	Use of Prior Conviction
evidence/proof	
satisfy	evidence of
defendant	not guilt
abiding belief/remaining doubt	weight/credibility/believe
innocence/guilt	defendant's testimony

a. Reasonable doubt

Paraphrases were classified as essentially correct if they included the minimum indication of doubt by an objective external standard; for example, "That there is a reasonable chance there is doubt of a crime," or "A valid reason to doubt." By comparison, paraphrases were classified as ambiguous if it was unclear whether or not there was an articulable standard for deciding on the evidence. Responses such as "Not enough evidence," "The facts are not clear," or "Some aspect of the case you are not sure about" fell into this category. Paraphrases that indicated too rigorous an objective standard (e.g., "Not 100% evidence of guilt," or "Absolute proof not present") or too subjective a standard (e.g., "Guilty or not guilty in my mind and consciousness," or "What's right in your mind") were rated as erroneous.

b. Intent

Correct paraphrases were easily discernible because of the small number of component units of meaning. Examples of correct paraphrases are "It is on your mind to commit a crime," or "Having the idea in mind of doing something unlawful." We rated answers that failed to mention an essential component (e.g., crime) as incorrect, despite the fact that other components were accurately defined (e.g., "Will to do right or wrong," "A preconception," or "Having consciously made a decision to do something or not to do something"). There were very few ambiguous paraphrases of intent.

c. Prior conviction

Correct paraphrases included the essential components noted in Table 6 (e.g., "Only as an aid in determining credibility," or "For weighting truthfulness of testimony"). Incorrect paraphrases were of three types. One type implied that the use of evidence of a prior conviction was absolutely impermissible; another, that the use of such evidence was proper on the issue of defendant's guilt or innocence; the third implied that the juror had no grasp of the concept at all.

d. Findings

Paraphrase data are summarized in Table 7. The clearest findings, appearing in the overall results of Table 7, were that correct paraphrases outnumbered incorrect paraphrases when revised instructions were given but not when pattern instructions were given. This result was most pronounced for jurors who deliberated.[76] Such findings lend strength to the pattern observed elsewhere in our results that revised instructions accompanied by an opportunity to deliberate tend to enhance understanding.

Several collateral findings help to complete the picture. First, jurors who did not deliberate tended to produce more purely subjective

TABLE 7

PERCENTAGE OF CORRECT, INCORRECT, AND AMBIGUOUS PARAPHRASE DEFINITIONS FOR REASONABLE DOUBT, INTENT, AND PRIOR CONVICTION INSTRUCTIONS COMBINED

	Correct	Incorrect	Ambiguous
Pattern Instructions Deliberation	31.7	49.3	19.0
Pattern Instructions No Deliberation	42.0	47.3	10.7
Revised Instructions Deliberation	47.7	36.7	15.7
Revised Instructions No Deliberation	45.7	43.7	10.7

76 While the trends are clear, these data were not significantly different.

definitions of reasonable doubt than jurors who did deliberate, using paraphrases such as "Guilty or not guilty in my mind and consciousness," "You honestly believe the defendant guilty," or "What's right in your mind." Second, jurors who receive revised instructions tended to respond in less formal language and to use the first person more often, suggesting that the use of simpler, more direct language promotes personal involvement and makes the task of jurors less abstract.[77]

E. DISCUSSION

Several themes recur in our data. First, jurors with greater experience and learning apparently comprehend and apply jury instructions better than those who are less experienced and/or less well educated. This general finding is demonstrated in comparisons of the more experienced and better educated ex-jurors with the less experienced and less well educated current jurors.

In addition to this basic tendency, there are effects due to the language of the jury instructions and the opportunity to discuss legal concepts in the course of deliberations. A fundamental trend that appears throughout the data is the tendency for juror understanding to be enhanced when the language is relatively clear *and* when there is an opportunity to discuss legal concepts through deliberation. Thus, those who deliberated after receiving revised instructions were found to better comprehend the legal concepts. Furthermore, the paraphrased instructions of jurors who received revised instructions, followed by deliberation, showed the highest percentage of correct responses.

Not surprisingly, the impact of clear language and an opportunity to deliberate is greatest for those who initially seem at the greatest disadvantage—the relatively inexperienced, less well educated current jurors. We found that it was current jurors, armed with revised instructions and an opportunity to deliberate, who perceived the judge's instructions to be most effective. Moreover, relative to current jurors, the advantage that ex-jurors showed in applying the legal concepts to novel fact patterns occurred only where there was no opportunity to deliberate.

Two of the three independent variables examined in this study affected verdicts. First, less experienced current jurors tended to be more lenient and also more certain than ex-jurors in reaching verdicts. This finding is analogous to the finding of Kalven and Zeisel that judges, who presumably have had a great deal of trial experience, are more apt to

[77] Compare the following concrete paraphrase of the revised reasonable doubt instruction, "If I have a doubt in my mind by the weight of the evidence, he or she is not guilty," with a more abstract paraphrase of the pattern instruction, "Based on the evidence, the uncertainty that a reasonable and prudent person would have about the guilt of the defendant."

convict a defendant than are jurors who watch the same trial.[78] Our data corroborate the inverse relationship between experience and leniency. Second, jurors who deliberated tended to be more lenient than jurors who did not deliberate. This finding suggests that the deliberation process may expose jurors to additional reasons for doubting the guilt of the defendant. At the very least, this result occurred for the particular facts of the case used in our research. Third, and most notably, the variations in instructions did not affect verdicts reliably. Thus, as a policy matter, it appears that the revisions we developed do not tip the scales of justice for or against the defendant in comparison to the language of the original pattern instructions. Inasmuch as the revised instructions enhance jurors' understanding of relevant legal concepts without biasing verdicts, our findings provide a clear basis for recommending the use of these simplified jury instructions in actual trials. This recommendation would, of course, require that the revised instructions maintain legal accuracy.

IV. Response of the Judiciary and Supersimplified Instructions

At the onset of our research, a review of appellate cases indicated that the wording of jury instructions is often fragile; minor variations in wording may be the basis of reversals for error in instructing the jury. Our initial efforts to revise the language of existing pattern instructions thus were tempered by two concerns: first, that extensive alterations from existing pattern instructions would be unacceptable to appeals-conscious trial court judges; and, second, that appellate judges might reject such substantially altered instructions as an excessive departure from established precedents.

An informal sampling of approximately ten state trial judges' opinions of our revised instructions, however, provided us with a different message. The judges indicated that our initial revisions did not seem to go far enough—that what was needed were instructions even more simplified than those of our initial efforts. Based on this response, we undertook to develop an even more simplified version of the targeted instructions. By further refining our revised instructions and, in some instances, reorganizing the format of instructions, we developed the "supersimplified" instructions that appear in Table 8.

---

78 H. Kalven, Jr. & H. Zeisel, The American Jury 109 (1966).

TABLE 8

EXAMPLES OF SUPERSIMPLIFIED INSTRUCTIONS

Topic	Supersimplified Instructions
Use of Prior Conviction to Impeach a Defendant	You may not use evidence of a prior conviction to decide if the defendant is guilty in the current case. But, you may consider a prior conviction when evaluating a defendant's credibility and how much weight to give his (or her) testimony.
Intent	A person acting with intent acts with the deliberate purpose of accomplishing a crime. Intent can be proven beyond a reasonable doubt by either direct or circumstantial evidence.
Burden of Proof; Presumption of Innocence; Reasonable Doubt	The defendant pleads "not guilty." The defendant is presumed to be innocent and need not prove his (or her) innocence concerning any element of the crime. You must wait until you have heard all the evidence before you come to a decision in this case. The defendant's plea of "not guilty" means that the state must prove each element of the crime beyond a reasonable doubt. A reasonable doubt about guilt is not a vague feeling or suspicion. It is a doubt that a reasonable person has after carefully considering all of the evidence. If you are satisfied that all of the elements of the crime are proven beyond a reasonable doubt, you must find the defendant "guilty." If you have a reasonable doubt about the proof of any element of the crime, you must find the defendant "not guilty."
General Introductory Instruction	You have three distinct duties as jurors in this case: 1) You must determine the facts in this case from the testimony and evidence presented during the trial; 2) You must accept and apply the law as I instruct you, regardless of what you believe the law should be; 3) You must find the defendant "guilty" or "not guilty" by applying the law to the facts that you have determined. First, to determine the facts in this case, you must consider all of the evidence admitted in court. Evidence consists of exhibits and testimony of witnesses. You must not consider any evidence that I have not admitted. Every party may benefit from evidence introduced by the opposing party. You are not to consider as evidence the mere fact that the defendant has been accused. You are the sole judges of the credibility of the witnesses. You must decide what

TABLE 8—Continued

Topic	Supersimplified Instructions
General Introductory Instruction (continued)	weight to give to the testimony of each witness. By law, my personal opinions about the facts or evidence in this case must not influence your judgment. I can offer some suggestions to help you evaluate each witness' testimony: (A) Consider the witness' ability to observe and remember facts. Ask yourselves: Could the witness see or hear clearly at the time? How accurate is the witness' memory? (B) Consider the witness' manner and attitude when testifying. Ask yourselves: Is the witness confident or hesitant? Does the witness appear biased or prejudiced in any way? How believable is the witness' testimony in light of all the evidence?
	Second, in accepting these instructions on the law, consider the instructions as a whole. One instruction should not take precedence over another. The order of the instructions has no significance.
	Third, in applying the law to the facts, remember that the lawyer's remarks, statements and arguments are not part of the evidence. They are intended to help you understand the evidence and apply the law. Disregard any remark, statement or argument which is not supported by the evidence or my instructions.
	Finally, you have absolutely nothing to do with the punishment of a convicted defendant. The fact that punishment may follow a conviction must not influence your verdict, except that it may tend to make you careful. Throughout your deliberation, do not allow sympathy or prejudice to influence you. You are officers of the court and must act fairly and with the sincere desire to determine the proper verdict. To reach a verdict, your decision must be unanimous.

Following the same procedures employed in our previous research, we presented two groups of students at the University of Washington, who were also registered voters, with the same videotaped burglary trial previously used and then gave them either pattern instructions or the supersimplified instructions. In this study, all subjects deliberated.

Our results showed no difference in comprehension between the two groups, but there was one significant difference between the groups in ability to apply the instructions to novel fact patterns: subjects who received the supersimplified instructions performed better in applying "reasonable doubt/presumption of innocence" than did subjects who received standard pattern instructions.[79]

While this study explored the possibility that substantial simplification of the language of pattern instructions may enhance juror understanding, it provided no basis for determining whether courts would be willing to accept alternative versions of the instructions, either revised or supersimplified, in actual trials. Our final study was directed toward answering this question.

V. Trial Judges' Evaluations of Alternatively Worded Criminal Jury Instructions

Underlying our attempts to draft understandable jury instructions was the concern that however clear to lay people our revised instructions might be, unless they were accepted by trial judges, they might never see their day in court. Because trial judges ultimately choose which instructions will be given to jurors, we decided to survey state court judges currently sitting throughout the United States to determine how they rated the language of the revised, supersimplified, and existing pattern instructions.

A. Methodology

In this study, 435 state superior court judges randomly selected from across the country were asked to complete a questionnaire designed to measure the legal adequacy and probable acceptance of our linguistic revisions in relation to the pattern instructions.[80] Each judge was sent one of four versions of our questionnaire. Mailing was done randomly so that each of the four versions was distributed evenly throughout the country.

Three versions of the questionnaire were quite similar (i.e., the "pattern," "revised," and "supersimplified" versions). In each version, the judges were asked to evaluate three instructions: intent, reasonable doubt/presumption of innocence, and the limiting instruction. These instructions were presented in either their pattern form, the revised form that we had developed in the earlier phases of this research, or the supersimplified form that was an attempt to radically simplify the language of the instructions. We asked several questions about each instruction, including:

---

79 $F(1,50) = 4.14$, $p = .047$.

80 We obtained a list of the names and addresses of all superior court judges in the United States. We thank the Honorable James E. Noe, King County Superior Court, for making this list available to us. Using a map of the United States that had been divided into Congressional districts, we placed each judge in his or her respective Congressional district, and then randomly selected one judge from each of the 435 districts.

1. In your opinion, is this instruction a legally adequate statement of the law?

2. How effective do you think the instruction will be in conveying the intended legal concepts to the jury?

3. What, if any, aspects of the instruction do you find particularly helpful or troublesome?

4. Overall, would you consider this a proper instruction to give to a jury?

5. Do you perceive bias favoring either party in the language of this instruction?

The fourth version of our questionnaire had a different format. Here, a judge was given all three forms (i.e., pattern, revised, and supersimplified) of a particular instruction, and then asked to rank-order the instructions along these lines:

1. Rank the instructions as legally adequate statements of the law in your jurisdiction. Which do you most prefer? Which do you least prefer?

2. Rank the instructions as to their effectiveness in conveying the intended legal concepts to a jury.

3. Rank the instructions as to the least amount of bias favoring either party in the language of the instruction.

4. Overall, which instruction would you choose to give to the jury?

5. What, if any, aspects of each instruction do you find particularly helpful or troublesome?

Overall, we received responses from 133 judges or 31% of the sample. Of these, 110 (25%) completed the questionnaire; others gave us only their comments or informed us that they tried civil cases exclusively. Of those responding, 22% answered the pattern version, 26% answered the revised version, 33% answered the supersimplified version, and 19% answered the comparison questionnaire.

B. RESULTS

1. Intent Instruction

Overall, judges preferred the revised version of the intent instruction over the pattern and supersimplified forms. When asked, "Is this instruction a legally adequate statement of the law?" more judges answered affirmatively for the revised version than for the other intent instructions.[81] For those judges who rank-ordered the three versions of

[81] On a scale from −2 to +2 where −2 = Positively no and +2 = Positively yes, the mean response to the revised version was .77; to the pattern version, .48; and to the supersimplified

intent according to their legal adequacy, the revised form was most preferred.[82]

In response to the question, "How effective do you think this instruction will be in conveying the intended legal concepts to the jury?" the revised version of intent received the highest mean score,[83] although judges who ranked the three instructions comparatively on the basis of perceived effectiveness did not differ significantly in their rankings of the three versions. When judges were asked which of the three versions they would prefer to give to the jury, however, the revised version was most preferred.[84]

In terms of the perceived bias inherent in the three versions of the intent instruction, the revised instruction was viewed as slightly more biased in favor of the prosecution, but the scores did not differ significantly for the pattern or supersimplifed forms.[85] This slight prosecution bias possibly can be attributed to the fact that the revised instruction included this statement: Intent can be proved by either direct or circumstantial evidence.

2. *Reasonable Doubt/Presumption of Innocence*

Like the intent instruction, the revised version of the reasonable doubt instruction was clearly favored by judges. Among judges who rated only one version, the revised instruction was given the highest mean score in terms of its legal adequacy[86] and was thought to be some-

---

version, −.28. Chi-square = 21.44, 8df, $p = .006$. The chi-square is used to determine whether a systematic relationship exists between two variables. This is done by arranging the data in a 2×2 table. The cell frequencies that would be expected were there no relationship between the variables are compared to the actual cell frequencies. The greater the discrepancies between the expected and actual frequencies, the larger the chi-square. The degrees of freedom (df) vary with the number of cells in the table.

82 On a ranking scale where 1 = Most preferred version and 3 = Least preferred version, the mean rank for the revised version = 1.76; for the pattern version = 2.38; and for the supersimplified version = 1.86. Friedman ANOVA on rank-order data, chi-square = 4.67, 2df, $p = .09$. The Friedman analysis of variance (ANOVA) by ranks is a statistical test to determine whether rank sums for different instructions, for example, differ at some predetermined level of significance (usually $p < .05$).

83 On a scale from 0 to 4 where 0 = Not at all effective, and 4 = Extremely effective, the revised instruction = 1.90; pattern instruction = 1.42; supersimplified instruction = 1.42. Chi-square = 17.07, 8df, $p = .03$.

84 On a scale from 1 to 3 where 1 = Most preferred version, and 3 = Least preferred version, mean rank for revised intent instruction = 1.68; pattern instruction = 2.47; supersimplified instruction = 1.84. Friedman ANOVA chi-square = 6.63, 2df, $p = .04$.

85 On a scale from −3 to +3 where −3 = strong defense bias, 0 = no bias, and +3 = strong prosecution bias, the mean score for revised instruction = .63; pattern instruction = −.16; supersimplified instruction = .13. Not significant by chi-square.

86 On a scale from −2 to +2, the revised instruction = .73; pattern = 0; supersimplified = .34. Chi-square = 12.47, 8df, $p = .13$.

what more effective at conveying the intended legal concepts to a jury.[87] The judges who saw all three versions and then ranked the instructions produced similar results. The revised version tended to be preferred on the dimension of legal adequacy,[88] and was seen as most effective in communicating the concept of reasonable doubt to the jury.[89] In response to the question, "Would you consider this a proper instruction to give to the jury?" the revised version received more affirmative votes[90] and was ranked as the most preferred form of the instruction.[91] Finally, in terms of the perceived bias of each version, the pattern instruction was thought to be slightly more biased in favor of the prosecution,[92] and the revised version was ranked as having the least amount of bias overall.[93]

3. Limiting Instruction

The judges found very few differences among the three versions of the limiting instruction. Although the revised limiting instruction received a slightly higher score for legal adequacy than did the other two versions, this difference was not statistically significant. However, there was a difference in the perceived effectiveness of the instructions, and here the revised instruction received the highest mean score.[94] For the questions, "Would you consider this a proper instruction to give to the jury?" and "Do you perceive bias favoring either party in the language of this instruction?" there were no statistically significant differences in judges' responses. Also, there were no differences in the rankings of the revised, pattern, and supersimplified instructions from judges who read all three versions and ranked the instructions in order of preference.

---

87 On a scale from 0 to 4, revised instruction = 2.19; pattern instruction = 1.48; supersimplified instruction = 2.03. Chi-square = 11.74, 8df, p = .16.

88 On a scale from 1 to 3, mean rank for revised instruction = 1.63; patten = 2.11; supersimplified = 2.26. Friedman ANOVA chi-square = 4.11, 2df, p = .12.

89 On a scale from 1 to 3, mean rank for revised instruction = 1.56; pattern = 2.17; supersimplified = 2.28. Friedman ANOVA chi-square = 5.44, 2df, p = .06.

90 On a scale from −1 to +1 where −1 = No, this is not a proper instruction, and +1 = Yes, this is a proper instruction, the revised version = .42; pattern version = −.28; supersimplified version = .19. Chi-square = 9.35, 4df, p = .05.

91 On a scale from 1 to 3, mean rank for revised instruction = 1.47; for pattern = 2.29; for supersimplified = 2.24. Friedman ANOVA chi-square = 7.18, 2df, p = .03.

92 On a scale from -3 to +3, revised instruction = .33; pattern = .52; supersimplified = .32. Chi-square = 16.04, 10df, p = .09.

93 On a scale from 1 to 3, mean rank for revised = 1.50; pattern = 2.25; supersimplified = 2.25. Friedman ANOVA chi-square = 6.00, 2df, p = .09.

94 On a scale from 0 to 4, where 0 = Not at all effective, and 4 = Extremely effective, revised version = 2.54; pattern version = 2.08; supersimplified version = 1.92. Chi-square = 16.70, 8df, p = .03.

VI. General Discussion

The strategy of the studies reported in this Article was (a) to identify certain criminal jury instructions that are difficult for jurors to understand, yet are crucial and used frequently in most jurisdictions; (b) to develop alternative language that would improve jurors' understanding; (c) to validate the use of the alternative language in a setting and with juror participants that approximate those of actual trials; and (d) to present information on trial judges' reactions to the alternatively worded instructions. The result is a set of alternatively worded instructions that both enhanced juror understanding and received favorable ratings by the trial judges included in our sample. We believe the revised language of the pattern instructions is appropriate for use in actual court cases and will preserve legal accuracy while also enhancing communication with jurors.

Although the findings generally seem clear, one caveat is in order. This concerns the notion of external validity, or the extent to which results of any experimental research can be generalized to other persons and situations. Because the experimental situation we used to test understanding of the pattern and revised instructions did not mirror exactly the conditions of an actual trial (for example, the trial was presented on videotape and thus not viewed live, our jurors were aware that their verdicts were not binding, and their deliberation time was limited), we must be cautious about overgeneralizing from the favorable results of these studies.[95]

There is, however, room for cautious optimism. First, results from the archival study enabled us to select jury instructions for revision that were indeed problematic—these instructions were frequently used but difficult for jurors to understand. Second, we tested our revised instructions in a setting that closely resembled that of a real trial, and we used actual jurors as our subjects. This closer approximation to reality is certainly an improvement over jury simulation studies of the past.[96] Finally, results from the trial judges' survey demonstrated that the language changes we proposed were acceptable to those trial judges who responded and were thought to communicate effectively crucial infor-

---

[95] For a general critique of jury simulation studies, see *Simulation Research and the Law*, 3 Law & Hum. Behav. 1 (1979).

[96] The resemblance of our simulation to a real trial was close, but still not complete. For example, jurors did not participate in voir dire—a portion of the trial in which counsel asks questions of potential jurors that relate to the law. However, mock jurors did hear closing arguments, in which counsel has the opportunity to argue and explain the law, interpreting legal issues so as to favor his or her side. Given the inevitably biased interpretations, the court has an even greater duty to provide neutral guidance so that jurors can indeed understand the relevant law.

mation to jurors. In many respects, the judges' evaluations provide the best test of the external validity of our research and lend confidence to the view that our findings are generalizable to actual jury trials and will improve jurors' understanding of their instructions.

As a policy matter, it is important to examine whether changes in the language of jury instructions such as those presented here are likely to affect verdicts. If, for example, verdicts of guilty dramatically increase or decrease as the result of language variations, we could assume that simplified language somehow was shifting the decision criteria used by jurors away from existing standards. The data reported here, however, showed reliable effects on verdicts of deliberation (i.e., those who deliberated were more likely to acquit) and of juror sample (i.e., less experienced jurors were more likely to acquit), but no reliable effects of instruction variations. These results suggest an interactive effect of jury instructions, such that jurors who have an opportunity to deliberate and who have little jury experience at the outset benefit the most from simplified language. In short, it appears that linguistic improvements in the instructions do not shift jurors' decision criteria relative to pattern instructions, though they do help jurors to comprehend and apply the instructions to facts more accurately.

More broadly, our results suggest that lawyers and judges need not despair that juries sometimes seem ill equipped to understand and apply the law. Our findings demonstrate that simplified language and organized presentations of legal concepts can effectively help jurors, particularly when coupled with the opportunity to discuss and deliberate. Proper attention to devising jury instructions that are meaningful to lay people, as well as legally accurate, can accomplish the important task of informing jurors of the relevant legal concepts.

Law and Human Behavior, Vol. 9, No. 1, 1985

On the Inefficacy of Limiting Instructions

When Jurors Use Prior Conviction Evidence to Decide on Guilt*

Roselle L. Wissler† and Michael J. Saks†

The rationale for allowing into evidence a defendant's criminal record asserts that such evidence can be used for the limited purpose of impeaching a defendant witness's credibility and, in accord with judges' instructions, will not be used to assess likelihood of guilt. The effect that the defendant's prior record has on mock jurors' assessments of credibility and guilt was tested in a two (cases) × four (type of prior conviction) factorial design. Adults' ratings of the defendant's credibility did not vary as a function of prior record and were consistently the lowest of the credibility ratings of all witnesses. Conviction rates did vary by prior record, however, with the highest conviction rate occurring when the prior conviction was the same as the present charge and the lowest conviction rate occurring in the no-prior-conviction condition. Defendants with a previous conviction for perjury or a dissimilar crime were convicted at an intermediate rate. We concluded that the risk of prejudice to the defense under existing policy is greater than the unrealized potential benefit to the prosecution.

INTRODUCTION

According to rule 609(a) of the Federal Rules of Evidence (1975),[1] evidence that an individual has been previously convicted of a crime may be admitted during

* Portions of this research were presented at the 90th Annual Convention of the American Psychological Association in Washington, D.C., August 23–27, 1982. The authors wish to thank Norman Berkowitz, Edward Krupat, and Marianne LaFrance for their comments on an earlier draft of this paper, and Hon. Robert J. Hallisey for providing us with sample instructions and for his counsel. Of course, the authors accept the responsibility for what they did, found, and concluded.

† Department of Psychology, Boston College, Chestnut Hill, Massachusetts 02167.

[1] Rule 609(a), the general rule for the use of evidence of prior convictions for impeachment purposes, "was one of the most hotly contested provisions in the Federal Rules of Evidence" in the Supreme Court's Advisory Committee as well as in Congress (United States v. Smith, 1976, p. 360). The adopted version reads as follows:

a trial "for the purpose of attacking the credibility of a witness." When such evidence is admitted for a defendant testifying on his or her own behalf, the judge instructs the jury that the defendant's prior record should be used solely to assess the credibility of the defendant (i.e., whether he or she is to be believed as a witness) and not to determine the defendant's propensity to commit the present crime or to determine guilt (Spector, 1979). In the terms of information integration theory (Anderson, 1974), the jury is allowed to use the prior conviction evidence to weight the defendant's testimony, but not to use it as an independent piece of information entering into the verdict.

Several courts and legal commentators have expressed concern, however, that the cautionary instructions may not enable the jury "to restrict the impact" of prior conviction evidence "to the issue of credibility" (*Gordon v. United States*, 1967, p. 939; *People v. Fries*, 1979). "Despite limiting instructions, the jury is likely to consider this evidence for the improper purpose of determining whether the accused is the type of person who would engage in criminal activity", in general, or would commit the specific crime charged (*People v. Antick*, 1975, p. 487; Margolis, 1972; *People v. Fries*, 1979). Thus, the defendant faces a substantial risk of prejudice "if the jury considers the prior conviction as evidence of present guilt" (*United States v. Toney*, 1980, p. 283). A 1968 survey indicated that 98 percent of the lawyers and 43 percent of the judges questioned expressed the belief that jurors are not able to follow an instruction to use prior conviction evidence only for assessing credibility (Note, 1968). Their intuition is supported by empirical research on jury behavior, which indicates both that the admission of evidence of prior criminal convictions increases the likelihood of conviction and that the judge's limiting instructions do not counteract the prejudice caused by the admission of the convictions.

In real cases where the inculpatory evidence in the different cases was approximately equal, Kalven and Zeisel (1966) observed that conviction rates were 27 percent higher for cases in which prior conviction evidence was presented than for those cases in which such evidence was not brought in. In simulation experiments, Doob and Kirshenbaum (1972) and Hans and Doob (1975) found, respectively, that individual jurors and four-person juries who were told that the defendant had previously been convicted of the same crime were significantly more likely to find the defendant guilty than were jurors who had no information on his prior record. Cornish and Sealy (1973) obtained mixed results depending upon the crime with which the defendant was charged. In addition, Doob and Kirshenbaum (1972) found that subjects were equally likely to find the defendant guilty whether or not they had received judges' limiting instructions. Hans and Doob (1975) also reported that even though subjects had received limiting instructions, tape recordings of their deliberations showed that groups informed of the

For the purpose of attacking the credibility of a witness, evidence that he has been convicted of a crime shall be admitted if elicited from him or established by public record during cross-examination but only if the crime (1) was punishable by death or imprisonment in excess of one year under the law under which he was convicted, and the court determines that the probative value of admitting this evidence outweighs its prejudicial effect to the defendant, or (2) involved dishonesty or false statement, regardless of the punishment.

defendant's prior record and those not informed did not differ in the amount of time spent discussing the defendant's credibility. In addition, some of the content of the deliberations reflected use of prior conviction evidence to estimate the likelihood of guilt in the present case.

While the previous studies, taken together, generally support the notion that evidence of a prior criminal record increases the likelihood of conviction and that judges' instructions do not prevent people from using such evidence to determine guilt, the possibility remains that subjects are using the information in a legally acceptable way. That is, the higher conviction rates in prior record conditions may be merely a consequence of the defendant's testimony being discounted by his decreased credibility. The present study attempted to rule out that possibility by using previous convictions of several different crimes: one which bears directly on the believability of the defendant's testimony (i.e., perjury) and others which relate to the defendant's propensity to commit the particular crime and not necessarily to his or her disposition to tell the truth.[2] If the law's rationale is correct, more convictions would result when the prior conviction is for perjury; but if jurors are misusing the information, more convictions would result from a prior conviction for the same crime; and an intermediate number of convictions would result from a prior conviction for a dissimilar crime.[3]

METHOD

Overview of Design

One hundred sixty male and female subjects were assigned to one of eight treatment conditions (i.e., 20 subjects per cell) in a 2 (cases) × 4 (prior convictions: same crime as present charge, different crime, perjury, no information about prior convictions) factorial design. In addition to a verdict, dependent variables included measures of certainty, credibility, and basis for the decision made.

Subjects

Subjects were 160 adult men and women who were approached at laundro-

---

[2] That this experimental strategy is consistent with the law's rationale in this area is reflected by Rule 609(a) and subsequent judicial opinions. The fact that crimes which "involved dishonesty or false statement" are listed separately in Rule 609(a) and were the only admissible convictions under an earlier version of the rule suggests that they are presumed to be "particularly probative of credibility" (United States v. Toney, 1980, p. 279; United States v. Smith, 1976). More specifically, several courts have stated that "different felonies have different degrees of probative value on the issue of credibility. Some, such as perjury, are intimately connected with the issue; others, such as robbery and burglary, are somewhat less relevant . . ." (People v. Rollo, 1977, p. 118). "Acts of violence on the other hand . . . generally have little or no direct bearing on honesty and veracity" (Gordon v. United States, 1967, p. 940).

[3] In a number of cases, the courts stated that when the prior conviction is the same as or similar to the present charge, the risk of prejudice is much greater (Gordon v. United States, 1967; People v. Antick, 1975; People v. Beagle, 1972; People v. Rist, 1976; United States v. Toney, 1980).

Table 1. Mean Ratings[a] of the Defendant's Credibility

Prior conviction	Case: Auto theft	Murder	Mean
None	4.45	2.95	3.70
Same	3.40	2.90	3.15
Dissimilar	3.20	4.20	3.70
Perjury	3.25	2.65	2.95

[a] Ratings range from 0 (not at all credible) to 10 (completely credible).

mats, supermarkets, airports, bus terminals, and private homes in the metropolitan Boston area and agreed to participate in the study. The sample of subjects was not selected in any systematic (i.e., biasing) fashion and was heterogeneous.

Cases

Written, two-page descriptions of two hypothetical cases, one involving auto theft and one involving murder, were given to the subjects. These case summaries included various facts of the case, the testimony of the defendant and several other witnesses, and instructions as to the elements which would be necessary in order to find the defendant guilty beyond a reasonable doubt. Through pilot testing, the cases were designed in such a way that the guilt or innocence of the accused was ambiguous. Four prior record conditions accompanied each case: no mention of the defendant's prior record,[4] previous conviction for the same crime, previous conviction for a dissimilar crime (murder in the auto theft case and auto theft in the murder case), and previous conviction for perjury. (The resulting stimuli consisted of eight present charge–prior conviction combinations.) Included in the case summaries of subjects in the latter three conditions were instructions by the judge that they were not to consider the evidence of the defendant's prior record as indicating that the defendant has criminal tendencies or dispositions but to use this evidence solely to assess the believability of his testimony.[5]

Procedure

Subjects were randomly assigned to one of the eight conditions before they were approached. Subjects were asked if they would be willing to participate in a study examining how people use information presented during a trial to reach a verdict. They were told that their participation in the study would involve reading a two-page case summary and answering a few questions. Persons who

[4] For the sake of brevity, the condition in which the defendant's prior record was not mentioned will be referred to as "no prior record" or "no prior conviction" throughout the rest of the paper.

[5] The instructions used in the case summaries are a shortened version of the actual instructions to jurors on the use of prior conviction evidence typically used in Massachusetts.

agreed to participate in the study were given a description of a hypothetical case and were asked to imagine that they were jurors deciding that case. After they had read the case summary, subjects were given a questionnaire which asked them to indicate: (1) whether they thought the accused person was guilty or not guilty of the charge; (2) how certain they were of their verdict on a ten-point scale; (3) the credibility of each witness, including the defendant, on a ten-point scale; (4) the major reasons they reached their decision in the case; (5) how much the defendant's prior conviction had influenced their guilty/not guilty verdict on a seven-point scale; and (6) their sex.

RESULTS

The findings pertaining to the defendant's credibility are presented in Table 1. The credibility ratings of the defendant did not vary as a function of prior conviction ($F(3,152) = .87$, $p = .46$) or case ($F(1,152) = .94$, $p = .33$). The interaction between prior conviction conditions and case was not significant, ($F(3,152) = 1.58$, $p = .20$). It is particularly important to note that the defendant's credibility was not significantly higher with no prior conviction nor significantly lower with a prior conviction for perjury, indicating that the evidence of prior convictions did not affect ratings of the defendant's credibility. In addition, the credibility rating of the defendant was significantly lower than that of the other witnesses in each case, $t(159) = 15.09$, $p < .001$, effect size $r = .77$.[6] On a scale from 0 (not at all credible) to 10 (completely credible), the average credibility rating of the defendant in the auto theft and murder cases, respectively, was 3.58 and 3.18, while the average credibility rating of the witnesses in each case was 7.52 and 7.30.[7]

Conviction rates varied as a function of prior conviction, $F(3,152) = 3.26$, $p < .05$, effect size $r = .15$ (see Table 2).[8] No significant main effect of case was found ($F(1,152) = 2.72$, $p = .10$) and no significant interaction was obtained between the prior conviction conditions and case ($F(3,152) = 1.92$, $p = .13$), indicating that the pattern of convictions among prior record conditions did not vary reliably between the auto theft and murder cases. Combining both cases, orthogonal a priori comparisons showed that defendants with no prior record had a significantly lower conviction rate than defendants with any of the three types of prior convictions, $t(156) = 2.25$, $p < .05$, effect size $r = .18$. Conversely, defendants previously convicted of the same crime had a significantly higher

[6] This test was conducted by comparing the defendant's credibility rating to the average credibility rating of the other witnesses. The same conclusion results from significance tests comparing the defendant with each other witness separately.

[7] The large difference between credibility ratings for the defendant versus other witnesses, and the lack of a difference in credibility ratings attributable to prior convictions, indicates that the nondifferences in Table 1 are not an artifact of insensitive measurement of credibility.

[8] The reports F's were computed by scoring guilty as 1 and not guilty as 0. The probability statements derived from this analysis do not differ from those yielded by traditional nonparametric tests for dichotomous data (e.g., see Cochran, 1950).

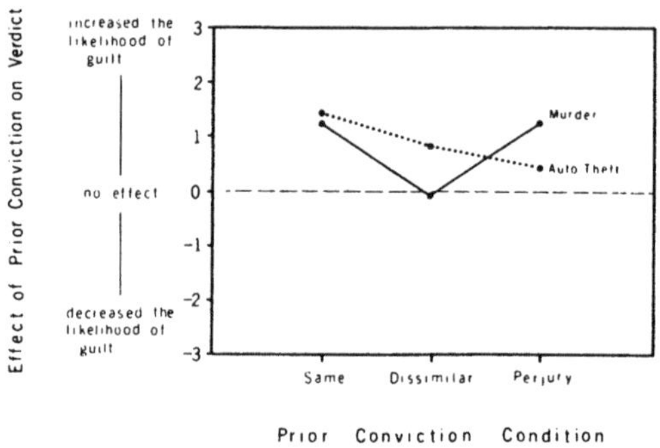

Fig. 1. Mean ratings of the effect of prior conviction on verdict.

conviction rate than defendants previously convicted of perjury or a dissimilar crime, $t(156) = 1.99$, $p < .05$, effect size $r = .16$.[9]

An analysis of covariance across both cases showed that prior record accounted for a significant portion of the variation in verdict over and above that which is explained by credibility, $F(3,155) = 2.90$, $p < .05$, effect size $r = .14$. That is, after controlling for the effect of credibility, prior record still had an effect on verdict. When each case was analyzed separately, this finding also obtained in the auto theft case ($F(3,75) = 2.90$, $p < .05$, effect size $r = .19$) but not in the murder case, $F(3,75) = 1.13$, $p > .10$.

Examining only those six cells where prior convictions were presented, fifty-six percent of the subjects reported they felt that the evidence of the defendant's prior conviction increased the likelihood that he was guilty, while thirty-eight percent reported that it did not influence the likelihood of the defendant's guilt. A significant main effect of prior conviction condition was found ($F(2,110) = 7.70$, $p < .001$, effect size $r = .26$) and a significant interaction was obtained between prior conviction conditions and case ($F(2,110) = 5.89$, $p < .005$, effect size $r = .22$), indicating that the effect of prior record on subjects' reports of how prior convictions had influenced their verdicts varied with each case and with each prior conviction (see Figure 1). Scheffé comparisons showed that subjects in the same-prior-conviction condition of the auto theft case reported that the previous conviction had a greater impact on their judgment of guilt than did subjects in the perjury condition, $p < .05$. In the murder case, subjects in both the same- and perjury-prior-conviction conditions reported that the previous conviction had a greater impact on their decision of guilty than did subjects in the dissimilar-prior-conviction condition, $p < .05$.

[9] Although it is statistically appropriate to collapse across the two cases because there is no significant interaction between prior record conditions and case (Keppel, 1973), these orthogonal a priori comparisons show different results when examined separately for each case. First, the lower conviction rate for defendants with no prior record compared to those with any of the three types of prior convictions holds for the auto theft case ($t(76) = 3.22$, $p < .005$, effect size $r = .35$) but not for the murder case, $t(76) = .13$, $p = .90$. Second, the higher conviction rate in the same-prior-conviction condition compared to the dissimilar or perjury conditions does not hold for the auto theft case ($t(76) = .79$, $p = .43$) but does obtain in the murder case, $t(76) = 2.02$, $p < .05$, effect size $r = .23$.

Table 2. Percent of Jurors Voting to Convict[a]

	Case		
Prior conviction	Auto theft	Murder	Mean percent
None	35%	50%	42.5%
Same	80	70	75.0
Dissimilar	70	35	52.5
Perjury	70	50	60.0

[a] $n = 20$ per cell

Thirteen percent of the subjects who found the defendant guilty stated that the prior conviction was the critical factor in reaching their verdict. Two-thirds of these subjects were in the same-prior-conviction condition while only one-third were in the perjury condition. The subjects' certainty of their verdicts did not vary by case ($F(1,152) = 1.62$, $p = .21$) or by prior record condition, $F(3,152) = .06$, $p = .98$. The interaction between case and prior record was not significant, $F(3,152) = 1.61$, $p = .19$. Male and female subjects did not differ on any of the variables.

DISCUSSION

According to the law's rationale, a defendant's criminal record is allowed into evidence for the limited purpose of impeaching the defendant's credibility. The prior record should, therefore, influence verdicts only to the extent that it decreases the believability of the defendant's testimony. If prior convictions were used to make only credibility judgments, we reasoned, the prior conviction for perjury would have done the most to vitiate the defendant's credibility. In fact, credibility judgments were unaffected by prior conviction condition. Indeed, the defendant's credibility rating was dramatically and unvaryingly the lowest of any of the witnesses. A field study by Linz and Penrod (cited in Penrod, 1983) also found that jurors rated defendant witnesses as less believable than other types of witnesses. The defendant's credibility is already so much lower than that of the other witnesses (because it obviously is in the defendant's self-interest to give testimony which favors his or her position) that the admission of prior convictions does not reduce the credibility of the defendant further (Margolis, 1972). Mock jurors do not appear to be using evidence of prior convictions to assess the defendant's credibility.

Although the defendant's credibility did not vary by prior record condition, conviction rates *did* vary as a function of the existence and type of prior record. Overall, the lowest conviction rate occurred in the no-prior-conviction condition and the highest conviction rate occurred when the prior conviction was the same as the present charge, corroborating the findings of Doob and Kirshenbaum (1972) and Hans and Doob (1975). Note that repetition in the defendant's behavior seems to make mock jurors feel that he is most likely to be guilty. At the same time, perjury prior convictions do not increase conviction rates more than the other prior convictions do. As shown in the covariance analysis, prior record had an effect on verdict even after controlling for the effect of credibility on verdict. Therefore, it appears that the mock jurors used the prior conviction evidence to help them judge the likelihood that the defendant committed the crime charged. Also interesting to note is that subjects were willing to state that the prior conviction evidence increased the likelihood of the defendant's guilt and was the reason they found him guilty, even though they had been instructed not to use the information for that purpose. The key finding, then, is that, at least for these mock jurors, prior conviction evidence does not have its impact on verdicts by way of an intervening impact on perceptions of credibility.

Cornish and Sealy (1973) hypothesized that jurors discount evidence of a prior conviction for a minor crime when it is introduced into a trial for a serious offense. The jurors may feel that the prosecution is unfairly trying to prejudice them by introducing evidence of a marginally relevant, less serious conviction and, hence, may be less likely to return a guilty verdict. By using auto theft as the prior conviction in our murder case and murder as the prior conviction in our auto theft case (both forming the dissimilar-prior-conviction condition), we were able to test this suggestion. Cornish and Sealy's hypothesis is consistent with the smaller percentage of convictions, the greater (although nonsignificant) degree of credibility, and the significantly lower impact of prior record on subjects' guilt judgments in the dissimilar prior conviction condition of the murder case. Perhaps most telling is that in the murder case, introduction of an auto theft prior conviction *reduced* the conviction rate 15 percentage points below the base rate (of 50%) while in the auto theft case, introduction of a prior conviction for murder *increased* the conviction rate 35 percentage points above the base rate (of 35%). Thus, the seriousness of the prior conviction relative to the present charge may be an important relationship.

Since credibility judgments do not account for the differences in conviction rates among prior conviction conditions, one must look for other plausible ways in which prior record may have affected jurors' verdicts. First, the prior record may have provided information which increased jurors' estimates of the likelihood of the defendant's guilt and, hence, increased the percentage of guilty verdicts for defendants with a prior record, especially for the same crime (Lempert, 1977; Nagao & Davis, 1980). Lempert (1977) suggests that jurors tend to give prior conviction evidence more weight than it deserves because, lacking base rate information, they are likely to overestimate the extent to which the defendant's criminal record is related to his or her propensity toward crime and to the probability that he or she committed a given crime. In addition, such evidence is redundant and tends to be double counted "because it probably has influenced the decisions to arrest and prosecute and so has figured in the jurors' initial estimation of the odds on the defendant's guilt" (Lempert, 1977, p. 1052). This is consistent with finding higher conviction rates for the prior record groups, with the largest percentage of convictions in the same-prior-conviction condition.

Second, knowing that the defendant has a prior conviction could change the meaning or significance of other evidence in the case (Hans & Doob, 1975; Thomas & Hogue, 1976). Hans and Doob (1975) found that the prior-record groups considered the evidence against the defendant to be stronger and were less likely to discredit it than were the no-prior-record groups. Third, knowing that the defendant has a prior record could decrease the standard of proof or the amount of evidence required to find him or her guilty. According to Lempert (1977), this occurs because the information of a defendant's prior record is likely to decrease the regret associated with the mistake of convicting a truly innocent person. The error of erroneous conviction has fewer negative consequences for a defendant with a record than for a defendant who had never been in trouble with the law because the former already has the stigma associated with a criminal record. In addition, "some may regard a convicted felon as essentially criminal and believe that if he did not commit the crime charged he probably has committed or will commit other crimes" (Lempert, 1977, p. 1039). For these reasons, jurors regret the mistake of convicting those with criminal records less than the mistake of convicting basically "good" people, with the resultant effect of lowering the level of probability of guilt, or level of reasonable doubt, necessary to vote to convict. This is consistent with finding a larger percentage of guilty verdicts for defendants with a prior record, with the largest percent for defendants previously convicted of the same crime.

Several social psychological concepts and theories provide a plausible basis for the apparent prejudice caused by the prior-record evidence. The larger percentage of guilty verdicts for defendants with a prior record could be due to subjects' generalizing negative characteristics—the reverse "halo effect." Rosenberg and Olshan (1970) cite several studies of evaluative or affective consistency in person perception which show that people tend to infer traits that are in the same direction (i.e., "good" versus "bad") as known traits. "It is likely, therefore, that a juror who has knowledge of one negative characteristic about the defendant (such as previous record) will be likely to infer other unfavourable characteristics about the defendant (such as guilt)" (Hans & Doob, 1975, p. 238). While this could account for the differences in conviction rates between the no-prior-record and combined prior-record groups, it does not explain the observed conviction rate differences among the three prior-record groups.

Whether jurors attribute the cause of the defendant's behavior (i.e., the commission of the present offense) to stable, internal characteristics of the defendant or to aspects of the particular situation could affect their evaluations and verdicts. People's general tendency to underestimate the situational, relative to dispositional, determinants of behavior can be observed in the public's perception of "the person who commits a criminal act . . . as *responsible* for that act, and further, the possessor of a *criminal* disposition" (Carroll & Payne, 1977, p. 193, emphasis in original; see also Jones & Nisbett, 1971; Kelley, 1971; Ross, 1977). One of the conditions under which people are more likely to attribute the causes of events to enduring personal dispositions than to environmental factors is when a particular individual has behaved the same on previous occasions (Jones & McGillis, 1976; Kelley, 1967; Kelley & Michela, 1980). Although such information may be logically redundant, it is regularly used by human decision-makers to increase their confidence in their judgments (Saks & Kidd, 1980–1981).

Therefore, subjects who know that the defendant has previously been convicted of a crime and is now charged with another crime would be more likely to make dispositional attributions about the reason he committed the present offense than would subjects who have no prior record information. This, in turn, could result in higher conviction rates. In fact, Lussier, Perlman, and Breen (1977) found that subjects attributed a crime more strongly to the defendant and less strongly to the circumstances when the defendant had previously committed similar crimes than when he was a first offender. Tanford and Penrod (1982) found that subjects judging joined trials rated a defendant charged with several crimes more negatively and as being more of a "criminal type" than did subjects judging defendants charged with a single crime. These ratings, in turn, were related to judgments of guilt. In addition, studies of parole board decisions found that the more stable and internal the subjects perceived the cause of the offense to be, the higher were their estimates of the risk of recidivism and the less favorable were their parole recommendations (Carroll, 1978; Carroll & Payne, 1977). Hence, the higher conviction rates for the three prior-record groups could be due to stronger dispositional attributions.

In addition, one would expect dispositional attributions to be more likely in the instance of highest consistency (i.e., previous conviction for the same crime) than in the dissimilar or perjury condition. This could explain (1) why a higher percentage of guilty verdicts obtained in the same versus dissimilar and perjury conditions; (2) why subjects in the same-prior condition reported that the previous conviction had a greater impact on their judgment of guilt than did subjects in the perjury condition of the auto theft case and subjects in the dissimilar-prior condition of the murder case; and (3) why two-thirds of those subjects who gave the prior record as the reason they reached their guilty verdict were in the same-prior condition, as compared with one-third in the perjury condition. Knowing that a person was previously convicted of the same crime appears to provide information that is more important than does a prior perjury conviction. The role of attributions should be directly investigated in future research.

One should be cautious in generalizing from the results of this study to jurors in a real trial. First, the ratio of trial evidence to prior conviction information is much lower in simulations than in actual trials. In an actual trial, the greater richness of evidence and actors probably provides jurors with more bases for forming credibility judgments than the subjects in our simulation had. Second, some factors operating in the courtroom were not present in the simulation (for a discussion of the well-known limitations of this methodological genre, see Bray & Kerr, 1982; Konečni & Ebbesen, 1982). It is unlikely, however, that the pattern of the obtained results is due to an interaction between the prior-conviction manipulation and something unique to these subjects or case materials. The findings are consistent with those of other studies which have found that subjects have not followed instructions to disregard inadmissible evidence (Sue, Smith, & Caldwell, 1973; Wolf & Montgomery, 1977) and to consider evidence pertaining to each charge of a joined trial independently (Greene & Loftus, 1981; Horowitz, Bordens, & Feldman, 1980; Kerr & Sawyers, 1979). This is not to say, of course, that a cognitive programming procedure of some sort could not be invented that would "correct" the jurors' processing of the information. A useful line of future research would be to try to discover *any* conditions under which jurors do not misuse prior-conviction information.

On the basis of the available data, we conclude that the presentation of the defendant's criminal record does not affect the defendant's credibility, but does increase the likelihood of conviction, and that the judge's limiting instructions do not appear to correct that error. People's decision processes do not employ the prior-conviction evidence in the way the law wishes them to use it. From a legal policy viewpoint, the risk of prejudice to the defense is greater than the unrealized potential benefit to the prosecution. A change of the rules to exclude evidence of prior convictions for defendants would protect defendants while not disabling the prosecutor. The defendant automatically has exceedingly low credibility for a jury, and the prosecution still has "other recognized means to challenge the credibility of a witness" (Margolis, 1972, p. 525).

REFERENCES

Anderson, N. H. Information integration theory: A brief survey. In D. H. Krantz, R. C. Atkinson, R. D. Luce, and P. Suppes (Eds.), *Contemporary developments in mathematical psychology*. San Francisco: Freeman, 1974.

Bray, R. M., & Kerr, N. L. Methodological considerations in the study of the psychology of the courtroom. In N. L. Kerr and R. M. Bray (Eds.), *The psychology of the courtroom*. New York: Academic, 1982.

Carroll, J. S. Causal attributions in parole decisions. *Journal of Personality and Social Psychology*, 1978, **36**, 1501–1511.

Carroll, J. S., & Payne, J. W. Judgments about crime and the criminal: A model and a method for investigating parole decisions. In B. D. Sales (Ed.), *Perspectives in law and psychology, Vol. I: Criminal justice system*. New York: Plenum, 1977.

Cochran, W. G. The comparison of percentages in matched samples. *Biometrika*, 1950, **37**, 256–266.

Cornish, W. R., & Sealy, A. P. Juries and the rules of evidence. *Criminal Law Quarterly*, 1973, **16**, 208–223.

Doob, A., & Kirshenbaum, H. Some empirical evidence on the effect of S.12 of the canada evidence act upon an accused. *Criminal Law Quarterly*, 1972, **15**, 88–96.

Federal rules of evidence, 1975.

Gordon v. United States, 383 F.2d 936 (DC Cir. 1967).

Greene, E., & Loftus, E. *When crimes are joined at trial: Institutionalized prejudice?* Paper presented at the convention of the American Psychology–Law Society, Boston, 1981.

Hans, V., & Doob, A. Section 12 of the canada evidence act and the deliberations of simulated juries. *Criminal Law Quarterly*, 1975, **18**, 235–253.

Horowitz, I. A., Bordens, K. S., & Feldman, M. S. A comparison of verdicts obtained in severed and joined criminal trials. *Journal of Applied Social Psychology*, 1980, **10**, 444–456.

Jones, E. E., & McGillis, D. Correspondent inferences and the attribution cube: A comparative reappraisal. In J. H. Harvey, W. J. Ickes, and R. F. Kidd (Eds.), *New directions in attribution research* (Vol. 1). Hillsdale, New Jersey: Erlbaum, 1976.

Jones, E. E., & Nisbett, R. E. The actor and observer: Divergent perceptions of the causes of behavior. In E. E. Jones et al. (Eds.), *Attribution: Perceiving the causes of behavior*. Morristown, New Jersey: General Learning Press, 1971.

Kalven, H., Jr., & Zeisel, H. *The American jury*. Boston: Little, Brown, 1966.

Kelley, H. H. Attribution theory in social psychology. In D. Levine (Ed.), *Nebraska Symposium on Motivation*. Lincoln: University of Nebraska Press, 1967.

Kelley, H. H. Attribution in social interaction. In E. E. Jones et al. (Eds.), *Attribution: Perceiving the causes of behavior*. Morristown, New Jersey: General Learning Press, 1971.

Kelley, H. H., & Michela, J. L. Attribution theory and research. *Annual Review of Psychology*, 1980, **31**, 457–501.

Keppel, G. *Design and analysis: A researcher's handbook*. Englewood Cliffs, New Jersey: Prentice-Hall, 1973.

Kerr, N. L., & Sawyers, G. W. Independence of multiple verdicts within a trial by mock jurors. *Representative Research in Social Psychology*, 1979, **10**, 16–27.

Konečni, V. J., & Ebbesen, E. B. Social psychology and the law: The choice of research problems, settings, and methodology. In V. J. Konečni and E. B. Ebbesen (Eds.), *The criminal justice system: A social–psychological analysis*. San Francisco: Freeman, 1982.

Lempert, R. O. Modeling relevance. *Michigan Law Review*, 1977, **75**, 1021–1057.

Lussier, R. J., Perlman, D., & Breen, L. J. Causal attributions, attitude similarity, and the punishment of drug offenders. *British Journal of Addiction*, 1977, **72**, 357–364.

Margolis, L. A. An eclectic approach to impeachment by prior convictions. *Journal of Law Reform*, 1972, **5**, 552–540.

Nagao, D. H., & Davis, J. H. The effects of prior experience on mock juror case judgments. *Social Psychology Quarterly*, 1980, **43**, 190–199.

Note. To take the stand or not to take the stand: The dilemma of the defendant with a criminal record. *Columbia Journal of Law and Social Problems*, 1968, **4**, 215–223.

Penrod, S. *Social psychology*. Englewood Cliffs, New Jersey: Prentice-Hall, 1983.

People v. Antick, 15 Cal.3d 79 (1975).

People v. Beagle, 6 Cal.3d 441 (1972).

People v. Fries, 24 Cal.3d 222 (1979).

People v. Rist, 16 Cal.3d 211 (1976).

People v. Rollo, 20 Cal.3d 109 (1977).

Rosenberg, S., & Olshan, K. Evaluative and descriptive aspects in personality perception. *Journal of Personality and Social Psychology*, 1970, **16**, 619–626.

Ross, L. The intuitive psychologist and his shortcomings: Distortions in the attribution process. In L. Berkowitz (Ed.), *Advances in experimental social psychology* (Vol. 10). New York: Academic Press, 1977.

Saks, M. J., & Kidd, R. F. Human information processing and adjudication: Trial by heuristics. *Law and Society Review*, 1980–1981, **15**, 123–160.

Spector, R. G. Impeachment by past convictions. *Loyola University of Chicago Law Review*, 1979, **10**, 339–362.

Sue, S., Smith, R. E., & Caldwell, C. Effects of inadmissible evidence on the decisions of simulated jurors: A moral dilemma. *Journal of Applied Social Psychology*, 1973, **3**, 344–353.

Tanford, S., & Penrod, S. Biases in trials involving defendants charged with multiple offenses. *Journal of Applied Social Psychology*, 1982, **12**, 453–480.

Thomas, E. A. C., & Hogue, A. Apparent weight of evidence, decision criteria and confidence ratings in juror decision making. *Psychological Review*, 1976, **83**, 442–465.

United States v. Smith, 551 F.2d 348 (1976).

United States v. Toney, 615 F.2d 277 (1980).

Wolf, S., & Montgomery, D. A. Effects of inadmissible evidence and level of judicial admonishment to disregard on the judgments of mock jurors. *Journal of Applied Social Psychology*, 1977, **7**, 205–219.

Guidelines for Drafting Understandable Jury Instructions: An Introduction to the Use of Psycholinguistics*

By Edward J. Imwinkelried**
and Lloyd R. Schwed***

It is shocking to learn just how little comprehension a jury has of instructions given in a criminal case. Lawyers and judges play it safe with the "stocks" and may fail to realize the disservice done to justice and the parties involved.

The authors review the literature on point and then go through the practical selection of words in jury instructions; the use of various phrases and clauses; sentence structure; and the overall organization of the instruction.

Using a psycholinguistic approach is not merely interesting, it can change the results in cases. Worth studying? What do you think!

"One area of trial practice that frequently seems to be shortchanged . . . is that of jury instructions."[1] Yet, experienced litigators realize that the judge's jury instructions can have a decisive impact on the outcome of the case.[2] In some cases in jurisdictions in which the judges give jurors written instructions, the instructions will be the only tangible thing the jurors take with them into the deliberation room.[3] Even if the jurors take other exhibits with them into the room, the jury instructions will be the only thing the jurors receive directly from the judge. The jurors may have doubts about the reliability

---

* A lengthier and revised version of this article will appear in *The Champion*, published by the National Association of Defense Lawyers.

** Professor of Law, University of California at Davis.

*** Private Practitioner, Coral Gables, Florida.

[1] Dombroff, "Jury Instructions Can Be Crucial in Trial Process," Legal Times, Feb. 25, 1985, at 26.

[2] *Id.*

[3] Greene, "A Jury Researcher Joins the Jury," Case & Comment, Jan.-Feb. 1986, at 34.

of some of the exhibits, since the exhibits come from the partisan attorneys. However, most jurors view the judge as the embodiment of impartial justice,[4] and they consequently attach great significance to the instructions. In principle, the instructions should have such great influence over the jurors. The purpose of the trial is to apply law to the facts determined by the jurors, and the instructions supply the jurors with the law to apply. Of course, the underlying assumption is that the instructions effectively communicate the legal rules to the jurors.

Since 1970, social scientists have undertaken numerous studies of the effectiveness of the instructions the judge reads to lay jurors during a trial.[5] For example, under the auspices of the National Science Foundation, Robert and Veda Charrow conducted six experiments in the mid-1970s.[6] Another line of research by Elwork and his co-workers led to the publication of *Making Jury Instructions Understandable* in 1982.[7] The research to date is by no means exhaustive,[8] but the data strongly indicates that there is extensive juror misunderstanding of instructions.

Experienced trial attorneys have long suspected that jurors have difficulty understanding the judge's instructions, but there is now far more than anecdotal support for the suspicion. There have been state[9] as well as national[10] studies. The studies have tested the effectiveness of criminal[11] and civil[12] instructions.

[4] Dombroff, note 1 *supra*.

[5] Perlman, "Pattern Jury Instructions: The Application of Social Science Research," 65 Neb. L. Rev. 520, 528 (1986).

[6] Charrow & Charrow, "Making Legal Language Understandable: A Psycholinguistic Study of Jury Instructions," 79 Colum. L. Rev. 1306 (1979).

[7] A. Elwork, B. Sales & J. Alfini, *Making Jury Instructions Understandable* (1982); see also Elwork, Alfini & Sales, "Toward Understandable Jury Instructions," 65 Judicature 432 (1982).

[8] Charrow & Charrow, note 6 *supra*, at 1307.

[9] *Id.* at 1311, 1316 (Maryland); Slonim, "Say Jury Instructions Hampered by Legalese," 66 A.B.A.J. 132 (1980) (Maryland and Virginia); M. Mahoney, *Jury Instructions for the Complete Idiot* 4 (1985) (five states) (unpublished manuscript on file in Professor Imwinkelried's office).

[10] Schwarzer, "Communicating With Juries: Problems and Remedies," 69 Cal. L. Rev. 731, 741 (1981).

[11] Severance, Greene & Loftus, "Toward Criminal Jury Instructions That Jurors Can Understand," 75 J. Crim. L. & Criminology 198, 202 (1984).

[12] *Id.*

The findings in the studies have been distressing. Some researchers discovered that the jurors understand barely half of the content of the instructions.[13] In several studies, jurors who had received no instructions performed as well as the jurors who heard the instructions.[14] The results in the criminal trial experiments have been particularly alarming. Roughly half of the subjects in the experiments do not understand the burden of proof instruction,[15] and some subjects even interpret the instruction as assigning the defendant the burden of proving her innocence.[16] The criminal trial experiments have attempted to assess the question whether lay jurors can follow limiting instructions, and as in the case of the experiments with burden of proof instructions, the results of the tests with limiting instructions call into question the assumption that the jurors comprehend the instruction.[17]

At first blush, on reviewing these findings, the reader may be tempted to conclude that the root problem is the conceptual difficulty of the legal doctrines described in the instructions: Lay jurors are simply not intelligent or sophisticated enough to appreciate the doctrines. However, the psycholinguistic research contradicts that conclusion.[18] The research indicates that the primary cause of juror misunderstanding is certain linguistic features in the instructions,[19] that is, problematic[20] structural defects[21] in the wording of the instructions. Several experiments

---

[13] "Proximate What? Only the Ph.D. Knew," 64 A.B.A.J. 660 (1978) ("The subjects understood an average of 54 per cent of the crucial elements of each instruction. . . .").

[14] Perlman, note 5 *supra*, at 528-529 ("traditional pattern jury instructions did not provide a significant measure of comprehension beyond that of the control group").

[15] Schwarzer, "Jury Instructions: We Can Do Better," Litigation Winter 1982, at 5.

[16] *Id.*

[17] Greene & Loftus, "When Crimes Are Joined at Trial," 9 Law & Human Beh. 193 (1985); Wissler & Saks, "On the Inefficacy of Limiting Instructions—When Jurors Use Prior Conviction Evidence to Decide Guilt," 9 Law & Hum. Behav. 37, 43 (1985).

[18] Charrow & Charrow, note 6 *supra*, at 1307, 1334, 1359; Schwarzer, note 15 *supra*, at 6.

[19] Charrow & Charrow, note 6 *supra*, at 1307.

[20] *Id.*

[21] Schwarzer, note 10 *supra*, at 740.

not only point to that cause; they also report that when that cause is removed by rewording the instructions, juror understanding improves markedly.[22] The results in one of the Elwork experiments are dramatic.[23] The subjects who received normal pattern instructions had an average comprehension rate of only 51 percent.[24] However, one revision of the instructions resulted in an average comprehension rate of 66 percent, and a further revamp of the instructions raised the rate to 80 percent.[25] In short, psycholinguistic research tends to show that these are techniques for making jury instructions appreciably more readable and understandable.[26] The balance of this article reviews those techniques. The techniques relate to word choice, the use of phrases and clauses, sentence structure, and the overall organization of instructions.

The Choice of Words

The psycholinguists have developed a number of norms to govern the choice of words in instructions for lay jurors.

To begin with, the draftsman should avoid legalese.[27] The draftsman should not view the task of writing an instruction as an excuse for displaying the extent of his technical vocabulary.[28] Including esoteric,[29] unfamiliar[30] legal terminology[31] can make the instruction incomprehensible to lay jurors. Legal jargon[32] may strike the jurors as gobbledygook[33] and mumbo

[22] Perlman, note 5 *supra*, at 531; Severance, Greene & Loftus, note 11 *supra*, at 213.

[23] Epstein, "A Threat to Justice: Jurors Who Don't Understand Instructions," San Francisco Examiner, June 7, 1981, § A, at 15.

[24] *Id.*

[25] *Id.*

[26] Charrow & Charrow, note 6 *supra*, at 1319.

[27] Goebel, "Defects in Jury Instructions: Can They Be Eliminated?" Cal. St. B.J., Sept. 1979, at 302.

[28] A. Elwork, B. Sales & J. Alfini, note 7 *supra*, at 176.

[29] Charrow & Charrow, note 6 *supra*, at 1359.

[30] Severance, Greene & Loftus, note 11 *supra*, at 208.

[31] *Id.* at 200.

[32] Perlman, note 5 *supra*, at 523.

[33] Epstein, note 23 *supra*.

jumbo.[34] It is preferable to use common words[35] that lay persons are most accustomed to.[36] In the Charrow experiments, jurors who were read "delegalized"[37] instructions had a comprehension rate 47 percent higher than that of jurors who heard typical pattern instructions.[38]

Like legalese, abstract words can confound the jurors. It is better to use concrete, case-specific terms.[39] Jurors can apply an instruction more effectively to the facts[40] when the instruction itself integrates the facts.[41] The words in the instruction should have real-world referents[42] that jurors can easily visualize.[43] The instruction should incorporate the evidentiary context for applying the rule of law embodied in the instruction: the relevant persons, places, and things.[44] For example, the draftsman should personalize the instruction[45] by referring to parties by name rather than by their legal role in the case ("the defendant").[46]

The use of nominalizations can similarly confuse jurors.[47] A nominalization is a noun formed from a verb. A nominalization can be constructed by adding the present participle ending "ing" to the verb stem or adding "tion" or "al" to the verb.[48] When the instruction uses a nominalization, the reader or hearer must work harder to decode the meaning. In the Char-

---

[34] Schwarzer, note 10 *supra*, at 732.

[35] Severance, Greene & Loftus, note 11 *supra*, at 207.

[36] Perlman, note 5 *supra*, at 532.

[37] Higginbotham, "Helping the Jury Understand," Litigation Summer 1980, at 5-6.

[38] Charrow & Charrow, note 6 *supra*, at 1336.

[39] Perlman, note 5 *supra*, at 532.

[40] Severance, Greene & Loftus, note 11 *supra*, at 201.

[41] Schwarzer, note 10 *supra*, at 741.

[42] A. Elwork, B. Sales & J. Alfini, note 7 *supra*, at 178.

[43] *Id.*

[44] Schwarzer, note 10 *supra*, at 741.

[45] Higginbotham, note 37 *supra*, at 6.

[46] A. Elwork, B. Sales & J. Alfini, note 7 *supra*, at 179.

[47] Charrow & Charrow, note 6 *supra*, at 1321.

[48] *Id.*

row experiments, the elimination of nominalizations significantly improved juror comprehension.[49]

The utilization of synonyms can also mislead the jurors. Polished prose stylists often use "elegant variation," but a juror "may [mis]interpret the use of synonyms [in an instruction] as an intentional attempt to distinguish between shades of meaning."[50] When in doubt, repeat the same word.

Synonyms and homonyms have a common denominator: the potential to lead jurors astray. A homonym is a word with more than one meaning.[51] The draftsman may have one meaning in mind, the judge may read the instruction with that meaning in mind, but another meaning may occur to the jurors hearing the instruction. Of course, it is difficult to find terms that can bear only one meaning. However, the draftsman can give the jurors contextual clues pointing the jurors to the intended meaning.[52] Elwork and his coauthors list five possible types of clues:

1. Definition through synonym: "The mean or midpoint score was 10.5."
2. Example: "The feline family includes cats, tigers, and lions."
3. Comparison and contrast: "Do not run; walk."
4. Contextual description: "The dirty, crowded slum."
5. Antonyms: "While she was sociable, he was reserved."[53]

Next, Elwork's research indicates that certain types of antonyms are more readily understood by jurors than other types.[54] Some antonyms such as polite-impolite share the same root. The draftsman forms the antonym by adding a negative modifier such as "im." Other antonyms, such as polite-rude, have different roots. After reviewing the literature, Elwork concludes that antonyms with the same root are "more difficult to comprehend and remember than those with a different root. . . ."[55] Suppose, for instance, that the defendant is on trial for crime no. 1 and there has been some testimony about crime

---

[49] *Id.* at 1322, 1336.

[50] A. Elwork, B. Sales & J. Alfini, note 7 *supra*, at 180.

[51] *Id.* at 179.

[52] *Id.*

[53] *Id.* at 180.

[54] *Id.*

[55] *Id.*

no. 2, an uncharged offense that is not mentioned in the indictment. The judge wants to instruct the jury to disregard the testimony if the jurors conclude that the defendant did not commit crime no. 2. The judge could use the word "disregard" in the instruction. However, that word is formed by adding a negative modifier to the antonym "regard." The word "ignore" is a much better choice.[56]

The above general guidelines apply whatever grammatical function the word serves in the sentence. There are additional guidelines for the words serving specific functions, such as the subject, verb, and negator in a sentence.

Just as it is generally preferable to use concrete terms, it is best if the subject of a sentence is human or animate.[57] The use of an inanimate subject can lead to jury confusion. Thus, whenever possible, avoid expressions such as "the law says . . ." or "the law is . . ."[58]

Verb choice can also be a source of jury confusion. In particular, there is potential for misunderstanding if the draftsman uses verbs "which can change from transitive to intransitive with the addition of an extra clause."[59] A transitive verb expresses action flowing from the subject to the object; transitive verbs ordinarily have direct object nouns. Hence, in the sentence "Mr. Jackson (the defendant) hit Ms. Martin," "hit" is a transitive verb. Intransitive verbs do not require direct objects. Elwork comments:

> Many verbs take on either form (e.g., "If you believe the defendant" versus "If you believe the defendant to be guilty"). The latter have been shown to cause confusion in comprehension because the reader/listener may make a transitive interpretation initially and then has to change it to an intransitive one upon hearing the last part of the sentence.[60]

While the draftsman should avoid verbs that can take on either transitive or intransitive form, he should resort to modal verbs.[61] A modal verb can be directive ("must" or "should")

---

[56] *Id.*

[57] *Id.* at 174.

[58] *Id.*

[59] *Id.* at 173-174.

[60] *Id.* at 174.

[61] Charrow & Charrow, note 6 *supra*, at 1324.

or permissive ("may").[62] Jurors tend to pay a great deal of attention to modal verbs because they help define the jurors' duties—they tell the jurors what to do.[63]

Finally, if possible, the draftsman should eliminate negators such as "not" in the sentence. Commentators on legal writing often assert that negators can confuse the reader.[64] However, the available research indicates that the assertion may be overstated. In the Charrow experiments, the use of double or triple negators significantly lowered jury comprehension,[65] but single negators had little impact on the level of jury understanding.[66] In some cases, the draftsman simply cannot avoid using a negator.[67] However, the draftsman should use only one negator in each sentence, and even then it is ideal if the sentence including the negator is followed by a sentence restating the same point in affirmative terms.[68] For instance, after instructing the jury that "direct evidence is not necessarily better than indirect evidence," the judge might add: "Some jurors assume that direct evidence is always better than indirect evidence. This is wrong."[69] The affirmative restatement of the point reinforces the preceding sentence containing the negator.

The Use of Phrases and Clauses

The last section reviewed the drafting norms for the selection of words, the smallest building block for the draftsman writing a jury instruction. This subsection addresses the norms for the next larger building block, phrases, and clauses.

Sometimes jury confusion arises because a subordinate clause is incomplete. Psycholinguists sometimes refer to this problem as the "whiz" phenomenon—a subordinate clause

---

[62] Severance, Greene & Loftus, note 11 *supra*, at 208 n.50.

[63] Charrow & Charrow, note 6 *supra*, at 1324.

[64] *Id.*

[65] *Id.* at 1325.

[66] *Id.*

[67] A. Elwork, B. Sales & J. Alfini, note 7 *supra*, at 172.

[68] *Id.* at 173.

[69] *Id.*

with a missing "which is."[70] The expression "question of fact submitted to you" is illustrative.[71] The expression is elliptical; the complete phrase would be "question of fact which is submitted to you." Both the relative pronoun "which" and the verb "is" are missing. The hearer's mind has to work harder to fill in the missing words to process the sentence. As a general proposition, the draftsman should insert the relative pronoun and verb.[72] Although the absence of the pronoun and verb may seem to be a minor sin of omission, the Charrow experiments bear out that reinstating the pronoun and verb can significantly increase juror understanding.[73]

There are also sins of commission in the use of phrases and clauses. A case in point is the use of the phrase "as to."[74] Most jurors find this prepositional phrase difficult to understand. The phrase is designed to connect two concepts, but the link is ambiguous.[75] The Charrow researchers found that eliminating the phrase enhanced comprehension by 19 percent.[76] In an uncharged misconduct instrument, the judge could refer to testimony "as to" crime no. 2. However, it would be better practice to refer to the testimony "about" crime no. 2. Jurors are much more accustomed to using and processing that preposition.

Another sin of commission is using an unduly long word list.[77] To help the jury understand an instruction, the judge sometimes gives the jury a string of examples.[78] Assume, for instance, that the judge wants to help the jury appreciate the permissible uses of uncharged misconduct evidence. Federal Rule of Evidence 404(b) defines the allowable uses of the evidence: "Evidence of other crimes, wrongs, or acts is not admissible to prove the character of a person in order to show that he

---

[70] Charrow & Charrow, note 6 *supra*, at 1323.

[71] *Id.*

[72] *Id.* at 1329; Severance, Greene & Loftus, note 11 *supra*, at 208.

[73] Charrow & Charrow, note 6 *supra*, at 1323.

[74] *Id.* at 1322.

[75] *Id.*

[76] *Id.* at 1336.

[77] *Id.* at 1326.

[78] Severance, Greene & Loftus, note 11 *supra*, at 208.

acted in conformity therewith. It may, however, be admissible for other purposes, such as proof of motive, opportunity, intent, preparation, plan, knowledge, identity, or absence of mistake or accident.''[79] The judge might give the jury a ''shotgun'' instruction,[80] listing several of the proper uses of uncharged misconduct evidence. Tracking the language of Federal Rule of Evidence 404(b), the judge might inform the jurors that they may consider the evidence for the purpose of determining ''motive, opportunity, intent, preparation, plan, knowledge, identity, or absence of mistake or accident.''[81] However, the use of long word lists in a sentence is counterproductive.[82] In the Charrow research, when the list exceeded two items, the jurors had great difficulty remembering any of the items.[83] By shortening the word lists to a maximum of two items, the researchers were able to increase jury comprehension by 17 percent.[84]

Finally, the crux of the problem may be that the phrase or clause is misplaced.[85] When the phrase is misplaced, it is difficult for the jurors to understand the meaning of the phrase. Worse still, the misplacement of the phrase can lead the jurors to misconstrue the entire sentence.[86] The Charrow researchers discovered that the misplacement of phrases causes a surprisingly large number of errors. Conversely, when they moved the phrases to their proper location in the sentence, juror comprehension increased 24 percent.[87]

Sentence Structure

The draftsman's next larger building block is the sentence. Like word choice and the use of phrases and clauses, the

---

[79] Fed. R. Evid. 404, 28 U.S.C.A.

[80] Slough, "Other Vices, Other Crimes: An Evidentiary Dilemma," 20 Kan. L. Rev. 411, 430 (1972); Note, "Evidence of Other Crimes in Kansas," 17 Washburn L.J. 98, 120 (1977); Note, "Admissibility of Evidence of Previous Crime Instructions to Jury," 35 Cal. L. Rev. 131 (1947).

[81] Fed. R. Evid. 404(b), 28 U.S.C.A.

[82] Charrow & Charrow, note 6 *supra*, at 1338.

[83] *Id.* at 1326.

[84] *Id.* at 1338.

[85] *Id.* at 1323.

[86] *Id.*

[87] *Id.* at 1336.

grammatical construction of the sentence can generate jury misunderstanding.[88] In constructing a sentence, the draftsman should be conscious of sentence length, the voice of the sentence (active or passive), and the complexity of the sentence structure.

Critics of jury instructions frequently declare that pattern instructions are too prolix and that this character is a major cause of jury confusion.[89] However, like the asserted dangers of using negators, these declarations may be exaggerated. In their research, the Charrows found that standing alone, the length of a sentence has little effect on jury comprehension.[90] Elwork concurs.[91] The real cause of jury confusion is not sentence length per se[92] but rather the complexity of the sentence structure.[93] A jury may find a long, simply structured sentence easy to comprehend, but the same jury may have tremendous difficulty understanding a shorter sentence with more complicated grammatical structure.

One of the most maligned sentence structures is the passive.[94] It is a commonplace observation that the use of the passive can introduce ambiguity into a sentence. When the juror hears "It is said . . ." the juror may wonder who said it. Or if the juror hears "It was done . . ." the juror may wonder who did it. The Charrow researchers studied the effect of the use of the passive on jury comprehension, but they reached equivocal results.[95] The use of the passive in main clauses resulted in little jury confusion, but the presence of the passive in subordinate clauses caused jurors considerable difficulty.[96] Overall, when the researchers eliminated the passive voice, jury comprehension improved markedly.[97]

---

[88] *Id.* at 1311.

[89] Schwarzer, note 10 *supra*, at 739.

[90] Charrow & Charrow, note 6 *supra*, at 1319-1320.

[91] A. Elwork, B. Sales & J. Alfini, note 7 *supra*, at 167-168.

[92] *Id.* at 168.

[93] Charrow & Charrow, note 6 *supra*, at 1320.

[94] *Id.* at 1325.

[95] *Id.*

[96] *Id.* at 1326.

[97] *Id.* at 1337.

Although the available data indicates that the use of the passive can contribute to jury confusion, the data shows that the presence of embeddings in a sentence is a more important cause of misunderstanding.[98] There are four basic types of sentence structures: simple sentences, compound sentences, self-embedded sentences (one independent clause with a subordinate clause), and compound self-embedded sentences.[99] Whenever possible, the draftsman should avoid using compound sentences.[100] The jurors are more likely to understand the two concepts if they are stated separately. Likewise, it is best to eliminate embeddings; the presence of a subordinate clause forces the jury to engage in mental gymnastics to understand the entire sentence.[101] The norm should be simple sentences with normal subject-verb-object order.[102]

The Overall Organization of the Instruction

The draftsman of a jury instruction must be concerned not only about the microcosm, individual building blocks such as words and phrases, but also about the macrocosm, the overall organization of the instruction.[103] There are three basic organizational strategies for jury instructions.

Hierarchical Organization

In this scheme, the draftsman breaks high-level concepts down into lower-level components.[104] The draftsman then integrates the components.[105] Elwork gives the following example: "[I]n defining an 'intent' to murder, we might explain that it must have four components: willfulness, premeditation, deliberation

---

[98] *Id.* at 1327.

[99] A. Elwork, B. Sales & J. Alfini, note 7 *supra*, at 168.

[100] Severance, Greene & Loftus, note 11 *supra*, at 208.

[101] Charrow & Charrow, note 6 *supra*, at 1340.

[102] *Id.*

[103] *Id.* at 1326 (discourse structure).

[104] Severance, Greene & Loftus, note 11 *supra*, at 208.

[105] *Id.*

and malice. Each of these components may, in turn, have to be broken down further into its sub-components."[106]

There are numerous examples in the uncharged misconduct doctrine. Suppose, for instance, that the prosecutor offers the defendant's uncharged misconduct on a motive theory: The defendant committed crime no. 2 (the uncharged act), the victim learned of crime no. 2, and the defendant committed the charged crime (the murder of the victim) to prevent the victim from reporting crime no. 2 to the police.[107] In some jurisdictions, when the prosecutor relies on this theory, the prosecutor must show both that the victim knew of the uncharged crime and that the defendant realized the victim knew.[108] The motive theory is the counterpart to the intent to murder in Elwork's hypothetical; the theory is the high-level concept. Just as the intent to murder breaks down into four elements, the motive theory breaks down into at least two lower-level components—the victim's knowledge and the defendant's realization.

Associational Organization

In associational organization, the draftsman groups connected topics together.[109] The topics must share some conceptual commonality.[110] For example, the draftsman can group evidentiary rules together if all the rules relate to how a particular item of evidence should be used.[111] He may do so even when one rule prescribes the proper use of the evidence and another proscribes a particular use of the evidence.[112] The draftsman of an uncharged misconduct evidence instruction can obviously capitalize on associational organization. Federal Rule of Evidence 404(b) announces two rules for the use of uncharged misconduct evidence. One is that the jury may not treat the uncharged misconduct as proof of the defendant's general

---

[106] A. Elwork, B. Sales & J. Alfini, note 7 *supra*, at 151.

[107] See generally E. Imwinkelried, *Uncharged Misconduct Evidence* § 3:16 (1984).

[108] *Id.*

[109] Elwork, note 106 *supra*, at 150.

[110] *Id.* at 161.

[111] *Id.* at 151.

[112] Mahoney, note 9 *supra*.

bad character and, in turn, infer the defendant's commission of the charged crime from his general bad character. The other rule is that the jury may use the evidence on certain noncharacter theories of logical relevance. Both rules relate to the same item of evidence and, more specifically, to the use of the item of evidence. The two rules should be grouped together by parallel construction.[113]

Algorithmic Organization

Topics should be organized algorithmically when one flows from the other.[114] One topic or concept builds on the other.[115] Algorithmic structure is especially effective when there is a causal or temporal relationship between concepts.[116] In the instruction, the sequence of the concepts should parallel the causal or temporal order.[117] Thus, the instruction should mention an earlier event before a later event[118] and a determination the jury must make before the consequences flowing from the determination.[119]

An algorithmically organized instruction should be a verbal flow chart[120] or logic tree.[121] The instruction should set out a decision-making process for the jury.[122] The instruction should inform the jury how to reach a decision or verdict[123] step by step.[124] The instruction should identify all the logical tasks the jurors must perform and guide the jurors to a decision task by

---

[113] A. Elwork, B. Sales & J. Alfini, note 7 *supra*, at 176.

[114] Perlman, note 5 *supra*, at 530; Severance, Greene & Loftus, note 11 *supra*, at 208.

[115] Charrow & Charrow, note 6 *supra*, at 1317.

[116] A. Elwork, B. Sales & J. Alfini, note 7 *supra*, at 151.

[117] *Id.* at 158.

[118] *Id.*

[119] Loftus & Severance, "Improving Jury Instructions," Wash. St. B. News, July 1982, at 18.

[120] A. Elwork, B. Sales & J. Alfini, note 7 *supra*, at 162.

[121] Strawn & Munsterman, "Helping Juries Handle Complex Cases," Case & Com., March-April 1983, at 45.

[122] *Id.*

[123] Charrow & Charrow, note 6 *supra*, at 1309.

[124] D. Herbert & R. Barrett, *Attorney's Master Guide to Courtroom Psychology; How to Apply Behavioral Science Techniques for New Trial Success* 1211 (1981).

task.[125] Although it is a mistake to include too many series of numbers in a set of instructions, the draftsman may want to enumerate or number the tasks in the most critical instructions.[126] Hence, when the jurors must complete a number of logical tasks, the draftsman can preface the description of the initial task with "The first thing you will be doing . . . ."[127] The numbers serve as mental signposts to ensure that the jurors perform the tasks in the correct sequence.[128] When the jurors must complete a large number of tasks, it is sometimes helpful to inform them beforehand[129]: "You must make three decisions. . . ."

These three organizational strategies are not mutually exclusive. In a given instruction, the draftsman may use some or all of the strategies. For example, the draftsman of an uncharged misconduct evidence instruction might initially employ an algorithmic structure:

1. Decide whether the defendant committed the act of uncharged misconduct.
2. If the defendant committed the act, determine how to use the evidence of the act.

The draftsman might then use associational organization to elaborate on the use of the evidence:

1. Decide whether the defendant committed the act of uncharged misconduct.
2. If the defendant committed the act, then determine how to use the evidence of the act.
   a. You may not use the evidence as proof of the defendant's general bad character.
   b. You may use the evidence on a noncharacter motive theory.

Finally, the draftsman can employ hierarchical organization to break the motive theory down into its component lower-level concepts:

---

[125] *Id.* a\ 1213.

[126] Char w & Charrow, note 6 *supra*, at 1327.

[127] A. Elwork, B. Sales & J. Alfini, note 7 *supra*, at 159.

[128] Charrow & Charrow, note 6 *supra*, at 1339.

[129] *Id.* at 1327.

1. Decide whether the defendant committed the act of uncharged misconduct.
2. If the defendant committed the act, determine how to use the evidence of the act.
   a. You may not use the evidence as proof of the defendant's general bad character.
   b. You may use the evidence on a noncharacter motive theory.
      i. Did the victim know that the defendant had committed the uncharged crime?
      ii. Did the defendant know that the victim knew?

The draftsman can thus use all three organizational principles to structure a limiting instruction on uncharged misconduct evidence.

It is the authors' hope that this article will help individual attorneys and judges draft more effective jury instructions. More broadly, it is our hope that the article will add momentum to the movement for reform of jury instructions.[130] That movement is still in its infancy.[131] Much more research must be done,[132] and attorneys and judges must devote greater effort to apply the research findings to the revision of jury instructions. However, there is good reason for at least cautious optimism.[133] The studies to date show that revised instructions can significantly enhance juror comprehension, and many trial judges have been receptive to revised instructions.[134] The task of reform may be a lengthy, difficult one, but as Judge William Schwarzer has written, psycholinguistics has given us confidence that "we can do better."[135]

---

[130] Perlman, note 5 *supra,* at 535, 541.

[131] *Id.* at 541.

[132] Charrow & Charrow, note 6 *supra,* at 1307.

[133] Severance, Greene & Loftus, note 11 *supra,* at 232.

[134] *Id.*

[135] Schwarzer, note 15 *supra.*

Effect of Particularized Instructions on Evaluation of Eyewitness Identification Evidence

*Michael H. Hoffheimer**

Abstract: The purpose of the research discussed in this article was to study the effect of instructions on subjects' evaluation of eyewitness identification evidence. One hundred seventy-seven law students were administered surveys that summarized evidence presented at two criminal trials. Critical inculpatory evidence in both cases included eyewitness identifications. The independent variable was the instructions. Subjects were directed to read the evidence and instructions and to indicate their verdict of guilty or not guilty. Survey variations included different instructions concerning proper evaluation of identification evidence. Results indicate that the particularized cautionary instruction used in a number of federal courts increased conviction rates for both cases as compared to subjects to whom a short burden of proving identity instruction was administered. ($P > .05$.) Results further suggest that the particularized instruction increased the conviction rate for the "violent" case and decreased the conviction rate for the "nonviolent" case as compared to subjects to whom no identification instruction was administered. The results conflict with assumptions made by courts and scholars that the particularized instruction reduces the conviction rate. Implications for jury instructions and the benefits of expert psychological testimony are discussed.

I. Introduction

Dangers of eyewitness identification testimony have been known for a long time and have received increased attention from courts and scholars since the late 1960s. Empirical studies have shown that persons without psychological training share assumptions that are not true about the influence of factors like stress or

* Assistant Professor of Law, University of Mississippi Law School; J.D. University of Michigan; Ph.D. & M.A. University of Chicago; B.A. Johns Hopkins University. Professors Ronald J. Rychlak and Joseph F. Rychlak provided helpful advice in the construction of the survey and in the formulation of strategy for its administration. I am grateful to Ms. Marilyn J. Bush for help with statistical analysis.

race on a witness's identification, and such assumptions prevent accurate evaluation of a witness's identification of a suspect.[1] Proposals for reducing dangers of inaccurate juror evaluation of eyewitness identification evidence include the use of expert psychological testimony on factors that aggravate risks of misidentification and the use of judicial admonitions or instructions to the jury on dangers of identification error.

Loftus has published results of empirical studies that show that use of expert testimony influences jury deliberation and reduces the conviction rate for both violent and nonviolent offenses.[2] Although the detrimental effect of certain identification instructions has been suggested on theoretical grounds, objections have been directed only against general credibility instructions that encourage jurors to use common sense and experience, which empirical studies have shown to be inaccurate.[3] Particularized cautionary instructions that articulate specific factors that militate against accurate identification have been approved by a number of federal appellate courts.[4] It has been assumed universally that

---

1. *See* Rahaim & Brodsky, *Empirical Evidence versus Common Sense: Juror and Lawyer Knowledge of Eyewitness Accuracy*, 7 LAW & PSYCHOLOGY REV. 1, 1-15 (1982).

2. Loftus, *Impact of Expert Psychological Testimony on the Unreliability of Eyewitness Identification*, 65 J. APPLIED PSYCHOLOGY. 9, 9-15 (1980).

3. General jury instructions direct jurors to evaluate a witness's credibility based on demeanor and to consider a witness's opportunity to observe those matters upon which he or she has testified. Critics object:

> This instruction, however, is not sufficient in a case involving uncorroborated testimony of a single eyewitness. By telling the jurors to use their own knowledge and life experiences, the court may actually be aggravating error if the life experiences of the jurors are erroneous. . . . many persons wrongly believe that cross-racial identifications are more likely to be accurate, that stress enhances one's ability to perceive, and that witnesses will remember more clearly the details of a violent crime than a nonviolent crime. The common credibility instruction may thus actually aggravate error.

E. Arnolds, W. Carroll, M. Lewis, M. Seng, EYEWITNESS TESTIMONY STRATEGIES AND TACTICS 345 (New York, 1984). It has also been suggested that general cautionary instructions on uncorroborated evidence that are used in English criminal proceedings increase the probability of conviction. Starkman, *The Use of Eyewitness Identification Evidence in Criminal Trials*, 21 CRIM. L.Q. 361, 377 n.78a. (1979).

4. *See generally* 1 D. Devitt & C. Blackmar, FEDERAL JURY PRACTICE& INSTRUCTIONS § 15.19 at 477-79 (1977); E. Devitt, C. Blackmar, Wolff, FEDERAL JURY PRACTICE & INSTRUCTIONS § 15.19 at 343-44 (3d ed. 1987 cumulative supp.);

such particularized identifications avoid the problems associated with general credibility instructions. There is, however, only one empirical study of the effect of such instruction.[5]

Demonstration of the influence of identification instructions is relevant to three controversial issues: 1) whether a trial court should give an identification instruction; 2) whether absence of the instructions at a trial detrimentally influences jury factfinding so

---

8A J. Moore, MOORE'S FEDERAL PRACTICE § 30.09[6] at 30-98 to 30-101 (2d ed. 1965) (1988 rev.); 2 C. Wright, FEDERAL PRACTICE & PROCEDURE § 495.1 at 771-73 (2d ed. 1982).

5. Greene, *Judge's Instruction on Eyewitness Testimony: Evaluation and Revision*, 18 J. APPLIED SOC. PSYCHOLOGY 252, 256 58 (1988). Greene studied student reactions to videotaped stimuli. Her between-subjects experiment involved two independent variables. There were two sessions of the trial of a defendant accused of assault (throwing a bottle in a bar). One session presented obstructed and poorly lit conditions; the other presented a strong identification. Half the subjects received particularized identification instructions and half received no identification instruction. Greene concluded that "jurors with weak evidence and [particularized instructions] differed significantly from both those with weak evidence and no instruction and those with strong evidence and [particularized instruction]." *Id.* at 258. While the overall difference was significant (as in the present study), she did not separately discuss the variance nor the degree of confidence associated with the variance. Green also attempted to evaluate the weight that subjects themselves attributed to the evidence as a function of the instruction and concluded that "[w]hen the instruction was presented in combination with a strong identification, more jurors chose the eyewitness as having the most important testimony." *Id.* at 261. In a second study, Greene measured the effect of two different particularized instructions and no instructions. By collapsing the results of one instruction and the no instruction, she concluded that the revised instruction reduced conviction rates at a statistically meaningful level. *Id.* at 265. Would collapsing the other particularized instruction with the no instruction have yielded the same result?

The work of Katzev and Wishart has also demonstrated that judicial commentary on identification testimony influenced mock jury deliberation and tended to reduce the probability of individual subjects' votes to convict. *The Impact of Judicial Commentary Concerning Eyewitness Identifications on Jury Decision Making*, 76 J. CRIM. L. & CRIMINOLOGY 733, 739-41 (1985). The extensive "commentary" in which the court engaged in their study, however, recited detailed conclusions of psychological investigations and was thus more comparable to expert opinion evidence. *See id.* at 738 n.19. It was not, as the authors emphasized, the kind of comment that courts would make in North American common-law jurisdictions. Such commentary violates some state constitutional provisions that preclude judicial comment on the evidence, and it may be prohibited as improper judicial notice under rules of evidence. *E.g.*, FED. R. EVID. 201(b) (facts subject to judicial notice must be either generally known or capable of accurate determination by resort to sources whose accuracy cannot be questioned).

as to warrant reversal of a conviction on appeal; and 3) whether expert psychological testimony about identification evidence should be admitted at trial when particularized instructions are given. The results of the present study raise for the first time a fourth issue that warrants further study: whether the widely used particularized instructions have a prejudicial effect on the factfinder's evaluation of identification evidence in cases of violent crime.

II. Method

The present study was conducted to test the influence of instructions on individual subjects' evaluations of eyewitness identification evidence. A written survey was administered to two groups of first-year law students (Groups A and B)[6] and one group of second-year law students (Group C).[7] The survey consisted of four variations (Survey 1, Survey 2, Survey 3, and Survey 4). Surveys were distributed randomly, subjects were informed that other subjects had different surveys, and subjects were asked not to consult with other subjects in completing the survey.[8]

---

6. Surveys were administered in two sections of the first-year class that were selected because they included no summer entrants (who had had Criminal Law). No students had had Criminal Procedure or Evidence. Law students who otherwise qualify are eligible to serve as jurors in local state and federal courts.

The survey was administered to group A (comprising 64 students) at the beginning of a class hour. Subjects were informed that participation was voluntary and all participated. The survey was administered to group B (56 students) at the end of a class hour. Subjects were informed that participation was voluntary and about six students chose not to participate.

7. Group C comprised first-semester second-year students, few of whom had enrolled in or completed a course in Evidence or Criminal Procedure. Because subjects constituting Group C had completed a substantive Criminal Law course and had completed or were contemporaneously enrolled in a trial practice course, the results raise additional problems of external validity and are recorded separately.

8. In addition to brief oral explanation, subjects read the following written directions at the start of the survey:

> You are asked to participate in a voluntary survey designed to explore the reactions of jurors to different fact situations. The survey consists of two different hypothetical fact situations followed by a series of instructions by a judge. Please read the facts and instructions and indicate whether you would find the defendant guilty or not guilty. Please read and decide Case I before starting Case II. Do not identify yourself on the survey. Different versions of the survey are being dis-

All variations of the survey consisted of two cases that summarized evidence presented in two unrelated criminal trials, Zeiler Case (bank robberies) and Greene Case (perjury).[9] The text summarizing the cases was identical for each survey variation. (Appendix A.) Eyewitness identification testimony was critical to the prosecution in both cases. Each case was followed by a series of jury instructions. The instructions following the cases were similar within each survey. The independent variable was the instruction on evaluation of identification evidence. All surveys contained the following instructions:

> The judge instructs you:
>
> 1. You must presume [defendant] to be innocent till proven guilty, and the fact that he is arrested and charged with a crime is not evidence of guilt.
>
> 2. You may return a verdict of guilty only if the government has proved that [defendant] committed the robberies beyond a reasonable doubt.
>
> 3. [Defendant] has no burden of proving his innocence and need not present any evidence. [You may not draw any inference about his guilt from the exercise of his constitutional right not to testify.] [The immediately preceding text in brackets was omitted from the Greene case instructions.]

Survey 1 contained only the three instructions. Survey 2 added a fourth instruction: "4. The government must prove [defendant's] identity [as the robber] beyond a reasonable doubt." Survey 4 substituted for the fourth instruction a particularized identification instruction in use in several federal courts. (Appendix B[10]) Survey 3 was similar to Survey 4 but switched the order of the cases.[11]

The method employed invites a number of objections. Subjects were not exposed to trial evidence in a realistic fashion. Because demeanor and confidence of eyewitnesses is known to affect

---

tributed to the group. Please do not consult with anyone before making your decisions. The results of the survey will be made available to you. Thank you for your cooperation.

9. The facts were derived freely from United States v. Zeiler, 427 F.2d 1305 (3d Cir. 1970) and United States v. Greene, 591 F.2d 471 (8th Cir. 1979).

10. The instruction was first promulgated prospectively as a model instruction in United States v. Telfaire, 469 F.2d 552 (D.C. Cir. 1972).

11. Survey 3, which presented the Greene case first, resulted in higher total conviction rates, but the conviction rates for Zeiler remained consistently higher regardless of the order.

powerfully the evaluation of identification testimony by jurors,[12] the textual description of evidence (especially identification testimony) and instruction to render a verdict excludes important factors that would influence decisionmaking.[13] The study is subject to the general objection that the subjects were not facing the hard choice that jurors face; consequently, none of the emotional stressors were present that militate against or encourage convictions. These objections must be met by confession and avoidance; they apply equally to those empirical studies that have tested mock juror deliberations based on written summaries of eyewitness identifications and expert psychological testimony.[14]

Further objections to external validity relate to the written rather than oral administration of the instructions and the fact that subjects' responses were measured individually rather than in interactive group dynamics (which can be reproduced in mock jury study).[15] The study is also vulnerable to the objection that the subjects were law students and might be more solicitous of certain rights or more attentive to certain defenses than average jurors.

While some force must be allowed to all the objections to the external validity of the methodology, the research was designed to test under controlled circumstances general effects of instructions on evaluations of evidence. Generalization of results to actual juror behavior is difficult or impossible because of the potential for unknown variables in individual cases. The results of the present research indicate, moreover, that external validity may be problematic because of the variable response accorded to different fact situations presented to test subjects.

---

12. Wells, Lindsay, & Ferguson, *Accuracy, Confidence, and Juror Perceptions in Eyewitness Identification*, 64 J. APPLIED PSYCHOLOGY 440, 440-48 (1979).

13. Eyewitness identification evidence need not, however, be introduced by the eyewitness. Identifications are not within the hearsay rule, and a third person may introduce evidence of an out of court identification by the eyewitness. Both the Confrontation Clause and good trial strategy place limits on such a practice.

14. The study by Greene, *supra* note 6, using videotaped stimuli presents fewer problems of external validity and is a more elegant study. But problems of external validity remain nonetheless where mock jury studies use actors as witnesses, because the subjects are never forced actually to judge credibility or to evaluate demeanor.

15. At the same time statistical assessment of group dynamics may present additional problems of internal validity. *See* Greene, *supra* note 6, at 258-259.

III. Results

The results are summarized as proportions of the numbers of verdicts in the charts below.

Group A: Zeiler Case

Not guilty: Guilty
Survey 1 (no instruction) 13:3
Survey 2 (burden proof of identity) 14:2
Survey 3 (particularized instruction) 13:3
Survey 4 (particularized instruction) 16:0

Group A: Greene Case

Not guilty: Guilty
Survey 1 (no instruction) 14:1
Survey 2 (burden proof of identity) 15:1
Survey 3 (particularized instruction) 16:0
Survey 4 (particularized instruction) 14:2

Group B: Zeiler Case

Not guilty: Guilty
Survey 1 (no instruction) 13:1
Survey 2 (burden proof of identity) 15:0
Survey 3 (particularized instruction) 6:6
Survey 4 (particularized instruction) 11:4

Group B: Greene Case

Not guilty Guilty
Survey 1 (no instruction) 12:2
Survey 2 (burden proof of identity) 15:0
Survey 3 (particularized instruction) 11:1
Survey 4 (particularized instruction) 15:0

Group C: Zeiler Case

Not guilty: Guilty
Survey 1 (no instruction) 10:5
Survey 2 (burden proof of identity) 13:0
Survey 3 (particularized instruction) 11:4
Survey 4 (particularized instruction) 10:4

Group C: Greene Case

Not guilty Guilty
Survey 1 (no instruction) 13:2
Survey 2 (burden proof of identity) 13:0
Survey 3 (particularized instruction) 15:0
Survey 4 (particularized instruction) 12:2

The mean probability of a guilty verdict for group A is 9.45%, for group B 12.50%, for group C 14.91%, for all verdicts 10.88%. The correlation of guilty verdicts by case and instruction type is set forth below.

Guilty verdicts for groups A & B

Zeiler Greene total (%)[16]
Survey 1 4/30 3/29 7/59 (11.86%)
Survey 2 2/31 1/31 3/62 (4.83%)
Survey 3 9/28 1/28 10/56 (17.86%)
Survey 4 4/31 2/31 6/62 (9.68%)
Survey 3 & 4 13/59 3/59 16/118 (13.56%)

Guilty verdicts for groups A, B, C

Zeiler Greene total (%)
Survey 1 8/45 5/44 13/89 (14.61%)
Survey 2 2/44 1/44 3/88 (3.41%)
Survey 3 13/44 1/43 14/87 (16.09%)
Survey 4 8/45 4/45 12/90 (13.33%)
Surveys 3 & 4 21/88 5/88 26/176 (14.77%)

The most striking result is the high acquittal rate for both groups and all versions of the survey.[17] While high acquittal rates

16. Percentage is calculated as a function of the number of guilty verdicts returned out of the total verdicts returned by each survey variation. Groups A and B are both included. The guilty results are added for both cases within each survey variation.

17. The high rate undoubtedly reflects aspects of the research method, including the absence of stressors associated with allowing a criminal, or dangerous suspect, to escape. The acquittal rate is higher, however, than comparable rates observed in some mock jury studies and may also reflect the decreased interest in outcome that attains when subjects passively complete a survey rather than participate actively in roleplaying.

The high acquittal rate may also derive from the tendentious elaboration of problematic identification evidence in the statements of evidence for both cases and from the fact that evidence was confronted in written and summary form. While raising problems about the external validity of the study for purposes of gauging juror response to evidence, the study may be of heightened validity for understanding the appellate judicial response to briefs and arguments that recite

have also been observed in mock jury studies and have been related to the difficulty of the cases presented to subjects,[18] the high acquittal rate also raises questions of external validity. Given the high background acquittal rate, the influence of the instructions initially appears to be minimal. The aggregate probability of guilty verdict for subjects who had no instruction was less than 0.2% lower than for those who had particularized identification instructions.

The lowest probability of guilty verdicts ocurred in all groups in Survey 2, among subjects to whom the short instruction on the burden of proving identity was administered. There was a statistically significant nonrandom increase in conviction rates with the administration of a particularized identification instruction as compared to the burden of proving identity instruction.[19] The result is ironic, because federal courts in promulgating particularized identification instructions rejected as inadequate older federal authority that required instruction on the burden of proving identity.[20]

---

in summary form alleged errors in identification evidence.

18. Katzev & Wishart, *supra* note 6, at 740, observed that "the more information the [mock] jurors received, the quicker they reached a verdict." The authors explained the high base rate of acquittal, however, as the result of a "weak case against the defendant." *Id.* at 742.

With a radically different design from the present study, Greene encountered the same phenomenon. Greene, *supra* note 6, at 256, designed stimuli that included "facts that were intentionally balanced so the defendant was not clearly innocent or guilty." Nevertheless, her overall conviction rate was only 13 percent. *Id.* at 257.

19. A statistically significant nonrandom increase obtained in the conviction rates for Zeiler: x-2 5.70, P .017, which excludes the null hypothesis at $P < .05$. The increase observed in the conviction rates for the Greene case did not exclude a null hypothesis at $P < .05$, whether calculated for Groups A and B or for A, B, C. (Fisher's two-tailed probability .664 for A,B,C.) The aggregate increase for both Zeiler and Greene, however, was significant. For A, B, C, x-2 6.50 (P .011) which excludes the null hypothesis at $P < .05$.

20. United States v. Telfaire, 469 F.2d 552, 556 (D.C. Cir. 1972), in promulgating prospectively the model particularized instruction used in the present study (surveys 3 and 4) (Appendix B), observed that "we are satisfied that the attention of the jury was significantly focused on the issue of identity." The Circuit considered the particularized instruction as a more effective method of avoiding wrongful conviction resulting from misidentification and did not return to older authority (which had become narrowly distinguished and limited in its applicability) to the effect that "the failure to say in plain words that if the circumstances of the identification were not convincing, [the jury] would acquit, was er-

Particularized instructions did not appear significantly to influence conviction rates as a whole as compared to the rates that resulted from subjects to whom no instruction was administered.[21] If, however, the rates are correlated separately for the two cases, the effort to generalize from the totals is rendered problematic. Percentages of guilty verdicts for Groups A and B are set forth below:

	Zeiler	*Greene*
Survey 1	13.33%	10.34%
Survey 2	6.45%	3.23%
Survey 3	32.14%	3.57%
Survey 4	12.90%	6.45%
Survey 3 & 4	22.03%	5.08%

The mean percentage for Zeiler is 16.21% (s19.19); that for Greene, 5.90% (s=5.41). Percentages for A, B, and C are:

	Zeiler	*Greene*
Survey 1	17.78%	11.36%
Survey 2	4.55%	2.27%
Survey 3	29.55%	2.33%
Survey 4	17.78%	8.89%
Survey 3 & 4	23.86%	5.68%

The mean percentage for Zeiler is 17.41% (s17.87), for Greene 6.21% (s=8.02).[22] Further analysis thus reveals that the small differences that resulted for the total were a function of two countervailing effects: particularized instructions in the Greene case reduced the probability of conviction from 10.34% (no instruction) to 5.08%; particularized instruction in the Zeiler case increased probability of conviction from 13.33% (no instruction) to 22.03%.[23]

---

ror." McKenzie v. United States, 126 F.2d 533, 536 (D.C. Cir. 1942). *

21. *x-2* for total verdicts is .001 (P .975) which fails to exclude the null hypothesis at P .05.

22. *x-2* for the difference between observed conviction rates for Zeiler and Greene (A,B,C) (8.43) excludes the null hypothesis at P .05 and P .01.

23. Because of the relatively low numbers of guilty verdicts (resulting from the high background acquittal rate), a null hypothesis can not be excluded at P < .05. Fisher's two-tailed probability .341 for A,B,C. Zieler yields *x-2* .422, for A,B,C. The same trend was observed in every group studied, and if a higher error rate were tolerated, the increase in the conviction rate (for Zeiler) and decrease (for Greene) were impressive. Although the values generated do not, in this case, support an affirmative theory at high levels of confidence, they do, I believe, most decidedly shift the burden to the party arguing that the instructions have no ef-

IV. Discussion

The test results indicate that instructions influence subjects' evaluation of identification evidence.[24] The short burden of proving identity instruction had the greatest observed effect on reducing conviction rates, and the reduction was statistically significant as compared to the conviction rates that were returned by subjects to whom the particularized identification instruction was administered. The results also suggest strongly that the effect of the particularized instruction depends on the nature of the case. The results confirm other studies that have indicated that jurors are more likely to convict when confronted with evidence of a violent crime.[25] Indeed, all instructions increased the difference between the conviction probability for violent as opposed to the nonviolent offense.[26] The greatest increase occurred (in absolute and relative terms) when subjects were given a particularized identification instruction. Studies of the influence of expert psychological evidence have indicated the opposite result: a narrowing of the difference between probabilities of conviction for violent and nonviolent of-

---

fect on subjects' behavior. If categories of responses to Surveys 1 and 2 are collapsed, and the conviction rates compared to Surveys 3 and 4, *x*-2 for the Zeiler case (3.44) (P .064) excludes the null hypothesis at P .10, and *x*-2 for the Greene case (.096) (P .77). The results indicate the absence of empirical support for the conclusion repeatedly made by appellate courts that the failure to give identification instructions was harmless error on the theory that the factfinder's evaluation of evidence was not influenced.

24. Combining the frequencies obtained in Surveys 3 and 4, and comparing the frequencies that resulted by instruction type for all groups (A,B,C) yields *x*-2 6.698, with 2 d.f., P .035, which excludes the null hypothesis at $P < .05$.

25. *See* Loftus, *supra* note 3, at 12. Though the summaries of evidence in the present study did not focus on circumstances of the criminal misconduct, subjects were informed that Zeiler was suspected of participation in a series of bank robberies. The extent of violence or threat of violence at the robberies was not disclosed, but suspects would in any event infer that the robber presented a greater danger than the suspected perjurer in the Greene case. Subjects were also aware in the *Zeiler* case that the defendant was suspected of a series of unsolved crimes, thus further increasing the potential regret they would suffer in acquitting.

Loftus's study actually observed different conviction rates that resulted from increase in violence. Though she characterized her two cases as violent and nonviolent, both were violent; both included an assault with a deadly weapon, but death resulted in one case while the assault was repelled in the other case.

26. The burden of proof instruction did not increase the absolute difference (which remained about 3%), but the 3% difference increased when considered a function of the probability of convicting.

fenses. While the consistently higher conviction rate for violent crimes can in part be attributed to the disutility calculus,[27] one would expect the effect of such disutility considerations to be less pronounced in a survey of the sort administered here than in a roleplaying test, where some psychological stressors are presumably engaged. But the differences observed in the present study were in fact considerably greater than those observed in mock jury studies.[28]

The higher conviction rate for violent crime and the aggravation of the rate in subjects to whom particularized instructions were administered suggests other possibilities. The particularized instruction, by identifying factors (like "strength of the identification" and "circumstances under which the identification was made") may encourage jurors to speculate and make inferences based on their own understanding, which studies have demonstrated to be inaccurate. For example, subjects may infer that eyewitnesses to a violent crime, being under stress at the time of observation, provide more accurate identifications. The particularized instruction may thus aggravate the error in precisely the manner that has been suggested for general credibility instructions. The different effect of instructions in violent and nonviolent cases may also result from the nature of the evidence itself. The robbery evidence may have suggested that the only evidence possible was eyewitness identification evidence. In the perjury case, however, there was exculpatory evidence, including the defendant's testimony.

The results of the present study, if confirmed by further empirical studies,[29] indicate that jury instructions on identification

27. The disutility of allowing a dangerous suspect to remain at large outweighs the disutility of convicting an innocent person. The difference is greater than the comparable difference for less violent offenses. For discussion of the operation of the regret matrix, *see* Lempert, *Modeling Relevance*, 75 MICH L. REV. 1021, 1032-41 (1977); Kaplan, *Decision Theory and the Fact-Finding Process*, 4 STAN. L. REV. 1065, 1073-74 (1968).

28. *Cf.* Loftus, *supra* note 3, at 12 (table one) (guilty verdicts as a percentage of the total verdicts ranged from 35% to 68%).

29. The most serious problem with the present test is one of external validity. I am grateful to Professor Richard Lempert for emphasizing to me the crucial problem of external validity that results both from the artificial format of the written survey test method and from the use of law students as subjects. He correctly identified the need for further research. Nevertheless, the present test results provide an important guide for further research. Future research might reduce but not eliminate problems of external validity by selecting subjects more

testimony have an influence on subjects' evaluation of identification testimony. At least in the case of violent crime, the instructions widely used by some federal courts did not have the same effect on evaluation of identification evidence as expert psychological testimony on eyewitness identifications. The availability of the instructions thus does not justify the exclusion of otherwise relevant expert opinion evidence. The recognized need to tailor instructions to particular cases appears to be especially important in identification cases, and the particularized instruction administered in the present study may not be adequate. Because the presence of instructions has an empirically demonstrated impact on the evaluation of critical inculpatory evidence, and because the nature of the impact varies in different types of cases, it would seem inappropriate to consider the omission of such instructions to be harmless error.

APPENDIX A: CASES IN THE SURVEYS

Case I

United States v. Zeiler

Evidence

The defendant Gary Zeiler has been charged with three separate bank robberies that occurred over a five-year period. The evidence against him at trial consist of identifications of Zeiler by three different eyewitnesses to the robberies. The robber did not wear any disguise and was dressed plainly. The three identifying witnesses observed the robber for time periods ranging from 30 seconds to 120 seconds under stressful circumstances.

Zeiler did not take the stand but attempted to show that he had been misidentified. The evidence disclosed that three days af-

---

representative of jurors, by presenting subjects with live or videotaped stimuli (testimony, arguments, and instructions), and by having subjects deliberate collectively in reaching verdicts. While the present study provides no basis for anticipating the data that would result from such research, it provides important suggestions for the structure of future testing. First, the differential effect of instructions in violent and nonviolent cases indicates the need for designing further testing to measure reactions to instructions in different types of cases. Second, the differential effect of nonparticularized instructions indicates the need for future research designs to incorporate as controls both instructions that omit any instruction and instructions that include a simple burden of proving identity instruction.

ter his arrest, Zeiler appeared at a lineup with five other persons. Fifty eyewitnesses to the robberies viewed the lineup. Three identified Zeiler as the robber, one identified another person in the lineup as the robber, and forty-six eyewitnesses were unable positively to identify any person in the lineup as the robber.

It was also disclosed during trial that before the lineup all the eyewitnesses were shown a series of eight photographs. Five of the photographs were police mugshots of persons other than Zeiler. Three of the photographs were ordinary snapshots of Zeiler. Zeiler was the only person in the photographs who wore glasses. The robber had worn glasses.

Case II

United States v. Greene

Evidence

Frank Greene was convicted of mail fraud and was released on bail pending his appeal. While he was released on bail, Greene was prohibited from traveling out of Kansas City without prior court permission. Greene obtained court permission to travel to Chicago, but a courthouse employee believed that she saw Greene on a flight to California. When Greene returned to Kansas City, the court conducted an evidentiary hearing to determine if Greene had violated conditions of his bail. At the hearing Greene testified under oath that neither he nor his mother had been on the scheduled flight to California.

Greene is charged with perjury for lying under oath to the court. He is specifically charged with two counts of perjury: 1) knowingly stating falsely that he was not on the flight; and 2) knowingly stating falsely that his mother was not on the flight.

Evidence against Greene at trial consisted of an identification of Greene by the courthouse employee who testified that she saw Greene on the flight. The government introduced evidence that a ticket had been purchased in Greene's mother's name and paid for by Greene's mother and that the ticket was used on the flight. No ticket had been purchased in Greene's name.

Greene introduced evidence that his wife and brother and several other family members were on the flight. He testified that he had helped them onto the plane but did not fly to California. Greene also introduced testimony from his landlord in Chicago that Greene had met with the landlord in Chicago the day after the flight to California. And Greene introduced into evidence various credit card receipts with his signature on them that had been charged in Chicago the two days after the flight to California. Greene's mother testified that she had purchased the ticket in her name but that Greene's brother and his family had used the ticket. The evidence further disclosed that Greene's brother is about the same age and height as Greene.

APPENDIX B: PARTICULARIZED INSTRUCTION

Identification testimony is an expression of belief or impression by the witness. Its value depends on the opportunity the witness had to observe the offender at the time of the offense and to make a reliable identification later.

In appraising the identification testimony of a witness, you should consider the following:

(1) Are you convinced that the witness had the capacity and an adequate opportunity to observe the offender?

Whether the witness had an adequate opportunity to observe the offender at the time of the offense will be affected by such matters as how long or short a time was available, how far or close the witness was, how good were lighting conditions, whether the witness had occasion to see or know the person in the past.

(2) Are you satisfied that the identification made by the witness subsequent to the offense was the product of his or her own recollection? You may take into account both the strength of the identification and the circumstances under which the identification was made.

If the identification by the witness may have been influenced by the circumstances under which the defendant was presented to him or her for identification, you should scrutinize the identification with great care. You may also consider the length of time that lapsed between the occurrence of the crime and the next opportunity of the witness to see the defendant as a factor bearing on the reliability of the identification.

You may also take into account that an identification made by picking the defendant out of a group of similar individuals is generally more reliable than one which results from the presentation of the defendant alone to the witness.

(3) Finally, you must consider the credibility of each identification witness in the same way as any other witness, consider whether he or she is truthful, and consider whether he had the

capacity and opportunity to make a reliable observation on the matter covered in his or her testimony.

I again emphasize that the burden of proof on the government extends to every element of the crime charged, and this specifically includes the burden of proving beyond a reasonable doubt the identity of the defendant as the perpetrator of the crime with which he stands charged. If after examining the testimony, you have a reasonable doubt as to the accuracy of the identification, you must find the defendant not guilty.

DO JURORS UNDERSTAND CRIMINAL JURY INSTRUCTIONS? ANALYZING THE RESULTS OF THE MICHIGAN JUROR COMPREHENSION PROJECT*

Geoffrey P. Kramer** and Dorean M. Koenig***

In our jury system, laypersons rather than legal experts determine the guilt or innocence of persons accused of crime by applying legal standards provided by a judge in the form of jury instructions. The complexity of some legal standards raises concern about the jurors' ability to perform their duties. Their responsibilities can be divided into three parts. First, jurors must determine the facts in the case before them.[1] Second, they must

* A grant from the Michigan State Bar Foundation and royalties from the Michigan Criminal Jury Instructions Committee of the State Bar of Michigan funded the project described in this Article. The Juror Comprehension Project (the "Project") is a subcommittee of the Michigan Criminal Jury Instructions Committee, a standing committee of the State Bar of Michigan. The Project was chaired by Professor Dorean M. Koenig, coauthor of this Article, and relied on the expertise of Michigan State University Professor Norbert Kerr, who was instrumental in developing the study discussed in this Article. For a list of Project members and a discussion of the origin of the Project and the Michigan Standard Criminal Jury Instructions, see Koenig, Kerr & Van Hoek, *Michigan Standard Criminal Jury Instructions: Judges' Perspectives After Ten Years' Use*, 4 COOLEY L. REV. 347 (1987).

We thank all the members of the Michigan Criminal Jury Instructions Committee for their assistance in constructing the questionnaire. We especially thank Joe Kimble and Janice Spodarek for work on the questionnaire and Judge William Caprathe, Dawn Van Hoek, and Elizabeth Jacobs for facilitating contact with various courts. We are also greatly indebted to Professor Norbert Kerr who provided valuable assistance throughout.

We are very grateful to the judges, clerks, and officers of the Detroit Recorder's Court and the Thirtieth Judicial Circuit Court of Lansing for their assistance in this Project and without whose help it could not have been done. For the additional assistance and enthusiasm of Judges Gershwin A. Drain and Clarice Jobes, who found time in their very busy schedules for this Project, we wish to give special thanks.

** Faculty Lecturer, Indiana University at Kokomo. B.S., Central Michigan University, 1975; M.A., Central Michigan University, 1977; Ph.D., Michigan State University, expected 1990. Mr. Kramer's background is in clinical and social psychology. He worked as a staff psychologist at the state prison in Jackson, MI from 1978 to 1984.

*** Professor, Thomas M. Cooley Law School. Ph.B., University of Detroit, 1956; J.D., University of Detroit Law School, 1967. Ms. Koenig is the original reporter of the Michigan Standard Criminal Jury Instructions and the author of the Commentaries. She is the chairperson of the subcommittee of the Michigan State Bar Committee on Standard Criminal Jury Instructions, which undertook the project reported in this article.

1. Jurors perform this function capably. *See, e.g.*, H. KALVEN & H. ZEISEL, THE AMERICAN JURY 149 (1966).

learn the relevant legal standards from the judge. Finally, they must apply those standards to the facts of the case. Confusion over the meaning of judicial instructions undermines the jurors' ability to fulfill their second function, that of learning the legal standards, and consequently affects their application of the law to the facts. The study of 600 actual jurors discussed in this Article sought to determine whether jurors are able to learn the law from complex instructions.[2] The study's data support the view that juror understanding of judicial instructions is flawed and that changes in the wording and presentation of judicial instructions may be required to improve juror comprehension.[3]

The use of laypersons to convict or acquit accused criminals was drawn from the English system into American law via the sixth amendment to the United States Constitution, which states in part: "In all criminal prosecutions, the accused shall enjoy the right to a speedy and public trial, by an impartial jury of the State and district wherein the crime shall have been committed. . . ."[4]

A jury trial in a criminal case[5] follows a set and orderly pattern.[6] At the end of the trial, after all the evidence and argu-

2. For a thorough description of the study, see *infra* Part I.

3. For a complete analysis of the results, see *infra* Part II.

4. U.S. CONST. amend. VI. In 1968, the sixth amendment right to a jury trial was "incorporated" as one of the fourteenth amendment's fundamental liberties and made applicable to any significant state criminal proceeding. Duncan v. Louisiana, 391 U.S. 145, 149 (1968). The standards for state and federal trials are not entirely congruent, however. In Apodaca v. Oregon, 406 U.S. 404, 406 (1972), for example, the Court concluded that a state law allowing a nonunanimous jury to return a verdict was constitutional. In a federal trial, however, absent a waiver, the Constitution requires a unanimous verdict for a criminal conviction. Johnson v. Louisiana, 406 U.S. 356, 369 (1972) (Powell, J., concurring).

The Court has allowed fewer than the usual 12 jurors in state trials, *see* Williams v. Florida, 399 U.S. 78 (1970), but has held that a conviction by 5 out of 6 jurors does not reflect adequately the sense of the community. Burch v. Louisiana, 441 U.S. 130 (1979). A unanimous five-person jury also fails to satisfy the right to a trial by jury. Ballew v. Georgia, 435 U.S. 223 (1978).

5. Criminal cases do not ordinarily go to jury trial. Almost 9 out of 10 criminal cases are disposed of prior to jury determination. Many of the cases are either dismissed during pretrial proceedings or result in a guilty plea by the defendant. *See* Y. KAMISAR, W. LAFAVE & J. ISRAEL, MODERN CRIMINAL PROCEDURE 21 (7th ed. 1990). Some defendants also opt for a determination by a judge instead of a jury, in which case no jury instructions are given. *Id.* at 19.

6. The petit jury is first impaneled from the larger panel of prospective jurors in a "voir dire" proceeding, at which either the attorneys or the judge questions the jurors to uncover any potential bias. *See* T. MAUET, FUNDAMENTALS OF TRIAL TECHNIQUES 25 (2d ed. 1988). The attorneys ordinarily make opening statements, although the defense attorney may wait until after the prosecution has presented his entire case. *See id.* at 51. The trial itself consists routinely of the following: 1) the prosecutor's direct examination of her witnesses; 2) the defense counsel's cross-examination of the prosecution's witnesses;

ments have been presented, the judge instructs the jury on the legal standards that they are to apply.[7] The jurors are told that they are the sole judges of both the facts of the case[8] and the credibility of the witnesses.[9] Most importantly, they are instructed on the elements or constituent parts that the prosecution must prove for each crime with which the defendant is charged.[10] They also are instructed on the concepts of reasonable doubt and the burden of proof.[11]

The jury is then sent to the jury room to deliberate without outside interference. Jury deliberations are not recorded and ordinarily postverdict statements or testimony by jury members may not be used to impeach the verdict[12] except in those few instances where it is shown that outside matters improperly influenced the jury.[13] Judges and attorneys may not contact the jurors during their deliberations, and jurors receive very little help when they are unclear about what is necessary to convict.[14] Thus, juror comprehension of judicial instructions upon recital is crucial to a legally correct verdict.

The function of the jury instructions, however, does not stop with recital of instructions to the jurors and application of in-

---

3) the prosecutor's redirect and the defense counsel's recross; 4) the repetition of the same process with the defense counsel now conducting direct examination on his witnesses, and so on. *See id.* at 151.

7. *See, e.g.*, FED. R. CRIM. P. 30. Unfortunately, judicial instructions given after the presentation of evidence come too late to assist jurors in analyzing and processing the facts of the case. *See, e.g.*, Kassin & Wrightsman, *On the Requirements of Proof: The Timing of Judicial Instruction and Mock Juror Verdicts*, 37 J. PERSONALITY SOC. PSYCHOLOGY 1877 (1979) (indicating that mock jurors who were given *pre-testimony* instructions on the requirements of proof demonstrated a reduced tendency to convict).

8. "[T]he factfinder's responsibility at trial, based on evidence adduced by the State, [is] to *find* the ultimate facts beyond a reasonable doubt." Francis v. Franklin, 471 U.S. 307, 316 (1985) (emphasis added) (quoting Ulster County Court v. Allen, 442 U.S. 140, 156 (1979)).

9. "The established safeguards of the Anglo-American legal system leave the veracity of a witness to be tested by cross-examination, and the credibility of his testimony to be determined by a properly instructed jury." Hoffa v. United States, 385 U.S. 293, 311 (1966).

10. "Lest there remain any doubt about the constitutional stature of the reasonable-doubt standard, we explicitly hold that the Due Process Clause protects the accused against conviction except upon proof beyond a reasonable doubt of every fact necessary to constitute the crime with which he is charged." *In re* Winship, 397 U.S. 358, 364 (1970).

11. *See infra* Appendix II.

12. *See* Y. KAMISAR, W. LAFAVE & J. ISRAEL, *supra* note 5, at 1408-10.

13. *Id.*

14. In fact, judges routinely respond to juror requests to explain instructions by merely rereading verbatim the same instruction. The judge is not obliged to give all of the instructions previously given and need only repeat those specifically asked for by the jury. *See* People v. Johnson, 167 Mich. App. 168, 175, 421 N.W.2d 617, 620 (1988).

structions to the perceived facts. Jury instructions in criminal cases form a basis for legal arguments raised on appellate review of a criminal conviction.[15] Thus, although appellate courts generally may not review jury determinations,[16] the instructions that were given to the jury are duly recorded and counsel may point to errors in the instructions as reason for reversal on appeal. Jury instructions thus form the basis on which the appellate courts shape the substantive criminal law. In order to minimize the use of jury instructions as a tool to obtain appellate reversal, "pattern" or "standard" instructions have been developed.[17] Perhaps the emphasis placed on technical accuracy explains why the primary role of jury instructions—to teach jurors about the law—has arguably been overlooked and underrepresented in the literature and in the cases.[18] Highly technical and relatively incomprehensible jury instructions that are legally

---

15. Appellate courts have been reluctant to reverse convictions following jury trials, basing their refusals on court rules as well as case law. They ordinarily will not reverse a conviction even if the jurors did not fully understand the jury instructions. *See* People v. Lee, 220 Cal. App. 3d 320, 329, 269 Cal. Rptr. 434, 439 (1990). *But see* Hoffert v. Florida, 559 So. 2d 1246 (Fla. Dist. Ct. App. 1990); People v. Tucker, 193 Ill. App. 3d 849, 550 N.E.2d 581 (1990).

One barrier to reversing convictions based on poorly comprehended instructions is that courts will read the instructions "as a whole." City of Minot v. Rubbelke, 456 N.W.2d 511 (N.D. 1990). A concurring judge in People v. Lee commented on this lack of concern over comprehension:

> One juror then noted: "We have read over several pages again and again and we are having a little bit of difficulty with when specific intent begins." After the judge stated that he could not further clarify the point, another juror asked: "How do you find intentions?" The question was not answered. . . . It is clear from the above the jurors were having difficulty with the concept of specific intent generally. . . . I am therefore unpersuaded by that too-oft employed bromide that failure to give a correct instruction may be cured by viewing the instructions as a whole.

220 Cal. App. 3d at 329, 320, 269 Cal. Rptr. at 434, 439 (White, J., concurring).

A second barrier, derived from court rules, precludes reversal if the defendant did not object adequately to the jury instructions, unless the alleged error in those instructions constitutes "plain error" or "fundamental error." *See, e.g.*, United States v. Jackson, 569 F.2d 1003, 1009 (7th Cir.), *cert. denied*, 437 U.S. 907 (1978) (finding that even the rejection by the court of twice-tendered valid instructions did not constitute grounds for reversal when the counsel failed to make a distinct objection); State v. Odom, 307 N.C. 655, 661, 300 S.E.2d 375, 379 (1983) (holding that, in applying the "plain error" test, the reviewing court "must examine the entire record and determine if the instructional error had a probable impact on the jury's finding of guilt").

16. Appellate courts may review the sufficiency of the evidence supporting a conviction by guilty verdict, but they may not substitute their own interpretation of the evidence for the jury's interpretation. *See, e.g.*, Jackson v. Virginia, 443 U.S. 307, 318-20 (1979).

17. *See* Koenig, Kerr & Van Hoek, *Michigan Standard Criminal Jury Instructions: Judges' Perspectives After Ten Years' Use*, 4 COOLEY L. REV. 347, 361 (1987).

18. Some authors, however, have recognized the importance of comprehensible jury instructions. For a thorough discussion regarding comprehensible jury instructions and

"correct" but less than useful in practice have supported guilty verdicts on appeal.[19] No matter how technically accurate an instruction is, it fails in its primary purpose if jurors are unable to use it to deliberate and determine verdicts.

In response to this concern, the Juror Comprehension Project ("the Project") sought to determine whether jurors understand judicial instructions. This Article reports the results of an empirical study growing out of that Project. The Project investigated how well 600 actual jurors in Michigan understood criminal jury instructions in actual trials. Part I describes the history of the study and explains the procedures and materials used in the study. Part II presents the results of the study, first analyzing juror comprehension of selected concepts, then discussing general factors that influence juror comprehension. Part III concludes that the results show a mixed juror understanding of complex judicial instructions, discusses this mixed understanding, and argues for changes in the current method of jury instruction, including the use of written instructions and simpler language.

I. THE STUDY

The study undertaken by the Juror Comprehension Project is the result of a collaboration between social science researchers from Michigan State University and legal professionals—judges, prosecutors and defense attorneys who were members of the Michigan Criminal Jury Instructions Committee (the "CJI Committee" or the "Committee").[20]

---

an alternative method of evaluation, see A. ELWORK, B. SALES & J. ALFINI, MAKING JURY INSTRUCTIONS UNDERSTANDABLE (1982).

19. Some of the most confusing instructions have been in the terms of art found in homicide law. *See, e.g.*, People v. Kelly, 423 Mich. 261, 292-303, 378 N.W.2d 365, 375-84 (1985) (Levin, J., concurring in part and dissenting in part) (asserting that trial judge gave incorrect felony-murder instruction, telling the jury that it might infer from defendant's participation in robbery that he had the requisite intent to support a conviction for murder); People v. Borgetto, 99 Mich. 336, 339, 58 N.W. 328, 329 (1894) (holding unobjectionable a jury instruction that stated that malice includes "not only anger, hatred and revenge but every other unlawful and unjustifiable motive"). The arguments against such language are discussed in People v. Morrin, 31 Mich. App. 301, 310-24, 187 N.W.2d 434, 438-46 (1971). *See also* Koenig, *Jury Instructions for Jurors: Proposals for the Simplification of Michigan Instructions on Murder*, 21 WAYNE L. REV. 1, 3-4 (1974); Purver, *The Language of Murder*, 14 UCLA L. REV. 1306, 1308-10 (1967).

For a case other than homicide, see People v. White, 168 Mich. App. 596, 604-06, 425 N.W.2d 193, 197-98 (1988) (upholding jury instruction as to whether defendant was armed with a weapon).

20. Koenig, Kerr & Van Hoek, *supra* note 17, at 347-49.

The collaboration began with a 1987 survey of Michigan judges. The 1987 survey helped identify perceived weaknesses in Michigan's standard criminal jury instructions, because judges giving instructions in criminal cases are in the best position to recognize difficulties that jurors might encounter.[21] Based on the results of the 1987 survey, certain instructions were targeted as likely candidates for juror confusion.

A. *Overview of the Study*

Once the 1987 survey identified potentially problematic instructions, the Project developed a short, easy-to-complete questionnaire. This questionnaire consisted of both true-false and open-ended questions.[22] Actual jurors received this questionnaire immediately after they finished serving on a trial. The Project assessed juror comprehension of instructions by comparing the responses of jurors instructed on a particular standard with jurors who had not received such an instruction. The presumption, of course, was that jurors exposed to instructions would score higher than the jurors not exposed.

This procedure yielded a great deal of data about the comprehension level of ordinary jurors. It also tested comprehension following actual trials and did so without interfering with appellate review of the instructions. Finally, it demonstrated that social science researchers and legal experts can work together productively to test empirically the effectiveness of jury instructions.

B. *The Questionnaire*

Each true-false question was intended to test comprehension of one jury instruction or one aspect of an instruction. The open-ended questions, which were designed to probe for additional sources of misunderstanding about jury instructions, allowed jurors to report their thoughts and experiences in trying to comprehend and use instructions.

The items contained in the questionnaire were developed in the following manner. First, Dorean Koenig, Geoffrey Kramer and Norbert Kerr wrote approximately seventy-five true-false

21. *Id.* at 369-71.

22. For a copy of the questionnaire, see *infra* Appendix I.

questions and submitted them to the CJI Committee for review by committee members. The committee members scrutinized these questions for legal accuracy and clarity. They recommended keeping or discarding each item, suggested rewording, commented about possible misinterpretations, and suggested alternate questions. Committee members also indicated whether the question, as worded, was true or false. Their responses for each question were tabulated and compared. The Committee only retained questions for which there was unanimity about a correct answer and for which there was a clear consensus on the question's relationship to the targeted instruction. The remaining questions were revised by the Committee, and this procedure was repeated with members of the Juror Comprehension Subcommittee of the CJI Committee, as well as a member of the Plain English Committee of the Michigan State Bar. The CJI Committee made every effort to word the questions in simple language. The questionnaire was again submitted to the CJI Committee for feedback and final approval.

The complexity of the items on the questionnaire varies considerably. This variation was intended for two reasons. First, it reflects a reality about jury instructions themselves. Some instructions seem straightforward while others engender considerable debate, even among legal professionals.[23] Second, it reflects the differing abilities of the jurors.

Some instructions are confusing because the underlying legal standards are vague and indefinite. This is indicative of an unwillingness in the law to refine difficult questions that produce substantial differences of opinion among lawyers and judges.[24] It is easier to leave technical and expansive jury instructions in a form that may be incomprehensible to the layperson because legal terminology is not ordinarily a ground for reversal of a conviction.[25] In other words, because juror confusion is not ordinarily grounds for reversal as long as the underlying instructions are technically correct, our legal system provides little incentive to correct errors in juror comprehension. Obviously, if jurors cannot ascertain what the law requires, their decisions will be

23. For an example, see the discussion of reasonable doubt, *infra* notes 45-56 and accompanying text.

24. *See* Koenig, Kerr & Van Hoek, *supra* note 17, at 354-55 (giving an example of judges' disagreement over "reasonable doubt"). Koenig, Kerr, and Van Hoek also discuss the history of the "reasonable doubt" instruction in Michigan, *id.* at 356-58, and summarize the four different methods used in the United States to explain the concept of reasonable doubt to juries, *id.* at 372-73.

25. *See id.* at 362.

tainted. Under our present system, however, there is no method to redress this confusion.

In addition, as a matter of test construction, it is desirable to include items that vary in difficulty.[26] A questionnaire with uniformly easy items probably would do little to assess jurors' comprehension of more difficult aspects of instructions, while uniformly difficult items might differentiate comprehension levels among only the brightest jurors. Variability in the difficulty of items, however, might reveal whether jurors comprehended the basic meaning of the instructions as well as their more subtle distinctions.

C. Procedure

Before using the questionnaire in earnest, we conducted a pilot test of it on undergraduate students in a jury simulation and on a small sample of actual jurors following trials. We hoped to identify questions that might present unforeseen problems. For instance, if virtually all jurors in the pilot sample answered a question correctly, further testing with that question probably would be uninformative. In that case, we would replace the question with another that might better reveal possible sources of juror misunderstanding. In addition, we conducted follow-up interviews with student pilot subjects to reveal unforeseen ambiguities in the wording of the questions. We made minor revisions as a result of this testing.

The first task in administering the questionnaire to actual jurors was to secure the cooperation of a number of courts. The Project contacted several judges from the Detroit Recorder's Court and the Thirtieth Judicial Circuit Court of Lansing, Michigan. These courts were selected because they hear a relatively high number of cases, which facilitated data collection. Specific judges were contacted in order to achieve a balance between judges who had defense-orientated backgrounds and judges who

26. The desirability of varying the difficulty of items in a test depends upon the purpose for which the test is given. Variability in item difficulties for our questionnaire was desirable because jurors' abilities were likely to vary broadly. Further, our purpose was to assess whether jurors understood both the elementary and complex aspects of particular instructions. Therefore, questions that varied in difficulty were constructed. It is worth noting that the overall test difficulty was very close to 50% (i.e., half of the items answered correctly), though the range of individual item difficulty varied roughly from 25% to 95% for uninstructed jurors. For a discussion of the relationship between test item difficulty and testing purposes, see A. Anastasi, Psychological Testing 205-06 (4th ed. 1976). *See also* J. Nunnally, Educational Measurement and Evaluation 133 (1964).

had prosecution-oriented backgrounds. Only those judges who routinely used the Criminal Jury Instructions verbatim participated. A total of twelve different courts eventually provided data, seven from Detroit and five from Lansing.

The Project administered the questionnaire to actual jurors immediately after they finished serving on a trial. Juror participation was entirely voluntary. At the completion of a trial, either the trial judge or the court clerk explained briefly the purpose of the questionnaire and requested that jurors complete it individually and at their own pace. The court exercised its discretion as to whether the judge or a court clerk administered the questionnaire and explained its purpose. Not surprisingly, higher percentages of jurors volunteered in the courts in which the judge administered and explained the questionnaire.[27] Completed questionnaires were collected and mailed to Michigan State University for analysis. A checklist, filled out by the court clerk, accompanied the questionnaires from each jury, indicating which criminal jury instructions those jurors had heard.

D. Design

The study focused on a comparison between instructed and uninstructed jurors. The instructed jurors were those who had been exposed to targeted instructions during the trial. The uninstructed (control) jurors were those who were not exposed to targeted instructions. Because all jurors were requested to answer every question on the questionnaire, each juror could function as an instructed juror for some questions and an uninstructed juror for other questions. For example, jurors who served on a felony murder case heard instructions about felony murder, but not about assault.[28] They served as instructed jurors for questions dealing with felony murder and uninstructed jurors for questions dealing with assault.[29] Persons who did not

27. The Lansing courts also requested that jurors complete a different, internal questionnaire. This additional request may have reduced participation in these courts.

28. Assault is not a felony that will support a conviction for felony murder in Michigan. *See* MICH. COMP. LAWS ANN. § 750.316 (West 1968 & Supp. 1989).

29. Unfortunately, we do not have any data comparing control jurors who never served with control jurors who served but were not exposed to particular instructions. It seems reasonable to suppose that the two groups are comparable in their responses to questions for which they did not hear instructions. Jurors who did serve were initially selected from the same pool as those jurors who did not serve, all jurors being selected via a random process, so there should be no systematic differences between the groups. It is also difficult to specify how exposure to some instructions (e.g., reasonable doubt, as-

serve on a jury comprised the control group for questions concerning reasonable doubt and witness credibility because reasonable doubt and witness credibility instructions are given to all jurors who serve in a criminal trial.[30] The rates of comprehension for uninstructed jurors, as revealed by the number of correct and incorrect responses, served as a baseline to evaluate the comprehension of instructed jurors and to make inferences about the effects of the instructions.

E. The Sample of Jurors

In total, 882 jurors, including those who served on a trial and control jurors who did not serve, were asked to complete the questionnaire. Of those requested, 600 completed the questionnaire, resulting in a compliance rate of approximately 68%. For the sample that completed questionnaires, the gender distribution was 50.2% female and 49.8% male. They ranged in age from 19 to 71, with a mean age of 39 and a median age of 37. Their educational level ranged from 7 to 20 or more years of education, with a mean of 13.4 years and a median of 12 years of education.

Testing actual jurors following actual trials has the advantage of realism, but it also presents certain limitations. Primary among these is the lack of control over a variety of factors that might influence juror comprehension. For instance, jurors who volunteer to take a questionnaire may be brighter and generally may have higher rates of comprehension than jurors who do not volunteer. This possibility does not have strong support. Of juries that returned questionnaires, 60% had all twelve members complete a questionnaire, and 75% had at least eleven of twelve members complete the questionnaire. Thus, self-selection within juries was relatively uncommon—either virtually all jurors from a jury completed the questionnaire or few or none did. Also, discussion of jury instructions may occur during deliberation, im-

sault, etc.) would influence responses to questions concerning instructions to which a juror had never been exposed (e.g., the elements of first degree felony murder). Still, it is possible that jurors who were instructed on some points of law during trials made inferences about other points of law that jurors who were never instructed at all did not make. Ultimately, this is an empirical question.

30. Certain instructions are given to all or nearly all juries (e.g., reasonable doubt). For those instructions, the uninstructed comparison group was a sample of jurors who were called to jury duty but who never actually served because of a surplus of potential jurors or last-minute settlements. These persons were asked to complete the questionnaire once it was clear that they would not be needed by the court.

proving the comprehension of jurors who initially did not understand an instruction. It is therefore difficult to make strong assertions about juror comprehension before deliberation, based on the results of a questionnaire administered after deliberation. One would hope that deliberation improves comprehension of instructions, but postdeliberation testing of juror comprehension may not provide an unambiguously clear picture of how comprehensible certain instructions are when they are given. Some of the limitations of testing actual jurors could be controlled by our procedures, but other limitations could not.[31]

An important question is whether our volunteer sample reflects a truly random sample of jurors. Neither the Detroit nor the Lansing courts keep records of juror demographics, so no direct comparison with their jury pools can be made. A sample of 205 jurors chosen at random over a 16-month period from the Lansing courts does provide a basis for comparison.[32] This random sample had a mean education level of 13.3 years,[33] nearly identical to the 13.4 mean for the volunteer sample. The mean age for that randomly chosen sample was 39.3,[34] again very close to the 39.0 mean age for the volunteer sample. Finally, the proportion of men and women in our volunteer sample does not differ significantly from the proportion in the general population.[35] We believe our volunteer sample, therefore, is representative of a random sample of jurors drawn from a metropolitan area in Michigan.[36]

The variation in volunteer rate was mostly a function of the courts from which the jurors came. Jurors frequently declined in some courts, while in other courts very few or no jurors declined. Follow-up telephone interviews with the personnel who administered the questionnaires revealed that declining was primarily related to who made the request. There was much greater com-

31. *See infra* notes 63-64 and accompanying text.

32. A comparison with one relevant population would be ideal. Unfortunately, such a population does not appear to be available. We could find no statewide demographics for jurors (which is not surprising because neither Detroit nor Lansing keep such records). Therefore, we used the sample from a study by Kramer, Kerr, and Carroll for comparison. *See* Kramer, Kerr & Carroll, *Pretrial Publicity, Judicial Remedies, and Jury Bias*, 14 LAW & HUM. BEHAV. ____ (forthcoming 1990) (draft on file at the *University of Michigan Journal of Law Reform*).

33. *Id.*

34. *Id.*

35. Michigan's population is 51.3% female and 48.7% male. BUREAU OF THE CENSUS, U.S. DEP'T OF COMMERCE, COUNTY AND CITY DATA BOOK 2 (1988).

36. The educational level of persons from Lansing is slightly higher than the educational level of persons from Detroit. *Id.* at 668. Thus, our volunteer sample might slightly overestimate the average education level of Detroit's juror pool.

pliance among Detroit Recorder's Court jurors, where judges typically made the request, than among Lansing Circuit Court jurors, where clerks typically made the request. In a few instances, court personnel indicated that declining also may have been related to time of day, with more jurors declining in the late afternoon after long deliberations. No one reported that declining seemed obviously related to juror characteristics such as helpfulness, age, intelligence, or reading ability.

II. Results of the Study: Juror Comprehension of Individual Instructions

To examine the effect of each instruction, the Juror Comprehension Project analyzed every question by comparing average percentage correct obtained by *uninstructed* jurors with average percentage correct obtained by *instructed* jurors. Only jurors who had heard the relevant instruction verbatim were included in the instructed group. Next, an analysis was undertaken that subdivided the uninstructed and instructed groups into into high and low education categories.[37] Such an analysis might reveal cases in which jurors at one education level were more (or less) influenced by instructions than jurors at another education level.

A few comments about interpretation should precede the analysis of specific results. First, because the questions are in a true-false format, mere guessing should result in a 50% correct response rate. Scores significantly above that level reflect at least some understanding of the concept tested. Scores significantly below 50% are more difficult to interpret, but probably indicate the presence of misconceptions—in other words, a belief that the wrong answer is correct rather than an absence of knowledge—or a problem with the question itself. This is important because scores for some of the questions are considerably below 50%. Second, differences among groups that have large sample sizes are more reliable than differences among groups that have small sample sizes.[38]

In the results reported below, questions are grouped and reported by topic area; for example, all questions concerned with reasonable doubt are listed under that heading. The Criminal

---

37. The groups were split at the median, resulting in one group with 12 or fewer years of education and one group with 13 or more years of education.

38. *See* J. Healey, Statistics 125-26 (1984).

Jury Instruction number(s) that apply to the relevant topic are in parentheses accompanying each question. Each question is then listed. Underneath each question appear the results for that question. An analysis of variance was performed on each question.[39] Results are presented in the following format:

Topic Area (Criminal Jury Instruction number(s))

Uninstructed = A% Instructed = B% Δ p

(number uninstructed) (number instructed)

A% = *the percentage correct* for uninstructed jurors, which serves as a baseline of comprehension for that particular question (group sample sizes appear below the percentage, in parentheses);

B% = *the percentage correct* for instructed jurors (group sample sizes appear below the percentage, in parentheses);

Δ = *the change* resulting from instruction; and

p = *the statistical significance of the difference*, which refers to the statistical probability that the observed difference would have occurred by chance alone. This statistic helps interpret the difference (Δ) between groups. As the p value increases, the likelihood that the observed difference has resulted from chance increases. For example, a p value of .3 indicates that there is a 3 in 10 chance that the observed difference is caused by chance or sampling error; a .5 indicates that there is a 5 in 10 chance that the observed difference is a result of chance. Conversely, smaller p values imply that the difference is unlikely to be caused by chance and more likely to be caused by the instructions. Social scientists have traditionally accepted a p value of less than .05 as statistically significant.[40] Values greater than .05 are generally considered nonsignificant. Thus, in judging whether an observed difference may be produced by an instruction rather than by chance, one should consider not only the size of the observed difference, but also the significance level.

A brief discussion of the results follows each series of questions. It should be reiterated that the instructions tested by this procedure were those identified as most problematic. The study's results, therefore, should not be used to draw overly generalized conclusions regarding juror comprehension of instructions.

39. Analysis of variance is a statistical test that allows one to infer whether an observed difference between groups is the result of random chance or the reliable result of some systematic difference in the way that the two groups were treated. In this case, the systematic difference is, of course, exposure versus no exposure to selected instructions.

40. *See* R. WONNACOTT & T. WONNACOTT, INTRODUCTORY STATISTICS 261 (4th ed. 1985).

A. *Reasonable Doubt* (03:1:04 or 03:1:05)

1. A REASONABLE DOUBT IS BASED ON YOUR COMMON SENSE. [TRUE]

Uninstructed = 68.8% Instructed = 84.6% Δ = 15.8 p = .005
(48) (526)

10. A REASONABLE DOUBT MUST BE BASED ONLY ON THE EVIDENCE THAT WAS PRESENTED IN THE COURTROOM, NOT ON ANY CONCLUSION THAT YOU DRAW FROM THE EVIDENCE. [FALSE]

Uninstructed = 48.0% Instructed = 31.8% Δ = -16.2 p = .020
(50) (510)

4. YOU HAVE A REASONABLE DOUBT IF YOU CAN SEE *ANY* POSSIBILITY, NO MATTER HOW SLIGHT, THAT THE DEFENDANT IS INNOCENT. IF SO, YOU SHOULD FIND THE DEFENDANT NOT GUILTY. [FALSE]

Uninstructed = 24.0% Instructed = 25.2% Δ = 1.2 p = .853
(48) (514)

22. TO FIND THE DEFENDANT GUILTY BEYOND A REASONABLE DOUBT, YOU MUST BE 100% CERTAIN OF THE DEFENDANT'S GUILT. [FALSE]

Uninstructed = 26.5% Instructed = 30.9% Δ = 4.4 p = .528
(49) (505)

Approximately 69% of uninstructed jurors believe that they are allowed to use their common sense to judge whether a reasonable doubt exists. The reasonable doubt instruction in either of the two forms increases this to approximately 85%. The amount of increase as a result of exposure to the instruction is identical for both high and low education groups.

Some confusion seems to exist, however, between reasonable doubt and any doubt. A majority of responses from uninstructed jurors revealed a belief that any doubt (or, alternately, anything less than 100% certainty) is equivalent to a reasonable doubt. Reasonable doubt instructions apparently did little to improve jurors' understanding that absolute certainty is not required.[41]

Question 10 suggests misunderstanding about whether jurors are allowed to draw inferences or conclusions from the evidence in order to reach a verdict. The comprehension rate actually de-

41. The high p values for questions 4 and 22 on reasonable doubt indicate that the observed difference between uninstructed and instructed jurors is likely the result of chance factors, such as random sampling error, and that the comprehension of the two groups of jurors do not differ in reality. Interestingly, uninstructed jurors with high education showed the most misunderstanding of all, responding correctly at a rate of 17%. Receiving instructions raised the high education group's correct response rate to only 31%.

clined as a result of exposure to instruction, though it is difficult to know if this effect comes from exposure to the instruction or from other factors that might be associated with reasonable doubt, such as repetition of the standard or conflict with other instructions.

The responses to questions 4 and 22 reflect a poor understanding of the reasonable doubt standard. Perhaps the questions did not test the information given in the instructions. Despite having been approved both by legal experts and by social scientists, the questions may differ importantly from the corresponding instructions. Questions 4 and 22 attempt to ask jurors about reasonable doubt as a quantifiable concept: question 4 speaks of "any doubt, no matter how slight," and question 22 speaks of "100% certain[ty]." The reasonable doubt instructions, on the other hand, are not cast in quantitative language but instead ask the jurors to examine the evidence qualitatively.[42] Jurors are instructed that a reasonable doubt is one that would cause them to hesitate in making an important decision in their own life, and that the decision is a moral one.[43] An alternative instruction also states that the evidence must convince them to a moral certainty of the defendant's guilt before they vote to convict.[44] Thus, the instructions given may have emphasized one concept while the questions presented may have asked something different—an apples and oranges situation. As stated by Professor Nesson:

> As long as the concept [of reasonable doubt] is left ambiguous, members of the observing public may assume that they share with jury members common notions of the kinds and degree of doubt that are unacceptable. . . . The closer reasonable doubt comes to quantification, the more any notion of it being a shared concept will break down.[45]

Indeed, some instructions that have attempted to define reasonable doubt in quantifiable terms have been declared reversible error.[46] Whether these questions test the true meaning of rea-

---

42. For a copy of the jury instructions on reasonable doubt see *infra* Appendix II.
43. *Id.*
44. *Id.*
45. Nesson, *Reasonable Doubt and Permissive Inferences: The Value of Complexity*, 92 HARV. L. REV. 1187, 1196-97 (1979).
46. *See, e.g.*, Commonwealth v. Sullivan, 20 Mass. App. Ct. 802, 804, 482 N.E.2d 1198, 1199 (1985) (reversing when jury instructions stated: "[I]f you put it in a one to hundred scale? I don't know. It's above fifty percent."); McCullough v. State, 99 Nev. 72,

sonable doubt is certainly debatable. Perhaps questions that addressed more qualitative distinctions would have been more informative, even though these questions are difficult to formulate because of the inherent ambiguity of reasonable doubt. Nevertheless, the minimal and even negative effects of these instructions should raise serious concern about whether instructed jurors understand a crucial element of their charge—the meaning of reasonable doubt.

B. *Witness Credibility* (3:1:11)

15. IN DECIDING WHETHER TO BELIEVE A WITNESS, YOU MAY CONSIDER NOT ONLY WHAT THE WITNESS SAID, BUT HOW HE OR SHE SAID IT. [TRUE]

Uninstructed = 91.7% Instructed = 84.1% Δ = -7.3 p = .121
(60) (496)

18. IF A WITNESS IS HONEST AND CONFIDENT, YOU CAN BE CERTAIN THAT HE OR SHE IS ACCURATE IN THEIR [SIC] PERCEPTION OF EVENTS. [FALSE]

Uninstructed = 77.6% Instructed = 69.0% Δ = -8.6 p = .181
(58) (442)

28. IT IS THE JUROR'S RESPONSIBILITY TO DECIDE IF THE WITNESSES ARE TRUTHFUL, NOT THE JUDGE'S OR THE ATTORNEY'S. [TRUE][47]

Uninstructed = 85.0% Instructed = 92.0% Δ = 7 p = .220
(77) (47)

Two things are apparent when one examines the responses to questions dealing with witness credibility. The first is that comprehension levels are generally high, and the second is that comprehension levels appear to decrease as a result of instruction. The latter result is puzzling.

74, 657 P.2d 1157, 1157 (1983) (reversing where the judge instructed "seven and a half, [on a scale of 0-10] if you had to put it on a scale"). *But see* Kagehiro & Stanton, *Legal v. Quantified Definitions of Standards of Proof*, 9 LAW & HUM. BEHAV. 159 (1985).

Some famous cases discussing reasonable doubt indicate that some of the best judges throughout history have experienced difficulty defining proof beyond a reasonable doubt. *Compare* Commonwealth v. Webster, 59 Mass. 295 (1850) (Shaw, C.J.) (providing a technical definition of proof beyond a reasonable doubt) *with* People v. Brigham, 25 Cal. 3d 283, 292, 599 P.2d 100, 106 (1979) (Mosk, J. concurring) (criticizing Chief Justice Shaw's definition from *Webster* as confusing, and concluding that proof beyond a reasonable doubt is not susceptible to a technical definition).

47. Questions 28-31 were omitted from the questionnaire given to most jurors after a preliminary analysis because both uninstructed and instructed jurors' understanding of these concepts was quite high.

One possible explanation is that the reduced comprehension for the instructed jurors is more apparent than real. Generally, social scientists regard significance levels above .05 as suspicious.[48] Because values for both questions 15 and 18 are above that level, it might be that comprehension for the instructed and uninstructed groups are actually the same and appear to differ only because of random sampling variation. If there is an actual difference between the groups such that instructed jurors comprehend less, two explanations may be advanced.

First, judicial instructions regarding witness credibility may actually mislead jurors. For instance, the results of question 15 are consistent with the results of question 22, which concerned reasonable doubt, in that both show instructed jurors endorsing the idea that they are not allowed to draw inferences. It may be that the instructions themselves lead jurors to endorse this idea.

Second, it may be that the repetition of standards stressing the presumption of innocence and proper use of evidence leads jurors to conclude that the law requires them to "stick to the facts" and not draw reasonable inferences from the facts. Why comprehension might decrease for instructed jurors in question 18 is less clear, particularly because in this question jurors seem to believe that they *are* allowed to draw inferences about credibility from paralinguistic cues.

In any event, the possibility that jurors are misled by the instruction or that the sum total of instructions causes jurors to believe the court requires an overly restrictive standard for drawing inferences is speculative. It cannot be determined conclusively from the present results. The most parsimonious conclusion is that the observed differences resulted from chance rather than that they represent reliable indicia of lower comprehension by the instructed group. Particularly for question 18, for which the p value of nearly .2 is far above what is traditionally regarded as indicating a reliable difference, this conclusion seems warranted.

C. *Mixed Direct and Circumstantial Evidence* (4:2:02)

5. FACTS CAN BE PROVEN THROUGH CIRCUMSTANTIAL EVIDENCE. [TRUE]

Uninstructed = 53.9% Instructed = 64.8% Δ = 10.9 p = .008
(290) (219)

48. See *supra* note 39 and accompanying text.

9. Suppose you see that your neighbor's drapes are closed. When you look a minute later, you see the drapes open and the lights on. The conclusion that someone is at home would be based on circumstantial evidence. [True]

Uninstructed = 81.4% Instructed = 86.7% Δ = 5.3 p = .113
(291) (218)

16. A witness's statement that he or she saw something is an example of direct evidence. [True]

Uninstructed = 74.8% Instructed = 75.4% Δ = .6 p = .893
(278) (215)

23. Suppose that a witness saw the defendant's automobile parked near the scene of a crime. The conclusion that the defendant was in the area would be based upon direct evidence. [False]

Uninstructed = 59.0% Instructed = 61.2% Δ = 2.2 p = .644
(244) (206)

19. The prosecutor may not build a case on circumstantial evidence alone. [False]

Uninstructed = 32.1% Instructed = 37.6% Δ = 5.2 p = .211
(280) (213)

The results from questions 5 and 19 suggest that uninstructed jurors believe that circumstantial evidence may be worthless. The instruction effectively communicates that circumstantial evidence can have value.

Although of marginal statistical significance, responses to question 9 suggest that instruction probably helps jurors distinguish between direct and circumstantial evidence only minimally. The factor that primarily determines a juror's ability to make this distinction is the juror's education level. Averaging across all three questions, uninstructed jurors with less education were 67% correct. Uninstructed jurors with more education averaged 78% correct. The instructions improved the performance of both groups by only about 3%.

The results from question 19, which is less tied to the wording of 4:2:02, suggest a belief by jurors that prosecutors must have more than circumstantial evidence. This is probably consistent with jurors' general belief that evidence must be quite strong as reflected in their responses to questions concerning reasonable doubt. Even for the high-education instructed group, the 54% correct response rate could have resulted from mere guessing.

D. Impeachment of Defendant by Prior Conviction (3:1:08)

7. YOU CAN NOT CONSIDER A DEFENDANT'S PRIOR CRIMINAL CONVICTIONS FOR ANY PURPOSE. [FALSE]

Uninstructed = 28.2% Instructed = 56.3% Δ = 28.1 p = .015
(539) (16)

25. YOU CAN CONSIDER A DEFENDANT'S PRIOR CRIMINAL CONVICTIONS IN DECIDING WHETHER TO BELIEVE THE DEFENDANT'S TESTIMONY. [TRUE]

Uninstructed = 26.2% Instructed = 50.0% Δ = 23.8 p = .035
(511) (16)

12. SUPPOSE YOU LEARN THAT A DEFENDANT HAS SEVERAL PRIOR CRIMINAL CONVICTIONS. BASED ON THIS FACT, YOU CAN ASSUME THAT THERE IS A GREATER CHANCE THAT THE DEFENDANT IS GUILTY OF THE CRIME WHICH HE IS NOW CHARGED WITH. [FALSE]

Uninstructed = 79.6% Instructed = 75.0% Δ = -4.6 p = .645
(539) (16)

Taken together, the results of these questions suggest that uninstructed jurors commonly believe that a defendant's prior record should not be used for *any* purpose. Roughly three out of four uninstructed jurors endorsed this view. The 23% and 28% increases in correct responses to questions 7 and 25, respectively, suggest that instruction may have reduced this misunderstanding. These increases, however, were only enough to raise correct responses to a level that could have resulted from mere guessing. The results for questions 7 and 25 were independent of educational level.

Question 12 indicates that most uninstructed jurors believe correctly that they should not use a defendant's prior convictions to imply an increased probability of guilt for the current offense. This conforms with the general "should not use" heuristic that most uninstructed jurors seem to employ when considering a defendant's prior record. When education level was accounted for, uninstructed persons with more education were correct more often and benefitted more from instruction. Responses improved from 84% to 100% correct. Persons with less education did not benefit from instruction, and in fact showed a decrease that was marginally significant.

E. Homicide (16:2:01, 16:2:02, 16:3:01, 16:3:02, 16:4:01, 16:4:02, 16:4:03)

i. First degree premeditated murder

24. FOR FIRST DEGREE PREMEDITATED MURDER, IT DOESN'T MATTER WHETHER THE DEFENDANT *INTENDED* TO KILL THE VICTIM. IF THE VICTIM WAS KILLED BY THE DEFENDANT'S ACTIONS, THAT IS ENOUGH. [FALSE] (16:2:01)

Uninstructed = 63.6% Instructed = 65.8% Δ = 2.2 p = .665
(418) (117)

21. SUPPOSE A DEFENDANT WAS STRONGLY PROVOKED BY A VICTIM, BUT KILLED THE VICTIM LATER, AFTER HE COOLED DOWN. THE MOST SERIOUS OFFENSE YOU CAN CONVICT THE DEFENDANT ON IS MANSLAUGHTER. [FALSE] (16:2:01, 16:4:02)

Uninstructed = 75.6% Instructed = 80.3% Δ = 4.7 p = .288
(427) (117)

3. ACTUAL INTENT TO KILL OR CREATE A VERY HIGH RISK OF DEATH IS REQUIRED FOR BOTH FIRST DEGREE PREMEDITATED MURDER AND VOLUNTARY MANSLAUGHTER. [FALSE] (16:2:01, 16:4:02)[49]

Uninstructed = N/A Instructed = N/A Δ = N/A p = N/A
(N/A) (N/A)

Roughly two out of three jurors answered correctly that intent is required for first degree murder. For more-educated jurors, the figure is closer to three out of four. This comprehension level is not impressive, considering that intent is a crucial aspect of first degree premeditated murder. The instructions did not improve substantially the comprehension for either low- or high-education jurors.

Question 21 indicates that three out of four uninstructed jurors answered correctly that if a defendant reflected on the killing, the defendant could be convicted of a crime more serious than manslaughter. Again, uninstructed jurors with more education grasp this concept quite well (85%). Instruction had a minimal impact on the small percentage of people who did not already understand the effect of reflection.

ii. First degree felony murder

6. SUPPOSE THAT A DEFENDANT WAS ROBBING A GAS STATION. HE HAD NOT PLANNED TO HURT ANYONE, BUT HE GOT SCARED BECAUSE HE THOUGHT THAT THE ATTENDANT WAS REACHING FOR A GUN. HE SHOT AND KILLED THE ATTENDANT. YOU CAN STILL

49. Jurors received two different versions of question 3. We thus cannot draw reliable conclusions from this question.

CONVICT THE DEFENDANT OF FIRST DEGREE FELONY MURDER. [TRUE] (16:2:02)

Uninstructed = 63.4% Instructed = 74.0% Δ = 10.6 p = .037
(431) (89)

Question 6 attempted to test comprehension of first degree felony murder by asking jurors to identify an example. Again, roughly two out of three jurors succeeded. Surprisingly, this time the uninstructed jurors with less education were more often correct (73% versus 52%). For the less-educated group, the instruction had no effect; for the more-educated group, the instruction had a large effect (from 52% to 72%). Thus, this instruction raised the comprehension level of the more-educated group to roughly 75%, which corresponds with the comprehension level of the less-educated group.

iii. Second degree murder; second degree murder as a lesser included offense

2. TO BE CONVICTED OF SECOND DEGREE MURDER, THE DEFENDANT *MUST* HAVE PREMEDITATED A KILLING; THAT IS, HE OR SHE HAD TO PLAN IT OUT BEFOREHAND. [FALSE] (16:3:01, 16:3:02)

Uninstructed = 71.5% Instructed = 83.5% Δ = 12 p = .007
(425) (127)

Question 2 tests jurors' understanding of a critical difference between first and second degree murder: premeditation. Each instruction produced a substantial improvement in comprehension for both less-educated jurors, who rose to 76% after instruction, and more-educated jurors, who rose to 92% after instruction.

iv. Voluntary manslaughter; voluntary manslaughter as a lesser included offense

26. TO BE CONVICTED OF VOLUNTARY MANSLAUGHTER, A DEFENDANT MUST HAVE KILLED WHILE INFLUENCED BY CIRCUMSTANCES THAT NORMALLY WOULD PRODUCE STRONG FEELINGS OR PASSION. THE KILLING MUST HAVE OCCURRED BEFORE A NORMAL PERSON WOULD HAVE HAD TIME TO STOP AND THINK ABOUT WHAT HE WAS ABOUT TO DO. [TRUE] (16:4:01, 16:4:02)

Uninstructed = 67.6% Instructed = 89.3% Δ = 21.7 p = .001
(414) (56)

27. SUPPOSE THAT A DEFENDANT WAS GROSSLY NEGLIGENT AND CARELESS IN HIS ACTIONS. HIS ACTIONS CAUSED SOMEONE'S DEATH. THOUGH THE DEATH WAS AN ACCIDENT AND NOT AT ALL

INTENDED, YOU CAN FIND THE DEFENDANT GUILTY OF INVOLUNTARY MANSLAUGHTER. [TRUE] (16:4:03)[50]

Uninstructed = 87.7% Instructed = 75.0% Δ = 12.7 p = N/A
(515) (4)

Question 26 tests jurors' recognition that voluntary manslaughter requires emotional arousal and an absence of premeditation. Though the majority of uninstructed jurors knew this, the instruction appeared highly effective in assisting those who did not. Again, the more-educated group scored higher than the less-educated group, but the instruction improved comprehension for both groups significantly.

F. *Attempt as a Lesser Included Offense* (9:1:02)

14. EVIDENCE THAT A DEFENDANT MADE DEFINITE PLANS TO COMMIT A CRIME IS ENOUGH TO PROVE THAT HE ATTEMPTED IT. [FALSE]

Uninstructed = 66.6% Instructed = 100% Δ = 33.4 p = N/A
(554) (4)

17. SUPPOSE THAT A DEFENDANT HAD PLANNED A ROBBERY OR CRIMINAL SEXUAL CONDUCT (RAPE). HE THEN BEGAN TO COMMIT THE CRIME. HOWEVER, HE WAS INTERRUPTED AND PREVENTED FROM COMPLETING THE CRIME. YOU CAN STILL FIND HIM GUILTY OF ATTEMPTED ROBBERY OR ATTEMPTED CRIMINAL SEXUAL CONDUCT. [TRUE]

Uninstructed = 93.0% Instructed = 100% Δ = 7 p = N/A
(558) (4)

Unfortunately, only four persons from one jury were exposed to this instruction and completed a questionnaire. Though the direction of the effect is encouraging and the comprehension of uninstructed jurors appears high, the sampling error from such a small group is likely to render a comparison of instructed versus uninstructed groups statistically insignificant.

G. *Specific Intent* (3:1:16)

8. SPECIFIC INTENT MEANS THAT A DEFENDANT HAD PLANNED TO DO AT LEAST *SOMETHING* ILLEGAL, REGARDLESS OF WHETHER HE HAD PLANNED TO COMMIT THE CRIME HE IS CHARGED WITH. [FALSE]

---

50. The sample size for the instructed group is too small to draw reliable conclusions from this question.

Uninstructed = 25.5% Instructed = 22.3% Δ = -3.2 p = .436
(192) (229)

This question was probably difficult for jurors because it is long and it addresses specific intent as an abstract definition, rather than as an element of a specific crime. More-educated jurors scored significantly higher than less-educated jurors, but even the instructed group with more education responded correctly only at a rate of about 36%. This can be interpreted as indicating that receiving the instruction did not significantly improve comprehension for the abstract meaning of specific intent. The poor rate of correct response merits attention.

H. *Assault* (17:1:02, 17:6:01, 17:6:02)

11. AN ASSAULT MUST INCLUDE ACTUAL PHYSICAL INJURY TO THE VICTIM. [FALSE]

Uninstructed = 49.6% Instructed = 32.3% Δ = -17.3 p = .060
(538) (31)

30. A DEFENDANT PURPOSELY AND VIOLENTLY STRUCK A VICTIM, CAUSING PHYSICAL INJURY. THIS FORCEFUL TOUCHING IS CALLED A BATTERY. [TRUE]

Uninstructed = 82.5% Instructed = 72.2% Δ = -10.3 p = .314
(97) (18)

The results for the two questions on assault appear rather counterintuitive and striking because the instructed group scored lower than the uninstructed group. The significance level for question 11 indicates that the decrease in juror comprehension after instruction on assault is a reliable measurement, by social science standards. For question 30, however, the significance level is well beyond that which indicates a reliable difference. The best conclusion for results from question 30 is that the two groups do not actually differ.

It is clear that the instructions for assault did not *improve* comprehension for the issues covered in either of these questions, and these instructions very likely worsened comprehension for the issue covered in question 11. One possibility is that the instructions are confusing to jurors. Postquestionnaire interviews with jurors would have helped determine the exact nature of juror misunderstanding; however, we were not able to do this.

An alternative possibility is that the instructions were not poor or misleading, but that unusual factors were present in one or two trials in which jurors were exposed to these assault instructions. Even if only one jury were confused or somehow misled, its responses might be enough to lower significantly the score of the entire instructed group, which had a sample size of only thirty-one.

We were not able to distinguish among these possibilities using our methodology. Nevertheless, it is clear that instructions do little to help jurors distinguish successfully assault from battery.

I. Criminal Sexual Conduct (20:3:01; 20:3:02; 20:5:01; 20:5:02; 20:2:11; 20:2:12)

13. SECOND DEGREE CRIMINAL SEXUAL CONDUCT ALWAYS INVOLVES PERSONAL INJURY AND PENETRATION. [FALSE] (20:3:01; 20:3:02)

Uninstructed = 64.4% Instructed = 100% Δ = 35.6% p = .026
(516) (9)

20. A JURY BELIEVES THAT A DEFENDANT COERCED A VICTIM INTO TOUCHING HIS GROIN TO GET SEXUAL GRATIFICATION. THERE WAS NO PHYSICAL INJURY TO THE VICTIM AND THE TOUCHING WAS ONLY THROUGH THE CLOTHES. THE JURY MUST FIND THE DEFENDANT NOT GUILTY OF ANY CRIMINAL SEXUAL CONDUCT. [FALSE] (20:5:01; 20:5:02)

Uninstructed = 0.0% No instructed jurors Δ = N/A p = N/A
(413) (0)

31. IN CRIMINAL SEXUAL CONDUCT CASES, YOU CAN CONSIDER MENTAL ANGUISH AS PERSONAL INJURY. [TRUE] (20:2:11; 20:2:12)

Uninstructed = 77.4% No instructed jurors Δ = N/A p = N/A
(124) (0)

Unfortunately, the questions that were asked about criminal sexual conduct did not correspond to the instructions that were most frequently given in such cases. Question 13 had one jury that received instructions 20:2:01 or 20:2:02, resulting in a very small sample size for the instructed group. Though the results for question 13 are encouraging and statistically significant, a reliable analysis of relevant characteristics among jurors is hindered by the small sample. For the other questions, comparisons between instructed and uninstructed groups can not be made.

J. Presumption of Innocence

29. IN A CRIMINAL TRIAL, A DEFENDANT IS CONSIDERED INNOCENT UNTIL PROVEN GUILTY. [TRUE]

Uninstructed = 95.8% Instructed = 97.4% Δ = 1.6 p = .460
(44) (77)

This question was presented originally as an example in the instructions to the questionnaire. Yet some CJI Committee members were curious about the rate of comprehension for this fundamental issue. It therefore was included in the questionnaire itself. After the first hundred or so questionnaires produced an extremely high uninstructed comprehension level, the question was omitted.

III. GENERAL FACTORS IN JUROR COMPREHENSION

The results from individual items seem discouraging. Comprehension levels are sometimes quite low for both uninstructed and instructed jurors. Instructions often had little impact on comprehension; sometimes, instruction actually decreased juror comprehension. Yet if one looks at the effects of the instructions across all items, the results are not quite as discouraging as they first appear.

If we examine only those instructions that demonstrate a statistically significant effect (those with a p value of less than 0.05), we note that eight questions showed a positive effect of instructions (questions 1, 2, 5, 6, 7, 13, 25, and 26) and only one showed a negative effect (question 10). Thus, it seems that when instructions do produce an effect they produce a positive effect on jurors' comprehension more often than they produce a negative effect. On the other hand, thirteen questions indicate that instruction had no statistically significant effect on juror comprehension (questions 4, 8, 9, 11, 12, 15, 16, 18, 19, 21, 22, 23, and 24).

A variety of other factors besides exposure to instructions may have affected the number of correct responses to this questionnaire. For instance, more-educated jurors might be expected to score higher than less-educated jurors. This was a difficult issue in constructing the questionnaire because the questions necessarily included some legal language or unfamiliar concepts.

In order to test which factors were associated with correct responses on the questionnaire, a score reflecting the total number of correct responses for each juror was calculated. Then, the total score was used as a dependent measure against which to test the influence of several factors. These included the total number of instructions heard by the juror, the juror's level of education, age, and gender, and whether written or audiotaped instructions were provided to the juror. Analysis of variance was used to test whether any of these factors, alone or in combination, affected juror comprehension.[51]

Not surprisingly, jurors who were exposed to more instructions generally answered more items correctly than jurors who were exposed to fewer instructions. This confirms that juror comprehension increased as a function of exposure to instructions. Though the difference between the means was highly significant, the magnitude of the increase as a result of exposure to more instructions was quite modest. This makes sense because

51. See *supra* note 39 for a brief description of analysis of variance. The number of instructions was divided at the median, resulting in one group that received 12 or fewer instructions and one group that received 13 or more of the instructions targeted by this study. Education and age were similarly dichotomized around their respective medians (13 years for education; 39 years for age). Gender and distribution of written copies are naturally dichotomized. Analysis of variance was performed on all the factors. An F statistic, which is "the ratio of the variance between categories to the variance within categories," J. Healey, *supra* note 38, at 163, was also calculated for each factor. The greater the F statistic, the less likely it is that an observation is due to random chance. *Id.* at 163-64. The following are the means (reported in percentage correct on the questionnaire), F statistics, and significance levels for each factor:

TABLE I

	Means	F	p
number of instructions	<13=47.1; 13 or more=51.7	4.63	.032
educational level	<13=46.8; 13 or more=53.9	18.18	<.001
age	<39=50.9; 39 or more=48.3	1.55	.213
gender	male=52.9; female=46.7	19.77	<.001
copies provided	no=49.3; yes=57.8	3.90	.049

These means cluster near 50%, which would suggest random guessing. However, nearly all of the means for individual items differ significantly from chance, which contradicts the notion that subjects guessed randomly on the questionnaire. Rather, the total score's closeness to 50% is an artifact of combining individual items that show high (e.g., witness credibility) and low (e.g., reasonable doubt) levels of comprehension.

There were no two- or three-way interactions except between age and educational level. Except for the effect of age, these are all significant main effects. This implies that each of these factors contributes independently to comprehension and no factor depends on levels of the other factors to have an influence.

Four factors affected overall comprehension: number of instructions heard, education, gender, and provision of copies. These factors did not interact with each other. We chose to discuss the effect of education level on the responses to individual questions because the influence of education on comprehension was, for the most part, not difficult to interpret. We did not discuss the effect of gender on responses to the individual questions because we had no sound theoretical reason for this effect. We did not discuss the effect of the provision of written copies on responses to individual questions because too few juries received written copies.

The following graph of the means from Table I is a useful illustration:

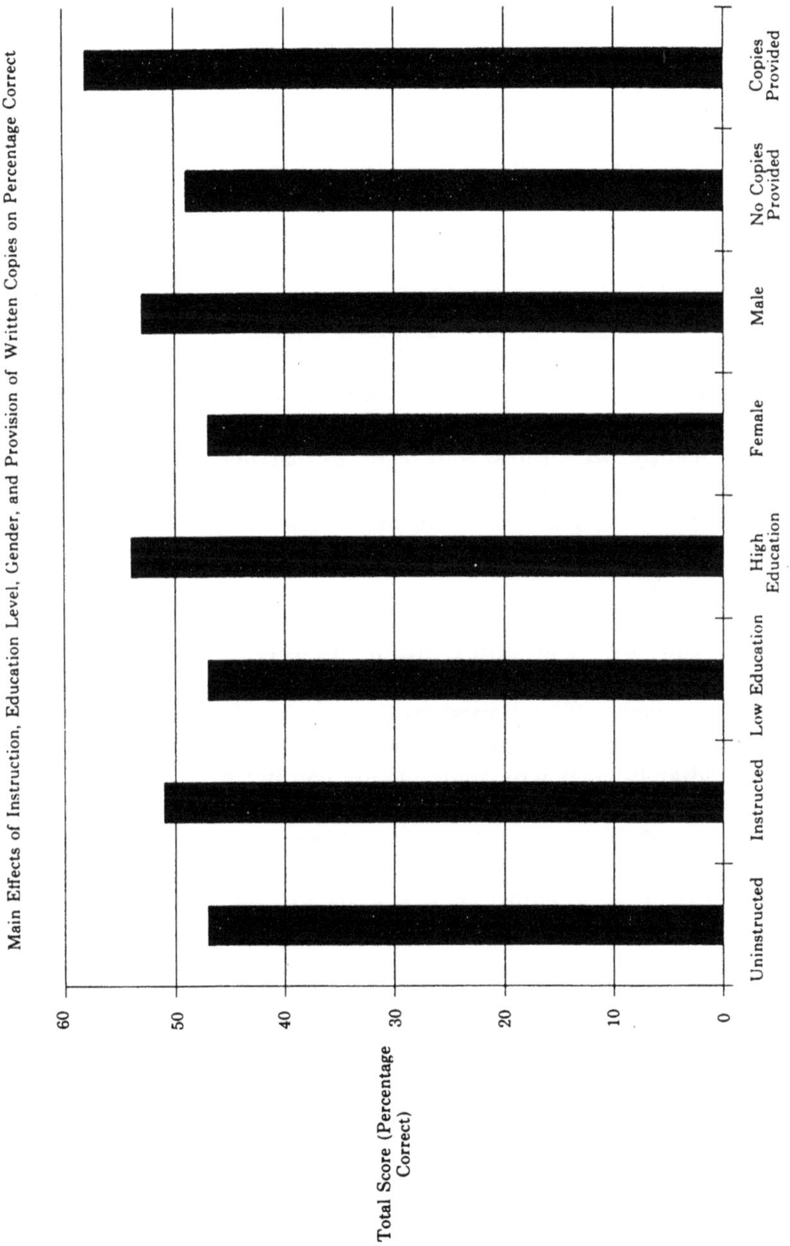

jurors who were exposed to many instructions would face more of a memory burden, particularly if the instructions were part of a complex trial, and may show a slower increase in comprehension, or even some decrease, as a result. Additionally, the number of instructions affected the total number of correct responses independently of each of the other factors. This suggests that the benefit of exposure to more instructions was about equal for all groups (e.g., more-educated and less-educated jurors, older and younger jurors, etc.).

Other factors influenced comprehension as well, including the jurors' educational level and the use of written instructions. Jurors with higher educational levels scored significantly higher than jurors with lower educational levels. Giving more instructions simply raised the scores of both groups equally. The provision of written instructions also affected comprehension levels significantly, with those who received instructions scoring higher than those who did not. The effect of written instructions was statistically significant despite relatively small sample sizes—only nine percent of the instructed jurors received written instructions.

The positive effect of written instructions conflicts with a recent study by Heuer and Penrod.[52] In a field study of Wisconsin jurors, they found that the provision of written instructions did not positively affect jurors' comprehension in criminal cases, as assessed on a nine-item multiple-choice questionnaire.[53] It is not immediately clear why their results conflict with the current results. In general, tests with more items are more discriminating, provided that the items in the test have some relationship to the dependent criterion (here, comprehension of particular instructions).[54] It is possible that our twenty-six-item measure was more sensitive to changes in comprehension as a result of written instructions than their nine-item measure. In any event, Heuer and Penrod do report that the provision of written instructions helped to resolve disputes among jurors over the meaning of the law, and therefore had some positive effects.[55]

The results of the questionnaire depended on gender. Men scored higher than women. This effect was not a result of differences in educational levels between men and women, so it remains unclear why men scored higher generally on this question-

52. Heuer & Penrod, *Instructing Jurors: A Field Experiment With Written and Preliminary Instructions*, 13 LAW & HUM. BEHAV. 409 (1989).

53. *Id.* at 420.

54. J. NUNNALLY, *supra* note 26, at 78.

55. Heuer & Penrod, *supra* note 52, at 421.

naire. Finally, age was not independently significant in the analysis of variance, although the number of correct answers increased as juror age decreased. Subsequent analysis revealed that younger persons in this study tended to have more education, and it may be that the difference in education rather than age produced this marginal effect.

IV. SUMMARY AND CONCLUSION

This research supports a growing body of literature suggesting that jury instructions are often lost on jurors, and can sometimes even backfire.[56] The relatively low rate of comprehension for some concepts, both among more- and less-educated jurors, the apparent ineffectiveness of instructions to improve comprehension, and the negative effect of certain instructions, constitute the most striking findings in the present study. Particularly startling are the results of instructions concerning reasonable doubt, defendant impeachment by prior conviction, and some aspects of mixed direct and circumstantial evidence.

Perhaps the study's results are not as surprising as they seem, given the complexity of the cognitive task confronting jurors, and the problematic nature of these particular instructions. One possible explanation for the ineffectiveness of instruction in these particular areas is that jurors come to court with preexisting beliefs about these issues that are resistant to change. For instance, jurors' beliefs about what the law requires may be derived from exposure to the media or other sources in the popular culture.[57] Ideas learned over a lifetime of exposure to these sources may be firmly entrenched and act as rules of thumb in directing jurors' decisions.[58] A few such "rules" may have driven how jurors responded to several questions on this questionnaire. For example:

---

56. *See, e.g.*, V. HANS & N. VIDMAR, JUDGING THE JURY 121 (1986); E. LIND, *The Psychology of Courtroom Procedure*, in THE PSYCHOLOGY OF THE COURTROOM 27-29 (N. Kerr & R. Bray eds. 1982).

57. Hastie, Penrod, and Pennington reported that videotaped mock jurors made inappropriate generalizations from television and film trials, and that "[n]ot even reinstruction on the law from the judge was sufficient to eliminate all of these errors." R. HASTIE, S. PENROD & N. PENNINGTON, INSIDE THE JURY 170 (1983).

58. Belief perseverance, even in the face of disconforming or inconsistent evidence, is well documented. *See, e.g.*, Ross & Anderson, *Shortcomings in the Attribution Process: On the Origins and Maintainance of Erroneous Social Assessments*, in JUDGMENT UNDER UNCERTAINTY: HEURISTICS AND BIASES 149 (D. Kahneman, P. Slovic & A. Tversky eds. 1982).

1. Jurors decide whom to believe and whom to disbelieve (witness credibility).
2. Jurors should not use circumstantial evidence (mixed direct and circumstantial evidence).
3. Jurors should not use a defendant's past record against him (defendant impeachment by prior conviction).

When such preconceived notions are congruent with instructions, both uninstructed and instruction-benefitted comprehension levels appear quite high. But when preconceived notions are incongruent with instructions, both uninstructed and instruction-benefitted comprehension levels remain low, well below chance levels for some issues.

Some support for this notion can be found in a recent study by Professor Ellsworth.[59] She videotaped deliberations of mock juries in order to investigate jurors' understanding and use of facts and instructions. She concluded that:

> Much of jurors' discussion of the law revolved around phrases they were likely to have known before they heard the judge's instructions. The instructions may have been effective in reminding the jurors of terms they had heard before, but the instructions were not very effective in educating them in new areas, or even in focusing their attention on the meaning of the familiar terms.[60]

Some jury instructions did raise comprehension. When jurors lack preconceptions or rules of thumb, they are perhaps more influenced by instructions, particularly if the instructions are central to the case and find their way into discussion during deliberation. For instance, distinctions between first and second degree murder are probably more obscure and therefore less entrenched and certain in jurors' minds. The jurors' open-ended comments support this interpretation: instructions involving homicide were often mentioned as being the most difficult to understand. Even though uninstructed comprehension may have been above chance, jurors' responses showed that they were influenced positively by these instructions.

---

59. Ellsworth, *Are Twelve Heads Better Than One?* 52 LAW & CONTEMP. PROBS. 205 (1989).

60. *Id.* at 219. Ellsworth also concluded that the jury benefitted little from the ability of its most able member to understand the meaning of instructions, *id.*, a finding consistent with our conclusion that it takes more than one person on a jury to understand an instruction for the instruction to have its intended effects.

A number of factors external to the instructions themselves can influence comprehension. Some factors that influence juror comprehension, such as jurors' educational level, are outside the control of courts. Other factors, such as whether written instructions are provided, are potentially within the court's control. In this sample, only nine percent of instructed juries received written instructions. Several judges commented that they would like to provide jurors with written instructions, but that the court lacked time and resources to do so. This is unfortunate because both the present results and the study by Heuer and Penrod suggest that written copies of judicial instructions can help juries to use the instructions.[61] In discussion of this issue within the CJI Committee, it was noted that the increased availability of computers might lead to greater use of written instructions. In particular, if criminal jury instructions were on file, one would need only to retrieve and print the instructions to be used in a given trial. Any modifications by the judge could be incorporated easily.

Clearly the more-educated jurors generally were likelier to grasp the concepts conveyed by an instruction. They generally had better uninstructed comprehension, and probably had better retention of spoken distinctions or concepts. Given the technical/legal nature of the jury instructions, this advantage for more-educated jurors will probably always be a factor. As one attempts to make instructions comprehensible to all jurors, including less-educated jurors, there is likely to be a trade-off between comprehensibility and technical accuracy. Providing written copies may narrow the comprehension gap between more- and less-educated jurors, but the current data suggest that more-educated jurors are more likely to comprehend legal concepts regardless of whether written instructions are provided.

Jurors do not individually attempt to apply instructions to a case but rather do so as a group. Therefore, the effects of jury deliberation on comprehension are important and relevant here. In the current study, the comprehension of instructed jurors was tested after jury deliberation. Thus, our measure could not be considered a pure measure of *individual* comprehension, because postdeliberation responses may also reflect the influence of group discussion.

The most optimistic theory about the influence of group deliberation on comprehension suggests that it takes only one person to understand an instruction at the time it is given. If jury in-

61. Heuer & Penrod, *supra* note 52, at 429.

structions are discussed later in deliberation, that person can then explain the instruction to the remaining jurors. An alternate theory is that a majority of jurors must understand an instruction at the time it is given. If the instruction is discussed, then the majority viewpoint will prevail in applying the instruction. This research does not directly address how deliberation influenced comprehension, but the current results are suggestive. Because data were collected *after* deliberation, and because open-ended questions revealed that most juries did discuss some instructions,[62] it appears that the more optimistic theory may be overly optimistic.[63]

This research could not address certain issues. First, we could not ascertain how variations in courtroom atmosphere or judges' behavior and presentation style influence jurors' comprehension of instructions. Presentation factors may be worth investigating in further research on comprehension of instructions. Second, the research could not confront the distinction between what jurors believe the law requires and what standards jurors actually use in making their decisions. We were careful to instruct jurors to respond to the questions based on what the law required, not on what *they* thought the law should be. Certainly most jurors are inclined to follow the law, if they understand it. But jurors sometimes do not conform their judgments to what the law requires, either because they lack the cognitive control to ignore certain variables,[64] or because they believe that the law conflicts with some fundamental notions of fairness or rationality.[65]

Finally, our procedure was designed to investigate the effectiveness of selected Michigan Criminal Jury Instructions currently in use. The Michigan Criminal Jury Instructions Committee constantly revises instructions, and it is uncertain whether differently worded instructions would result in similar rates of comprehension among actual jurors.

At least two goals—legal accuracy and juror comprehension—underlie the choice of wording in judicial instructions. There

---

62. Reasonable doubt was mentioned most frequently.

63. *See* Ellsworth, *supra* note 59, at 219.

64. *See* Kramer, Kerr & Carroll, *supra* note 32.

65. The jury has the power to nullify a judge's instructions. *See* Y. Kamisar, W. LaFave & J. Israel, *supra* note 5, at 1295-97. As Justice Holmes stated: "[T]he jury has the power to bring in a verdict in the teeth of both law and facts." Horning v. District of Columbia, 254 U.S. 135, 138 (1920). For a case presenting both sides of this issue, see United States v. Dougherty, 473 F.2d 1113, 1137 (D.C. Cir. 1972) (upholding refusal to instruct jury of its right to acquit defendants without regard to law and evidence) and see *id.* at 1139 (Bazelon, C.J., dissenting) (asserting that the jury should be told of its nullification power).

seems to exist an inherent tension, however, between communicating to jurors the requirements of the law, and insuring that instructions are technically complete and not reversible on appellate review. This tension has become more strained, for as law becomes more developed and differentiated, it also becomes more difficult for the layperson to understand. Designing instructions to improve comprehension may increase the chance of appeal, but designing technical instructions to guard against appeals may reduce juror comprehension, as indicated in the present study. A misunderstanding of the law precludes jurors from fulfilling their duties to the best of their abilities, as they sit in judgment of their peers.

APPENDIX I

Jury Instructions Study Questionnaire

Today's Date ________________________ Male or Female ____

Age ____ Education (highest grade completed) ______

Did you serve on a jury today? __Yes __No
Have you *ever* served on a jury before today? __Yes __No

If you have served on a jury, list the *dates* you served (as best you can recall). Also list the crime(s) the defendant was *charged* with.

Date ________ Charge ________________________
Date ________ Charge ________________________
Date ________ Charge ________________________

Below are some True-False questions based on criminal jury instructions. Please answer each question by circling either T (for True) or F (for False).

EXAMPLE:

T F A defendant has a right to remain silent.

You are not being tested. Rather, we are testing how clear the criminal jury instructions are. When answering these questions, assume that you are a juror. If you have heard jury instructions on the questions below, try to recall what you heard. If you have not heard instructions or are not sure, pick the answer that you think is the correct one.
Please answer every question.

T F 1. A reasonable doubt is based on your common sense.

T F 2. To be convicted of second degree murder, the defendant *must* have premeditated a killing; that is, he or she had to plan it out beforehand.

T F 3. Actual intent to kill or create a very high risk of death is required for both first degree premeditated murder and voluntary manslaughter.

T F 4. You have a reasonable doubt if you can see *any* possibility, no matter how slight, that the defendant is innocent. If so, you should find the defendant not guilty.

T F 5. Facts can be proven through circumstantial evidence.

T F 6. Suppose that a defendant was robbing a gas station. He had not planned to hurt anyone, but he got scared because he thought that the attendant was reaching for a gun. He shot and killed the attendant. You can still convict the defendant of first degree felony murder.

T F 7. You can not consider a defendant's prior criminal convictions for any purpose.

T F 8. Specific intent means that a defendant had planned to do at least *something* illegal, regardless of whether he had planned to commit the crime he is charged with.

T F 9. Suppose you see that your neighbor's drapes are closed. When you look a minute later, you see the drapes open and the lights on. The conclusion that someone is at home would be based on circumstantial evidence.

T F 10. A reasonable doubt must be based only on the evidence that was presented in the courtroom, not on any conclusion that you draw from the evidence.

T F 11. An assault must include actual physical injury to the victim.

T F 12. Suppose you learn that a defendant has several prior criminal convictions. Based on this fact, you can assume that there is a greater chance that the defendant is guilty of the crime which he is now charged with.

T F 13. Second degree criminal sexual conduct always involves personal injury and penetration.

T F 14. Evidence that a defendant made plans to commit a crime is enough to prove that he attempted it.

T F 15. In deciding whether to believe a witness, you may consider not only what the witness said, but how he or she said it.

T F 16. A witness's statement that he or she saw something is an example of direct evidence.

T F 17. Suppose that a defendant had planned a robbery or criminal sexual conduct (rape). He then began to commit the crime. However, he was interrupted and prevented from completing the crime. You can still find him guilty of attempted robbery or attempted criminal sexual conduct.

T F 18. If a witness is honest and confident, you can be certain that he or she is accurate in their perception of events.

T F 19. The prosecutor may not build a case on circumstantial evidence alone.

T F 20. A jury believes that a defendant coerced a victim into touching his groin to get sexual gratification. There was no physical injury to the victim and the touching was only through the clothes. The jury must find the defendant not guilty of any criminal sexual conduct.

T F 21. Suppose a defendant was strongly provoked by a victim, but killed the victim later, after he cooled down. The most serious offense you can convict the defendant on is manslaughter.

T F 22. To find the defendant guilty beyond a reasonable doubt, you must be 100% certain of the defendant's guilt.

T F 23. Suppose that a witness saw the defendant's automobile parked near the scene of a crime. The conclusion that the defendant was in the area would be based upon direct evidence.

T F 24. For first degree premeditated murder, it doesn't matter whether the defendant *intended* to kill the victim. If the victim was killed by the defendant's actions, that is enough.

T F 25. You can consider a defendant's prior criminal convictions in deciding whether to believe the defendant's testimony.

T F 26. To be convicted of voluntary manslaughter, a defendant must have killed while influenced by circumstances that normally would produce strong feelings or passion. The killing must have occurred before a normal person would have had time to stop and think about that he was about to do.

T F 27. Suppose that a defendant was grossly negligent and careless in his actions. His actions caused someone's death. Though the death was an accident and not at all intended, you can find the defendant guilty of involuntary manslaughter.

Please answer the following questions. Feel free to write on the back if you would like more room. Your thoughts and opinions are important.

Were there any instructions which you or any of the other jurors found confusing? If so, please list what these instructions were about. Also, for each instruction, please tell us what made the instruction confusing.

1. Instruction: ____________________

1a. What made the instructions confusing or hard to understand? ______

____

2. Instruction: ____________________

2a. What made the instructions confusing or hard to understand? ______

____

3. Instruction: ____________________

3a. What made the instructions confusing or hard to understand? ______

____

4. Instruction: ____________________

4a. What made the instructions confusing or hard to understand? ______

____

If you sat on a jury today, did your jury discuss the meaning of the jury instructions? _____ Yes _____ No If yes, which instructions were discussed?

A. ____________________

B. ______________________________

C. ______________________________

D. ______________________________

We would welcome any comments about the jury instructions or your experience with them.

Comments: ______________________________

____

APPENDIX II: COMPOSITE INSTRUCTIONS

CJI 3:1:04

Definition of Reasonable Doubt

A reasonable doubt is a fair, honest doubt growing out of the evidence or lack of evidence in this case or growing out of any reasonable or legitimate inferences drawn from the evidence or the lack of evidence. It is not merely an imaginary doubt or a flimsy, fanciful doubt or a doubt based upon the mere possibility of the innocence of the defendant or a doubt based upon sympathy, but rather it is a fair, honest doubt based upon reason and common sense. It is a state of mind which would cause you to hesitate in making an important decision in your own personal life. By stating that the prosecution must prove guilt beyond a reasonable doubt, I mean there must be such evidence that causes you to have a firm conviction to a moral certainty of the truth of the charge here made against the defendant.

USE NOTE: The jury *must* be instructed on the concepts of the presumption of innocence, burden of proof and reasonable doubt.

CJI 3:1:05

Definition of Reasonable Doubt (Alternate)

A reasonable doubt is a fair doubt growing out of the testiomony, the lack of testimony or the unsatisfactory nature of the testimony in the case. It is not a mere imaginary or possible doubt, but a fair doubt based on reason and common sense. It is such a doubt as to leave your minds, after a careful examination of all the evidence in the case, in the condition that you cannot say you have an abiding conviction to a moral certainty of the truth of the charge here made against the defendant.

Journal of Applied Social Psychology, 1980, 10, 5, pp. 444-456

A Comparison of Verdicts Obtained in Severed and Joined Criminal Trials[1]

IRWIN A. HOROWITZ,[2] KENNETH S. BORDENS, MARC S. FELDMAN[3,4]
The University of Toledo

An experiment was conducted to determine the possible prejudicial effect of joining two similar criminal offenses in one trial, as compared to severing those offenses into separate trials. Levels of evidence (clear case for the prosecution, or a close case), trial mode (severed, combined with a clear or a close case), and position of case presentation in the joined trial (first or second) were combined in two 2 x 3 x 2 designs. The results indicated that clear cases received more guilty verdicts than close cases; joined trials obtained more guilty verdicts than severed trials; and first cases in joined trials received higher guilt scores than their severed counterparts or their joined counterparts presented second. The position effect seemed particularly strong when a close case was presented first and combined with a clear case in a joined trial.

Criminal prosecutions are initiated by formal accusation, an indictment or affadavit. The accusation serves to inform the accused of the charge or charges against him. It informs the trial judge of the nature of the prosecution so that he may rule properly on the admissibility of the evidence entered at the trial, and the accusation further serves as a basis for determining the extent to which jeopardy is attached (Kelley, 1976-1977).

It is a general rule that two or more offenses committed by the same person may be joined in the same indictment where the offenses are of the same general nature or class of crimes. The mode of trial and nature of punishments for

[1]This research was sponsored, in part, by a grant from the University of Toledo Graduate School.

[2]Requests for reprints should be sent to Dr. Irwin A. Horowitz, Department of Psychology, The University of Toledo, 2801 W. Bancroft St., Toledo, OH 43606.

[3]The authors would like to thank Professor Thomas Willging of the Toledo University Law Faculty and Mr. Fred McDonald of the U.S. Attorney's office for Northern District of Ohio, for their advice and assistance.

[4]Dr. Marc Feldman is now on the staff of St. Elizabeth's Hospital, Washington, D.C.

these crimes must be the same or similar (Daly vs. U.S., 1964). Criminal Rule 8(A) of the Ohio rules of criminal procedure provides four separate grounds for the joining of offenses in one indictment. It provides that two or more offenses may be charged in one indictment where the offenses:

> (1) Are of the same or similar character;
> (2) Are based on the same act or transaction;
> (3) Are based on two or more acts or transactions connected together or constituting parts of a common scheme or plan;
> (4) Are part of a course of criminal conduct.

Cipes (1965) suggests that the likelihood of conviction increases with the number of offenses cumulated in one trial. The rules regulating joinder of offenses within an accusation are among the most crucial in the administration of criminal justice. The determination of whether to allow joinder of offenses within a single accusation or to permit a severance of these offenses involves the competing interests of judicial conservation and efficiency and fairness to the accused (Kelley, 1976–1977).

Rule 14 of the Federal Rules of Criminal Procedure states that if it appears the defendant or the government is prejudiced by a joinder of offenses in an indictment, the trial court may order a separate trial of counts, grant a severance of counts, or "provide other relief" (Cipes, 1965). Generally, the trial court has full and complete discretion in deciding whether to grant or deny a motion to severe offenses charged in one indictment to a defendant (Holderman, 1978). The trial court's determination that joinder is or is not prejudicial is virtually irreversible, in that an appellate court will intervene only upon finding clear abuse (U.S. vs. Johnson, 1973).

The possibility that it is inherently prejudicial to be forced to defend several counts at the same time because they tend to reinforce one another, aside from clear abuse or prejudice, has not been an effective argument or rationale in appellate courts. In State vs. Nance (1976), the Nebraska Supreme Court ruled that the proper test for severance of counts was whether or not "actual" prejudice had occurred. The court held that severance was clearly a matter of judicial discretion, and in the absence of "actual" prejudice the defendant's appeal was rejected.

An empirical definition of "actual" prejudice has not been offered by the court. The United States Supreme Court in Spencer vs. Texas (1967) accepted the argument that all joint trials allow for opportunities for unfairness, particularly when evidence submitted as to one charge may influence the jury as to a different charge. Thus, the prejudicial effects of Rule 14 are acknowledged to inhere in the practicing of joining offenses in a single trial. The court justified or accepted the prejudicial effects on the grounds that the jury will follow the instructions to consider the evidence pertaining to each charge separately and independently, and by advocating the concept of judicial efficiency. Furthermore, the court consoled itself with the notion that as the crimes charged must be of a similar nature, concurrent sentences are meted out. Therefore, the defendant is not unduly punished by the possible prejudice in joinder of offenses. Given the Supreme Court's support of liberal joinder, the federal courts have been reluctant to order severance of counts for trial purposes under Federal Rule 14. Indeed, in many states the issue of joinder is within the discretion of the trial court, and that discretion, generally, has not been relinquished except for clear abuse.

There are a number of empirical questions suggested by the preceding discussion, which, if answered, would aid trial and appellate courts in determining whether or not joinder of offenses was clearly prejudicial to the defendant. Among the most basic assumptions made by the court is the proposition that a juror can fairly follow the instructions to weigh the evidence for each count separately and come to an independent decision on each count. The social psychological literature on information processing would lead us to believe that the above assumption is not psychologically valid. Concomitantly, the question as to the cumulative effect of evidence over a number of counts has yet to be addressed empirically. We would be interested in the effect of not simply the number of offenses charged in an indictment, but the nature and strength of the evidence for each count.

Prosecutors will freely admit the joinder of strong and weak cases within a single indictment with the hope that the sheer amount of evidence presented cumulates, yielding a guilty verdict on at least some of the counts. (McDonald, Note 1) Obviously, prosecutors do not make the law and are therefore perfectly willing to use the current liberal joinder rulings to their advantage.

Evidence obtained from the legal literature does not permit a determination as to whether or not the various prosecutorial joinder modes are abusive. There is not a clear, a priori test, empirical or otherwise, as to whether or not joinder of certain offenses of varying evidential modes is prejudicial to the defendant.

The present research is designed to test the possible cumulative effects of joinder of offenses in one indictment. Verdicts will be obtained from jurors under conditions where offenses are joined and compared to verdicts obtained on those same charges and evidence where the offenses are severed and considered separately and independently. The study will also test the impact of joining cases of different evidentiary strength on the final verdict. Specifically, we are interested in testing, within various combinations, the effects of joining strong evidential and close evidential cases on jurors' decisions.

There is a considerable psychological literature that is concerned, within various contexts, with the effects of one set of stimuli upon another set. Various theoretical models have been advanced to account for these effects. The application of various social psychological models and data to the present study requires a consideration which involves the relatively sequential ordering of criminal charges within one indictment. The court obliges the juror to regard the evidence pertaining to the first charge, hold it in abeyance, and then consider the evidence for the succeeding charges. The first judgment(s) are unanchored. The juror is not required to make a judgment concerning the evidence relevant to the first charge until the entire trial is completed.

Pepitone and DiNubile (1976), in an excellent and informative article, have demonstrated that where sequential judgments concerning criminal charges are required, an unanchored first judgment freely influences succeeding judgments. A proactive summative effect has been demonstrated in sequential judgments of crimes that are equal in magnitude. The effect seems to occur in a simple, additive manner such that the effect is cumulative over a series of crimes of high and equal magnitude of seriousness.

What occurs when the charges joined are of differential evidentiary strength? Redundant information, such as two criminal charges in one indictment in which the evidence is clear, may simply summate as Pepitone and DiNubile (1976) report. A number of studies have demonstrated that the addition of nonredundant information leads to greater shifts in an individual's judgment than the addition of redundant information (Schmidt, 1969; Wyer, 1968, 1970). A juror may be faced with a situation in which the evidence for the second count of a two-count indictment may be inconsistent with the evidence submitted for the first count. Simply put, the juror may have decided on the basis of the initially presented evidence that the defendant is guilty. However, the information presented for the second count might cast doubt upon the defendant's probable guilt.

Several possibilities may be considered as to the processing of the divergent information. The new information may affect the inferences formed on the basis of the initial evidence. The evaluation of the defendant might be averaged over the two cases, increasing or decreasing the probability of guilty verdicts depending upon the strength of the evidence, the nature of crimes, and the attendant thresholds of reasonable doubt for these crimes. The averaging model, of course, is a linear model of information integration, based partly on a conception of the organism as an analog computer of stimulus averages. This model suggests, unlike the Pepitone and DiNubile (1976) findings, that judgments are averaged rather than added. Anderson (1974) has given the averaging model support at both the qualitative and quantitative levels.

Another possibility is that the inconsistent information will be discounted. There is a tendency to accept stimulus information that is presented earliest more than inconsistent information presented later (Jaccard & Fishbein, 1970). The inconsistent information presented later would be given lower weight in the decision making process. As Fishbein and Ajzen (1975) note, inconsistently resolution could be achieved just as well by discounting the inconsistent information presented earlier. However, it appears that it is easier to discount later information than to change the impression evoked by the initial information (Hendrick & Constantini, 1970). Therefore, the discounting hypothesis would predict a primacy effect. The initial evidence should be the determining factor in the juror's decision making process. Thus, the effect of a strong initial case on a close second case would be to increase the probability of guilty verdicts with respect to the close case as compared to the juror's evaluation of the close case separately and independently. The discounting hypothesis would, it seems, predict that the effect of a weak initial case on a strong second case is to decrease the probability of guilty verdicts with respect to the strong case as compared to the strong case separately and independently.

Whatever the process, all of the above models predict a proactive effect. The evidence for the first offense modifies the effect of the second. One would therefore expect a primary effect. Clear and strong evidence for the first case, for example, would yield more guilty verdicts for a second, weaker case as compared to the second case being judged alone (severed).

Kaplan (1972), in contrast, has suggested that initial beliefs are modified when new information, particularly conflicting new information, is presented. Adapting Kaplan's model for the juror decision process, a retroactive effect would be predicted, particularly when the evidence for the second of two joined cases is discrepant from the first. Kaplan hypothesized that initial beliefs would be adjusted on the basis of acceptance of new information. Research based on Kaplan's (1972) model has suggested that maximal change in a juror's decision making would occur at moderate discrepancy levels from initial attitudes. One would expect then, based on Kaplan's model, that the evidence presented last, in a two-count indictment, would modify the effect of the earlier evidence, particularly at moderate levels of discrepancy, as for example between a relatively clear evidentiary case and a relatively close evidentiary case.

The present study is designed to test whether or not joinder of offenses of various evidentiary modes prejudice the defendant. Specifically, we ask if joinder yields significantly more guilty verdicts as compared to verdicts yielded by the same offenses when severed.

METHOD

Subjects

Undergraduates (312 male and female) at the University of Toledo, whose participation fulfilled a course requirement, were paid $7.50 to take part in a 1-hour (severed) or 2-hour (joined) mock trial.

Trial Materials

Mock trial materials were based upon two cases which were tried under one indictment in Lucas County, Ohio in the spring of 1977. The names and dates involved in the original cases were altered, but the mock trial materials adhered as closely as possible to the transcript of the original trial.

Two versions of each of the two cases were prepared and recorded on audiotape. The audiotapes summarized the trial materials. One version of each case indicated strong evidence for the prosecution (clear case), while a second version contained evidence which suggested evidential ambiguity (close case).

In addition to the two levels of evidentiary strength, two types of mock trials, joinder of offenses or severance of offenses, were prepared. Each severed trial consisted of one of four rape cases; Clear Foster, Close Foster, Clear Richards. [The names *Foster* and *Richards* refer to the names of the victims. Cases will henceforth be referred to by the victim's name.] Each case was comprised of an opening statement by Prosecution and Defense, prosecution evidence, defense evidence, closing statements by Prosecution and Defense, and judicial instructions.[5]

The four severed trials were combined to produce the following eight joined trials: (1) Clear Foster-Clear Richards; (2) Clear Foster-Close Richards; (3) Close Foster-Clear Richards; (4) Clear Foster-Close Richards; (5) Clear Richards-Clear Foster; (6) Close Richards-Close Foster; (7) Close Richards-Clear Foster; (8) Clear Richards-Close Foster. Each joined trial included opening and closing statements encompassing both cases, prosecution evidence, defense evidence, and judicial instructions. Each case in the joined trial was presented separately and the judicial instructions emphasized to the jurors that the cases were to be considered separately.

Each case was pre-rated by a separate sample of subjects for evidentiary strength.

Design

A. Evidentiary strength in Foster: clear or close.

B. Trial mode: severed (foster clear and Foster close presented separately), and joined (Foster clear or close presented along with Richards clear or close).

C. Ordinal position of Foster (first or second) in the joined trial.

In order to maintain a balanced factorial design, it was necessary to employ each severed case twice within each 2 x 3 x 2 design. Therefore, in the Foster design, each severed case, Foster close and clear, was run twice, independently and separately. The ordinal position manipulation *does not* apply to the severed cases.

[5]Judicial instructions were taken from *Ohio Jury Instructions*, 1974.

In the Foster design, thus, the data were analyzed for the effects of Richards on Foster. The data from the joined Foster cases were compared with the severed Foster cases within the 2 x 3 x 2 design.

The same procedures were followed for the counterbalanced 2 x 3 x 2 Richards design.

Procedure

Subjects were randomly assigned to one of the 16 experimental conditions within the two 2 x 3 x 2 designs. Subjects were run in small groups ranging in size from two to four.

Subjects were escorted into a laboratory designed to resemble a judge's chambers. They listened to the audiotaped trials, either joined or severed. Subjects were informed that they would listen to a taped trial based upon an actual case tried in Lucas County, Ohio, and that all names and places had been altered. Subjects were requested to assume the role of jurors and to render a verdict(s) at the completion of trial. Subjects did not deliberate and were told not to converse with each other.

Following the termination of the joined trials, subjects were required to indicate a separate verdict for Foster and for Richards. The order of completing the dependent measure followed the order of case presentation.

One verdict was required in the severed trial.

Dependent Measure

A bracketed 6-point vertical scale was employed. Points 1 through 3 were bracketed as a not guilty verdict and indicated that the evidence was variously below the level of reasonable doubt, while points 4 through 6 were bracketed as a guilty verdict and indicated that the evidence was variously above the level of reasonable doubt.

RESULTS

Foster Case

A 2 x 3 x 2 ANOVA was performed on the guilt ratings of the Foster case. The analysis revealed significant main effects of trial mode, $F(2,144) = 11.36$, $p < .001$, ordinal position of the Foster case, $F(1,144) = 25.13$, $p < .001$, and the strength of the Foster evidence, $F(1,144) = 59.26$, $p < .001$. Additionally, the trial mode by position interaction and the position by strength of evidence interactions were significant, $F(2,144) = 4.49$, $p < .05$ and $F(1,244) = 4.62$, $p < .05$, respectively.

Close inspection of the means presented in Table 1 demonstrates that when the Foster case was presented first, the defendant received higher guilt scores

TABLE 1

MEAN GUILT SCORES FOR ALL EXPERIMENTAL CONDITIONS IN FOSTER[1]

Position of presentation	Evidence close			Evidence clear		
	Trial severed[2]	Richards close	Richards clear	Trial severed[2]	Richards close	Richards clear
Foster first	3.46_a	4.69_{bc}	4.92_{bc}	4.53_b	5.23_{cd}	5.69_d
Foster second	3.31_a	3.30_a	3.38_a	4.38_a	5.00_{bc}	4.85_{bc}

[1]n = 13. Means without common subscripts are significantly different at $p < .05$. Scores ranging from 1 to 3 indicate a not guilty verdict, while 4 to 6 reflect a guilty verdict.

[2]The severed trial was run twice to maintain balance in the factorial design. Ordinal position does not apply to the severed cases.

(M = 4.76) than when the Foster case was presented second (M = 4.04). The means presented in Table 1 include the values for the severed cases along with the joined cases. When the joined cases are viewed alone, the impact of ordinal position increases. When the Foster case is presented in the first position in the joined trials, the defendant received higher guilt ratings (M = 5.14) than when the Foster case was presented in the second position (M = 4.14).

The trial mode manipulation resulted in the defendant, in joined trials, receiving higher guilt scores than in the comparable severed case. When the Foster case was combined with the Richards close case, the defendant was more likely to be found guilty (M = 4.56) than the defendant in the severed Foster case (M = 3.93), $F(1,144) = 13.09$, $p < .001$. Similarly, when the Foster case was combined with the clear Richards case, the defendant was more likely to be found guilty (M = 4.72) than the defendant in the severed case (M = 3.93), $F(1,444) = 20.20$, $p < .001$. The difference between the Foster cases when combined with Richards clear or close did not differ significantly, $F(1,144) = 1$.

It was also found that the defendant in the clear Foster case received higher guilt ratings (M = 4.95) than the defendant in the close Foster case (M = 3.85).

Analysis of the simple main effects of the trial mode by position interaction showed that the joined and severed trials differed when the Foster case was in the first position, $F(2,144) = 14.91$, $p < .001$, but not when the Foster case was presented in the second position, $F(2,144) = < 1$. Finer analyses revealed that when the Foster case was combined with both the Richards close (M = 4.96) or the Richards clear case (M = 5.31) and presented in the first position, the defendant received higher guilt ratings than in the severed Foster case (M = 4.00), $F(1,144) = 15.02$, $p < .001$ and $F(1,144) = 27.79$, $p < .001$, respectively. The Foster case (when presented first) in the joined trials did not differ significantly, $F(1,144) = 1.95$.

Analysis of the position by evidence interaction showed that the difference between the Foster close and Foster clear was presented in the second position (M = 3.33 and 4.36, respectively) rather than if Foster was presented first (M = 4.74 and 5.15, respectively). Once again, if the influence of the severed cases is removed, this effect becomes more striking. In this instance, when Foster is presented first the close case (M = 5.46) is seen as more similar than if Foster was presented in the second position (M = 4.80 for the close case and M = 3.35 for the clear case).

Richards Case

The 2 x 3 x 2 ANOVA performed on the Richards data revealed a similar pattern of results. Once again, the main effects of trial mode, $F(2,144) = 9.14$, $p < .001$, case position (position of Richards case), $F(1,144) = 5.53$, $p < .025$, and strength of the Richards case (clear or close), $F(1,144) = 52.10$, $p < .001$ were significant. Additionally, the trial mode by ordinal position interaction was found to be significant, $F(1,144) = 7.54$, $p < .001$. The position by strength of case interaction was marginally significant, $F(1,244) = 3.40$, $p < .07$.

Further, in depth analyses of the main effect of trial mode, as seen in Table 2, revealed that the defendant in the joined trial, whether combined with the Foster close (M = 4.75) or the Foster clear (M = 4.89) case, received higher guilt ratings than the defendant in the severed Foster case (M = 4.14), $F(1,144) = 10.82$, $p < .001$ and $F(1,144) = 16.07$, $p < .001$, respectively. No difference was found in the joined trials, $F(1,244) = < 1$.

TABLE 2

MEAN GUILT SCORES FOR ALL EXPERIMENTAL CONDITIONS IN RICHARDS[1]

Position of presentation	Evidence close			Evidence clear		
	Trial severed[2]	Foster close	Foster clear	Trial severed[2]	Foster close	Foster clear
Richards first	3.31_a	4.62_{bc}	5.15_{cd}	4.69_{bc}	5.08_{cd}	5.77_d
Richards second	3.77_a	3.92_{ab}	3.46_a	4.77_{bc}	5.38_{cd}	5.15_{cd}

[1]n = 13. Means without common subscripts are significantly different at $p < .05$. Scores ranging from 1 to 3 indicate a not guilty verdict, while 4 to 6 reflect a guilty verdict.

[2]The severed trial was run twice to maintain balance in the factorial design. Ordinal position does not apply to the severed cases.

It was also found that if the Richards case was presented in the first position ($M = 4.76$) the defendant received higher guilt ratings than if the Richards case was presented in the second position ($M = 4.41$). Once again, the data as presented in Table 2 include the influence of the severed case. If the effect of the severed case is removed, the magnitude of the difference between the Richards case presented first ($M = 5.16$) and the Richards case presented second ($M = 4.48$) increases. Additionally, the defendant in the Richards clear case ($M = 5.14$) received higher guilt ratings than the defendant in the Richards close case ($M = 4.04$).

Analysis of the trial mode by ordinal position interaction showed a simple main effect of trial mode when the Richards case was presented first, $F(2,444) = 15.38$, $p < .001$. Further analysis of the simple main effect of trial mode when the Richards case was presented first showed that when the Richards case was combined with the Foster close ($M = 4.85$) or Foster clear ($M = 5.46$) case, the ratings of guilt were higher than in the severed Richards case ($M = 4.00$), $F(1,144) = 10.23$ and 30.52, respectively, $p < .001$. Also, the Richards cases in the joined trials differed significantly, $F(1,144) = 5.40$, $p < .01$.

Inspection of the means involved in the marginally significant ordinal position by evidentiary strength interaction shows a pattern of results similar to the one found in the Foster case analysis. When the Richards case was presented first, the difference between the clear Richards ($M = 5.18$) and the close Richards ($M = 4.36$) case is less than when the Richards case was presented second ($M = 3.72$ for Richards close and $M = 5.10$ for the Richards clear case). Once again, if the influence of the severed Richards cases is removed, then the magnitude of the above effect increases. In this instance, when Richards is presented before the Foster case the clear Richards ($M = 5.43$) and close Richards ($M = 4.89$) are seen as more similar than if the Richards case was presented after the Foster case ($M = 3.69$ for the Richards close case and $M = 5.63$ for the Richards clear case).

DISCUSSION

The major finding in this study is that when two cases, with one and the same defendant, are joined in one trial, the first of these cases is evaluated differently than the same case presented alone (severed). The first case in the joined trial consistently receives higher guilt scores than that same case when tried separately (severed). The second case in the joined trial does not receive higher guilt scores than its severed counterpart.

Several possibilities exist as explanations for this retroactive effect. All are clearly speculative and open to empirical verification.

It is possible to consider the second case of the two joined cases as an "anchor." It is an anchor in only a tenuous sense, but an argument can be made for this conceptualization. Mock jurors, or indeed actual trial jurors, are warned by the court to evaluate each case separately and independently.[5] This instruction comes most forcefully after all the evidence has been rendered. Furthermore, the evidence for the second case is fresh and recent. Mock jurors, in the present study at least, seem able to fairly evaluate the second case relative to the comparable severed case as baseline. Whatever "prejudice" inheres in the joinder of two charges in one trial falls on the "unanchored" first charge. The first charge is unanchored in the mock jurors, indeed actual trial jurors, are not required to make any formal judgment at the end of the presentation of the evidence for that charge. In the absence of explicit judgment standards, one expects judgments to be less stable. Therefore, the judgment of the first case is free to vary according to later information. The combination of judicial instruction, the recency effect of evidence presented for the second charge, and the request for a verdict soon after the second case is presented, "anchors" the second judgment, and it is the first, unanchored case which obtains the greater guilt scores over and above its severed counterpart.

The question remains as to why prejudice should inhere in a joined trial, or at least in a joined trial with the present parameters. It is clear the courts believe that the evidence for each charge should be evaluated independently. The evidence for each charge should be "distinct and separate."[5] Against the possibility that jurors do not obey the judicial injunction to keep the evidence separate, the court metes out concurrent sentences, as we have noted. The issue of whether the evidence for various charges brought against the same defendant ought to be considered independently in light of the countervailing rights of the defendant and society is for the legal philosophers, and is not the purpose of this empirical examination of the effects of joinder.

The defendant receives higher guilt scores in the first case of a joined trial than in its evered counterpart. That is clear. What is unresolved is exactly what process mock jurors utilize to arrive at these higher guilt scores. Initially, we took guidance from various models which show how sequential ordering effects occur. We found both the Pepitone and DiNubile (1976) and the Kaplan (1972) models to be most instructive and suggestive of possible outcomes. Nevertheless, these models do not deal with some features found in the joinder of two bodies of evidence tied to one and the same defendant. Thus, while the Pepitone and DiNubile model found that an anchored judgment enhances or depresses the judgment of the unanchored stimulus, there are some very specific differences between the situation they employed and the present context. Their model dealt with two different crimes involving two different defendants. Pepitone and DiNubile explicitly anchored the first case and found that it was the second, unanchored case which was evaluated differently based upon the severity of that first crime.

Our assumption is that the mock juror does stay a final judgment concerning the first case until all the evidence is presented. We have suggested that the second case serves as an anchor. The anchoring concept allows for a common thread (albeit tenuous) of analysis between the Pepitone and DiNubile model and our own. Nevertheless, the issue of exactly how two bodies of evidence attached to the same defendant interact is unresolved and open to empirical resolution.

We do not have data bearing on the mock jurors' perception of the evidence, nor do we know, independently of subjects' response, whether the evidence was viewed separately or was mutually reinforcing. To endeavor to obtain these data, at least in the present context, could have altered the decision process. Procedurally, the evidence for each charge was presented to mock jurors independently. The body of evidence for each case was always presented separately from the other case in a joined trial. The judge's instructions and lawyers' summaries did, perforce, intertwine the evidence to a degree. This clearly follows courtroom procedure. Evidence for each case in a courtroom must be separate and distinct, but judge's instructions, lawyers' summaries, and possibly the presence of the arresting officer presenting evidence, separately but for both charges, lead ineluctably to some intertwining of evidence. What we do not know, despite the attempt at procedural independence, is whether the mock jurors were able to deal with each charge independently of the other charge.

REFERENCES

Anderson, N. H. Information integration theory: A brief survey. In D. H. Krautz, R. C. Atkinson, & R. D. Luce (Eds.) *Contemporary developments in mathematical psychology*. San Francisco: W. H. Freeman, 1974.

Cipes, R. M. *Moore's federal practice: Rules of criminal procedure* (2nd ed.). New York: Matthew Bender & Co., 1965.

Daly vs. United States, 342 F 2d 932 (D.C. Cir. 1964).

Fishbein, M., & Ajzen, I. *Belief, attitude, intention and behavior: An introduction to theory and research.* Reading, Mass.: Addison-Wesley, 1975.

Hendrick, C., & Constantini, A. F. Effects of varying trait inconsistency and response requirements on the primacy effect in impression formation. *Journal of Personality and Social Psychology*, 1970, **15**, 158–167.

Holderman, L. Joinder of criminal offenses in Nebraska: Judicial discretion vs. fair and impartial trial. *Nebraska Law Review*, 1978, **56**, 399–409.

Jaccard, J. J., & Fishbein, M. Inferential beliefs and order effects in personality impression formation. *Journal of Personality and Social Psychology*, 1970, **15**, 158–167.

Kaplan, K. J. From attitude formation to attitude change: Acceptance and impact as cognitive mediators. *Sociometry*, 1972, **35**, 448–467.

Kelley, D. S. Joinder of offenses: Louisiana's new approach in historical perspective. *Louisiana Law Review*, 1976–1977, **37**, 203–233.

Pepitone, A., & DiNubile, M. Contrast effects in judgements of crime severity and the punishment of criminal violators. *Journal of Personality and Social Psychology*, 1976, **33**, 448–459.

Schmidt, C. F. Personality impression formation as a function of relatedness of information and length of set. *Journal of Personality and Social Psychology*, 1969, **12**, 6–11.

Spencer vs. Texas, 385 U.S. 554 (1967).

State vs. Nance, 197 Neb. 95, 246 N.W. 2d 868 (1976).

U.S. vs. Johnson, 487 F. 2d, 1129, 1131 (5th Cir. 1973).

Wyer, R. S. The effects of information redundancy on evaluation of social stimuli. *Psychonomic Science*, 1968, **13**, 245–246.

Wyer, R. S. Information redundancy, inconsistency and novelty and their role in impression formation. *Journal of Experimental and Social Psychology*, 1970, **6**, 111–127.

REFERENCE NOTE

1. McDonald, Fred. Assistant U.S. Attorney for the Northern District of Ohio. Personal communication, May, 1980.

JOURNAL OF EXPERIMENTAL SOCIAL PSYCHOLOGY 17, 1–15 (1981)

The Effects of Consensus Requirements and Multiple Decisions on Mock Juror Verdict Preferences

JAMES H. DAVIS

University of Illinois

ROBERT W. HOLT

George Mason University

CRAIG E. SPITZER

Quaker Oats Company

AND

GAROLD STASSER

Miami University

Received May 10, 1979

After watching a simulated rape trial, prerecorded on videotape, mock jurors either did or did not expect to sentence a defendant following deliberation with or without a group verdict required. Both sentencing expectation and verdict requirement significantly elevated jurors' preference for conviction (and average ratings of guilt likelihood). Closer analyses of personal changes (before and after deliberation) in the distribution of opinions suggested that majorities favoring not guilty were more influential than guilty-favoring majorities; and, somewhat unexpectedly, minorities in juries which deliberated without a verdict required were more likely to change personal opinions than minorities in juries required to render a verdict. The overall social decision scheme confirmed earlier observations about the importance of the initial majority in determining the verdict; but the majority did not always prevail and there was a marked asymmetry ("defendant protection") in its action.

The research reported here was supported by National Science Foundation Grant BNS 77-15216, James H. Davis, Principal Investigator. We are especially indebted to David Vollrath and Blair Sheppard for several comments and suggestions on earlier drafts. Address reprint requests to Dr. James H. Davis, Department of Psychology, University of Illinois, Champaign, IL 01820.

It is sometimes convenient to distinguish informally two kinds of task-oriented groups. In one case social interaction is primarily a factor in developing or influencing the position, the decision, or solution of the *individual member.* Attention is directed at the level of the individual, and there are *r* opinions recognized in a group of size *r*. For example, discussion among panel members may aid individuals in checking recall of information, interpreting facts, and applying relevant principles when evaluating a grant proposal. However, there may not be a single rating adopted by the group acting as a whole. The second kind of group produces a *collective* decision, solution, or some other product following discussion, and may sometimes require a fairly formal set of rules to resolve disputes about what the group response should be. The jury provides an example; a verdict is reported after deliberation if there is unanimous agreement (or sometimes as low as two-thirds agreement). There seems to be no wide use of groups of decision makers who must somehow reach a consensus but engage in no preceding discussion. (Delphi groups, Dalkey (1969), designed to eliminate conformity influences from social interaction may be something of an exception.) And, of course, the fourth possibility defined by the conjunction of a consensus requirement or not with discussion or not is no more than a set of noncommunicating individuals who respond independently. A set of jurors before they repair to deliberate corresponds to such a "group"; the individual condition in most experiments on group and individual problem solving is another example.

Most group decision studies have required both discussion and consensus, perhaps because most analogs in society at large (juries, organizational work groups, study commissions, etc.) are groups of this general character. Whatever the reason, we have surprisingly little information with which to evaluate separately the consequences of discussion and consensus on some task of interest (Anderson & Graesser, 1976). Evidence has only gradually accumulated on how group tasks may determine the kind of process which is relevant to producing a social decision (see the analysis by Steiner, 1972, and the research summary by Davis, Note 1.) Thus, the task, especially one with significant social content or implications, constitutes an important class of social parameters which define the context within which discussion/consensus effects may be evaluated.

The Jury

The jury offers a convenient referent for rationalizing our initial exploration; and one which illustrates as well the problems associated with human (social) engineering efforts in institutions of long-standing. For example, why should a jury be required to reach consensus upon a verdict?[1] Besides avoiding any consensus pressures on individual jurors, a discussion-only jury would convey more information to the court at the end of deliberation; the distribution of guilt-convinced and guilt-unconvinced jurors might provide a useful measure of the extent prosecution or defense had "established its case." As far as we know, there are currently no strong philosophical or legislative proposals to remove consensus requirements from jury procedures. However, the question is compelling both from a fundamental interest in group performance and in light of its implications, even if somewhat remote, for jury functioning.

If every juror prefers exactly the same verdict, the group decision follows directly, and the verdict contains all the available information. But, suppose there is a division of opinion, and the jury follows an assigned social decision scheme (see Davis, 1973; Davis, 1980; Stasser, Kerr, & Davis, 1980) other than unanimity (e.g., two-thirds majority), or dissidents acquiesce (without personal change) to a majority. The group decision would not now contain information about the actual division of opinion actually existing. In the former case, a dissenting minority is legally tolerable, and the nonunanimous majority may generate only moderate pressures on a losing minority to yield. The latter case is one in which dissenters publicly comply to maintain unanimous agreement but remain privately unconvinced.

Whether motivated by the possibility of procedural reform or by more basic concerns, the separate evaluation of discussion and consensus effects implies the comparison of guilt preferences of group members who had deliberated without reaching a verdict and those who were required to reach a verdict. The study to be described also permitted the observation of guilty—not guilty distributions, $(r_G, r_{NG}) = \mathcal{S}_i$, of jurors' opinions in the two kinds of groups, and the *pattern* of movement from one state, $\mathcal{S}_i$, to another, $\mathcal{S}_j$ (Davis, Stasser, Spitzer, & Holt, 1976). We may observe that the latter comparison of interest requires an $m \times m$ state matrix, S, in which $m = n + r - 1/r$), and n is the number of response alternatives and r is group size. The ijth entry $[s_{ij}]$ represents the probability that a group moves from state S_i to state S_j, and a state is defined as the distinguishable distribution of members' preferences $(r_1, r_2, \ldots, r_n)$. The present application found $r = 6$ mock jurors who could prefer one of $n = 2$ outcomes. Hence, $m = 7$, since $(r_G, r_{NG}) = (6,0), (5,1), \ldots, (0,6)$ were the possible member distributions of opinion.

Mock juries which reached a verdict, however, could decide for guilty or not guilty, but also might not arrive at a verdict, i.e., "hang." The conditional probabilities, d_{ik} of the kth outcome, given the ith distribution

[1] We shall consider only criminal juries here, but much of the same could be said about civil juries, which have interesting properties in their own right.

of prior opinion may be cast into an $m \times n' = 7 \times 3$ matrix, D. The social decision scheme matrix, D, (Davis, 1973; Stasser *et al.*, 1980) provides a gross description of the social decision process in terms of input and outcomes.[2]

Multiple-decision expectations. Another procedural issue, somewhat different from the consensus requirement, concerns the prospect of subsequent decisions. Many kinds of groups must make, independently, a sequence of decisions. A jury required to render a verdict on each of several charges is supposed to deliberate each independently. Yet, there is clearly an opportunity to compensate on a later response (whether intended or not) for any discomfitting acquiescence, "overreaction," or the like, which might linger after an earlier decision. Nagao and Davis (1980) studied a somewhat different kind of decision sequence, in which their subjects decided guilt successively in two different cases; they observed a significant order effect although mock jurors had been instructed to treat the cases independently—after the fashion of jurors who may serve for more than one trial although perhaps in juries of different composition.

Yet another kind of question about sequence effects on decisions arises in connection with juries in capital cases, where a sentencing decision or recommendation is rendered subsequent to the verdict. It is this latter procedural question involving successive decisions which we have chosen to investigate in this study. Our interest was restricted to asking simply whether or not the expectation of later meting out a sentence, in the event of conviction, might influence the verdict itself. For example, French juries in the 19th century were reportedly reluctant to convict defendants because they feared judges would impose excessive sentences subsequently (Gleisser, 1968). Although we are aware of no ground swell of interest in extending jury sentencing (or sentencing recommendations) to noncapital cases, there has been some controversy surrounding the general question (see the Presidential Task Force Report, 1967, for a summary of arguments for and against jury sentencing.) At present a majority of states allow the jury to fix or recommend sentence in capital cases at life imprisonment, and Tennessee requires that the jury fix sentence in all cases. The common law provides for sentencing by judge, and the U.S. Constitution is mute on the subject.

The question of sentencing expectation effects on verdict rendering may be conveniently pursued at both the individual and group level, given the experimental procedure implied by our earlier discussion. Foregoing various elaborations because of the cost in subject hours, we used a 2×2 design in which juries were asked (or not) to reach a group verdict after

[2] See Davis (1973) and Stasser et al., (1980) for a more detailed description of social decision scheme theory and Davis (1980) for a summary of related research on mock juries. Further comments on social decision schemes will be given in the results section.

discussion, and were instructed (or not) that a sentencing recommendation would be required following the verdict. An additional sample of noninteracting individuals also heard the same mock trial (closed circuit TV) in which the defendant was accused of rape (Davis, Kerr, Atkin, Holt, & Meek, 1975).

METHOD

Subjects

All 659 subjects (373 males and 286 females) participated for 2 hr each as part of a class exercise in an introductory social psychology course. Some subjects (618) were randomly assigned to six-person mock juries, and the remainder (41) served as individuals, interacting with no one.

Design and Procedure

A jury was randomly assigned to one of 2 × 2 experimental conditions formed by crossing (a) a requirement to deliberate to a verdict or deliberate without reaching a verdict, with (b) an instruction to recommend, if appropriate, a sentence after deliberation about guilt or no such instruction.

All subjects received in turn: (a) Instructions that they would serve as a juror in a mock rape trial to be presented by means of video and audio tape recordings; (b) a "Voir Dire Questionnaire," the content of which paralleled in some respects the voir dire examination prior to seating (such as items soliciting opinions toward rape, punishment for the convicted, and the like); and (c) a prerecorded enactment of a rape trial (modified from Norris, 1965), lasting approximately 50 min.[3] (d) All subjects then privately answered questions concerning their beliefs about the innocence or guilt of the defendant and the sentence they regarded as appropriate if he were to be found guilty. (e) Everyone then went to smaller rooms and deliberated as members of six-person juries. Any subjects remaining after the maximum number of juries were formed were assigned to the individual condition. The six positions around the table in each jury room were labeled form A to F. For juries in the verdict contition, the juror at the seat designated A acted as foreman. Juries in the no verdict condition were not assigned foremen.

In the *verdict* conditions, juries deliberated until a poll showed five of the six jurors agreed on a verdict. (A maximum of 30 min was allowed for deliberation, and a jury not decided by this time was declared hung.) The *no verdict* juries discussed the case for 20 min; then jurors presented evidence that supported their position, and in turn listened to evidence presented by jurors with opposing positions. (Several ways of organizing no verdict juries are possible, but preliminary studies suggested that some discussion plan is necessary in the absence of a group decision if discussion is to develop sufficiently to parallel the verdict condition.) Finally, jurors again individually recorded their personal beliefs about the guilt or innocence of the defendant.

Juries in the *sentencing* condition were instructed, before they began deliberation, that should they find the defendant guilty (as a jury or as a juror depending upon their assignment to the verdict or no verdict condition) it would also be necessary to sentence the defendant

[3] The trial was a condensed version of an actual case in which the defendant was accused of rape. He had allegedly impersonated a police officer in stopping the victim with the ruse that she had run a red light. The victim further charged that he had raped her after luring her into his car under the pretense of going to the local police station. The defendant admitted to sexual relations, but denied it was without consent or that he had impersonated a police officer. (See Davis *et al.* (1975), for a more comprehensive account of the trial.) Additional information provided upon request.

subsequently. Verdict condition juries later decided sentence as a group, and in the no verdict juries individual jurors recommended sentence.

Subjects in the individual condition were asked to reflect on the trial, and write down all the evidence they could recall which supported (a) the prosecution, and (b) the defense. After this reflection period, subjects again indicated their belief regarding the guilt or innocence of the defendant. Half were required to sentence the defendant if they found him guilty, and half did not.

Finally, all subjects answered a postsession questionnaire soliciting (as appropriate to the condition) opinions about the case, jury activities, and the experimental situation in general. Everyone was then thanked and dismissed; lengthy debriefing followed in that considerable class discussion was devoted to the whole exercise as an illustration of various phenomena in social psychology.

RESULTS

Jury Decisions

The effects of a sentencing expectation on mock jury verdicts was assesssed by comparing juries receiving such instructions with those not so instructed. The observed verdict distributions, $\hat{P} = (\hat{P}_G, \hat{P}_{NG}, \hat{P}_H)$, for juries from both experimental conditions are given in Table 1, along with individual and juror predeliberation results. Juries with a sentencing expectation yielded a higher proportion of guilty and a lower proportion of not guilty and hung verdicts—but, this difference was not significant, $\chi^2(2) = .481$. The decisions obtained from the two kinds of verdict-rendering juries were then pooled to give a verdict distribution, $\hat{P} = (.47, .18, .35)$, based upon all 51 juries.

We may characterize the interpersonal decision process in an overall way by tracing the relative frequency of each outcome of guilty, not guilty, or hung $(\hat{P}_G, \hat{P}_{NG}, \hat{P}_H)$, given each possible distribution of opinion among juror members at the outset, viz., (r_G, r_{NG}), where $r_G + r_{NG} = r = 6$. These observations may be cast in an opinion distribution by outcome matrix, $\hat{D}$, a 7 × 3 social decision scheme matrix. Tht is, there are $(r_G, r_{NG}) = (6,0), (5,1), \ldots, (0,6)$ initial distributions of (guilty, not guilty) opinions

TABLE 1

VERDICT DISTRIBUTIONS FOR MOCK JURIES WITH AND WITHOUT A CHARGE TO SENTENCE SUBSEQUENTLY THE DEFENDANT IF FOUND GUILTY, AND VERDICT PREFERENCE OF JURORS PRIOR TO DELIBERATION AND INDIVIDUALS NOT IN JURIES

	Jury verdicts			Juror verdict preferences	
Decision outcomes	Sentencing	No sentencing	Total	Pre-deliberation	No deliberation
Guilty, G	.52	.42	.47	.63	.65
Not guilty, NG	.16	.19	.18	.37	.35
Hung, H	.32	.38	.35		
(N)	(25)	(26)	(51)	(614)	(40)

TABLE 2
SOCIAL DECISION SCHEME MATRIX OBSERVED FOR COMBINED SENTENCE AND NO SENTENCE JURIES, $N = 48$[a]

	Group outcome		
(r_G, r_{NG})	G	NG	H
(6,0)	1.00	.00	.00
(5,1)	.82	.00	.18
(4,2)	.47	.11	.42
(3,3)	.14	.00	.86
(2,4)	.00	1.00	.00
(1,5)	.00	1.00	.00
(0,6)	—	—	—[b]

[a] One or more members from three juries failed to respond appropriately, leaving 48 juries for which data were complete.

[b] No juries with this initial distribution were observed.

which result ultimately in jury outcomes of guilty, not guilty, or hung. Such a matrix of observed values estimates the social decision scheme matrix, D, summarizing the social decision process in terms of personal decision preference patterns among group members and task outcomes. The ikth entry, $[\hat{d}_{ik}]$, is an estimate of the conditional probability that the kth group outcome will occur, given the ith initial distribution of member opinion, $i = 1, 2, \ldots, 7$ and $k = 1, 2, 3$, or G, NG, H for juries. (Notice that we have adopted here an approach not of *model testing*, but of *model fitting*,[4] in which we attempt to *estimate* the social decision scheme matrix, D.)

Inspection of the observed entries, $[\hat{d}_{ik}]$, given in Table 2 suggests that interaction may be summarized as a type of majority process. But the majority was not "pure" and not symmetrical. That is to say, when a majority existed favoring one or the other verdict, there was a large, but not certain, likelihood of the jury rendering that verdict; and, the effect was much stronger when the majority favored a not guilty than a guilty verdict. The social decision scheme data reported in Table 2 differ slightly in detail but resemble in overall pattern those reported by Davis, Kerr, Stasser, Meek, and Holt (1977)—the only earlier study which is comparable in this way. Majority social decision schemes of one sort or another

[4] A *model testing* strategy emphasizes the prediction of group decisions from a priori assumptions about the social processes at work; these assumptions, whether derived from previous research, axiomatic theory, conventional wisdom, or intuition, often take a highly idealized form, such as "majority wins," which may require later amendment to less tidy form in the face of data. A *model fitting* approach attempts to achieve a best description of obtained data; this a posteriori account of the social decision process emphasizes the *estimation* of parameters defined by the theoretical system rather than testing hypotheses about them. (See Kerr, Stasser, & Davis, 1979, for a further discussion of the distinction.)

have been observed before in mock juries (Davis *et al.*, 1975; Davis *et al.*, 1977), real juries (Kalven & Zeisel, 1966), and other kinds of task-oriented groups (e.g., Davis, Kerr, Sussmann, & Rissman, 1974). However, the *pattern* of the majority is of interest partly because of the direct implications of the strength levels and asymmetry observed, and partly because these results hint that even under otherwise quite constant conditions a shift in social decision schemes might occur. (See Nagao and Davis, 1980b, for a discussion of temporal trends in these and other parameters, and the methodological and conceptual implications of such parameter changes over time.)

Guilt Preferences of Exjurors

We next examined the effects of verdict consensus and sentencing expectations on individuals' guilty/not guilty preferences and guilt likelihood ratings (10-point scale), reflecting the primary concern of the study. The proportion, $\hat{q}_G$, of jurors' postdeliberation guilty judgments observed in each experimental condition are given in the first line of Table 3. An analysis of variance was carried out on the (arcsin) transformed proportions. The verdict requirement produced a significantly larger guilty preference rate, $F(1, \infty) = 4.16$, $p = .04$, and the sentencing expectation also gave a significantly higher proportion of guilty judgments, $F(1, \infty) = 5.19$, $p = .02$. The interaction was not significant, $F(1,\infty) = .830$. Thus, the impact of a sentencing expectation was not sufficient to influence the

TABLE 3

PROPORTION, $\hat{g}_g$, OF EXJURORS WHO PERSONALLY PREFERRED A GUILTY VERDICT, AND THE MEAN LIKELIHOOD OF GUILTY AND MEAN CRITERION OF GUILT JUDGMENTS IN EACH EXPERIMENTAL CONDITION[a]

	Verdict jurors			No verdict jurors		
Exjuror responses	Sentence (149)	No sentence (153)	Total	Sentence (161)	No sentence (150)	Total
Guilty verdict preferences, r.f. of guilty	.678	.575	.626	.553	.520	.537
Mean likelihood of guilt, 0–10% [0], ..., 90–100% [9]	6.25	5.68	5.96	5.51	4.91	5.22
Mean criterion for guilty preferences, 0–10% [0], ..., 90–100% [9]	6.24	6.62	6.43	6.16	5.60	5.89

[a] Collapsed over sex.

verdicts of juries, as we noted earlier, but did influence the judgments of individual jurors. (Observe, however, that individuals are more numerous than groups, and the resulting difference in statistical power must be considered in interpretations.) The "verdict variable," of course, has no counterpart at the group level.

The mean guilt rating (0 = 0-10% likely, . . ., 9 = 90-100% likely the defendant committed the crime) for each condition is also reported in Table 3, second line. An analysis of variance, which included sex as a (nonsignificant) variable, revealed a significant effect due to verdict, $F(1, 604) = 9.88$, $< .002$, a significant effect due to sentencing, $F(1, 604) = 4.47$, $p < .04$, and no significant interaction, confirming the pattern of results from the dichotomous guilty/not guilty judgments reported above. When subjects' average judgments of the guilt criterion (last line of Table 3) were analyzed in the same fashion, no significant differences were observed. (A "criterion" judgment was obtained in response to the request to mark that category of the likelihood rating scale which "would divide your opinion such that anything above would be 'guilty beyond a reasonable doubt' and anything below would be 'not guilty.' ") Thus, there is no evidence that the manipulations altered the perceived guilty/not guilty threshold.

Perceptions of Exjurors from Verdict-Rendering Juries

The average reaction of exjurors suggested that they were fairly certain of the correctness of their jury's verdict; the overall mean was 2.92, on a 1 (certain) to 8 (uncertain) scale. The sentencing requirement did not significantly affect the certainty judgment.

Exjurors' perceptions of the final poll taken in their jury prior to verdict revealed a higher degree of perceived consensus than was actually recorded on that poll; jurors perceived .69 dissenters on the average (either for guilty or not guilty), whereas there were actually 1.26 dissenters on the average. Though small in magnitude, the sentencing requirement significantly increased *perceived* consensus; .59 dissenters on the average were perceived for juries in the sentencing condition and .79 for those in the no sentencing condition, $F(1, 197) = 8.52$, $p < .004$. Such a relative difference is consistent with the actual opinion change observed.

Social Influence and Social States

We have discussed in the preceding two sections the postdeliberation, verdict-related responses of exjurors and some of their personal reactions to the situation. For these analyses we aggregated data across juries within conditions, a strategy consistent with the usual treatment of data from group members in experiments on small groups. (See Anderson & Ager (1978) for relevant comments on using the analysis of variance in a somewhat similar situation.) Although individuals were randomly assigned to conditions and to groups within conditions (thereby guarding as usual against systematic groupings of particular personality traits, prior experience, and the like, being correlated with experimental conditions), some effects on individuals may be attributable to the *particular* group membership, stemming from unique social interaction events. The most prominent class of such events might be those associated with discussion of the defendant's guilt, which is after all the organizing purpose of the group's existence. Our next aim is thus to describe in more detail those changes in verdict preferences of jurors before and after deliberation.

Recall that the second assessment of individual preferences took place *after* deliberation for all juries and after a group verdict for some juries. Effects of this consensus requirement were further assessed by comparing "social state matrices" from the two kinds of juries. A 7 × 7 social state matrix, S, was constructed for the verdict juries by relating the ith initial opinion distribution or *state*, $\mathcal{S}_i$, to the final opinion distribution or state, $\mathcal{S}_j$, following the verdict, $i, j = 1, 2, \ldots, 7$, where the states were the distributions $(r_G, r_{NG}) = (6, 0), (5, 1), \ldots, (0, 6)$. The entry, $[s_{ij}]$, denotes the probability that a jury begins in $\mathcal{S}_i$ and ends in $\mathcal{S}_j$. The state matrix for the no verdict juries, S^*, with entries $[s^*_{ij}]$, has the same interpretation; rows and columns refer to the opinion distribution before and after deliberation. (See Davis et al. (1976), for discussion of a somewhat similar approach in which mock jury members repeatedly gave their personal responses throughout the deliberation period.)

The relative frequencies, $[\hat{s}_{ij}]$ and $[\hat{s}^*_{ij}]$, estimating the probabilities described above were obtained by counting the groups whose members followed the particular before–after path as defined by the intersection of the particular row and column; these are given in Table 4. Inspection of the two obtained state matrices reveals a great many empty cells, although we have collapsed over the sentencing-expectation variable to create larger samples. The true relative frequencies for many such cells for cases such as we are studying are in fact probably very near zero. For example, neither intuition nor previous data (e.g., Davis *et al.*, 1977) lead us to expect extreme reversals such as a (1, 5) jury at the outset going to a (6, 0) array at the end of deliberation. (Indeed, we have never observed such a turnabout.) Thus, in view of the sparse data available for an overall comparison of the two data matrices, we focused on the entries along the main diagonal of each array, viz., $[\hat{s}_{ij}]$ with $[\hat{s}_{ij}]$. Entries in cells along the main diagonal are large when there is little change, and small when advocates of one verdict or the other change—thus indexing social influence by majority or minority as the case may be. The most striking dissimilarity occurs for juries which initially had no majority (viz., the (3, 3) row) or had a nonunanimous majority favoring not guilty (viz., the (2, 4) and (1, 5) rows). For these cases, *no-verdict* juries were more likely to shift off the main diagonal, suggesting more social influence in the absence

TABLE 4

STATE MATRICES TRACING MOVEMENT OF OPINION FROM PRE- TO POSTDELIBERATION IN VERDICT JURIES (N = 47) AND NO-VERDICT JURIES (N = 50), POOLING OVER SENTENCING VARIABLE

Experimental condition	(G,NG)	Postdeliberation state, $\mathcal{S}_j$ (6,0)	(5,1)	(4,2)	(3,3)	(2,4)	(1,5)	(0,6)	r.f. in $\mathcal{S}_i$
Verdict juries, state matrix, S	(6,0)	.750	.250	.000	.000	.000	.000	.000	.085
	(5,1)	.300	.600	.100	.000	.000	.000	.000	.213
	(4,2)	.053	.263	.368	.105	.053	.158	.000	.404
Predeliberation state, $\mathcal{S}_i$	(3,3)	.000	.000	.143	.714	.143	.000	.000	.149
	(2,4)	.000	.000	.000	.000	.400	.200	.400	.106
	(1,5)	.000	.000	.000	.000	.000	1.000	.000	.043
	(0,6)	—	—	—	—	—	—	[1.000]	—[a]
	r.f. in $\mathcal{S}_j$	.149	.255	.191	.149	.085	.128	.043	
No verdict juries state matrix, S^*	(6,0)	1.000	.000	.000	.000	.000	.000	.000	.140
	(5,1)	.250	.625	.000	.125	.000	.000	.000	.160
	(4,2)	.077	.077	.462	.231	.077	.077	.000	.260
Predeliberation state, $\mathcal{S}_i$	(3,3)	.000	.000	.000	.444	.222	.222	.111	.180
	(2,4)	.000	.000	.000	.125	.000	.500	.375	.160
	(1,5)	.000	.000	.250	.000	.000	.250	.500	.080
	(0,6)	.000	.000	.000	.000	.000	.000	1.000	.020
	r.f. in $\mathcal{S}_j$	.200	.120	.140	.180	.060	.160	.140	

[a] No juries exhibited an initial (0,6) distribution, but the most plausible inference is that this entry would have been near 1.00.

of a verdict requirement. The result is somewhat counterintuitive; intuition suggests that the increased social pressure toward consensus would produce more shifts in juries required to reach a verdict. It is interesting to note that in the absence of an initial majority, *no verdict* juries exhibit a substantial defendant bias that does not occur for verdict juries. Similarly, when an initial nonunanimous majority favors not guilty, no verdict juries are more likely to shift further in the not guilty direction than those juries required to reach a verdict.

DISCUSSION

Jury Decisions

There was no clear theoretical prediction, a priori, about how a subsequent sentencing responsibility might influence the verdict itself. However, sequential decisions offer the possibility of "balancing" outcomes, although ostensibly the two actions are to be independent in the present role. We noted at the outset (Gleisser, 1968) that juries in 19th-century France were reportedly reluctant to convict in view of the harsh sentences which judges of the time were inclined to impose subsequently. Thus, jury control of sentencing the convicted might similarly induce a greater willingness to convict. Indeed, we observed a higher proportion of guilty verdicts given by juries in the sentencing than no sentencing condition, but the discrepancy was not significant.

A more important result was the form of the observed social decision scheme matrix. Recall that the "majority rule" of everyday usage makes no provision for nonmajorities, such as (3, 3). Moreover, the idea usually implies that the majority influence is (a) symmetrical in that guilty and not guilty verdicts are similarly determined; and (b) "pure," in the sense that the majority-favored alternative occurs with near certainty (i.e., probability near 1.00). Task-oriented groups often perform according to social decision schemes other than majorities (see Davis, Note 1, for a comprehensive discussion of this point), and we have in past research on mock juries regarded majority effects observed to be less than pure (i.e., <1.00), and displaying any asymmetry, as probably the result of sampling error, since these departures were quite small. The entries in the social decision scheme matrix observed here (Table 2), however, seem to contradict such notions. We have previously observed suggestions of asymmetric and "impure" majority effects (Davis et al., 1977), but not so clearly as in the present case. Departures from ideal social decision scheme forms seem less likely than heretofore to be attributable to sampling errors—especially in view of the asymmetry being consistent with norms and instructions about reasonable doubt.

Convenient verbal summaries of "majority rule," like any other historical convention may not serve well to capture the social complexity actually present. We must therefore be prepared to find in data evidence for complex and untidy social decision schemes—whether a near majority or not.

Postdeliberation Preferences

Both the sentencing expectation and verdict requirement had the overall effect of elevating the proportion of guilty verdict preferences and mean likelihood ratings. The two findings bear on rather fundamental questions of group performance which are usually ignored: the effects of one task upon another in a decision sequence and the very issue of requiring a group level consensus at all. Explanations as to the nature and direction of action probably cannot be sought independently of the particular task content and social context. For example, sentencing after a verdict might be interpreted within the task-role setting as we discussed at the outset.

Thus, jurors who have the option of managing the severity of the sentence subsequent to the verdict may be more willing to convict than those who do not have such an expectation. Whether or not procedural changes which increase the part played by the jury in sentencing are desirable constitute judgments lying well beyond the scope of our discussion. Not now common, especially outside of capital crimes, jury sentencing is certainly consistent with the philosophy of increased citizen participation and public accountability which is very much a part of contemporary social thought. In this connection, it is important to bear in mind that no single study, whether with role-playing undergraduates or actual jurors, should be interpreted as endorsing or providing sufficient justification for social policy bearing on complex social institutions. To the extent that results here are relevant, they are only part of the large accumulation of data and arguments which would necessarily be considered prior to legislative or judicial action. (Again, see the Presidential Task Force Report (1967), for an array of pro and con arguments concerning jury sentencing.)

The custom of a single overall verdict being reported probably stems from the idea that if each and every juror has come to have the same opinion (or at least a strong majority is convinced beyond a reasonable doubt), then conviction or acquittal rests on a sound "empirical" base. Such a view, however, does not adequately take into account the possibilities for interpersonal influence, mere acquiescence, and related phenomena, associated with consensus-reaching per se. However, since consensus pressures can in principle move members *either* toward acquittal or conviction, it is important to supplement with pattern information the overall finding of a significant verdict effect. (Any particular direction to an overall verdict effect may be due to the initial disposition of jurors' preponderance of majorities in any one direction and the way the subscheme sorts the nonmajorities if a majority is the primary social decision scheme determining verdicts. See Davis (1980), for a more comprehensive discussion.)

The pattern of yielding among the various initial opinion distributions was less similar in the two kinds of groups than we anticipated. Both data sets, as summarized by the state matrices, S and S^*, confirmed the decision asymmetry (whereby not guilty majorities are the more powerful) we noted earlier. Furthermore, this asymmetry favoring not guilty was more pronounced for no-verdict juries than verdict juries, especially when no majority existed (i.e., for juries initially in the (3,3) state).

In summary, a single overall verdict may indeed mask disagreement among jurors, and the process of reaching that verdict may foster less flexibility among minority members to change their opinion, even though they may acquiesce in the verdict as reported. Although several plausible conjectures to explain such an effect might be constructed, prudence dictated by the small samples at hand would suggest that further speculation await larger data sets. Sufficient data are likely to accumulate only through abandoning the random assignment of subjects to groups, such as we used in this study, since that potentially leads to consideration of all possible opinion arrays; an alternative strategy would be the controlled composition of groups having only a few of the possible majority/minority opinion arrays—thereby allowing larger samples.

REFERENCES

Anderson, L. R., & Ager, J. W. Analysis of variance in small group research. *Personality and Social Pscyhology Bulletin,* 1978, **4,** 341–345.

Anderson, N. H., & Graesser, C. C. An information integration analysis of attitude change in group discussion. *Journal of Personality and Social Psychology,* 1976, **34,** 210–222.

Dalkey, N. An experimental study of group opinion: The Delphi method. *Futures,* September 1969, 408–426.

Davis, J. H. Group decision and social interaction: A theory of social decision schemes. *Psychological Review,* 1973, **80,** 97–125.

Davis, J. H. Group decision and procedural justice. In M. Fishbein (Ed.), *Progress in social psychology.* Hillsdale, N.J.: Erlbaum, 1980.

Davis, J.H., Kerr, N. L., Atkin, R. S., Holt, R., & Meek, D. The decision processes of 6- and 12-person juries assigned unanimous and 2/3 majority rules. *Journal of Personality and Social Psychology,* 1975, **32,** 1–14.

Davis, J. H., Kerr, N. L., Stasser, G., Meek, D., & Holt, R. Victim consequences, sentence severity and decision processes in mock juries. *Organizational Behavior and Human Performance,* 1977, **18,** 346–365.

Davis, J. H., Kerr, N. L., Sussmann, M., & Rissman, A. K. Social decision schemes under risk. *Journal of Personality and Social Psychology,* 1974, **30,** 248–271.

Davis, J. H., Stasser, G., Spitzer, C. E., & Holt, R. Changes in group members' decision preferences during discussion: An illustration with mock juries. *Journal of Personality and Social Psychology,* 1976, **34,** 1177–1187.

Gleisser, M. *Juries and justice.* New York: Barnes, 1968.

Kalven, H., Jr., & Zeisel, H. *The American jury.* Boston: Little, Brown, 1966.

Kerr, N. L., Stasser, G., & Davis, J. H. Model testing, model fitting, and social decision schemes. *Organizational Behavior and Human Performance*, 1979, **23**, 399–410.

Nagao, D. H., & Davis, J. H. Effects of prior experience on mock juror case judgments. *Social Psychology Quarterly*, 1980, **43**, 190–199 (a).

Nagao, D. H., & Davis, J. H. Some implications of temporal drift in social parameters. *Journal of Experimental Social Psychology*, 1980, **16**, 479–496. (b)

Norris, H. Rape; assault with intent to commit rape: Gross indecency; assault and battery, People vs. Haney. In *A casebook of complete criminal trials*. Detroit, Mich.: Citation, 1965.

Presidential Task Force Report. *Task force report: The courts*. Washington, D.C.: U.S. Govt. Printing Office, 1967.

Stasser, G., Kerr, N. L., & Davis, J. H. Group performance and decision making. In P. Paulus (Ed.), *Psychology of group influence*. Hillsdale, N.J.: Erlbaum, 1980.

Steiner, I. D. *Group process and productivity*. New York: Academic Press, 1972.

REFERENCE NOTE

1. Davis, J. H. *Social interaction as a combinatorial process in group decision*. Paper presented at the Castle Reisensburg Conference, West Germany, 1978.

Journal of Applied Social Psychology, 1982, 12, 6, pp. 453-480

Biases In Trials Involving Defendants Charged With Multiple Offenses[1]

SARAH TANFORD[2] AND STEVEN PENROD
University of Wisconsin–Madison

Under federal and state laws, a defendant who has been charged with more than one offense can be tried for all the offenses in a single "joined" trial. It was predicted that the probability a defendant would be convicted would increase as a function of the number of joined offenses. Legal theories, research on memory, and social psychological models of information integration and attribution led to three hypotheses as to why this bias might occur: (1) confusion of evidence, (2) accumulation of evidence, and (3) inference of a criminal disposition. Subjects read and judged written trial summaries presented as joined or single trials. In Study 1, joinder resulted in higher rates of conviction and in confusion of evidence. In Study 2, the conviction results were replicated, and subjects judging joined trials also rated the evidence as more incriminating and made negative attributions about the defendant. These ratings were strongly related to judgments of guilt. A sequential judgment process was also found to affect jurors' judgments.

Under federal and state laws, a defendant who has been charged with more than one related offense may be compelled to defend against those charges in a single trial (known in the law as "joining" the charges). However, a prosecutor's decision to try several offenses in the same trial can be challenged at several points in the legal process. Even before the trial begins, the defense may ask that the charges be "severed" and tried separately. If this request is denied and the defendant is convicted of one or more of the offenses, the convictions may be appealed on the grounds of prejudice resulting from the

[1]This research was supported by grants to the second author from the Graduate School of the University of Wisconsin and the National Institute of Justice Grant #81-LJ-CX-0048.

[2]Requests for reprints should be sent to Sarah Tanford, Department of Psychology, University of Wisconsin, W. J. Brogden Psychology Bldg., 1202 W. Johnson St., Madison, WI 53706.

joinder. In both the initial motion for severance and the appeal following conviction, the court must decide whether the joinder sufficiently prejudiced the defendant to warrant separate trials. Although some courts have gone so far as to demand demonstrations of "actual" prejudice (*State v. Nance*, 1976), the appellate courts have provided trial court judges with very little guidance on how to make such determinations. Inevitably, judges are reduced to making intuitive judgments on such questions.

The leading federal case on joinder is *United States v. Foutz* (1976), where a successful appeal was made on the grounds of prejudice under Rule 14 of Federal Rules of Criminal Procedure. The federal rule recognizes three possible types of prejudice to a defendant in a joined trial: (1) jurors may confuse the evidence presented in proof of different charges; (2) jurors may incorrectly combine or accumulate the evidence they are presented; and (3) jurors may inappropriately infer that the defendant has a criminal disposition.

While it is perfectly satisfactory, from a legal point of view, for judges to use introspection and speculation in their assessments of the likelihood that a defendant will be prejudiced by the joinder of multiple offenses, this is an issue that can be investigated empirically. In fact, the present research began as a result of an inquiry from a criminal defense attorney who was seeking empirical evidence that would support a motion of severance for a case in which the defendant had been charged with four different offenses. The case was eventually severed into two trials of two charges each, so the *number* of joined offenses was apparently a factor in the court's assessment of potential prejudice.

The theories of prejudice expressed in the legal rules lend themselves to empirical investigation and research in the areas of cognitive and social psychology offers some evidence in support of the legal intuitions. Type 1 prejudice (confusion) suggests that memory processes might be different in single and joined trials. Research on interference in long-term memory has shown that when subjects learn multiple lists of word pairs, they make intrusions (i.e., confuse items) between lists when recalling the lists (Postman & Underwood, 1973). The same sort of interference might occur when a juror is exposed to a series of joined charges, resulting in confusion of evidence among charges.

Literature on impression formation shows that the amount of information we have about a person affects our overall impression (Schneider, Hastorf, & Ellsworth, 1979). Anderson's (1974) information integration model has received considerable support, suggesting that our impression is a weighted average of the information received, with each piece of information having some scale value on the dimension to be judged. The information integration model has been applied to the juror decision-making task by Kaplan and Kemmerick (1974) and Ostrom, Werner, and Saks (1978). Joinder might affect the weights and/or scale values assigned to information presented at the trial, resulting in accumulation of evidence or Type 2 prejudice.

Attribution theory (Kelley, 1967, 1972) provides a plausible basis for the hypothesized Type 3 prejudice, the inference of a criminal disposition. The behavior of a defendant charged with several different crimes can be viewed as low in distinctiveness–the person is charged with an act with respect to several different entities (victims, situations, times, places)–and high in consistency–the person has allegedly displayed criminal behavior on more than one occasion. These are the two key elements for an internal attribution. The third factor of consensus information has received less support (Nisbett, Borgida, Crandall, & Reed, 1976), suggesting that people do not always use such information. However, criminal behavior in all instances should be low in consensus (most people are not criminals); thus, the third component of an internal attribution is probably typically present.

Empirical Evidence

Three studies (Greene & Loftus, 1981; Horowitz, Bordens, & Feldman, 1980; Kerr & Sawyers, 1979) have directly examined the impact of joining two charges on jurors' assessments of defendant guilt. Horowitz et al. found that a juror's ratings of defendant guilt were higher when two offenses were joined than when the offenses were tried separately. Horowitz et al. report that this effect occurred primarily for offenses presented first rather than second, and suggest that this may arise because the jurors suspend judgment on the first case until they have received evidence on the second offense, which serves as a kind of anchor. However, in examining their results, it appears that in some conditions the joinder effect was also operating in the second case. Also, the severed case was always judged individually, and so technically could not appear in the second position, but was treated as such in order to complete the factorial design. Therefore, comparisons between the second severed and joined offenses could not meaningfully be made. Even so, the joinder effects obtained were quite strong–our estimates of effect size (epsilon–Cohen, 1977) for their two cases were .36 and .35 overall. Horowitz et al. offer no evidence as to which of the four types of prejudice might operate in their joined cases.

Greene and Loftus (1981) also found that a defendant was more likely to be convicted if two charges were joined than if charged with a single offense. Judges' instructions to consider charges separately were ineffective in removing this effect. They also found that subjects judging joined charges made negative inferences about the defendant's character, providing support for what we have called Type 3 prejudice.

Kerr and Sawyers (1979) examined the independence of judgments of multiple charges, and found that as the strength of evidence on one charge increased, the probability of conviction of the other charge tended to decrease. All of Kerr and Sawyers' conditions were joined conditions of two charges, and the variable of interest was the *combination* of verdicts produced on the two charges, rather than a comparison of verdicts in joined and single offenses. However, a point which was not central to their study is central to the present one. Conviction on the weak charge alone was determined to be about 25% through pretesting. The conviction rate was much higher (57%) in the experimental conditions, all of which consisted of two charges. A joinder effect was not obtained for strong charges, where the mean conviction rate was 77% in the experimental conditions and 75% when pretested alone. This suggests that the effect may operate mostly in weak cases (although the possibility of a ceiling effect cannot be ruled out). Greene and Loftus (1981), Horowitz et al. (1980), and Kerr and Sawyers (1979) all offer evidence that joining two charges will lead to a higher conviction rate.

In addition to empirical evidence on joinder, there is related research on juror decision making. Nagao and Davis (1980) studied the effects of previous experience judging unrelated crimes of differing relative severity. They found that subjects with previous experience judging a mild vandalism case) were *less* likely to convict the defendant in a more severe rape case than subjects without experience. Subjects with previous experience judging rape were *more* likely to convict in a vandalism case than those without experience. The research on prior experience suggests that making one decision will affect subsequent decisions.

As a safeguard against prejudicc in joined cases, the trial judge typically instructs the jury to consider the evidence for each charge separately, although there is no rule governing what form those instructions should take. The legal assumption is that these instructions will reduce the chance of prejudice, although the study by Greene and Loftus (1981) suggests that this may not be the case. In a recent review of research concerning judge's instructions on other factors such as burden of proof, inadmissible evidence, and previous convictions, Lind (1982) has concluded that some instructions are followed whereas others are ignored and that further research is needed on the instruction process.

Hypotheses

Greene and Loftus (1981), Horowitz et al. (1980), and Kerr and Sawyers (1979) demonstrated a higher probability of conviction in the judgment of two charges than in the judgment of a single charge. The present experiments were designed to extend this finding to the judgment of more than two charges, and to test the hypotheses of confusion, accumulation, and criminal inference suggested in the legal literature and supported indirectly in the psychological literature.

1. It was predicted that joinder would increase the likelihood that a defendant would be convicted on any charge when compared to the same charge judged alone. The proportion of guilty verdicts on each offense was predicted to increase as a positive function of the number of charges with which it was joined. Of subsidiary interest was a comparison of the magnitude of the joinder effect, where decisions are made at the end of the trial, and a sequential judgment effect, where decisions are made following each charge. The concern here is the effect of making one decision on subsequent decisions.

2. Confusion of evidence. It was predicted that recall of material from the offenses would be affected by joining charges. Subjects judging joined charges were predicted to confuse evidence between charges, as the legal theories and theories of interference in long-term memory suggest.

3. Accumulation of evidence. It was predicted that jurors judging joined trials would assign more weight to evidence against the defendant, and might assign more weight to certain kinds of evidence. Joinder might also affect the scale value assigned to all items of information, making the evidence appear more incriminating. Moreover, it was predicted that jurors would combine both evidence about the defendant's character and factual trial evidence in forming their impressions. This would support an information integration model of juror decision making (Kaplan & Kemmerick, 1974).

4. Criminal attribution. It was predicted that jurors judging joined offenses would rate the defendant more negatively on personality and behavioral characteristics. This could be the result of attributing the criminal behavior to internal dispositions of the defendant.

5. Instructions. Another research question was whether instructions to consider charges separately could reduce or remove the biasing effects of joined charges. Greene and Loftus (1981) found that such instructions were not effective. The research on instructions in related areas has shown that judge's instructions have reduced mock juror bias in some situations but not in others (Lind, 1982), so no prediction was made as to how effective our instructions would be.

Two experiments were designed to test these hypotheses. Both studies used the same written case summaries, a simulated jury trial and undergraduate "jurors." The study did not include group deliberation. Analysis of group verdicts would have increased the number of subjects needed by a factor of 6 or 12. Furthermore, in previous studies of this kind, it has been found that group verdicts can be predicted with substantial accuracy from knowledge of the distribution of individual juror preferences prior to deliberation (Davis, 1973, 1980; Penrod & Hastie, 1979). Hypotheses 1 and 2 were tested in Study 1. Subjects judged joined or separate offenses and the number of joined cases presented to the subjects to decide was manipulated. Additionally, instructions to the mock jurors were manipulated to assess their effectiveness and recall measures collected to test for a confusion effect. Study 2 tested the hypotheses of accumulation of evidence and criminal inference by obtaining ratings of the evidence and the defendant.

STUDY 1

Method

Subjects

Subjects were 68 male and 85 female undergraduates at the University of Wisconsin who received course credit for participation. One female was excluded from the analysis because she asked questions about how to respond which related to the purpose of the study, leaving 68 males and 84 females.

Independent Variables

Joinder and sequential judgment. Subjects were presented with two, three, or four trial summaries and asked a series of questions about the offenses charged in each trial. The trial summaries included two charges of sexual assault involving rape, one charge of sexual assault involving the touching of the victim's breast, and one charge of criminal trespass. These charges represented distinct crimes, which occurred at different times and places and with different victims. The evidence concerning each charge was independent, such that evidence on any one charge was not directly related to the other two charges. The joinder and sequential judgment manipulations consisted of the way in which the charged offenses were presented and judged. In the joined conditions, two, three, or four offenses were merged into a single trial, and judgments for all the joined offenses were made after the evidence for all the charges had been read. In the sequential or "non-joined" conditions, subjects read three separate case summaries presented as individual trials consisting of one charge each, and were asked to make judgments about the charged offense immediately after reading each case.

Within each condition, the order of the cases was varied to produce six combinations of joinder and sequential judgment. Because a full factorial design was not manageable (e.g., there is no "third" offense for a joined trial with two offenses), combinations were selected on the basis of theoretical interest and susceptibility to analyses based on planned contrasts. The six combinations, along with a letter code by which they will subsequently be identified, were:

1. single offenses (sequential judgment): sexual assault [first rape case(1)–R], sexual assault [touching breast–B], and criminal trespass [T]–designated RBT;
2. single offenses (sequential judgment): trespass, touching breast, rape(1)–designated TBR;
3. two joined offenses: trespass and rape(1)–designated *TR*;

4. three joined offenses: trespass, touching breast, rape(1)–designated *TBR*;
5. four joined offenses: rape(1), touching breast, rape(2) and trespass–designated *RBRT*;
6. four joined offenses: trespass, touching breast, rape(2) and rape(1)–designated *TBRR*.

The first offense in the sequential judgment conditions also served as a control group with which to compare both joinder and sequential judgment effects, since it simply involved reading and judging a single trial.

Instructions. The instruction manipulation was included in two of the conditions, separate TBR and joined *TBR*. Following the general experimental instruction, subjects in the instructions condition were given the following instructions:

> Be sure to judge each case individually in making your decision–treat each offense as a separate crime.

Thus, there were eight conditions altogether, with six combinations of joinder and sequential judgment and two instructions conditions. In coded form, the eight conditions were: (1) RBT; (2) TBR; (3) Instructions-TBR (I-TBR); (4) *TR*; (5) *TBR*; (6) *RBRT*; (7) *TBRR*; and (8) I-*TBR*. The charges in each condition appeared in the order specified.

Stimulus Materials and Procedure

The experimental materials consisted of proceedings of trials based on actual cases, each involving the same defendant. The materials were prepared by the defendant's attorney and the second author who also has a law degree. The trial materials included summaries of the indictments, opening statements by the prosecution, direct examination and cross-examination of witnesses, the opening statement and case for the defense and closing arguments by prosecution and defense, followed by the judge's instructions on the law. This order of presentation matches actual trial sequencing. For the sequential judgment conditions, the sequence was repeated separately for each charge, followed by judgments made by the subject. When the charges were joined into a single trial, the sequence occurred once, i.e., all the indictments were presented, followed by opening statement and presentations of the evidence for all the offenses, etc. This represents the manner in which joined trails actually are conducted. In all conditions, the charges represented distinct offenses, each containing unique evidence. The wording of the proceedings was the same regardless of method of presentation. The average length for individual trials was 2,500 words.

All materials were assembled in packets representing the experimental materials and were prearranged in a random order for males and females separately in order to obtain a sex balance across experimental cells. Subjects were run in group sessions and the materials were handed out to the subjects as they reported to the experimental room. In the conditions where recall information was collected, subjects were given recall questionnaires after turning in the trial materials. The experimental sessions lasted between 30 minutes and 1 hour.

Dependent Variables

Judgment measures. Subjects were asked to make several judgments about each of the cases they read. Only two judgments were of particular interest to the present study. (1) *Verdict*–Subjects were asked how they would vote, guilty or not guilty, if they were a juror on the trial by answering whether they thought the defendant was guilty beyond a reasonable doubt. (2) *Probability of guilt*–Subjects were asked to rate the probability that the defendant actually did commit the offense on a continuous scale from 0% (definitely did not commit the alleged offense) to 100% (definitely did commit the alleged offense). Responses were coded into discrete intervals from 1 to 9. In addition to the verdict and probability of guilt measures, subjects provided several other judgments. They were asked to rate confidence in their verdict and the severity of the consequences to the victim for each of the charges. Those subjects whose verdict was guilty were also asked to assign prison and/or probation sentences. The results of these measures will not be discussed in order to simplify the presentation of the results and focus on the variables of primary interest. (A full summary of the results is available from the authors.)

Recall measures. Subjects in four of the conditions were also asked to recall facts about each case. Recall measures were collected from some of the TBR and *TBR* subjects and all of the instructions-TBR and *TBR* subjects. For each case, subjects were first asked to list briefly as many pieces of evidence against the defendant as they could remember and then to do the same thing for evidence in favor of the defendant. A separate sheet, with the charge labeled at the top, was provided for each offense to make it clear that subjects were to list evidence for that charge only (as opposed to evidence on all the charges). These measures were collected in the order the offenses were presented.

Recall was scored so as to obtain two dependent measures for each case. (1) *Percentage intrusions against* was the percentage of all items generated against the defendant that were intrusions. Intrusions were defined as items from other cases that were recalled as facts in a case in which they did not appear. (2) *Percentage intrusions in favor* was the proportion of items generated in favor of the defendant that were intrusions. These two dependent measures were scored separately for each case.

Personal information. After all other measures were collected, subjects answered questions concerning age, year in school, political orientation, and attitudes towards rape. These items were not used in the analysis and will not be considered further.

Results

Overview

Since a number of different dependent measures were collected, a brief overview should help clarify the results. First the results from the *judgment measures* (verdict and probability of guilt) will be presented. The means (adjusted for the covariate) for each of the three cases are presented in Table 1. Following preliminary analyses, the results for the effects of interest will be presented in the following order: (1) joinder effects, (2) sequential judgment effects, (3) joinder vs. sequential judgment, (4) instructions. Following the judgment, results will be the results for the *recall measures*.

Judgment Measures

Verdict and probability of guilt results were analyzed separately for three of the criminal cases (sexual assault-rape(1), secual assault-touching breast, criminal trespass). Data from the rape(2) case (which only appeared in the two four-case conditions) were not analyzed. Data from one subject was eliminated from this part of the analysis because of failure to respond appropriately to some of the measures, leaving 151 subjects. Since the sexual assault (touching breast) case did not appear in one of the conditions (*TR*) its analysis included only 135 subjects.

Preliminary analyses. Because several researchers have reported gender differences in mock juror reactions to rape trials (Davis, Kerr, Stasser, Meek & Holt, 1977; Feldman-Summers & Lindner, 1976; Rumsey & Rumsey, 1977; Thornton, 1977), and since gender was not a variable of interest in the present study, all analyses were performed with analysis of covariance using gender as the covariate. The effect of the covariate was found to be significant as expected for both of the variables in both cases of sexual assault. In the sexual assault (rape) case, there were significant gender differences for verdict, $t(142) = 2.81$, $p < .01$, and probability of guilt, $t(142) = 2.56$, $p < .05$. In the sexual assault (touching breast) case, there were again gender effects for verdict, $t(127) = 3.87$, $p < .001$, and probability of guilt, $t(127) = 2.71$, $p < .01$. In the criminal trespass case, the only effect for gender was on verdict, $t(142) = 2.06$, $p < .05$. Gender did not interact with any other variable, and all the gender effects were in the direction of harsher judgments by females than by males.

The overall analysis could not simultaneously examine the conditions of interest, namely joinder, sequential judgment, and instructions. Since these

TABLE 1

ADJUSTED MEANS FOR JUDGMENT MEASURES

Dependent variable	Experimental condition									Overall F
	RBT	TBR	I-TBR	TR	TBR	RBRT	TBRT	I-TBR	MSE	
1. Sexual assault (rape)										
Verdict	.06	.38	.08	.06	.29	.28	.39	.08	.16	2.47*
Probability of guilt	3.22	5.51	3.75	3.63	4.32	4.56	4.33	4.25	6.50	1.57
2. Sexual assault (touching breast)										
Verdict	.06	.17	.08		.25	.28	.28	.08	.14	1.08
Probability of guilt	3.78	3.97	3.00		4.00	3.67	4.07	3.42	4.63	.52
3. Criminal trespass										
Verdict	.39	.10	.08	.07	.29	.28	.33	.17	.16	1.78
Probability of guilt	5.11	3.38	3.00	3.63	4.29	4.89	4.34	4.33	5.50	1.75
n =	18	29	12	16	28	18	18	12	* = $p < .05$	

three variables were not completely crossed, all the data could not be analyzed in a factorial design. Instead, several nonorthogonal but theoretically relevant planned comparisons were made which did allow a test of the main hypotheses (Keppel, 1982). Table 1 presents an overall F test from a one-way ANOVA by condition, as well as the error term used in the contrasts.

The nature of the design requires comment on one other statistical consideration. Data for each case had to be analyzed separately even though case was a repeated measure within subjects. This was necessary for two reasons. First, all cases did not appear in all conditions. Second, the contrasts of interest were different depending on the case to which they were applied. It would have been meaningless to perform these contrasts on cases where they were not relevant. Therefore, since there were only 7 between-groups degrees of freedom, a Modified Bonferroni test was used to control the error rate of the 10 comparisons. This test set the acceptable level of significance at .035.[3]

Joinder effects. The main hypothesis of interest was the effect of joinder of offenses. Linear trends were predicted as the number of charges increased from a single case to two, three, and four joined offenses. The trend analysis for the sexual assault (rape) case was performed on the four cells in which the rape appeared in the first, second, third, and fourth positions (i.e., rape was last in each of these cells). A linear trend was found for verdict, $t(75) = 2.94$, $p < .01$. The trend analysis for the criminal trespass (using the four conditions in which trespass was tried first) again yielded a linear trend for verdict, $t(86) = 2.43$, $p < .01$. The linear trends for probability of guilt did not reach statistical significance, although the trends in both cases were as predicted, with means increasing as number of joined offenses increased. In the criminal trespass, the mean probability of guilt ratings were 3.38, 3.63, 4.29, and 4.34 with 1, 2, 3, and 4 offenses, and in the rape case the means were 3.22, 3.63, 4.32, 4.33. Figure 1 shows the linear trend for guilt verdicts in the sexual assault (rape) and criminal trespass.

Sequential judgment. A comparison between the two sequential judgment conditions (RBT and TBR) examined the effect of prior decisions on subsequent ones in the rape and trespass cases. In the rape case, the effect was significant for verdict, $t(142) = 2.66$, $p < .01$, and probability of guilt, $t(142) = 2.84$, $p < .01$. Subjects who had previously decided two charges assigned more guilt verdicts ($M = .38$ vs. .06), and rated the probability of guilt as higher ($M = 5.51$

[3]The Modified Bonferroni test is suggested by Keppel (1982, p. 147-148) as a method for controlling the error rate with planned comparisons. The significance level of the present study was obtained using the following formula:

7 (between subjects d.f.) × .05 (significance level) = .35
.35/10 (number of comparisons) = .035 (new significance level).

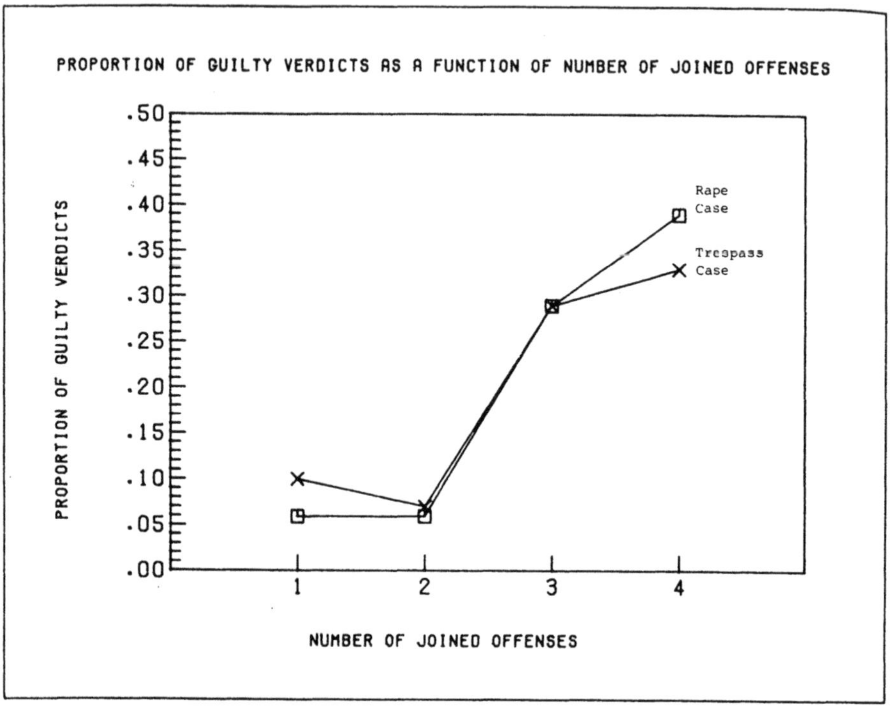

Fig. 1. Proportion of guilty verdicts as a function of the number of joined offenses.

vs. 3.32) than subjects making their first judgment. In the criminal trespass case, the effect of sequential judgment again was significant for verdict, $t(142) = 2.38$, $p < .02$, and probability of guilt, $t(142) = 2.48$, $p < .01$. Subjects making their third decision again assigned more guilty verdicts (M = .39 vs. .10) and rated the probability of guilt as higher (M = 5.51 vs. 3.38) than those deciding their first case.

Joinder vs. sequential judgment. While these results suggest both joinder and sequential judgment of non-joined offenses, it is not clear whether joinder and sequential judgment represent two distinct processes. Since each of the three single offenses involved the same defendant, some of the same biases may be operating in both conditions. Subjects judging joined offenses had *read* evidence prior to making their first decision, whereas subjects judging cases sequentially made each decision prior to reading the next case. To compare these two effects, an analysis of covariance was performed on a portion of the data (TBR and *TBR*) with type of judgment (joined or sequential) as a between-subjects factor and case as a within-subjects factor. There was no main effect for type of judgment, and there were case main effects on verdict,

$F(2,110) = 4.38$, $p < .02$, and probability of guilt, $F(2,110) = 6.97$, $p < .01$. More interesting was the interaction between case and type of judgment, $F(2,110) = 3.75$, $p < .03$ for verdict and $F(2,110) = 5.59$, $p < .01$ for probability of guilt. In the sequential judgment condition, the proportions of guilty verdicts were .10, .17, and .38 for the first, second, and third charges, and probability of guilt was rated as 3.38, 3.97, and 5.41. In the joined condition, the proportions of guilty verdicts were .29, .25, and .29, and the guilt ratings were 4.29, 4.00, and 4.32. Thus the sequential judgment effect was cumulative, increasing as subjects progressed from the first charge to the second and third charges, whereas the joinder effect was equally strong regardless of the position of the offense. This suggests that the joinder effect may be a result of accumulating evidence across the three charges.

Instruction effects. The results reported so far indicate that joinder results in consistently harsher judgment of a defendant. An important question is whether this bias can be removed by specifically instructing subjects to consider the evidence for each case separately. Two contrasts were designed to determine the effect of such instructions. A contrast to determine the effect of instructions in joined cases compared the joined *TBR* and instructions (I-*TBR*) conditions and there were no effects in any of the cases. A second comparison was made between the joined instructions condition (I-*TBR*) and its single case counterpart (TBR for the trespass and touching breast cases and RBT for the rape case). Again there were no significant differences. Thus there is some evidence that the instruction was partially effective, since there were no differences between joined (with instructions) and single conditions.

Recall Measures

The recall measures collected at the end of the experiment were designed to further investigate the decision-making process in terms of the confusion hypothesis. The two dependent measures for each case were (1) percentage of items generated against the defendant that were intrusions (facts from other cases), and (2) percentage of items generated in favor that were intrusions. A percentage score was used because the total number of evidence items available varied somewhat depending on the case. There were so few errors other than intrusions (such as listing a fact that appeared in none of the cases, n = 6) that these were not scored.

Recall measures were collected in four of the conditions: TBR, I-TBR, *TBR*, and I-*TBR*. They were analyzed in a 2 (joinder) × 2 (instructions) × (3(case) × 2(type of intrusion)) analysis of covariance with gender as the covariate. Joinder and instructions were crossed factorially with type of intrusion (against or in favor) as repeated measures within subjects. There were main effects for joinder, $F(1,44) = 34.60$, $p < .001$; intrusion type, $F(1,45) = 10.82$,

$p < .01$; case, $F(2,90) = 9.78$, $p < .001$ and a case × joinder interaction, $F(2,90) = 4.15$, $p < .02$. There was no effect for instructions and no other interactions. Joined offenses led to a higher proportion of intrusions (M = .13) than separate offenses (M = .04). There were also more intrusions against the defendant (M = .12) than in favor (M = .06). In this analysis, case is confounded with order, since the cases always appeared in the same order, and the case effect could best be considered a recency effect, since the mean proportion of intrusions in the first, second, and third offenses respectively were .15, .08, and .04. The recency effect also explains the case × joinder interaction, in that joinder led to less intrusions in more recent cases.

The specific nature of these overall effects was examined with six simple effects analyses. Each case was analyzed for intrusions against and in favor separately in order to examine the effect of most interest–joinder. For intrusions against the defendant, a separate analysis on each case showed that the joinder effect was significant for criminal trespass, $F(1,44) = 13.02$, $p < .001$, and sexual assault (touching breast), $F(1,44) = 5.41$, $p < .01$, but not for sexual assault (rape), $F(1,44) = 1.79$, $p > .10$. Figure 2 illustrates the case recency effect, showing that joinder did not cause a large increase in intrusions in the most recent case, sexual assault (rape), where the means were .02 in sequential cases and .08 in joined cases. There was a substantial increase in the middle case, sexual assault (touching breast), means = .05 for sequential cases and .18 for joined cases. Joinder produced the largest increase in intrusions in the first case, criminal trespass, means = .10 and .26 for separate and joined cases respectively.

For proportion of intrusions in favor of the defendant there was a significant joinder effect in the first case, criminal trespass, $F(1,44) = 13.36$, $p < .001$, where the means for separate and joined cases were .02 and .20 respectively. There was no effect in either the sexual assault (touching breast) case, means = .02 and .06, or the sexual assault (rape) case, means = .03 and .04.

Since recall measures were collected after all judgments were made, these results suggest that joinder and sequential judgment may involve different processes. All subjects had made all their judgments the time of recall, and yet subjects who had judged sequential trials produced significantly fewer intrusions than subjects who had judged the same offenses in a joined trial. Subjects in both groups were given the same instructions to lists facts from each charge individually, so the results cannot be explained by a failure to understand the task. It does appear that making judgments on each case before going on to the next one allowed subjects to separate the facts from different charges.

While the results have shown that joining cases results in systematic errors in recall, the real question is how these errors reflect biases in the judgment process. It was predicted that the balance of intrusions against the defendant vs.

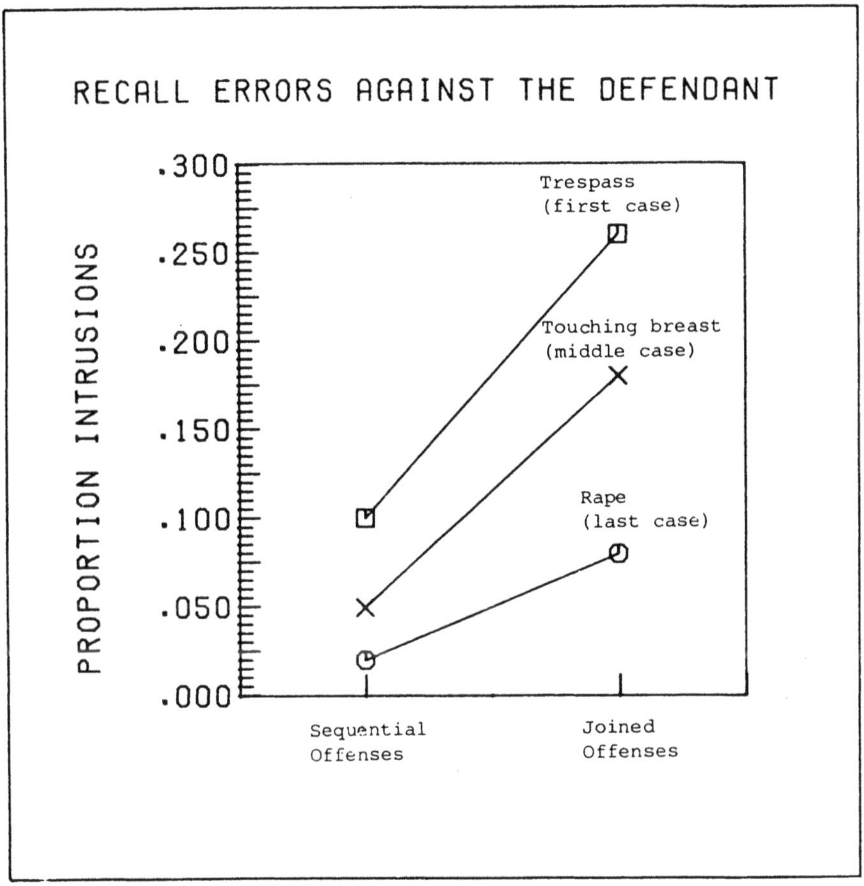

Fig. 2. Proportion of recall errors against the defendant in joined and sequential offenses.

intrusions in favor might be reflected in judgments of guilt. In other words, subjects who were more confused about evidence against the defendant than in favor might make harsher judgments. A difference score was computed for each subject between proportion of intrusions against and in favor of the defendant, and this was correlated with the verdict and guilt measures. For the rape case, the values were $r(47) = .18$ for verdict and .22 for probability of guilt; for the sexual assault (touching breast) case, $r = .23$ for verdict and .23 for probability of guilt; and in the criminal trespass, $r = .09$ for verdict and .01 for probability of guilt (all values nonsignificant). These correlations, although generally in the right direction, were low, and together with the lack of type of intrusion × joinder interaction, do not support the hypothesis that confusion of evidence is the key biasing factor in joinder. At this point it can only be concluded that joinder does lead to both conviction biases and to confusion.

STUDY 2

Study 1 was designed to demonstrate the biasing effects of joinder and to provide a test of Type 1 prejudice, confusion of evidence. While supporting the hypothesis that conviction rate would increase with the number of joined offenses, a direct relationship between confusion and conviction bias was not found. The study also did not provide a direct test of the other two types of prejudice: accumulation of evidence and inferences about the defendant's criminal disposition. Study 2 was designed to provide such a test and to further test the generality of the joinder effect by including three key control conditions, namely measures on each of the offenses judged alone. In these conditions, neither joinder nor sequential judgment was a factor. Study 2 also tests two additional hypotheses: (1) joinder might raise jurors' prior probabilities of guilt, and thus violate the legal requirement of presumption of innocence; (2) joinder might lower the amount of evidence needed to convict a defendant "beyond a reasonable doubt."

Method

Subjects

Subjects were 60 female and 55 female undergraduates at the University of Wisconsin who received course credit for participation.

Design and Procedure

Subjects read and judged written trial summaries of three different offences: criminal trespass, sexual assault (touching victim's breast), and sexual assault (rape) in one of three conditions. In the *single offense* condition, subjects read and judged only one of the three offenses. In the *joined* condition, the three offenses were merged into a single trial and judgments for the joined offenses were made after all the evidence for the three charges had been read. In the *sequential judgment* condition, subjects read the three cases presented as individual trials consisting of one charge each and were asked to make judgments about the charged offense immediately after reading the case. In both joined and sequential judgment conditions, the offenses were always presented in a fixed order. The materials were identical to those used in the first experiment. Using the previous notation, the experimental conditions were: single offenses–(1) T, (2) B, (3) R; (4) joined offenses–*TBR*; (5) sequential judgment –TBR. The procedure was identical to Study 1.

Dependent Variables

Judgment measures. As in the previous study, subjects were asked to render a verdict (guilty or not guilty) and to rate the probability of guilt on a scale from 0% to 100%.

Prior probabilities. Before reading the case summary, subjects were asked to rate the probability that the defendant had committed the act based solely on the charge information. Subjects judging three separate trials made their ratings immediately before each trial, while subjects judging joined offenses rated prior probabilities on all three charges before reading the joined trial. Subjects judging a single trial made only one judgment. The ratings were made on a scale of 0% (definitely did not commit the alleged offense) to 100% (definitely did commit the alleged offenses), and were coded into discrete intervals from 1 to 9.

Criterion for conviction. Subjects were asked to rate the lowest probability of committing the act that would be necessary in order to convict the defendant beyond a reasonable doubt on a scale of 0% (definitely did not commit the offense) to 100% (definitely did commit the offense).

Weight of evidence. Subjects rated eight individual pieces of evidence from each of the offenses they judged on a scale of 0% (strongly indicates innocence) to 100% (strongly indicates guilty). This evidence was divided into four categories: (1) *character* evidence *against* the defendant (e.g., a prior criminal record); (2) *character* evidence *in favor*; (3) *trial* evidence *against* (e.g., an eyewitness identification); and (4) *trial* evidence *in favor*. The evidence was chosen on the basis of the recall results from the previous experiment, using items listed most frequently as evidence against and in favor of the defendant.

Defendant ratings. Subjects were asked to rate the defendant on a 9-point bipolar scale on each of the following characteristics: honest-dishonest, respectable-not respectable, likely to commit a crime in the future-unlikely to commit a crime in the future, moral-immoral, responsible-not responsible, good-bad, believable-not believable.

Judgment Measures

Planned comparisons were used to examine the differences in verdicts and probability of guilt between the joined, single, and sequential conditions.

Joinder effects. In the criminal trespass, there were joinder effects for verdict, $t(65) = 1.82, p < .04$, and probability of guilt, $t(65) = 2.52, p < .01$ (one-tailed tests). Subjects judging joined offenses returned a higher proportion of guilty verdicts than subjects judging separate offenses, $M = .30$ vs. .13, and rated the probability of guilt as higher, $M = 4.74$ vs. 3.28. In the sexual assault (touching breast) case, there were also joinder effects for verdict, $t(63) = 1.70$, $p < .05$, and probability of guilt, $t(63) = 1.93$, $p < .03$ (one-tailed). Subjects judging joined offenses again returned a higher proportion of guilty verdicts, $M = .22$ vs. .04, and rated the probability of guilt as higher, $M = 4.26$ vs. 3.09, than subjects judging single offenses. In the rape case, there was a marginal joinder effect for verdict, $t(63) = 1.40$, $p < .10$ and a significant effect for probability of guilt, $t(63) = 2.01$, $p < .025$ (one-tailed), which again were higher in joined than single offenses–$M = .30$ vs. .13 for verdict and $M = 4.26$ vs. 3.00 for probability of guilt.

Sequential judgment. In the sexual assault (touching breast) case, there was a sequential judgment effect for probability of guilt, $t(63) = 1.68$, $p < .05$, one-tailed, which was judged to be higher when judged second in the sequence ($M = 4.14$) than when judged alone ($M = 3.09$). In the rape case, there was again a sequential judgment effect of probability of guilt, $t(63) = 2.47$, $p < .01$, one-tailed. Subjects who had made two previous decisions rated the probability of guilt as higher than subjects judging a single offense ($M = 4.62$ vs. 3.00). The verdict results in each of the two sequential judgment conditions were not statistically significant but were in the predicted direction, with a mean conviction rate of .13 for the single rape case and .24 for the sequential one. In the sexual assault (touching breast) case, the means were .04 for single offenses and .14 for sequential offenses. A final contrast compared the effects of joinder vs. sequential judgment and no significant differences were found on either judgment. The analyses reported so far essentially replicate the previous results showing that both joinder and sequential judgment bias jurors towards guilt.

Prior probabilities and *conviction criterion.* There were no significant effects of joinder or sequential judgment on prior probability of guilt, although the prior probabilities, whose means ranged from .5 to .55, suggest that jurors are not presuming innocence as the law prescribes. Rather, they appear to assume chance probabilities. These results should be interpreted with caution, however, since direct measures of the variables may not be reliable. Ostrom et al. (1978) have shown, using a statistical estimation procedure, that in some situations jurors do presume innocence. There were also no joinder or sequential judgment effects on criterion for conviction.

Defendant ratings. Table 2 presents the mean ratings of the defendant on the 7 bipolar rating scales in single, sequential, and joined offenses. These data were collapsed across offenses in the single-offense conditions, since subjects in the joined condition rated the defendant only once after judging three charges, and therefore case-by-case comparisons could not be made. However, preliminary analyses on individual cases (comparing each single offense to the same joined and sequential ratings) yielded the same pattern of results.

TABLE 2

DEFENDANT RATINGS

	Single	Sequential	Effect size	Joined	Effect size
Negative items[1]					
Honest-dishonest	3.62a	5.39b	.40	4.71b	.28
Moral-immoral	4.39a	5.43b	.24	4.84ab	.11
Responsible-not responsible	3.48a	4.91b	.27	4.63b	.22
Believable-not believable	3.97a	5.30b	.26	4.76b	.16
Positive items[2]					
Not respectable-respectable	6.19a	5.00b	.27	4.71b	.34
Bad-good	6.09a	4.61b	.38	5.21b	.24
Future crime likely-unlikely	5.55a	4.26b	.25	5.00ab	.11
n =	69	23		24	

For each item, means without common subscripts are significantly different at $p < .05$.

[1]Higher scores indicate more negative ratings.

[2]Lower scores indicate more negative ratings.

For the first four items on Table 2, a higher score indicates a more negative rating, e.g., honest-dishonest, where honest is anchored at 1 and dishonest at 9 on the 9-point scale. For the last three items in Table 1, a lower score indicates a more negative rating, e.g., bad-good with bad anchored at 1 and good at 9. A 3 (joinder) × 2 (gender) analysis of variance revealed gender main effects for believable, $F(2,110) = 3.92$, $p < .05$, and responsible, $F(2,110) = 4.82$, $p < .05$. Both were rated lower by females than by males, and there were no interactions with gender. Therefore, the effects of joinder and sequential judgment were tested with analysis of covariance using gender as the covariate. These results are presented in Table 2, along with effect sizes and significance levels. Subjects judging joined or sequential trials rated the defendant more negatively on all ratings than subjects judging single trials. In the sequential judgment condition, all differences were statistically significant ($p < .05$); in the joined condition, all except two were significant; and all ratings were in the predicted direction. There were no significant differences between the joined and sequential conditions. The results of the defendant ratings show that one of the sources of bias involved in both joinder and sequential judgment is the attribution of more negative characteristics to the defendant, suggesting the inference of a criminal disposition. In attribution theory terms, this suggests that subjects are indeed attributing the criminal behavior to internal characteristics of the defendant. An alternative explanation could be offered, however. Subjects could derogate the defendant to justify the judgments they have previously made.

Weight of evidence. The evidence ratings were analyzed in a 3 (joinder) X 3 (case) X 2 (type: trial or character) X 2 (direction: in favor or against) X 2 (replicates) analysis of variance with joinder as a between subjects variable and case, type and direction as repeated measures within subjects. Although cases were actually between subjects in the single case conditions, they were not in the joined and sequential conditions, so the within-subjects analysis was chosen since it provides the more conservative estimate of error variance.[4] There were no gender effects or interactions, so analysis of covariance was not used and the data were collapsed across gender.

The analyses revealed main effects for joinder, $F(2,66) = 15.32$, $p < .001$; type, $F(1,66) = 8.64$, $p < .01$; direction, $F(1,66) = 284.27$, $p < .001$; and a type X direction interaction, $F(1,66) = 58.52$, $p < .001$. The strong direction main effect was essentially a manipulation check, showing that subjects rated evidence against the defendant as more incriminating ($M = 5.47$) than evidence in favor of the defendant ($M = 3.61$). The effect of joinder was of most interest, showing that subjects judging joined offenses rated the evidence overall as more incriminating ($M = 4.63$) than subjects judging single offenses ($M = 3.95$). Subjects judging sequential offenses rated the evidence to be even stronger ($M = 5.04$). The type main effect revealed that subjects rated trial evidence as more incriminating ($M = 4.66$) than character evidence ($M = 4.42$). Finally, the type X direction interaction showed that trial evidence differentiated between guilt and innocence more strongly than character evidence. For trial evidence, the mean ratings were 3.40 for evidence in favor and 5.92 for evidence against; and for character evidence, the mean ratings were 3.81 in favor and 5.02 against.

There were also interactions for case X direction, $F(2,132) = 5.91$, $p < .01$, and joinder X case X type, $F(4,132) = 3.98$, $p < .01$, and a main effect for individual evidence items, $F(12,132) = 12.68$, $p < .01$. No other interactions reached significance. The case X direction interaction is not particularly informative, showing simply that the direction effect varied somewhat across cases, although in all cases the direction manipulation exerted a strong effect. The joinder X case X type interaction was not readily interpretable. A calculation of the effect size yielded an epsilon of .28, revealing that this interaction accounts for much less variance than the strong effect found for joinder, epsilon =

[4]The variance accounted for by the effects is identical whether offenses are treated as different groups or as repeated measures within subjects. The only difference is the error term used for the tests of significance, which is larger in a within-subjects analysis since it includes both within- and between-subjects error variance.

.54. The effect size for type of item was .32, and for the type × direction interaction, epsilon = .66.

The main finding of the analysis of weight of evidence is that joinder causes subjects to rate all evidence as more highly incriminating, regardless of the direction of the evidence. This provides support for the legal theory of accumulation of evidence. Instead of affecting the *weight* of evidence in the information integration equation (Anderson, 1974), it appears that joinder affects the *scale value* of evidence, such that all items are given values more towards the negative end of the scale.

Correlations between defendant ratings and guilt. The present study strongly supported the conclusion that joinder leads to more negative ratings of the defendant and to higher ratings of evidence strength. The crucial question becomes, "How are they reflected in judgments of guilt?" Correlations between defendant ratings and judgments of verdict were computed separately for joined, sequential, and single offenses. (The same defendant ratings in the joined and sequential conditions were used in the correlations with judgments on each of the three charges, since subjects in these conditions rated the defendant only once.) The results indicate a positive relationship between undesirable defendant characteristics and judgments of guilt. This relationship was strong and consistent in joined and sequential offenses and weak and less consistent in single offenses. For probability of guilt in joined offenses, 18 of the 21 correlations reached the .05 significance level, with r's(23) ranging from .42 to .75. The remaining three r's of .40 were marginally significant at the .06 level. The mean correlation in the joined condition was .53. In the sequential judgment condition, 19 of 21 correlations were statistically significant, with r's ranging from .43 to .80, and the remaining two r's were .28 and .29 (n.s.). The mean correlation in the sequential condition was .55. Correlations between probability of guilt and defendant ratings in single cases varied according to the case. In the criminal trespass, there was a single significant correlation between probability of guilt and the "bad" rating, $r(23) = .46$, $p < .05$. The remaining nonsignificant correlations ranged from .00 to .25, and the mean correlation was .18. In the sexual assault (touching breast) case, there were significant correlations between probability of guilt and "dishonest", $r(23) = .44$, $p < .05$; "not believable", $r(23) = .52$, $p < .01$; and a marginal correlation with "bad", $r(23) = .39$, $p < .06$. The remaining correlations ranged from .03 to .29, and the mean r overall was .26. In the single rape case, the relationship between defendant ratings and probability of guilt was as strong as in the joined and sequential rape cases, with r's ranging from .42 to .77, mean = .54, all p's $< .05$.

In terms of guilt verdicts, the same correlational patterns emerged, although not as strongly, probably due to the dichotomous nature of the verdict measure (Cohen & Cohen, 1975, p. 177). In joined cases, the r's ranged from .11 to .57,

TABLE 3

CORRELATIONS BETWEEN MEAN RATINGS OF EVIDENCE STRENGTH AND GUILT JUDGMENTS

Measure	Case								
	Criminal trespass			Touching breast			Rape		
	Joined	Sequential	Single	Joined	Sequential	Single	Joined	Sequential	Single
Probability of guilt	.58xx	.56xx	.47x	.48x	.53xx	.42x	.48x	.47x	.67xxx
Verdict	.26	.47x	.43x	.32	.52xx	.46x	.51xx	.50x	.46x

$n = 23$.
x = $p < .05$.
xx = $p < .01$.
xxx = $p < .001$.

mean = .34, although only seven of these reached statistical significance ($p <$ .05) and three approached significance ($p < .10$). In sequential cases, 11 correlations were significant and 4 were marginal, with r's overall ranging from -.10 to .80, mean = .44. In single offenses, the correlations ranged from -.22 to .29 (n.s.) in the criminal trespass and sexual assault (touching breast) with a mean r of .10. Again the relationship was stronger in the single rape case, with r's ranging from .25 to .43, mean = .35, although the relationship was even stronger in the joined and sequential rape cases with r's ranging from .31 to .67, mean = .49. It could be that as offenses become more severe (e.g., rape), all jurors begin to evaluate defendants negatively, so that joinder might produce stronger biases with less severe offenses.

Correlations between evidence ratings and guilt judgments. Table 3 presents the correlations between subjects' mean ratings of evidence strength and judgments of guilt. The results are a strong positive relationship between ratings of evidence strength and probability of guilt in joined, sequential, and single trials. All correlations between probability of guilt and evidence ratings were statistically significant, while two of the verdict-evidence correlations were positive but not significant. There is no apparent pattern of differences between joined, sequential, and single offenses—all exhibit a consistent positive relationship between ratings of evidence strength and judgments of guilt.

The fact that the correlations between evidence strength and guilt judgments are equally strong in joined, sequential, and single offenses shows that all jurors are, as indeed they should be, basing their judgments of guilt on the strength of the evidence. However, since subjects judging joined offenses rate evidence overall to be stronger, this will be reflected in higher guilt judgments. Furthermore, the fact that the correlations between *defendant ratings* and judgments of guilt are stronger in joined than single offenses suggests that these jurors are, in addition to the evidence, inappropriately basing judgments on attributions about the defendant.

DISCUSSION

The results provide compelling evidence that joined trials significantly influence mock jurors' judgments. The joinder effect supports the hypothesis that the decision process in a joined trial results in a higher probability that a defendant will be convicted on a particular charge, and that the effect increases with the number of charges joined. Thus, the results obtained by Greene and Loftus (1981), Horowitz et al. (1980), and Kerr and Sawyers (1979) using two charges have been extended to trials with three and four charges.

A sequential judgment process was also found to affect judgments of later charges, such that subjects who made judgments on prior, severed cases were more likely to convict. What is not yet clear is whether joinder and sequential judgment represent two distinct processes. The recall results suggest that they are distinct, since there were more recall errors in joined than in sequential trials; however, these errors were not strongly related to guilt judgments. Also, the defendant and evidence ratings were not significantly different in joined and sequential trials, indicating that the two processes are quite similar. The results from Study 1 indicate that the sequential judgment effect is cumulative, with guilt verdicts increasing as subjects progress from the first charge to the second and third charges, whereas the joinder effect is equally strong on all charges. The mean effect size for verdicts in Study 1 was .29 for joinder and .21 for sequential judgment; in Study 2, the effect size was .20 for joinder and .12 for sequential judgment. Future research is needed, however, to conclusively separate the effects of joinder and sequential judgment. Existing case law hypothesizes several sources of the biasing effects detected in these studies. We have labeled these the confusion, accumulation of evidence, and criminal inference hypotheses.

The recall measures collected at the end of Study 1 provide support for the hypothesis that joinder can promote confusion about evidence. Joined charges led to a higher percentage of intrusions of facts from other offenses than did separate charges. This confusion occurred despite the fact that written trial summaries were used, so there was much less evidence to confuse than there would be in an actual trial. The confusion was likely due to interference processes in long-term memory (e.g., Postman & Underwood, 1973). Memory processes are further implicated by the finding of a recency effect, such that intrusions were not affected by joinder in the rape case, which had been read last in the offense sequence, while the largest number of intrusions occurred in the joined criminal trespass, which was the first of three. A recency effect in long-term memory has also been found in other free recall tasks (Bjork & Whitten, 1974). Of course, a defendant might not have the benefit of a recency effect in an actual trial that extended over a longer period of time. Furthermore, in the present study, recall measures were collected immediately following trial judgments, and the recency effect might have disappeared if there had been a delay between trial presentations, judgments, and recall tasks. It is also possible that deliberation would influence recall. A jury discussing the charges might be able to set the facts straight or might become even more confused. Future studies should include group deliberation to examine its effects on all judgmental processes. Although Study 1 demonstrated that the joinder of offenses does appear to affect memorial processes, it should be emphasized that a direct relationship between confusion and conviction bias could not be established.

The second study examined the other two hypothesized sources of bias: accumulation of evidence and criminal inference. Both joinder and sequential judgment yielded shifts in juror ratings of evidence strength. Jurors in both conditions rated all evidence, whether positive or negative, as being more incriminating. This supports the hypothesis of accumulation of evidence. Within an information integration model, one could say that jurors' scale values for *all* evidence items increased. However, neither joinder nor sequential judgment affected prior (pretrial) probabilities of guilt or criterion for conviction. Interestingly, the relationship between perceived evidence strength and guilt judgments was equally strong in joined and single cases. Thus, all subjects used strength of evidence in assessing guilt, as should be expected, although the evidence was subjectively stronger for subjects in joined cases.

With respect to the third hypothesized source of bias, Study 2 also showed that jurors judging joined offenses made more negative attributions about the defendant, supporting the hypothesis of criminal inference (although the idea that subjects may have been justifying their verdicts cannot be ruled out). Subjects did consider a person charged with several crimes to be more of a "criminal type." That is, they appear to have attributed his criminal behavior to internal factors. Moreover, these ratings bear a strong relationship to judgments of guilt, stronger than the relationship found in single cases. At this point the hypothesis that the inference of criminal disposition is responsible for the joinder effect receives the strongest support.

In actual trials where charges have been joined together, the trial judge sometimes gives jurors special instructions designed to offset possible biases that may arise from joinder. Instructions in the present study were partially effective in removing the bias towards conviction. Instructions may be more effective in the courtroom, since instructions in the present study were given as part of the general experimental instructions, and the instructions were quite short. Appellate court cases show that at least some trial judges give very elaborate instructions. The study therefore does not show *how* effective instructions can be in the courtroom, although Greene and Loftus (1981) found that even more realistic instructions were not effective. Since the results have demonstrated that bias can arise from joinder, an important area for future research is to investigate ways of removing the bias, perhaps through more effective instructions.

Though experience dictates prudence in generalizing results from mock jury studies to actual cases (Bray & Kerr, 1982; Linz, Slack, Kaiser, & Penrod, 1981; Weiten & Diamond, 1979), the results from these studies do raise questions about the guidelines trial judges should apply when deciding whether offenses should be joined for trial. If judges are to successfully avoid bias to defendants, then an understanding of the process underlying joinder effects is essential.

A question which may have to remain unanswered is the external validity of this or any other mock juror study, since ethical and legal constraints prohibit the conducting of experiments in the courtroom (see, especially, Special issue: Simulation research and the law, *Law and Human Behavior*, 1979). Several general criticisms have been raised which must be considered when assessing the generalizability of simulation results. First, the present study used undergraduate jurors and so was not a representative sample of the actual juror population. However, we have no reason to believe that students differ from other adults in their decision-making processes. Second, the verdicts rendered had no real consequences to the defendant, but we surmise that varied consequences affect the overall probability of conviction and would not interact with the joinder effects. Finally, subjects judged written trial summaries as opposed to being involved in an actual courtroom trial, and the study did not include group deliberation. However, the stimulus materials were carefully patterned after actual courtroom procedures, and research on group polarization effects suggests that deliberation might actually aggravate the joinder effect (see Lamm & Myers, 1978). Despite these limitations, we can still make some tentative suggestions concerning the legal implications of the results.

The present study has demonstrated empirically what the legal system has recognized intuitively: that a defendant can be prejudiced by the joinder of offenses and that confusion, accumulation of evidence, and criminal inference are all involved. The latter two processes were demonstrably related to judgments of guilt. While recognizing the possibility of prejudice resulting from joinder, the law is ambiguous about the circumstances under which prejudice will operate, and traditionally the decision to grant severance is left to the intuition of the court. Further research should be devoted to the task of identifying situations that might aggravate the problem of joinder and judicial actions that might reduce the problems. Further research to establish the causal links between methods of trial presentation, attribution processes, integration of evidence, and judgmental biases is also warranted.

REFERENCES

Anderson, N. H. Information integration theory: A brief survey. In D. H. Krantz, R. C. Atkinson, R. D. Luce, & P. Suppes (Eds.), *Contemporary developments in mathematical psychology*. San Francisco: Freeman, 1974.

Bjork, R. A., & Whitten, W. B. Recency-sensitive retrieval processes in long-term free recall. *Cognitive Psychology*, 1974, **6**, 175–189.

Bray, R. M., & Kerr, N. L. Methodological considerations in the study of the psychology of the courtroom. In N. L. Kerr & R. M. Bray (Eds.), *The psychology of the courtroom*. New York: Academic Press, 1982.

Cohen, J. *Statistical power analysis for the behavioral sciences*. New York: Academic Press, 1977.

Cohen, J., & Cohen, P. *Applied multiple regression-correlation analysis for the behavioral sciences*. Hillsdale, NJ: Erlbaum, 1975.

Davis, J. H. Group decision and social interaction: A theory of social decision schemes. *Psychological Review*, 1973, **80**, 97–125.

Davis, J. H. Group decision and procedural justice. In M. Fishbein (Ed.), *Progress in social psychology* (Vol. 1). Hillsdale, NJ: Erlbaum, 1980.

Davis, J. H., Kerr, N. L., Stasser, G., Meek, D., Holt, R. Victim consequences, sentence severity, and decision processes in mock juries. *Organizational Behavior and Human Performance*, 1977, **18**, 346-365.

Feldman-Summers, S., & Lindner, K. Perceptions of victims and defendants in criminal assault cases. *Criminal Justice and Behavior*, 1976, **3**, 135-150.

Greene, E., & Loftus, E. *When crimes are joined at trial: Institutionalized prejudice?* Paper presented at the convention of the American Psychology-Law Society, Boston, 1981.

Horowitz, I. A., Bordens, K. S., & Feldman, M. S. A comparison of verdicts obtained in severed and joined criminal trials. *Journal of Applied Social Psychology*, 1980, **10**, 444–456.

Kaplan, M., & Kemmerick, G. Juror judgment as information integration: Combining evidential and nonevidential information. *Journal of Personality and Social Psychology*, 1974, **30**, 493–499.

Kelley, H. H. Attribution theory in social psychology. In D. Levine (Ed.), *Nebraska symposium on motivation*. Lincoln: University of Nebraska Press, 1967.

Kelley, H. H. *Causal schemata and the attribution process.* Morristown, NJ: General Learning Press, 1972.

Keppel, G. *Design and analysis: A researcher's handbook* (2nd ed.). Englewood Cliffs, NJ: Prentice-Hall, 1982.

Kerr, N. L., & Sawyers, G. W. Independence of multiple verdicts within a trial by mock jurors. *Representative Research in Social Psychology*, 1979, **10**, 16-27.

Lamm, H., & Myers, D. G. Group-induced polarization of attitudes and behavior. In L. Berkowitz (Ed.), *Advances in experimental social psychology* (Vol. 11). New York: Academic Press, 1978.

Lind, E. A. The psychology of courtroom procedure. In N. L. Kerr & R. M. Bray (Eds.), *The psychology of the courtroom*. New York: Academic Press, 1982.

Linz, D., Slack, A., Kaiser, K., & Penrod, S. *Meta-analysis of defendant characteristic studies.* Paper presented at the convention of the American Psychology-Law Society, Boston, 1981.

Nagao, D. H., & Davis, J. H. The effects of prior experience on mock juror case judgments. *Social Psychology Quarterly*, 1980, **43**, 190-199.

Nisbett, R. E., Borgida, E., Crandall, R., & Reed, H. Popular induction: Information is not necessarily informative. In J. S. Carroll & J. W. Payne (Eds.), *Cognition and social behavior.* Hillsdale, NJ: Erlbaum, 1976.

Ostrom, T. M., Werner, C., & Saks, M. J. An integration theory analysis of jurors' presumptions of guilt or innocence. *Journal of Personality and Social Psychology*, 1978, **36**, 436–450.

Penrod, S., & Hastie, R. Models of jury decision making: A critical review. *Psychological Bulletin*, 1979, **86**, 462–492.

Postman, L., & Underwood, B. J. Critical issues in interference theory. *Memory and Cognition*, 1973, **1**, 19–40.

Rumsey, M. G., & Rumsey, J. M. A case of rape: Sentencing judgments of males and females. *Psychological Reports*, 1977, **41**, 459–465.

Schneider, D. J., Hastorf, A. H., & Ellsworth, P. C. *Person perception* (2nd ed.). Reading, MA: Addison-Wesley, 1979.

Special issue: Simulation research and the law. *Law and Human Behavior*, 1979.

State v. Nance, 197 Neb. 95, 246 N.W. 2d 868 (1976).

Thornton, B. Effect of rape victims' attractiveness in a jury simulation. *Personality and Social Psychology Bulletin*, 1977, **3**, 666–669.

United States v. Foutz. 540 Federal Reporter 2d 733 (4th Cir. 1976).

Weiten, W., & Diamond, S. S. A critical review of the jury simulation paradigm: The case of defendant characteristics. *Law and Human Behavior*, 1979, **3**, 71–93.

RUNAWAY VERDICTS OR REASONED DETERMINATIONS: MOCK JUROR STRATEGIES IN AWARDING DAMAGES*

Jane Goodman†, Edith Greene††, and Elizabeth F. Loftus†††

ABSTRACT

In tort cases, once a liability determination is made, jurors face the difficult task of determining appropriate damages to award the plaintiff. Few instructions or guidelines are provided on how to award damages, and jurors must rely on their common sense and experience to translate the plaintiff's loss and harm into financial compensation. Often, complex economic issues are involved, such as estimating the future stream of income of a young plaintiff. This study examines mock jurors' common sense considerations in awarding damages in a wrongful death case. Jurors from King County, Washington read brief case summaries of a product liability, automobile negligence, or medical malpractice suit, in which the defendant's liability was established. The gender and age of the decedent were systematically varied. Jurors awarded damages and responded to questions about the strategies used and factors considered. Case type had little impact on the magnitude or the process of awarding damages. Male decedents were awarded

---

*This research was supported in part by Grant #SES-8600638 from the National Science Foundation, Law and Social Sciences Division, to Elizabeth F. Loftus. Opinions, findings, conclusions, or recommendations stated in this document are those of the authors and do not necessarily represent the official position or policies of the National Science Foundation. Special thanks are extended to Robert Cannon, Gary Tomlinson, Judy Rutledge, and Nicola Hommel, Administrators of the King County Superior Court in Seattle, Washington, for their cooperation and assistance in facilitating data collection.

†Jane Goodman, J.D., and Ph.D., Postdoctoral Research Associate, University of Washington Psychology Department, Adjunct Professor of Law at the University of Puget Sound, and Associate at the law firm of Frank and Rosen, Seattle, Washington.

††Edith Greene, Ph.D., Assistant Professor of Cognitive and Social Psychology, University of Colorado, Colorado Springs.

†††Elizabeth F. Loftus, Ph.D., Professor of Psychology and Adjunct Professor of Law, University of Washington, Seattle, Washington.

significantly more than similarly situated female decedents. Younger males were awarded significantly more than older males. Jurors were more likely to consider exponential strategies and factors when the decedent was a younger male. Most jurors conservatively multiplied annual earnings by a fixed number of years, often fewer than the decedent's projected age of retirement. Certain strategies and factors used varied in response to the characteristics of the decedent.

I. INTRODUCTION

Robert N. Williams died instantly when he was struck in the head by the mechanical arm of a robotic vehicle designed by Litton Industries.[1] He was survived by three young children and his wife, Sandra Williams, who filed a wrongful death suit against Litton. The case came to trial before a working class jury of six, and lasted eight days. Trial testimony fell into two categories. First, there was evidence concerning Litton's liability. The second category, accorded little emphasis by comparison, concerned the plaintiff's damages and was intended to guide jurors in determining fair compensation to the Williams family. The jury learned Robert Williams' age, his annual salary and educational background. Williams' lawyers called no expert, and suggested no specific factors the jurors should consider in determining an appropriate amount in damages. In closing, the plaintiff's attorney emphasized the loss of Williams to his wife and children, and asked for two million dollars for each of Williams' three children.

The jury deliberated just a few hours before returning a verdict against Litton. Post-deliberation interviews revealed that five jurors found Litton's liability clear; one juror dissented. Apparently, deliberations centered on an appropriate amount to award in damages, with the dissenting juror voting against any monetary award. The others reported that they tried carefully to assess the value of numerous items. They argued that life was expensive; they tried to apportion money for a variety of foreseeable events. For instance, they took into account that the family might have to pay income taxes on the damage award.[2] Other factors which entered into their decision included compensation for (a) the agony of the loss of a loved one; (b) the lifetime potential of income earned by Robert Williams; (c) the cost of college tuition for the children; and (d) funds to cover some future, unknown accident that might prevent Sandra Williams from working. However, the jurors did not consider that the sum awarded to the wife and children might earn interest or have other investment potential. At one point, jurors apparently calculated damages as high as twenty million dollars. This amount was reduced after the dissenting juror joked that they might as well award the Williams family the entire Litton Corporation and let them run it as a family business. Finally, the jury arrived at a total of ten

[1]P. DIPERNA, JURIES ON TRIAL 197-209 (1984). Information in this article concerning the Williams case is taken from DiPerna's summary and observations of that case and its jurors. The Williams case is based on Michigan law.

[2]*See infra* note 12.

million dollars, allocating two million dollars for each of the three surviving children, three million dollars for the surviving wife, and one million for other members of the closely knit Williams family. How can we evaluate their verdict?

Determining Economic Losses in a Wrongful Death Case

In a wrongful death action such as the *Williams* case, in which death was immediate, there can be no claims for decedent's pain and suffering according to Michigan law.[3] Instead, the focus is on special compensatory damages for the lost future income of the decedent. In the state of Washington, the venue for the hypothetical used in our study, the personal representative of the decedent's estate can recover lost wages, assuming the decedent had a normal life expectancy, plus documented medical and funeral expenses, if any.[4] An increasing number of jurisdictions now permit recovery for the lost value of household services provided by the decedent, and for employer contributions to fringe benefits.[5] As in Washington, there may be a separate statutorily created right of the spouse and children of a decedent to recover damages for their own pain and suffering, loss of consortium, and the like.[6] The law, however, generally does not permit speculation about future potential needs of the survivors.[7]

Anecdotal information gathered from interviews of the *Williams* jurors indicated that the primary focus of the jurors' attention in determining damages was the decedent's family and their future needs. These post-trial interviews were not fully informative as to how sums were awarded for pecuniary and non-pecuniary losses. For instance, did the three million dollars awarded to Sandra Williams include consideration of a certain sum for loss of consortium, a certain sum for her own pain and suffering, and a certain sum for lost future income based on her husband's potential wages? There was no indication that the jury attempted any calculations involving the decedent's salary and potential worklife. Interviews of the *Williams* jurors served to highlight a number of interesting but unanswered questions. Would they have increased the award by four million dollars if Williams had five and not three children? In deciding what amount to award to Sandra Williams, did jurors consider that she had to pay attorneys' fees? Did jurors consider whether Litton carried insurance against product liability claims?

Historically, judicial skepticism concerning the competency of the jury led to the doctrine that life expectancy tables and annuity tables should be used with great caution, if at all.[8] For instance, a Pennsylvania court reviewing a wrong-

---

[3]MICH. STAT. ANN. 27A.2922 (1988).

[4]WASH. REV. CODE 4.20.10 and 4.20.20 (1987) (wrongful death statutes).

[5]M. Brookshire, ECONOMIC DAMAGES (1987).

[6]WASH. REV. CODE 4.20.010 (1987).

[7]Brookshire, *supra* note 5.

[8]Broeder, *The Functions of the Jury: Facts or Fictions?*, 21 U. CHI. L. REV. 386-424 (1954).

ful death case noted in 1930: "The less jurors are burdened with complicated tables and the necessity of complex calculations, the more likely will they be to do substantial justice."[9] Court decisions to exclude evidence about lost future income were often motivated in part by judicial fear of "swollen verdicts."[10] Accordingly, jurors who could only speculate about the amount of lost income, would tend to underestimate the amount of damages, denying full recovery to the plaintiff.[11] Simplistic estimates of lost income derived by multiplying annual salary by future worklife may be very inaccurate if the major variables that can affect earning capacity are ignored, such as wage trends, productivity rates, fringe benefits, interest rates, inflation, income taxes, and worklife expectancy factors.[12]

Runaway Verdict or Reasoned Determination?

The *Williams* case was one of a group of approximately 360 cases tried in 1983 in which jury verdicts of one million dollars or more were returned.[13] Escalating jury awards have been cited as a major factor underlying a crisis in the insurance industry, allegedly because jury behavior is too erratic and unpredictable for insurance companies to maintain stability.[14] Whatever the merits of the facts marshalled by proponents or opponents of tort reform, one by-product of the debate has been to shed doubt on the competence of jurors to make a reasoned determination in awarding damages in civil lawsuits.[15] In this contentious atmosphere, judges and lawyers are calling for empirical research to show "what does and does not need fixing."[16] For instance, one commentator notes that "providing rational guidelines for damage awards is an important element" to solve the current litigation crisis.[17] The question of juror compe-

---

[9]Moore v. Leininger, 299 Pa. 380, 385 (1930).

[10]*Id.* at 361.

[11]Broeder, *supra* note 8.

[12]In many jurisdictions, special rules exist concerning allowable wage growth rates and discount rates (the "offset rule"), whether payment of federal and state income taxes on lost income may be considered by jurors; whether the amounts the decedent would have expended on personal consumption must be deducted from the award; whether pre-judgment interest may be added to the award; and whether income from collateral sources must be included in the analysis of lost future income. Legislative and judicial modifications have not been uniform. Accordingly, there are considerable differences among the states concerning permissible elements of recovery, in particular, regarding inflation and discounting, income taxes, deduction of personal consumption, household services, and collateral source income.

[13]Insurance Information Institute, *Crisis in the Courts*, AIDE MAG., Winter, 1986 at 8-12.

[14]P. Parker, *Crisis? What Crisis: Liability Insurance and Tort Reform*. Paper presented at the Law and Society Annual Meeting, June, 1987, Washington, D.C.

[15]M. Galanter, *Jury Shadows: Reflections on the Civil Jury and the "Litigation Explosion,"* The 1986 Chief Justice Earl Warren Conference on Advocacy: The American Civil Jury, Washington, D.C.: The Roscoe Pound Foundation.

[16]Wald, *Litigation in America: Introduction*, 31 U.C.L.A. L. REV. 1-3 (1983).

[17]Civiletti, *Zeroing in on the Real Litigation Crisis: Irrational Justice, Needless Delays, Excessive Costs*, 46 MD. L. REV. 40-48 (1986).

tency with or without expert testimony on damages is ripe for investigation.[18] Surprisingly little empirical evidence exists concerning jury damage awards. Little is known about the way in which jurors approach the task of allocating money to redress the injuries—physical, monetary, or psychological—of a prevailing plaintiff. One issue of interest in assessing juror competency is evaluation of the strategies jurors employ when awarding damages. Are similar strategies used in similar cases? Do jurors adjust the way in which they approach the task of awarding damages in response to the characteristics of the parties?

Prior Research on Jury Damage Awards

Prior investigations of jury decision-making in civil cases have generally addressed the liability phase of the lawsuit, rarely inquiring into damage awards. Some information on jury damage awards has come from post-verdict interviews in actual cases. One post-verdict interview case study concerned an antitrust suit that was tried twice;[19] thus, comparisons could be made of the two different juries' responses to the damages testimony presented by an expert witness, an economist. Overall, evidence about the calculation of damages was either ignored or forgotten by the jurors, and jurors were reportedly ill-prepared to assume the task of allocating damages. One jury fared far better than the other in terms of understanding the evidence. Information from another post-verdict interview study showed jurors used a more precise strategy to award damages in an asbestos trial. Jurors told interviewers they determined each component of damages separately, and then summed the components to derive a final amount.[20]

In the handful of empirical studies which have examined jurors' damage awards, the focus has generally been the relative magnitude of the award. Little is known about the strategies or cognitive processes used by jurors in determining damages. A few researchers have examined the influence of juror demographics, such as gender, on damage awards. For instance, Nagel and Weitzman analyzed data collected by the Jury Verdict Research Corporation of Cleveland, Ohio, from actual personal injury cases, to assess whether jurors favor plaintiffs of their own gender in determining liability and awarding damages.[21] While juror gender made no significant difference with regard to liability, male dominated juries gave more to male plaintiffs and less to female plaintiffs; female dominated juries favored women to a lesser extent than male dominated juries favored men.[22] One limitation of such archival research is the

[18]Lempert, *Civil Juries and Complex Cases: Let's Not Rush to Judgment*, 80 MICH. L. REV. 68-131 (1981); E. Greene, J. Schooler, & E. Loftus, *Expert Psychological Testimony*, in THE PSYCHOLOGY OF EVIDENCE AND TRIAL PROCEDURE 201-52 (S. Kassin & L. Wrightsman, eds. 1984).

[19]D. AUSTIN, COMPLEX LITIGATION CONFRONTS THE JURY SYSTEM: A CASE STUDY (1984).

[20]M. SELVIN & L. PICUS, THE DEBATE OVER JURY PERFORMANCE: OBSERVATIONS FROM A RECENT ASBESTOSIS CASE (1987).

[21]Nagel & Weitzman, *Sex and the Unbiased Jury*, 56(3) JUDICATURE 108-11 (1972).

[22]*Id.*

lack of controls over the strength of the evidence or type of injury. For instance, injuries to male plaintiffs were notably more serious than those to females. The researchers also hypothesized that the differential earning power of males and females might account for the results, without specifying whether this factor would cause female jurors to award lower damages in general, or would produce lower awards for lost income to female plaintiffs by both male and female jurors. The study provided no information about processes in determining damages for male versus female plaintiffs.

In studying deliberations of actual jurors, one researcher noted that a variety of topics were raised about which jurors had received no previous instructions.[23] This led him to wonder whether jurors often consider factors which are not part of the formal evidence before them, factors such as taxes to be paid, attorneys' fees, inflation, the investment potential of the award, whether the defendant was insured, what the defendant could afford to pay in damages, and so forth.[24] Analysis of Rand Corporation data and a nationwide sample of automobile insurance claims supported the notion that jurors may deviate from the standards of black letter law by responding to factors the substantive law regards as irrelevant, such as what the defendant can afford to pay.[25] It was also observed that different juries used many different strategies to determine the amount to award in damages.[26] For instance, one jury estimated the costs of the prevailing plaintiff's attorney fees, then multiplied by ten to derive the final damage award.[27] Little is known about factors which may lead jurors to employ one strategy over another.

Psychological Theories Which Bear on Jury Decisions About Damage Awards

One area of psychological inquiry which bears on the issue of jury damage awards is research on people's abilities to deal with exponential growth problems. Work by Wagenaar and Sagaria investigated how subjects perceive exponential growth, represented by numbers and graphs, when asked to make

[23]Kalven Jr., *The Dignity of the Civil Jury*, 50 VA. L. REV. 1055-75 (1964).

[24]Compensatory damages are intended to provide the plaintiff with the financial equivalent of the loss or harm suffered, and to restore the plaintiff to the position occupied before the tort. *See* W. PROSSER, J. WADE & V. SCHWARTZ, CASES AND MATERIALS ON TORTS 537 (1982). Awards for personal injuries are not subject to federal income tax, but generally, jurors are not informed of this fact. *Id.* at 551. Nor are jurors informed about contingent fee arrangements to pay the lawyers who represent the plaintiffs in personal injury lawsuits. *Id.* at 552-53. In most jurisdictions, juries are instructed to reduce lost future earnings to "present value." *Id.* at 543. While some courts permit juries to consider the impact of inflation on future damages, others regard this evidence as too speculative. *Id.* Damages for future pain and suffering are rarely reduced to present value.

[25]Hammitt, Carroll & Relles, *Tort Standards and Jury Decisions*, 14 J. LEGAL STUD. 751-62 (1985).

[26]Kalven, *supra* note 23.

[27]*Id.*

intuitive as opposed to arithmetic estimates of future growth processes.[28] Without arithmetic rules, two-thirds of the subjects produced estimates at or below 10% of the value prescribed by exponential extrapolation, 90% estimated below half of the normative value.[29] Interestingly, the absolute magnitude of the numbers used in the series did not determine the degree of underestimation of exponential growth.[30] Moreover, subjects who had more experience with growth problems were just as likely to underestimate the exponential growth as were subjects who had no daily experience working with such problems.[31] Follow-up studies by Timmers, Wagenaar, and Keren confirmed that people grossly underestimate the impact of exponential growth functions when making computations about everyday matters, such as estimates of the price of a loaf of bread, given a certain inflation rate.[32]

These research findings left us wondering whether jurors typically consider the influence of exponential factors, such as inflation or investments, when awarding damages. Would the exponential growth bias demonstrated in the laboratory generalize to legal settings? We hypothesized that without special instruction, jurors would tend to use a more linear approach in calculating damages. If so, their bias would favor the defendant.

II. METHOD

Overview of the Research

To investigate strategies that mock jurors adopt when awarding damages in a civil case, we used a between-subjects jury simulation design. Mock jurors were asked what monetary damages to award a plaintiff, assuming the defendant was liable. Wrongful death cases were selected for study to obviate the possibility that mock jurors' damage awards would include sums for non-pecuniary damages, such as pain or suffering of the plaintiff, which might be difficult to distinguish from other sums.[33]

A major question addressed in the experiment was whether jurors are affected by factors which, based on the law alone, should not influence decisions about damages. Two types of ostensibly irrelevant information were selected for study:

---

[28]Wagenaar & Sagaria, *Misperception of Exponential Growth*, 18(6) PERCEPTION & PSYCHOPHYSICS 416-22 (1975).

[29]*Id.*

[30]*Id.*

[31]*Id.*

[32]Timmers & Wagenaar, *Inverse Statistics and Misperception of Exponential Growth*, 21 PERCEPTION & PSYCHOPHYSICS 558-62 (1977); Wagenaar & Timmers, *Extrapolation of Exponential Time Series is Not Enhanced by Having More Data Points*, 24(2) PERCEPTION & PSYCHOPHYSICS 182-84 (1978); Keren, *Cultural Differences in the Misperception of Exponential Growth*, 34(3) PERCEPTION & PSYCHOPHYSICS 289-93 (1983).

[33]In addition to wrongful death cases, other civil causes of action which typically involve similar damage claims are employment discrimination, personal injury, antitrust, and some contract and tort cases.

(a) the identity of the decedent; and (b) facts leading to the liability of the defendant. The latter factor was included to determine whether the strategies that mock jurors adopt and the factors they consider generalize across different case types.

A second major question was the extent to which mock jurors take economic factors into account. Do jurors spontaneously consider inflation rates, the potential of a decendent for higher earnings in the future, or the investment potential of a jury award? Our hypothesis, based on the findings of Timmers, Wagenaar, and Keren,[34] was that jurors would ignore or substantially undervalue factors, such as inflation or periodic increases in income, that contribute to an exponential growth function in determining compensatory damages, thereby establishing a judgmental bias lower than the damages due. We hypothesized that jurors—if they attempted any calculations at all—would use linear measures in computing damages. That is, they might simply multiply the decedent's expected worklife by annual earnings. In the case of an older decendent who had few remaining years of worklife, jurors might be more inclined to attempt an exponential growth calculation, as the numbers would not be so unwieldy and the task less onerous than it is to make analogous computations over a thirty-five year or forty year period, as would be required in the case of a younger decedent.

Materials

Experimental materials consisted of consent forms, instructions, a case synopsis, and a written questionnaire. Mock jurors read a brief synopsis of facts leading to the wrongful death of the plaintiff's decedent. In all versions, the decedent was described as married, self-employed, and earning $25,000 annually at the time of the fatal accident. Subjects were informed that liability had been determined in favor of the plaintiff,[35] and that their task was to determine an appropriate sum to award in damages.[36] The base condition was a product liability case in which a thirty year old male has a fatal accident when the accelerator pedal of his car malfunctions:

[34]*See* sources cited *supra* note 32.

[35]Standards for liability vary from one court to another. The three major liability rules are negligence with contributory negligence, negligence with comparative negligence, and strict liability. W. HIRSCH, LAW AND ECONOMICS 181 (1988). In 32 states, some form of comparative negligence applies. *Id.* at 185. However, as many as eight possible liability rules were distinguished by Brown, *Toward an Economic Theory of Liability*, 2 J. LEGAL STUD. 323-49 (1973): no liability, strict liability, negligence, strict liability with contributory negligence, negligence with contributory negligence, strict liability with dual contributory negligence, relative negligence, and comparative negligence.

[36]No explicit jury instructions on how to determine an appropriate amount in damages were provided as the goal of this study was to explore considerations which jurors bring to the task. In actual trials, the guidance jurors receive in awarding damages varies. In some jurisdictions, the law prohibits attorneys from suggesting an amount to the jury. Typically, jurors receive little help from the judge. Kalven, *The Jury, the Law, and the Personal Injury Award*, 19 OHIO ST. L. J. 158-78 (1958). Essentially, they are instructed to make the plaintiff "whole." J. Guinther, THE JURY IN AMERICA 96 (1988).

> Kevin Klemmer, a self-employed thirty year old, was driving his newly purchased Ford Escort[37] on an L.A. freeway at four a.m. the morning of December 31, 1983, when he swerved into an embankment and crashed into a fence about sixty-five feet from the roadway. Kevin suffered severe head injuries and died at the scene. A wrongful death suit was brought by his wife, Karen Klemmer, against the Ford Motor Corporation. The California Highway Patrol investigating the accident reached the following conclusion about what must have happened. Just prior to the accident, the car had been going slightly uphill, requiring acceleration. At the crest of the hill, the accelerator failed to return to its normal position due to a broken spring. Upon further investigation, Ford admitted that indeed there had been a design flaw in the acceleration system. Therefore, the defendant's liability has been established and the issue before the jury is to determine what dollar amount to award Kevin Klemmer's estate to compensate for his death. His 1983 income at the time of the accident was $25,000. He is survived by his wife, Karen Klemmer, who is the sole beneficiary of his estate.

This condition was compared with two conditions in which different circumstances led to the wrongful death: (1) a negligence case in which a fatal automobile accident is caused by a driver who failed to stop for a pedestrian; and (2) a medical malpractice case, in which a fatal accident occurs when a patient is injected with a substance to which he or she is known to be allergic. These three conditions formed a 2 x 3 factorial design in which the first factor was gender of the decedent (male or female), and the second factor was case type (product liability, negligent driving, medical malpractice).

The "base" condition involving the thirty year old male in the product liability case was compared with two additional conditions. First, to assess whether jurors were more likely to take exponential factors into account when the lost future income involved fewer years, and calculations were therefore more straightforward, the age of the male decedent in the product liability scenario was varied, so that the decedent had either five to ten future work years at the time of the accident, or thirty-five to forty future work years (decedent age sixty versus age thirty). A final comparison was designed to test the application of "norm theory," which predicts that compensation increases in cases in which the victim is injured as the result of actions which vary from normal, typical conduct.[38] This manipulation was introduced by varying the typicality of the behavior leading to the wrongful death in the product liability scenario. Instead of driving his own car, in one version the thirty year old male borrows a friend's car in which the fatal accident occurs when the accelerator pedal malfunctions.

---

[37]No adverse inferences, real or imagined, concerning any parties named in this research scenario, are intended. The case of Klemmer v. Ford is entirely fictional.

[38]Miller & McFarland, *Counterfactual Thinking and Victim Compensation: A Test of Norm Theory*, 12 PERSONALITY & SOC. PSYCHOLOGY BULL. 513-19 (1986).

Procedures

Following roll call in the jury room at the King County Courthouse in Seattle, Washington, jurors were invited by the jury administrator to participate in a study requiring approximately thirty minutes of their time. Volunteers were handed written trial summaries and questionnaires and were instructed to work independently. No time limit was prescribed. Participants were assigned to one of the eight experimental conditions described below on a random basis.

Subjects awarded damages, and responded to open-ended questions by writing a brief explanation of how they decided what amount to award. To further assess strategies jurors used in computing damages, a checklist of possible strategies was provided. Subjects checked those they employed. If none applied, they specified the strategy they used. We asked subjects to indicate whether they (a) used a calculator; (b) performed mental arithmetic; (c) made pencil and paper calculations; (d) made no precise calculations; (e) multiplied expected earnings by expected worklife; (f) without calculation, picked an amount that seemed just and fair; (g) started with one amount, then increased it because it seemed too low; (h) started with one amount, then decreased it because it seemed too high; (i) based the decision on other cases they knew of; or (j) used none of these strategies. Finally, subjects reviewed a list of seventeen substantive factors which might have entered into their mental deliberations, and were asked to check those factors which they had considered. The listed factors included items such as the age of the decedent, the decedent's salary and expected worklife, what the defendant could afford to pay, the investment potential of the award, inflation, attorney's fees, and taxes on the damage award. Subjects ranked the three most important factors.

Subjects were 202 potential or experienced jurors on call at the King County Superior Court in Seattle, Washington during September and October, 1986. Basic demographic information was gathered from the 202 subjects who participated in this experiment. The study sample included more females (62%) than males (38%). The marital status of the jurors surveyed broke down as follows: 15% single, 63% married, 4% remarried, 2% separated, 11% divorced, and 5% widowed. The mean age of the mock jurors was 47 years, with approximately 10% of the group under age 28, and 10% of the group over age 65. Approximately 36% had completed a university degree, and an equal number had completed some college courses. Many jurors had some prior exposure to the judicial system. About 30% of the jurors surveyed had served on a trial before at some time, evenly divided between civil and criminal cases. Approximately 26% of the jurors reported that either they or a close friend or member of the family had been personally involved in litigation before. Fourteen per cent of the jurors in the sample had been plaintiffs before in a lawsuit; 10% had been defendants.

III. RESULTS

Overview of Damage Awards

Damages were awarded by 191 of the 202 mock jurors. The median award was $399,975; the mode was $250,000. Awards ranged from a low of $1000 to a high of $10 million, with one award of $1 billion. To facilitate meaningful analysis, variance attributable to either unusually low or extremely high individual awards was reduced by trimming the lowest 5% (amounts less than $25,000) and the highest 5% (amounts exceeding $2 million) of the awards from the data. Data analysis was performed on the remaining 90% of the responses, from 67 males and 101 females, plus 17 mock jurors who did not reveal their gender (N = 185). First, we report data from the six conditions comprising the 2 x 3 factorial study to examine the influence of case type and gender of the decedent (N = 125). Then, we report data derived from the two comparisons with the basic "male product liability" condition, in which the influence of the age of the decedent and atypical behavior are examined. Finally, we report results of analyses of strategies used by mock jurors and factors considered in awarding damages.

Influence of Case Type

To determine whether mock jurors were influenced in the amount they awarded by the facts underlying the liability of the defendant, we compared awards in the three types of cases: product liability, automobile negligence, and medical malpractice. The grand mean was $624,502; the median award was $410,000. Damage awards were somewhat higher in the product liability and automobile negligence cases than in the medical malpractice case, but not statistically so. (See Table 1.) A one-way analysis of variance revealed no main effect of case type, ($F(2,122) = 1.9$; MSe = .32; $p > .10$).

TABLE 1
Damage Awards by Case Type (Dollars)

	Product Liability	Automobile Negligence	Medical Malpractice	Grand Mean
Mean	709,900	639,438	522,857	624,502
Median	500,031	506,250	251,250	410,000
N	43	40	42	125

Influence of Gender of the Decedent

When the decedent was male, the overall mean award was $788,337; when the decedent was female, the award was 58% of that amount. (See Table 2.) Awards by case type for male versus female decedents are displayed in Table 3. Across all cases types, male decedents were awarded more than female decedents. Statistical confirmation of the impact of decedent gender came from

TABLE 2
Damage Awards by Gender of Decedent (Dollars)

	Male Decedent	Female Decedent	Combined
Mean	788,337	458,024	624,502
Median	750,036	451,607	410,000
N	63	62	125

t-tests comparing awards when the decedent was male to those when the decedent was female within each case type. In two of the three fact patterns, contrast tests revealed statistically significant differences, with higher awards to male decedents—namely, product liability case: $t(41) = 2.15; p<.05$; automobile negligence case: $t(38) = 2.48; p<.02$. In the medical malpractice case, the male decedent received more money, but the difference in awards to male and female decedents did not achieve statistical significance: $t(41) = 1.5; p>.1$.

Table 3 further reveals that the pattern of larger awards in the case of male decedents was true of both male and female jurors. In other words, we found no evidence that the mock jurors favored decedents, or surviving spouses, of their own gender. Statistical confirmation was derived from a two by two (gender of decedent by gender of juror) analysis of variance, revealing a main effect of decedent gender, ($F(3,112) = 16.2$; MSe $= .45; p < .001$), but no other statistically significant effects.

TABLE 3
Mean Awards for Male and Female Decedents by Case Type and Gender of Mock Juror (Dollars)*

Gender of Mock Juror	*Gender of Decedent* Male	Female	Combined Mean
Product Liability Case			
Male	894,444	481,250	700,000
Female	985,455	521,520	743,261
total (n = 40)	944,500	505,250	724,875
Automobile Negligence Case			
Male	827,000	625,000	692,958
Female	843,636	333,750	600,833
total (n = 36)	838,436	479,375	638,958
Medical Malpractice Case			
Male	591,364	191,967	450,294
Female	706,818	225,455	466,136
total (n = 36)	649,091	213,529	459,230
All Case Types			
Male	747,600	468,750	611,020
Female	845,303	365,833	605,568
Total (n = 112)	803,190	409,167	607,891
N	58	57	115

*Data from ten jurors who did not disclose their gender were excluded from this analysis.

Influence of Age of Decedent

The base scenario presented to one group of mock jurors described information about a product liability case in which the decedent was a male, aged thirty. Another group of mock jurors received the identical case synopsis except for the fact that the male decedent was twice as old, aged sixty years. Mock jurors awarded significantly less money to the older decedent. The mean award was $366,717 when the decedent was sixty years of age (n = 26), but was $905,466 when the decedent was thirty years of age (n = 22). (These are trimmed means.) A t test was statistically significant, $t(46) = 3.3; p < .01$.

At first glance, it may seem reasonable to award more money when a young man dies than when an older man dies. After all, younger men can look forward to a longer productive life than can older men. On the average, the stream of income to a younger man might amount to three to ten times more than that of an older man. But, looked at another way, this may be less reasonable. A higher award to a male decedent implies that more money is received by a female surviving spouse. A younger female spouse presumably has more opportunities to attain financial security than are available to an older female spouse.

Influence of Atypical Behavior

The base scenario involving a product liability case in which the decedent aged thirty years was driving his own car was compared to a similar synopsis, factually different only in that the decedent was driving a friend's car rather than his own car at the time of the fatal accident. We refer to the friend's car condition as the exceptional or "atypical" condition. From norm theory,[39] we predicted that damage awards would be higher in the atypical condition. The mean damage award when the male decedent was driving his own car was $905,466 (n = 22), not statistically different from the mean damage award of $788,542 (n = 24) in the case of the atypical behavior, $t(39) = 0.6; p > .1$.

Strategies in Awarding Monetary Damages

A major purpose of this research project was to examine the strategies and factors people use in determining monetary damages. To accomplish this, mock jurors described in their own words how they arrived at their award. First, all longhand responses were examined to determine the types of statements made by jurors. A listing of all factors considered was compiled. Then, items on the list were grouped into five broad classes or categories: (1) picked a fair and reasonable number without computation; (2) linear multiplication of work-life by annual salary; (3) multiplication, then adjustment upward to in-

[39]Kahneman & Miller, *Norm Theory: Comparing Reality to its Alternatives*, 93(2) PSYCHOLOGICAL REV. 136-53 (1986).

TABLE 4
Jurors Strategies in Awarding Damages as Determined by Judges (Percentages)

	Experimental Condition		
Strategy	Male Decedent age thirty	Female Decedent age thirty	Male Decedent age sixty
picked a reasonable amount	26	30	23
worklife x salary	28	47^{d}	27^{d}
multiply then increase	18	15	27
multiply then decrease	3	3	0
exponential	25^{a}	5^{a}_{b}	23_{b}
N	63	62	26

Note: Pairs of superscripts and subscripts denote statistically significant differences as follows: a indicates $p < .001$, b indicates $p < .01$, c indicates $p < .05$ (two-tailed test of significance), d indicates $p < .05$ (one-tailed test of significance). (For example, reading the "exponential" line under the "strategy" column, 25 is compared to 5, resulting in a statistical difference of a, then 5 is compared to 23, resulting in a statistical difference of b).

crease the total; (4) multiplication, then adjustment downward to decrease the total; (5) computation including some exponential growth factor. A few uncodable responses were excluded from the percentages reported in each category in Table 4. A team of three raters coded the responses independently, resolving any disparities by discussion.

The most common strategy was to multiply the decedent's annual salary by an expected worklife of some period. In the case of a decedent aged thirty years, earning $25,000 per year, simple multiplication of the annual salary by the expected worklife to age sixty-five yields an award of $875,000 in lost future income. In the case of a decedent aged sixty years, this strategy yields an award of $125,000 in lost future income. However, very few jurors awarded damages on the assumption that the decedent would continue working until age sixty-five. Often, the worklife-times-annual salary multiplication strategy was used as a starting point, and then adjustments were made to the product. More than a quarter of the responses showed no evidence of calculation. Only a very modest number of the jurors took into account factors which would lead to an exponential growth in income, such as inflation or future salary increases. Sample responses within the five coded categories are listed below. Then we discuss the influence of characteristics of the decedent on the strategies used to award damages.

Approximately 27% of the mock jurors arrived at a damage award without engaging in any calculations, but by "picking a fair number." Examples included:

- Each person that dies in an accident has a different value. Karen Klemmer made $25,000 in 1983. She was only thirty years old and had many productive years ahead of her. Maybe $20,000 would be sufficient.

- Seems to be a reasonable amount, his wife will probably remarry or find suitable employment, and this amount should carry her through her adjustment period. If there were children my decision would have been for more money.
- I feel this is a fair sum to both parties due to the apparent guilt and negligence of the Ford Company. While the dollar sum will not replace the loss of a human being, husband, and loved one, it will give the deceased's wife a sufficient amount for security, and a new beginning.
- A random number, it's tough to put a price for someone's life.

Approximately 31% of the mock jurors multiplied the decedent's salary by an expected future worklife, though not all subjects assumed the same number of future working years. For instance, several mock jurors opted for ten years future worklife, stating that the goal was to provide just enough funds to stabilize the surviving spouse, but not to award a full lifetime of lost future wages based on the stream of income the decedent would have earned but for the fatal accident. Examples of the simple linear multiplication strategy included:

- The victim dies at age thirty through no apparent fault of his own. Thirty years income would place him at sixty years—a more than likely age for him to live and produce. 30 x 25 is 750.
- Although difficult to determine fault with the limited evidence given us, this would be approximately twenty years of her present salary, which would take her to age fifty.
- Mr. Klemmer at sixty years of age would most probably work if he had lived for another five years, so his wife should be granted the above amount ($125,000).
- Took average life expectancy of seventy-eight times yearly income.

A third category was comprised of approximately 22% of the responses in which damages were determined by engaging in some salary times worklife calculations, and then adding a sum to the total to increase the final award. Examples included:

- Monies the man would have earned at $25,000 per year for five years plus Social Security at his rate to a male's life expectancy (roughly ten years after sixty-five).
- Five years of income, assuming that Klemmer would have worked until age sixty-five, for $100,000. An additional $50,000 for legal fees, emotional duress, inflation, *etc.* I think it is irrelevant that the Ford Company could afford to pay much more. It seems wrong to me to "go after" a big company—it doesn't bring the deceased back to life.

The fourth distinct strategy was exhibited by a small group of responses—about 4%—in which some preliminary calculations were made, and the product was reduced to come up with a final award. For instance, some jurors regarded the worklife times annual income method as excessive. Responses included:

- He had approximately thirty more years of employment. $25,000 present income times thirty years = $750,000. I gave him one third of that amount.

- Had she worked only twenty more years she would have earned the amount. His working years are actually about thirty-five more. Since she has no children I reduced the amount.
- I figured thirty-five years of future wage earning minus about 25% consumption of earnings by late husband. Additional amount was added for medical costs.
- Liability is established. Kevin is thirty. Assume another thirty years working. Annual salary is 25,000 x 30 = 750,000. This seems an excessive amount unless malice was indicated—apparently this was just an accident. I would divide by three.

A fifth strategy used by approximately 15% of the mock jurors involved multiplying the decedent's annual salary by future worklife and specifically increasing the sum because of factors which produce an exponential function. Awards in this group tended to be higher than those in the other three groups. Examples included:

- Kevin was only thirty years old. He had approximately thirty-five—forty years of work years and income earning years ahead of him. Taking into account a gradual increase in salary plus inflation and thirty-five years of work time plus savings and investments on part of this capital, the amount would approximate $1.5–2 million dollars.
- Age at time of wrongful death deducted from remaining life expectancy (75-60) times annual income 25,000 factored for inflation over fifteen years plus replacement car, plus legal and funeral costs = $1,145,000.
- $25,000 x 5 years = retirement age. I allowed .03 annual inflation rate. Not knowing the wife's age I assumed it to also be sixty. I estimated her life expectancy at eighty, so figured 1/2 of her husband's annual salary, plus estimated annual inflation rate. These two amounts were added together.
- He died at thirty, average working age is sixty-five, which left him thirty-five years he could have earned a living. Thirty-five times his yearly income of $25,000 = $575,000—times two to cover projected increased income and inflation.

Certain strategies were more likely than others to be elicited in response to variations in the gender and age of the decedent. Subjects were more inclined to "pick a fair number" when the decedent was a female. The damage award was more frequently adjusted upwards after a preliminary calculation was performed when the decedent was an older male (29% versus 17%), and was never adjusted downwards in this condition. Exponential factors were considered both in the case of the younger and the older male decedent. Mock jurors were dramatically less likely to consider exponential factors such as salary increases, inflation, investment potential of damage award, or the like when the decedent was a female. Interestingly, mock jurors for the sixty year old male decedent were less likely to adopt an exponential growth strategy than jurors for the thirty year old male decedent.

Subjects reviewed a list of ten possible strategies to determine damages, and indicated whether they used any of them in reaching their decision. More than one item could be checked from the following list: (a) performed some mental arithmetic; (b) used a calculator; (c) made some pencil and paper calculations; (d) made no precise calculations; (e) multiplied expected earnings by expected worklife; (f) without calculations, picked an amount that seemed just and fair; (g) based my decision on awards in other cases I know of; (h) started with one amount, then increased it because it seemed too low; (i) started with one amount, then decreased it because it seemed too high; (j) none of these strategies really fits what I did. (Subjects who used other strategies than those listed were asked to describe them. Few used such strategies.)

Very few subjects resorted to use of a calculator (1%). Approximately one third of the subjects stated they used a pencil and paper to make some calculations. The remainder of the group relied on mental arithmetic, or less precise estimates to reach a conclusion. Overall, approximately 14% of the subjects indicated that they simply picked a fair number; 55% multiplied worklife by annual income; 20% multiplied worklife by salary and then increased the total; and 12% made some calculations and then decreased the amount to reach a final award. Results by gender and age of decedent are presented in Table 5. Subjects reported multiplying worklife by income most often in the case of the older decedent, when there were fewer years left to work. Subjects more frequently reported decreasing the award derived by multiplication when the decedent was a female.

Factors Considered in Determining Damages

Mock jurors reviewed a list of seventeen factors (for example, decedent's age, inflation) which might have entered into their deliberations, and checked those that they considered. Table 6 reports the percentage of subjects in each of three conditions who claimed to have considered each factor. Overall, the decedent's annual salary and age were the most frequently cited factors. Certain factors featured less prominently when the decedent was a female versus a young male or older male. For instance, when the decedent was a female only 16% of mock jurors took into consideration what decedent's spouse would need to live on. However, when the decedent was a male, over half of the jurors took this factor into consideration. When the decedent was a female, mock jurors were less likely to consider economic factors such as inflation or investment potential of an award. Moreover, it was less likely that they would consider the financial loss of the surviving male spouse. Nor were mock jurors as likely to consider the expected worklife of the female decedent in determining damages.

Comparisons between the older male and younger male decedent conditions revealed that when the decedent was older, mock jurors were less likely to consider that the spouse might remarry, or to consider lost raises or promotions of the decedent. One limitation with the indirect process measures used in this study is how to interpret the fact that subjects simply checked the factors that they claim to have considered. Some subjects may have checked factors that

TABLE 5
Jurors' Self-Reported Strategies in Awarding Damages (Percentages)

	Experimental Condition		
Strategy	Male Decedent	Female Decedent	Older Decedent
performed some mental arithmetic	62	74	77
used a calculator	2	0	0
made some pencil and paper calculations	41^{b}	20^{b}	31
made no precise calculations	3^{b}	15^{b}_{b}	19_{b}
multiplied expected earnings by expected worklife	57	44^{b}	73^{b}
without calculations, picked an amount that seemed just and fair	21	20	12
based my decision on awards in other cases I know of	2	2	0
started with one amount then increased it because it seemed too low	16	23	19
started with one amount then decreased it because it seemed too high	6^{d}	15^{d}	8
none of these strategies really fits what I did	7	2	4

Note: Pairs of superscripts and subscripts denote statistically significant differences as follows: a indicates $p < .001$, b indicates $p < .01$, c indicates $p < .05$ (two-tailed test of significance), d indicates $p < .05$ (one-tailed test of significance).

were not actually considered, but which subjects may regard as socially desirable responses, prompted by the questions. This is invariably a problem with a checklist approach. Thus, to obtain some idea of factors subjects spontaneously mention, we coded the open-ended responses for the mention of specific factors. These results are reported in Table 7.

Spontaneous mention was made most frequently of the decedent's annual salary and age. Certain factors featured more prominently in the decision when the decedent was female than male, or when the decedent was an older male. For instance, when the surviving spouse was a young female, 23% of the jurors awarded money to provide the spouse with income during an "adjustment" period and 11% of the jurors awarded money to rehabilitate the spouse. No funds were spontaneously designated for this purpose when the surviving

TABLE 6
Factors Checked by Mock Jurors (Percentages)

Factor	Male Decedent	Female Decedent	Older Decedent
decedent's age at the time of the accident	81	75^{d}	92^{d}
decedent's salary at the time of the accident	94	87	92
how many years decedent might have continued working	70	58^{b}	85^{b}
future raises and promotions decedent might have received had he continued working	40^{b}_{b}	20^{b}	8_{b}
the likelihood that decedent might have changed careers	5	7	0
loss of companionship to decedent's spouse	57	57	50
emotional loss to decedent's spouse	57	59	46
financial loss to decedent's spouse	75^{c}	57^{c}	89
whether the defendant could afford a large amount	5	10	8
what decedent's spouse would need to live on	54^{a}	16^{a}_{a}	62_{a}
that decedent and spouse had no children	43^{d}	38	23^{d}
that decedent's spouse might remarry one day	33^{b}	30_{c}	8^{b}_{c}
the impact of inflation on decedent's annual salary had he continued working	38^{b}	15^{b}	23
the value of the amount in the future if invested now	25^{d}	12^{d}_{c}	31_{c}
that attorney's fees must be paid for bringing the lawsuit	18	15	27
taxes to be paid on the amount awarded in damages	14	8	15
other thoughts not listed above which entered your mind, if any	3	8	11

Note: Pairs of superscripts and subscripts denote statistically significant differences as follows: a indicates $p < .001$, b indicates $p < .01$, c indicates $p < .05$ (two-tailed test of significance), d indicates $p < .05$ (one-tailed test of significance).

TABLE 7
Judges' Coding of Factors in Open-Ended Responses (Percentages)

	Experimental Condition		
Factors	Male Decedent	Female Decedent	Older Decedent
attorneys fees	3	8	8
inflation	18^{b}	3^{b}	4
salary increases	23^{b}_{b}	7^{b}	0_{b}
future stream of income	48	43	50
spouse's loss of companionship	32^{d}	30	15^{d}
actual funeral costs	8	5	8
insurance coverage	3	2	4
rehabilitate spouse	11^{b}_{d}	0^{b}	0_{d}
tide over adjustment period (minimum compensation)	23^{b}	13_{d}	0^{b}_{d}
investment growth	5	3	4
dependents, no children	8	13^{d}	0^{d}
retirement needs	2^{b}	0	20^{b}
refer to other cases	0	3	4

Note: Pairs of superscripts and subscripts denote statistically significant differences as follows: a indicates $p < .001$, b indicates $p < .01$, c indicates $p < .05$ (two-tailed test of significance), d indicates $p < .05$ (one-tailed test of significance).

spouse was a young male or an older female. Loss of companionship was more prevalent in deliberations over a younger decedent than an older male decedent. Discussions of expected increases in the future income of the decedent through promotions or cost-of-living increases were considerably more frequent when the decedent was a young male.

Analysis of factors spontaneously mentioned similarly revealed the influence of the characteristics of the decedent. When the decedent was female, mock jurors were less likely to consider factors contributing to an exponential growth in the amount of money awarded in damages. Inflation and cost of living increases came to mind in the case of a male decedent, irrespective of the male's age. Several mock jurors mentioned retirement needs in awarding damages, particularly in the case of the older male decedent. Insurance coverage was mentioned by a small percentage of jurors in all conditions.

IV. DISCUSSION

Several major findings emerged. Mock jurors arrived at a damage award by picking a reasonable number, without computation, about one quarter of the time. The rest of the time they attempted some semblance of calculation. Simple linear multiplication of worklife by salary was a common strategy, although few jurors assumed the decedent would have continued working until normal retirement age of sixty-five years. Consideration of exponential growth in computing damages was rare. The amount of money mock jurors awarded in damages and the factors considered in reaching a decision fluctuated in response to the characteristics of the decedent or the characteristics of the surviving spouse.

Consider the situation that arose when the decedent was a young male versus a young female. With a young male, mock jurors were more likely to use an exponential growth strategy, and factors such as the number of years of the decedent's future worklife, future raises and promotions, the impact of inflation on the decedent's salary, and so forth. When the surviving spouse was female, mock jurors gave considerably more weight to factors such as her financial losses and needs than they did when the survivor was male.

The finding that damage awards are higher when the decedent is a male raises the question as to whether mock jurors perceive that a woman's life is worth less than a man's, or whether they award more because of the greater perceived needs of a surviving female spouse. One way to resolve this dilemma would be to assess whether jurors consider the financial needs of the surviving spouse. For example, do they tend to allocate funds to rehabilitate a surviving female spouse, but not a surviving male spouse? If so, this may explain the differential emphasis on the surviving spouse depending on whether the decedent is male or female. The foregoing data are consistent with this idea.

The characteristics of the decedent affected the strategies used and factors considered in awarding damages to a younger versus an older male. In some ways, it may seem more reasonable to award less to the older male with perhaps five more years before retirement, than to his younger counterpart with a future worklife of thirty-five years. On the other hand, there are reasons one may want to give more money to the surviving spouse of a sixty year old decedent than to the spouse of a thirty year old decedent. After all, the surviving spouse of a thirty year old has a statistically greater likelihood of remarriage, developing a new career, and other options not as available to a women in her sixties. A women aged approximately sixty years might conceivably live another twenty or thirty years without the benefit of remarriage, a new source of financial and emotional support, or companionship. A more rosy future might exist for a younger woman in terms of the probabilities of remarriage or career development. This line of reasoning was not engaged in by our subjects. Ironically, factors prominent when awarding damages to an older male did not include speculations on the likelihood of remarriage by the surviving spouse, nor on future raises and promotions the decedent might have earned.

Older decedents and female decedents were awarded significantly lower amounts than was a male aged thirty years. This pattern of responses emerged for both male and female jurors. Surprisingly, while prior researchers have found gender differences in the way in which money is allocated by men and women, this study provided no evidence supportive of such differences. Awards by males and females were similar. One possible explanation for this finding is that the age and gender of the decedent cause jurors to think of different factors that are subsequently incorporated into the damage award, and to make different inferences about the needs of the surviving spouse. For instance, a male decedent caused more jurors to consider the impact of future career changes and inflation, which may have led jurors to award more money to male decedents. Female decedents were more likely to elicit consideration of factors such as whether or not there were young children to take care of. From an economic standpoint, the basic techniques for estimating lost earning capacity do not vary depending upon whether the decedent is male or female.[40] However, worklife expectancy of female employees is typically less than that of males, because women frequently enter and exit the workforce.[41] In cases in which females devote a portion of their time or full-time service to the household, this element of damages may comprise a major element of economic loss.[42] It is tempting to conclude that mock jurors awarded less to female decedents by basing their decisions on probabilistic assumptions about the participation of females in the labor force, ignoring the value of their service to the household. However, the written explanations provided by the subjects showed that no subjects allocated funds for the economic value of loss of household services when the decedent was female. One possible explanation for the disparate awards by decedent gender comes from Kalven who, in observing actual jury deliberations in a wrongful death case involving a male decedent, noted that economic damages due to the attractive widow were substantially reduced because her chances of remarrying were deemed high.[43] Jurors commented that if she did not remarry and thus suffered economically, that would be her fault, not theirs.[44] Similarly, in a personal injury case not resulting in death but involving an elderly plaintiff whose children were wealthy, damages awarded were substantially less than the plaintiff's entitlement under the law because his children could afford to care for him.[45] Kalven hypothesized that jurors' considerations of fairness and equity lead them to ignore legal guidelines.[46]

Only a small number of subjects spontaneously considered factors common to expert economic testimony in computing lost future income—namely, factors that would lead to an exponential growth in the income over a period of

---

[40]Brookshire, *supra* note 5.

[41]Bureau of Labor Statistics of the Department of Labor's 1982 tables. Note, however, that experts question assumptions in these tables, such as the fact that the tables assume that anytime a person wants a job, he or she will obtain a job and keep it.

[42]Brookshire, *supra* note 5.

[43]Kalven Jr., *The Jury, the Law, and the Personal Injury Damage Award*, 19 OHIO ST. L. J. 158-78 (1958).

[44]*Id.*

[45]*Id.*

[46]*Id.*

years. Few subjects took into account the fact that the decedent would have spent a large portion of the future earnings to support himself; for example, deductions were not made for personal consumption by the decedent, as is common in expert testimony on lost future income. Absent expert testimony to guide them, jurors tended to consider a wide range of factors, based on their own experiences and their suppositions about the parties. Many mock jurors inferred that a surviving female spouse was less well-equipped to be self-supporting than a male surviving spouse. Considerations about future promotions or salary increases were less likely to enter spontaneously into the decision for female decedents than for male decedents. Even those who opted for a "fair number" without computation nonetheless considered a variety of factors; others adopted a more componential approach to determining damages, allotting a separate sum for each factor they considered.

This study is instrumental in showing that when the court is silent concerning factors such as attorneys' fees, taxes, insurance, and interest rates, some individual jurors will take these factors into consideration in awarding damages. The likelihood that factors such as these will enter into group deliberations and discussions over damages may be greater. The variability observed in mock jurors' damage awards in all conditions indicates that subjects do not uniformly translate liability for injury into monetary compensation. As shown in the written justifications provided by the subjects for the awards they made, a wide variety of strategies and factors influenced the damage awards. Even when subjects considered similar elements, such as annual income, subjects' use of this information in reaching a damage award was not uniform.

The finding of no significant differences between awards in the product liability case in which the decedent drives his own car versus a friend's car may be attributable to the fact that it is not so unusual to borrow a friend's car. Miller and McFarland suggested that "outcomes that follow unusual actions are easier to undo mentally or to imagine otherwise, than outcomes that follow routine actions."[47] For example, the unexpected death of someone in an airplane crash after switching flights at the last minute may evoke greater sympathy or a stronger affective reaction than that of someone who suffers a similar fate preceded by a more usual or routine sequence of events. Perhaps our scenario did not product the strong affective response to an exceptional event which Kahneman and Miller theorize can result in increased compensation to victims.[48] Our fact pattern did not emphasize the fact that the decedent routinely drove his own car, and that it was exceptional for him to borrow and drive a friend's car. Accordingly, variation in the ownership of the car may not have caused subjects to generate the readily available alternative of no accident if the decedent were driving his own car in lieu of the friend's defective car. In a study by Miller and McFarland, more compensation was recommended in cases in which a ques-

---

[47]Miller & McFarland, *supra* note 38, at 514.

[48]Kahneman & Miller, *supra* note 39.

tion suggested the events "could have been otherwise."[49] Further research needs to be done to assess specifically what kinds of variations in facts come within the class of exceptional events which produce a heightened sense of injustice. Another possibility is that the defective automobile scenario represented an extreme value on a scale of exceptional injustice as far as male decedents are concerned. Many of the subjects who received the product liability scenario commented on the deterrent value of a substantial damage award against the defendant who might put other drivers in danger.

Overall, the research shows that jurors attempted to make equitable awards, but not necessarily based on legally permissible means of computing economic damages. The task of awarding damages prescribed by legal doctrine differs from the perceptions of the task held by jurors in a number of ways. In particular, where the broad purpose and intent of wrongful death statutes is to compensate survivors, the law nonetheless determines the amount of compensation due based on the stream of income the decedent would have earned but for his or her untimely death. Many jurors focus more directly on the survivors than does the law, basing their awards on the circumstances of the survivor. In so doing, their considerations are less legally rational, but perhaps this is what the law intends by allocating such decisions to jurors rather than economists. One possible reason for such variability is that the meaning assigned to different sums of money in relative, since not everyone has the same idea as to what constitutes a large or a small amount of compensation. Variability attributable to different interpretations of the unit of measurement may be confounded with variability attributable to the facts of the particular cases in issue. Also, people may hold very different ideas as to what is adequate compensation in a wrongful death case, irrespective of the particular decedent in issue.

Kalven wrote that "jury handling of damages is an extraordinarily interesting topic. It would take a full lifetime of empirical research to document the many nuances of this corner of jury 'law' ."[50] This report has highlighted several fruitful areas of investigation in that direction. First, the study revealed that absent guidance from an expert on statistical projections of exponential growth to future income, jurors tend to underestimate lost future earnings, to the detriment of the plaintiff. This fact should be of interest to those engaged in the debate over the merits of tort reform. Second, jurors' written explanations of the factors they considered when awarding damages revealed that some jurors hold misconceptions about their task. For instance, several jurors believed they were required to place a monetary value on human life. Other jurors approached the task of awarding damages as one of providing minimum financial aid to the surviving spouse in a time of crisis rather than compensation for loss of a stream of future income. Third, jurors making decisions under conditions of uncertainty may rely on stereotypical or prototypical social knowledge, such

[49]Miller & McFarland, *supra* note 38.

[50]Kalven, *supra* note 43.

as that derived from the parties' gender, to make adjustments to reach an equitable damage award. Fourth, jurors' written explanations indicated that they considered many factors which are strictly "extra-legal," or on which the law is silent, such as taxation, attorneys' fees, the income of the surviving spouse, what the defendant can afford to pay, and so on. Possibly, in a situation in which there is less ambiguity about the circumstances of the decedent and the surviving spouse, if any, jurors' mental inferences and interpretations may differ. However, not all of the items represented in jurors' deliberations over the evidence constitute admissible evidence in the context of a full wrongful death trial, thus there always will be elements of ambiguity and uncertainty from which jurors may draw inferences in awarding damages.

LAWYERS' PREDICTIONS OF SUCCESS

Elizabeth F. Loftus*
Willem A. Wagenaar†

ABSTRACT

Can lawyers predict the outcome of their cases? In a group of eighty-four criminal defense lawyers, we found that just under half predicted that lawyers would be overconfident in their chances of winning. The remainder incorrectly predicted that lawyers would be well calibrated or underconfident in their predictions.

The actual ability to predict was assessed in one hundred eight-two other lawyers, ninety-three of whom primarily practiced criminal law, and the remainder primarily focused on civil defense. These lawyers were asked to think of a case that would be going to trial soon, to provide their minimum goal, and their chances of obtaining that goal. Verdicts were submitted spontaneously or after prompting. We found that in general lawyers were overconfident in their chances of winning, especially so in cases in which they had been highly confident to begin with. These results have implications for the decisions that lawyers routinely make about whether to settle or litigate a case, and if they litigate, what case strategies they pursue.

INTRODUCTION

To practice law with facility requires substantial education and training. Even after formal education is completed, lawyers continue to learn about their profession. From experience, continuing legal education seminars, reading, and colleagues, they presumably learn more about how to practice law well. With increasing amounts of experience, lawyers presumably get better at framing arguments, spotting important issues, and persuading triers of fact. But do these educational experiences also improve lawyers' ability to predict the outcome of their cases?

---

*Professor, Department of Psychology, University of Washington. Professor Loftus received a Greyhound Research Award for the 1987–88 academic year for her work on this article.

†Dean of the Faculty of Social Sciences and Professor of Experimental Psychology, Leiden University, The Netherlands.

The question of whether lawyers can predict an uncertain future is important from both a theoretical and practical standpoint. Theoretically, the question is important since it relates to a body of literature in psychology on the errors that people make in life. The study of error is a "hot topic"[1] since learning about errors is a way to gain valuable insights into normal processes of human judgment. The study of error in judgment provides us with valuable information on how the mental system handles, absorbs, and distorts incoming information in the process of making judgments.

The issue of whether lawyers can predict the outcome of their cases also relates to another important topic in psychology, namely the mental capabilities of experts and novices. Cognitive psychologists have become enamored with trying to understand how experts acquire their expertise, and how experts think differently from novices about their topic.[2] While much of this research has been criticized for using student subjects performing relatively unimportant tasks,[3] or for using unfamiliar and poorly comprehended judgment tasks that are far removed from the types of judgments that govern important everyday decisions and actions,[4] there has been a growing interest in whether similar results would occur with professionals performing tasks that are normal in their job.[5] For example, in their work, many experts are required to assess the probability that a proposition is true. Doctors diagnose diseases from X-rays, and must assess the probability that a particular X-ray indicates cancer, benign fibroids, or other diseases. Clinical psychologists gather information from clients, reach diagnostic conclusions, and perhaps even venture to predict future behavior.[6] Weather forecasters are continually asked to predict the probability of precipitation. How well do they perform their jobs?

I. EXPERT PREDICTIONS OF SUCCESS

To find out how well experts predict success we must do more than ask a single expert his or her opinion. If a single expert claims that there is a 0.8 probability that a certain proposition is true, and later finds out that the proposition is

[1]Funder, *Errors and Mistakes: Evaluating the Accuracy of Social Judgment*, 101 PSYCHOLOGICAL BULL. 75-90 (1987).

[2]LESGOLD, *Acquiring Expertise*, TUTORIALS IN LEARNING & MEMORY 31-60 (J. Anderson & S. Kosslyn eds. 1984).

[3]Einhorn & Hogarth, *Behavioral Decision Theory: Processes of Judgment and Choice*, 32 ANN. REV. PSYCHOLOGY 53-88 (1978).

[4]DUNNING, MILOJKOVIC & ROSS, THE OVERCONFIDENCE EFFECT IN SOCIAL PREDICTION (1988).

[5]Neale & Northcraft, *Experts, Amateurs, and Refrigerators: Comparing Expert and Amateur Negotiators in a Novel Task*. 38 ORGANIZATIONAL BEHAV. & HUM. DECISION PROCESSES 305-17 (1985).

[6]Oskamp, *Overconfidence in Case-Study Judgments*, 29 J. CONSULTING PSYCHOLOGY 261-65 (1965).

false, this in itself does not mean that the assessment is invalid.[7] Something unexpected or unpredictable could have occurred in that one case. However, suppose the expert assigns a 0.8 probability to 1000 propositions, and only five of them are found to be true. Then something is wrong with the assessments of this expert. Similarly, something is wrong if each of 1000 experts assigns a 0.8 probability to a single personal proposition, and only five of them turn out to be correct. We would say that these experts as a group are "poorly calibrated." By contrast, experts would be called "well calibrated" if, for example, 80 percent of all propositions assigned a probability of 0.8 turned out to be correct.

Weather forecasters have been found to be very well calibrated. When professional weather forecasters were asked to assess the probability of precipitation for nearly 25,000 forecasts made in Chicago in the mid 1970s, the proportion of precipitation days was approximately equal to the assigned probability. For instance, when forecasters said they were 80 percent certain it would rain, it rained about 80 percent of those times.[8] Figure 1 illustrates the excellent calibration of weather forecasters.

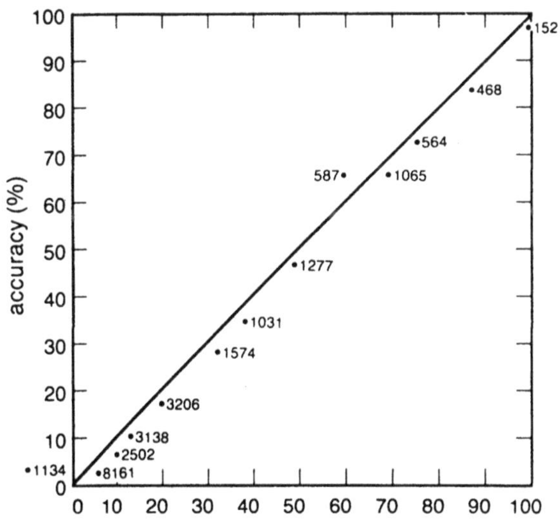

FIGURE 1

[7]Lichtenstein, Fischhoff & Phillips (1984) *Calibration of Probabilities: The State of the Art to 1980*, in JUDGMENT UNDER UNCERTAINTY: HEURISTICS AND BIASES 306-34 (D. Kahneman, P. Slovic & A. Trersky eds. 1984).

[8]Murphy & Winkler, *Forecasters and Probability Forecasts: Some Current Problems*, 52 BULL. AM. METEOROLOGICAL SOC. 239-47 (1971); Murphy & Winkler, *Can Weather Forecasters Formulate Reliable Probability Forecasts of Precipitation and Temperature?* 2 NAT'L WEATHER DIG. 2-9 (1977).

Other professional experts such as psychologists, on the other hand, have been found to be poorly calibrated. Oskamp asked experienced clinical psychologists to review the MMPI profiles of men admitted to a Veterans Administration hospital for either psychiatric or purely medical reasons.[9] All experts had to decide what type of patient the profile described, and to state the probability that their decisions were correct. The psychologists tended to be overconfident in their ability to predict. Similarly psychologists who were given only historical background and then answered questions about individual persons were overconfident about their predictions and became increasingly overconfident the more information they were given.[10] Physicians too have been found to be poorly calibrated. In one study, nine of them were asked the probability of a diagnosis of pneumonia in 1500 patients with coughing symptoms. While physicians were 80 percent certain of a diagnosis of pneumonia, their diagnosis was correct only 20 percent of the time.[11]

When psychologists and physicians were found to be overconfident, at least one professional group tends towards underconfidence. Practicing auditors in public accounting were asked to perform a task akin to developing an opinion about the fairness of a client's financial statement. The study revealed that the auditors tended to underestimate the accuracy of their predictions.[12]

A. Lawyers' Predictions of an Uncertain Future

Are lawyers well calibrated like weather forecasters, or overconfident like physicians? Or, are they underconfident like the auditors? When lawyers claim to be 50 percent certain that they will win an upcoming case, do they actually win 50 percent of the time? Evidence shows that many lawyers believe that their colleagues are overconfident, while many others believe that their colleagues are underconfident (to be presented in detail later). Whether lawyers in fact are over- or underconfident has some important practical implications. If lawyers are underconfident, they might look like heroes to their clients if in fact they ultimately do better than their prediction. On the other hand, they might perform less optimally than they would otherwise. The phenomenon of "self-fulfilling prophecy" is well known in psychology. People tend to find what they are looking for, and they may even unwittingly create what they seek. A lawyer who is pessimistic about an upcoming case might inadvertently express

---

[9]Oskamp, *The Relationship of Clinical Experience and Training Methods to Several Criteria of Clinical Prediction*, 76 PSYCHOLOGICAL MONOGRAPHS (28 Whole 547) (1967).

[10]Oskamp, *supra* note 6.

[11]Christensen-Szalanski & Bushyhead, *Physicians' Use of Probabilistic Information in a Real Clinical Setting*, 7 J. EXPERIMENTAL PSYCHOLOGY: HUM. PERCEPTION & PERFORMANCE 928-35 (1981).

[12]Tomassini, Solomon, Romney & Krogstad, *Calibration of Auditors' Probabilistic Judgments: Some Empirical Evidence*, 30 ORGANIZATIONAL BEHAV. & HUM. PERFORMANCE 391-406 (1982).

a pessimistic attitude in court which influences the decision that a jury makes. Research dating back to more than twenty years ago has shown that even when we are fully aware that self-fulfilling prophecies can occur, we sometimes inadvertently create the results we expect to see.[13]

On the other hand, if lawyers are found to be overconfident, this could profoundly influence their settlement activities. As is now well known, the majority of cases, both civil and criminal, are disposed of without a trial because the parties reach a settlement.[14] In civil cases, attorneys invariably explore the possibility of settlement.[15] Although estimates vary, we can roughly say that for an average lawyer, four out of five cases will be settled through negotiation, while only one will actually go to trial.[16] While a dispute exists in the literature about which cases actually do go to trial and which do not,[17] we are concerned here with the possibility that erroneous predictions about an uncertain future might lead a lawyer to make the wrong decision about whether to proceed with further litigation or to settle.

Why lawyers and their clients resist settlement and go to trial concerns many judicial administrators with clogged courtroom calendars. In recent years, economists attempted to explain lawyers' decisions to litigate versus settle. Their analysis assumes that a lawyer considers the probable outcomes of further litigation steps and weighs those outcomes against economic benefits that are likely to be obtained without further litigation.[18] When we think about a lawyer "considering the probable outcomes" we naturally ask whether such consideration is done in an optimistic or pessimistic way, not only by a single lawyer, but also by the opposing advocate. Thus, one possible reason for the failure of negotiation is that the parties are inherently at odds concerning the "expected value of the claim in litigation."[19] Put another way, both sides believe that the outcome of litigation will be more favorable than their opponent's best settlement offer. In the language of calibration, both sides overconfidently assess their chances of success.

Apart from settlement activities, there are other reasons why we should care about lawyers' ability to predict the future. Economists say that the anticipated size of a settlement or verdict is a major factor in the decision to seek particular kinds of experts.[20] Lawyers must ask themselves whether the anticipated "return" from the use of an expensive expert witness will be worth the cost of the expert's fees. A lawyer who thinks that the chances are 80 percent of

[13]R. Rosenthal, Experimenter Effects in Behavioral Research (1966).

[14]I. A. Horowitz & T. E. Willging, The Psychology of Law: Integrations and Applications (1984); H. L. Ross, Settled Out of Court (1970).

[15]J. A. Tanford, The Trial Process (1983).

[16]G. R. Williams, Effective Legal Negotiation (1978).

[17]Wittman, *Is the Selection of Cases for Trial Biased?*, 14 J. Legal Stud. 185-214 (1985).

[18]Johnson, *Lawyers' Choice: A Theoretical Appraisal of Litigation Investment Decisions*, 15 L. & Soc'y Rev. 567-610 (1980–81).

[19]*Supra* note 12, at 163.

[20]M. L. Brookshire, Economic Damages (1987).

winning a verdict of $100,000 may be far more willing to spend $3,000 on an expert witness than one who thinks the chances are low. Thus subjective probabilities of success influence major aspects of a lawyer's handling of a case.

The foregoing discussion makes it evident that calibration of lawyers is a worthwhile topic for scientific study. What is needed first are direct empirical tests of whether lawyers are well or poorly calibrated, and if poorly calibrated whether they err on the side of over- or underconfidence. This article reports what we believe to be a unique study of whether lawyers can predict the outcome of their cases.

II. THE EXPERIMENTS

A. Experiment 1

One problem with measuring calibration is that each data point on a calibration plot represents a percentage. Thus each data point should rest on a sufficient number of observations, preferably 100 or more. With eleven data points on a calibration plot, at least 1100 predictions should be collected, either from one single lawyer, or from 1100 different lawyers. In practice, these goals are virtually impossible to achieve, at least within a reasonable time period. In the present research we opted to ask a sizable sample of individual lawyers to each contribute one prediction, and to garner as many predictions as we could in a reasonable period of time. Some of our techniques for gathering data failed (we discuss these later), but at least one technique, while not providing sufficient predictions for the construction of a reliable fine-grained calibration plot, did produce sufficient data for the estimation of an overall degree of calibration.

1. Subjects

The participants in this study were practicing lawyers who were attending a continuing legal education seminar. We collected data at national meetings, such as a 1985 criminal defense seminar conducted in Houston, Texas, sponsored by the Association of Trial Lawyers of America. We collected other data at regional meetings, such as a highly popular 1986 criminal defense seminar in Atlanta sponsored in part by the Atlanta Bar Association.

2. Procedure

Before a scheduled lecture by one of the authors, a one-page questionnaire was handed out. The questionnaire asked the lawyer to "think of a criminal case that you are currently handling. It should be a case that you are fairly certain is going to trial in the near future or is in trial at the moment. Enter a code name for the case so that you will be able to recognize it." Lawyers were then asked what outcome, if it or something better were achieved, would be considered a win situation. Put another way, they were asked what was their minimum goal. In many criminal cases, lawyers stated that acquittal or mistrial was the desired outcome, however in some cases a life sentence rather than the death penalty could also constitute a win. Finally, the lawyer was asked, "What is the probability that you will achieve this outcome, or something better? You should respond with a number between 0 and 100 percent." The lawyer recorded all of this information on the top half of the questionnaire, which was handed in immediately.

The bottom half of the questionnaire was to be used for recording the verdict when the trial was over. On it, the lawyer recorded his or her name, the code name, and the goal, so that the outcome could be later matched with the earlier supplied prediction. Lawyers were asked to keep the bottom half in their wallet or briefcase until the trial was over, then to report the actual outcome, whether it was equal to or better than the goal. The attorneys were to mail the outcome reports to the lecturer at her university.

3. *Results*

The lawyers who responded had chosen a wide range of cases. Sometimes they characterized their case in very general terms (e.g., murder, robbery). Others characterized them quite specifically (e.g., "thirteen count burglary; assault with intent to kill") or with acronyms (e.g., PWID/PCP). Out of those who completed the first half of their questionnaires, a total of ninety-six returned outcomes. This constituted approximately 37 percent of those who had initially submitted the first half of the questionnaires. In three cases, the lawyer indicated that the outcome was "equal to or better than" the goal, but a comparison of the outcome and goal proved otherwise. These three questionnaires were eliminated from further analysis.

Our major question of interest, of course, is whether there is any relationship between lawyers' confidence estimates and their likelihood of actually winning. Figure 2 presents a calibration curve, but because of the paucity of observations, only three data points are presented. The three data points reflect data provided by lawyers whose confidence levels were below 50 percent, n=34, between 50 and 65 percent, n=33, and above 65 percent, n=26.

Figure 2 reveals two aspects of calibration. The first aspect can be called "sensitivity." It is related to the degree of correspondence between confidence and accuracy. When accuracy increases with confidence, it can be said that subjects were at least sensitive to probability of success. The second aspect, under- or overconfidence, is represented by the mean vertical distance between the observations and the line of good calibration, the identity line.

As a group, the lawyers seemed to be somewhat sensitive to the probability of success. Those who had expressed high confidence in their chances of winning actually won 58 percent of the time. Those who expressed low confidence in winning won about half as often, 29 percent of the time.[21]

As a group, the lawyers were overconfident. The simplest measure of overconfidence is mean confidence minus obtained percentage of accuracy. As can be seen in Figure 2, this figure was 3 percent for those expressing low confidence, 8 percent for those expressing moderate confidence, and 21 percent for those expressing high confidence. Thus, highly confident predictions tended to be especially overconfident. In the group of lawyers who expressed high confidence, a significant amount of overconfidence was found; $z=2.65$, $p<0.01$.

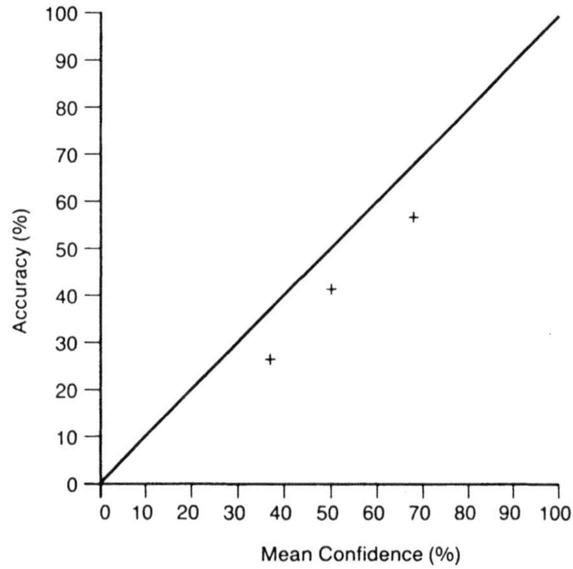

FIGURE 2

4. *Discussion of Potential Problems*

The ninety-three criminal lawyers who participated in this study revealed overconfidence in their chances of winning. While they were more likely to win in cases in which they had expressed high confidence rather than low confidence, they were also prone to be the most overconfident in these cases.

Before discussing the implications of these findings, a potential problem with seminar studies should be acknowledged. Not all subject-lawyers com-

[21]Standard statistical tests were conducted. The statistical association between confidence and accuracy in a 3 × 2 contingency table was modest, 0.22, but only marginally significant; $x^2(2)=4.89$, $.10>p>0.05$. *See, generally* M. H. DeGroot, Probability and Statistics, 451-54 (1975).

plete the first part of the questionnaire, and even a smaller proportion complete and return the second part. The specifics of the current procedure dramatically curtailed this first potential problem. In our first attempts to gather predictions from lawyers, we placed the questionnaires at a registration desk and had the seminar moderator request participation by the lawyers. At three seminars in which we employed this technique less than 5 percent of lawyers turned in the first portion of the questionnaire. For Experiment 1, and all subsequent studies, we modified the procedure by eliciting participation from seated lawyers before the lecture began. With this "captive audience" approach, we increased compliance to over 80 percent, at least as far as the return of the first portion of the questionnaire was concerned.

There still remained the problem that not all lawyers returned the second portion of their questionnaire. In Experiment 1, less than 40 percent did so. What bias might this introduce? Assuming that lawyers would tend to return the second portion of the questionnaire when their predictions were successful, the effect of the present procedure could only be that the overconfidence we observed is underestimated. Thus the resulting calibration curves should indicate even greater optimism.

The ideal study of this sort would employ a random selection of lawyers and cases, and a 100 percent response in the posttrial phase. For a preliminary study, this approach was not practical. As an alternative, we decided to conduct a second study in which we would collect the addresses of lawyers, and personally contact each lawyer who failed to return the second portion of the questionnaire. This was done in Experiment 2. In this way we could assess the possibility that lawyers who responded on their own tended to be more successful than those who did not. A second goal of Experiment 2 was to extend our findings to civil lawyers.

B. Experiment 2

1. Subjects

The participants in this study were practicing lawyers who were attending a continuing legal education seminar. We collected most of the data at two 1985 seminars sponsored by the Washington Association of Defense Counsel and the Colorado Defense Lawyers Association. Thus, these data came from lawyers with a primary interest in defense of civil cases.

2. Procedure

Before a scheduled lecture by one of the authors, a one-page questionnaire was handed out. Both the top and bottom half of the questionnaire asked for the lawyer's full name and address. The top half additionally asked the lawyer to "think of a case that you are currently handling. It should be a case that you are fairly certain is going to trial soon." The lawyer was asked to enter a code name for the case so it could be recognized later. Lawyers were then asked: "What outcome, if you achieved it or better, would you consider to be a win situation? Put another way, what is your goal? (e.g., defense verdict; plaintiff verdict of no more than $5,000 award)." As in the previous study, the lawyer defined what constituted a win. Finally, the lawyer was asked: "What is the probability that you will achieve this outcome or something better?" They were told to respond with a number between 0 and 100 percent. The attorney recorded all of this information on the top half of the questionnaire and handed it in immediately.

The bottom half of the questionnaire was to be returned when the case was over. It requested information about the verdict, and whether the goal was achieved.

About one year after the initial data had been collected, in the fall of 1986, each lawyer who had failed to return the second half of the questionnaire received a letter. The letter politely reminded the lawyer about the lecture that had been given, and the request to participate in the study. A copy of the top portion of the questionnaire was included with the letter to remind the lawyer of the case that had been chosen. The letter went on to ask for the outcome of the case and whether it was better, equal to or less good an outcome than the goal. The lawyer was also asked, even more politely, to provide the reason why the outcome information had not been spontaneously provided.

3. Results

The lawyers who responded had chosen a wide variety of cases. There were numerous auto accident cases in the set, but also industrial accidents, product liability cases, medical malpractice, construction cases, contract cases, and other types. Occasionally a lawyer specified the case only in general terms (e.g., personal injury), and occasionally more specifically (e.g., "slip and fall"—negligence). A total of fifty-three lawyers without reminder returned the bottom half of the questionnaires by the fall of 1986. This was about 33 percent of those who had completed the first portion of the questionnaire. In response to the reminder letter, an additional thirty-six responses were obtained.

The first question we ask is whether the lawyers who spontaneously returned their outcome information were more likely to win their cases than lawyers who did not. In fact the "spontaneous" lawyers were slightly, but not significantly, more likely to win. Of those who spontaneously returned their questionnaires, 58 percent achieved their stated goal, while of those who responded only after a reminder, 44 percent achieved their goal. These percentages are not significantly different, indicating that the reason why lawyers did not return their outcome information was not a massive loss of their cases.

Why did the lawyers fail to return the outcome information? Several explanations were given, the most common of which was a variation of "I forgot" (89 percent).

"Sorry for not returning the outcome information sooner. The reason is simply that I forgot, with the crush of other business occupying the available remainder of my memory." (Lawyer from Aurora, Colorado)

Another common reason was that the lawyer did not realize that he or she still had an obligation to do anything (33 percent). The percentages sum to more than 100 since many lawyers supplied several reasons.

There were a few relatively idiosyncratic reasons.[22]

Next we examined how confident the lawyers were about their chances of winning. How often did they choose a confidence level above 50 percent? How often was it below 50 percent? Those who spontaneously returned their outcomes tended to be somewhat less confident than those who had to be reminded. Among the spontaneous lawyers, 49 percent displayed a confidence level about 50 percent, whereas among the reminded lawyers, 61 percent did so. However, our major issue is whether there is any relationship between lawyers' confidence estimates and their likelihood of actually winning. In Figure 3, we present two calibration curves. Because of the paucity of observations only two data points are presented for the "spontaneous" lawyers, and two for the "reminded lawyers." The two data points reflect data provided by lawyers whose confidence levels were 50 percent or below, twenty-seven spontaneous and fourteen reminded and lawyers whose confidence levels were above 50 percent, twenty-six spontaneous and twenty-two reminded.

Figure 3 reveals two aspects of calibration. The "sensitivity" aspect relates to the degree of correspondence between confidence and accuracy. The spontaneous group of lawyers was completely insensitive. This means that their probability of success was constant, no matter how much confidence in success the lawyers had previously displayed. The reminded lawyers were somewhat more sensitive.

In terms of under-versus overconfidence, three of the four groups show overconfidence. The data once again show a tendency toward overconfidence among both spontaneous and reminded lawyers who had initially expressed relatively high degrees of confidence. Unfortunately because of the small number

[22]For example, a failure to respond because the verdict had not been reached, or because the response sheet had been misplaced, or because the lawyer thought the interest was in jury verdicts and the case had settled without trial. One lawyer from Denver gave a very lengthy explanation: "I failed to respond to your initial request for the outcome information for two reasons. First of all, while I do not consider this to be a particularly legitimate or valid excuse, the press of my practice in the last several months has left me with what sometimes appears to be inadequate time to carefully manage my existing caseload. I have been traveling a great deal and have been spending more time than I like on weekends, trying to keep on top of matters. For that reason, as well as the fact that it took me some time to associate the "code name" with the actual case, your request for outcome information simply got shifted to the bottom of the pile! Please accept my apologies. Secondly the case has not yet been resolved. . . ."

Among the more interesting responses was one from a Seattle lawyer who blamed the investigator (EL) for his failure to return the form: " . . . The reason that I didn't send in the 'outcome information' was that you never asked for it."

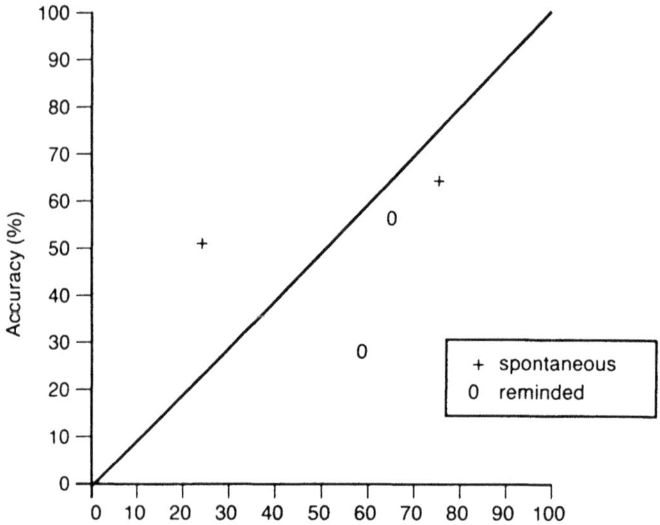

FIGURE 3

of observations in each of the four groups, statistical significance could not be achieved. However, if we combine the high confident spontaneous and reminded lawyers, together they demonstrate significant overconfidence; $z=2.34$, $p<0.05$.

4. Discussion

Calibration was relatively poor for the fifty-three spontaneous lawyers. They achieved their declared goals in 58 percent of the cases, but this proportion was independent of their prior confidence rating. The situation improved somewhat for the thirty-six reminded lawyers, although they tended to display overconfidence.

A question arises about whether lawyers know that as a group they tend to be poorly calibrated or overconfident. It is easy with data in hand that demonstrate overconfidence to say "I could have told you that." Such tendencies towards hindsight bias are well established.[23] In order to discover whether lawyers as a group would predict in advance that our experiments would show optimism (overconfidence), pessimism (underconfidence) or neither, we conducted Experiment 3.

[23] Fischhoff, *Perceived Informativeness of Facts*, 3 J. EXPERIMENTAL PSYCHOLOGY: HUM. PERCEPTION & PERFORMANCE, 349-58 (1977).

C. Experiment 3

1. Subjects

The subjects were trial lawyers attending an educational seminar sponsored by the Tennessee Association of Criminal Defense Attorneys in Nashville, Tennessee in December 1987. Approximately 100 lawyers were in attendance at the time the study was conducted.

2. Procedure

Again we used the "captive audience" approach. At the beginning of a scheduled lecture, the assembled lawyers were asked if they would take a minute before the lecture began to participate in an experiment. Pre-prepared questionnaires were not used. Rather, each lawyer was asked to take out a piece of paper, and write down on the first five lines of the page, the numbers one through five. Five pieces of information were requested. First, they were asked for the number of years they had been in practice, to be written on line one. Next they were asked to think of a criminal case that they thought would go to trial soon and to write, on line two, the type of case, e.g., murder. The next question requested that they write down what they hoped to achieve in the case, the minimum win situation. They wrote this goal on line three. Next, on line four they wrote down their subjective probability of achieving that goal. It was explained to them that this should be a number between 0 and 100 percent. Thus, at this point in the procedure, the lawyers had participated in a task that was virtually identical to that engaged in by seminar attendees in Experiments 1 and 2. They had thought of a case and a goal, and had provided a confidence level. This experience set the stage for the final question.

The fifth question posed to the lawyers was critical. The lawyers were asked to imagine that I had gathered together the predictions from a group of 100 lawyers all of whom had said that their chances of achieving their goal was 50 percent or better. "When the case is resolved, how many of these lawyers will in fact win?" It was explained that if they chose a number less than fifty, it meant that they believed that lawyers as a group were too optimistic. On the other hand, if they chose a number greater than fifty, it meant that they believed that lawyers as a group were too pessimistic.

3. Results

A total of eighty-eight lawyers turned in their sheets. Four sheets were unusable because question five was not answered, n=2, a civil case was chosen, n=1, or the participant was not a lawyer, n=1. Of the eighty-four sheets that were usable, thirty-nine, or 46 percent, of the lawyers chose a number below fifty; twenty-two, or 26 percent, of the lawyers chose exactly fifty; and twenty-three, 27 percent, chose a number above fifty. These data suggest that just over half of the sample (26 percent + 27 percent) incorrectly predicted that lawyers would be well calibrated or underconfident in their predictions.

III. GENERAL DISCUSSION

To our knowledge, this is an unusual preliminary study comparing lawyers' subjective expectations of success with their actual performance. We found that lawyers tended to be overconfident, in general, but especially so in cases in which they initially made highly confident predictions. The observation that the greatest overconfidence occurs when confidence is high to begin with has been found in other domains.[24] What is especially striking about the data reported here is that the overconfidence we observed has occurred in a domain that is very familiar to lawyers, namely their chosen profession.

A natural question to ask at this point is why lawyers express more confidence than would prove justified by the levels of accuracy they achieved? Other investigators[25] suggest that overconfidence may be an inevitable by-product of the whole range of human inferential shortcomings that have been documented in the recent past. The shortcomings occur in part because of the development and maintenance of specific stereotypes and beliefs. In the case of lawyers, overconfidence could occur because the lawyer can bring readily to mind a similar case in which a favorable verdict was achieved, or because the lawyer fails to bring to mind similar cases in which unfavorable verdicts were achieved. A related reason for overconfidence in lawyers may arise from a failure to process feedback in a systematic and formalized manner.[26] Although some lawyers might keep a record of their win percentage, few probably perform any kind of systematic analysis of the discrepancies between their prior predictions and the actual outcomes. In short, they might record how often they lose, but fail to fully analyze what went wrong. Finally, overconfidence can be a result of systematic neglect of important predictors, relevant law, precedence, personality of the judge, and that in turn can lead to the adoption of suboptimal strategies in the courtroom.

What purpose does overconfidence serve? It is possible that lawyers need to feel and display overconfidence in order to attract clients, and, later, to keep those clients convinced that their interests are well served. Overconfidence might also function as a psychological support that helps lawyers maximize their performance in court. Great confidence could be a factor that helps convince judges and juries to adopt the lawyers' point of view.

On the other hand, there is a cost to overconfidence. If two opposing lawyers are both overconfident, this would adversely impact settlement activities.

[24]In similar ongoing work being carried out by the authors in The Netherlands, over 100 Dutch lawyers, both civil and criminal, have already made predictions of success and provided verdicts. Although the legal system is very different from that in the United States, nonetheless, the Dutch lawyers who express the greatest degree of subjective confidence are also the most overconfident.

[25]Dunning, *supra* note 4.

[26]Wagenaar & Keren, *Does the Expert Know? The Reliability of Predictions and Confidence Ratings of Experts*, in INTELLIGENT DECISION SUPPORT IN PROCESS ENVIRONMENTS, 87-103 (Hollnagel, Mancini & Woods eds. 1986).

The decision to resist settlement is, to a considerable degree, based on the lawyers' expectation of success in court. The lawyer goes to trial if settlement is not reached, with a good chance that suboptimal strategies will be followed. The chances of winning at trial may be accordingly reduced.

Assuming we wanted to reduce the "overconfidence bias," could we? Psychological studies show a few techniques that can successfully reduce the overconfidence bias.[27] One technique involves training people by giving them prompt feedback on the accuracy of their judgments. One reason why weather forecasters, and those who predict the odds at horse racing, are so well calibrated in their work is that they receive prompt, unambiguous feedback on the accuracy of their predictions. Another way to reduce the overconfidence bias is to encourage people to generate reasons why their initial judgment might not be correct. When people are forced to consider discomforting information their predictions become more realistic.

This study constitutes but a first step towards understanding the ability of a significant professional group, namely lawyers, to predict an uncertain future. We found that lawyers as a group were overconfident, but there is still much more to be learned. For example, is the overconfidence bias reduced as lawyers become more experienced? Studies in other domains show that overconfidence actually increases with the degree of expertise that individuals believe themselves to have;[28] but this might not be true with lawyers. Is the overconfidence bias greater with certain kinds of cases rather than others? We made too few observations to answer these questions at the current time.

One final comment concerns the methodological difficulties of conducting this sort of research. Our findings here come from 182 practicing lawyers, and it took nearly three years to gather these data. Before settling on the "captive audience" seminar approach, we failed with a number of other attempts. To spare other researchers from experiencing our frustrations, we mention these briefly. One failed technique involved gaining permission from administrators in three public defender offices, Seattle, Columbus, and San Diego, and one prosecutor's office, Seattle, where deputies would be asked to make their predictions on the first day of the trial and verdicts would be gathered from office personnel after the trials were concluded. Unfortunately despite the deputies' good intentions, they were too busy and harassed to be relied upon to fill out the questionnaires on the first day of the trial. A second failed technique involved sending students to the courthouse to personally contact lawyers on the first day of their trials, with the idea that the verdicts would be obtained later from official records. Unfortunately lawyers were too busy to spare time to talk with students, and disinclined to reveal to a student stranger their goals and probabilities lest this impair possible settlement opportunities. A third failed technique involved placing the questionnaire in a widely read lawyers' newspaper.

[27]Fischoff, *Debiasing* in JUDGMENT UNDER UNCERTAINTY: HEURISTICS AND BIASES. (D. Kahneman, P. Slovic & A. Trersky eds. 1982).

[28]Bradley, *Overconfidence in Ignorant Experts*, 17 BULL. PSYCHONOMIC SOC'Y 82-84 (1981).

The questionnaire appeared below an enticing story entitled "Can you predict the outcome?" written by a prominent lawyer in the state of Washington. The story gave some background about the study, and asked lawyers to fill out the following two-part questionnaire. We looked forward to receiving hundreds of responses, but alas, we received only one—from the wife of the prominent lawyer who had authored the "Can you predict the outcome?" piece.

Despite the difficult beginning, the final version of our seminar approach produced useful data from 182 individual lawyers. We hope that future research might use this and other techniques for gaining more data so as to be able to answer some of the questions posed above. Further researchers might find themselves grappling as we did with the definition of a "win situation." In our study, we left the definition to the individual attorney, but this easy solution was not without problems as it occasionally elicited protest from some lawyers. This is because many cases are subject to a range of solutions. For example, do we consider a plaintiff verdict below $50,000 to be a "win" if common jury verdicts have been below $5,000 for similar circumstances? What if the client cannot afford to pay $50,000? Is a manslaughter verdict a "win" when a lawyer knows that the client should be guilty of first degree murder? What if the lawyer knows that the client will be emotionally destroyed by even a year in prison? Given our procedures, lawyers in our study did not have much time to work out these difficult issues.

Another aspect of the "win" terminology is the fact that lawyers' definitions change throughout the course of litigation. During the course of the trial, or afterwards, lawyers may revise their estimates of what it means to "win." If events went very badly at trial, what might have been characterized as a "loss" before trial now appears to be a "win." Thus the lawyer might respond that he did win after all. This could explain the few instances in the present study in which a lawyer said that the outcome was "equal to or better than" the goal, but a comparison between the goal and the outcome indicated otherwise. Careful inquiry as to the precise result obtained is essential to eliminate this problem.

As cases become increasingly complex one can anticipate an additional problem and that is evaluating the outcome of the case and determining whether it did exceed the goal or not. This was made clear in one auto accident case in our sample in which a Denver civil defense lawyer predicted a 65 percent chance of obtaining a verdict of less than $25,000 to the plaintiff. In response to the letter requesting the outcome information, she said it was difficult to evaluate the outcome of the case and went on to explain that it:

> . . .involved three defendants, an employer, an employee, and a manufacturer. I represented the employee. Because of negotiations with the Plaintiff's attorney concerning certain motions to which other defense counsel objected, I was able to have my client dismissed from the action in exchange for supporting the Plaintiff's motions. My client was dismissed the morning of trial and shortly thereafter the case was settled for a total

amount of $10,000. Since my client and the employer were represented by the same carrier, we had thought a good outcome would be $50,000 which was approximately $25,000 for each of the defendants, i.e., employer and employee. Since my client was dismissed, the $50,000 was actually paid by the employer, however, because of theories of liability, he was responsible for any negligence of the employee. The total settlement amount of $110,000 was contributed $50,000 by the carrier for the employer and employee, $50,000 by the carrier for the manufacturer and $10,000 directly from the manufacturer. Overall, I think that the total amount paid to the Plaintiff was in excess of what I consider a good result for this case, but keeping our client's contribution to $50,000 was a favorable result. Obviously, having my client dismissed entirely was a much better result than I ever anticipated. Because of the nature of the resolution of this matter it is difficult for me to say whether or not the actual outcome was better or worse than my actual goal. . . .

For purposes of analysis we classified this as a victory. Its convoluted nature points to the even greater difficulties that lawyers will have in predicting the outcomes of complex cases, and in assessing whether those predictions were in fact borne out.

Law and Human Behavior, Vol. 14, No. 4, 1990

Determining Damages

The Influence of Expert Testimony on Jurors' Decision Making*

Allan Raitz,† Edith Greene,‡ Jane Goodman,§ and Elizabeth F. Loftus§

How do jurors accomplish the task of awarding damages in a civil lawsuit? To what extent are they influenced by expert testimony? These questions were addressed in a mock juror simulation in which jurors from El Paso County (Colorado) read one of three versions of a trial manuscript involving an age discrimination claim in which liability was already determined. They awarded damages and answered follow-up questions. In one version, there was no expert testimony; in a second version, they received plaintiff expert testimony on lost future wages and other economic matters; and in the third version, they received both plaintiff and defense expert testimony. Monetary awards were significantly higher when expert(s) testified. Moreover, jurors were strongly influenced by the expert testimony: Nearly half of them selected a damage award that exactly matched the amounts suggested. Finally, jurors infrequently considered exponential calculations in assessing damages.

Jurors in civil cases face a difficult task when they determine damage awards. The difficulty arises for several reasons. First, the instructions that jurors receive

---

* This research was supported by a grant from the Law and Social Sciences Program at the National Science Foundation. The paper is based on a master's thesis submitted to the University of Colorado by the first author. We thank Colorado Fourth Judicial District Presiding Judge Donald Campbell, Court Administrator Douglas Haxton, and Jury Commissioner Eldene Mosbarger for allowing us access to jurors and Valerie Stromquist and Alisa Cohen for their research assistance. Please direct correspondence to Edith Greene, Department of Psychology, University of Colorado, Colorado Springs, Colorado 80933.

† Denver University.

‡ University of Colorado.

§ University of Washington.

regarding damages and what amounts are acceptable contain virtually no guidelines as to how damages should be determined. In fact, the instructions inform jurors that no guidelines exist (Kalven, 1958).

Second, in cases involving personal injury, discrimination, trademark infringement, and antitrust, the evidence concerning lost income is often probabilistic in nature. For example, future rates of interest and inflation, as well as chances for promotion and salary increases, may all be discussed. Recent research suggests that jurors have difficulty understanding and using probabilistic concepts (Goodman, 1986; Thompson & Britton, 1988).

A third factor contributing to jurors' difficulty concerns the use of expert economic testimony. Increasingly, cases are being brought that include claims for damages totaling millions of dollars (Samuelson, 1986). To substantiate these large claims, attorneys often rely on experts who proffer complex economic testimony. Because these cases often involve *conflicting* expert testimony, jurors may be exposed to contrasting economic models which lead to very different outcomes.

In this study, we examined the impact of requests for large sums of money, complex economic forecasting, and conflicting claims for damages on jurors' decision making. Several questions were addressed: What impact would an expert economist have on jurors' decisions? How would jurors resolve conflicting expert testimony? Would they endorse the experts' amounts? Would they consider exponential concepts (e.g., interest compounding) in their decision making?

On the basis of previous research, we expected that jurors might place considerable weight on the testimony of an expert. Jurors may rely on the belief that experts can be trusted or believe that expert opinions are valid and thus fail to consider reasonable arguments against the expert (Chaiken & Stangor, 1987; Eagly & Chaiken, 1984).

The hypothesis that jurors blindly accept expert testimony was evaluated in a study that examined the use of evidence obtained from polygraph tests (Cavoukian & Heslegrave, 1980). Results indicated that mock jurors who heard expert testimony that the defendant was telling the truth when he said he did not commit the crime were less likely to convict than those in the control group who did not hear expert testimony. These researchers also examined jurors' reactions to a "battle of the experts." Their data indicate that the prosecution's expert nullified the effect of the defendant's expert.

Although instructive, results from studies of decision making in criminal trials may not generalize to civil cases. In criminal cases, jurors usually have only two verdict options (guilty, not guilty). In civil cases, they can award any amount of money to a prevailing plaintiff that they deem reasonable. Thus, jurors exposed to conflicting expert testimony in a civil suit might resolve the controversy by selecting a compromise award. But even in that situation, the expert testimony has influenced them.

Other research suggests that a request for a specified amount in monetary damages may serve to "anchor" jurors' assessments. Broeder (1959) reported data from posttrial interviews with jurors in 11 civil cases. One question examined the effects of the *ad damnum* (the amount requested by the plaintiff's counsel as damages) on the amount awarded. Results from the interviews indicate that the *ad damnum* served as a "jumping-off place for jurors" (p. 756). In fact, jurors usually jumped *down* from the plaintiff's requested sum by consistently awarding less money than requested. However, none of the cases examined by Broeder involved expert testimony to support the *ad damnum*, nor did the defendant's case include countervailing requests. Thus, the question of whether the *ad damnum* is always viewed as excessive was not addressed.

A more complete answer came from a mock juror study in which the *ad damnum* was systematically varied while the facts of the case were held constant (Zuehl, 1982). Jurors in a simulated personal injury case received one of four damage requests: a low request of $10,000, a fair request of $75,000 (the mock trial was based on an actual case in which the jury awarded $65,000), an excessive request of $150,000, or a request for "substantial compensation" with no specific dollar amount suggested. The mean awards for the four groups were $18,000, $62,800, $101,400, and $74,600, respectively. These figures are consistent with Broeder's (1959) findings and provide evidence that jurors can be strongly influenced by specified requests for damages.

Further evidence for this influence can be seen by examining the modal awards. Fully one half of all juries that heard cases requesting a specific amount determined awards that matched the *ad damnum* exactly. As in Broeder's research, this study did not include testimony by experts, nor did the defendant counter the plaintiff's request.

Finally, some research has shown that when people are asked to make predictions based on incomplete data, they have a tendency to underestimate amounts of exponential growth (Keren, 1983; Wagenaar & Timmers, 1978). Because many civil cases involve considerations of lost *future* earnings, jurors' computations should theoretically involve exponential factors (e.g., raises and promotions). If jurors lack an appreciation for exponential growth patterns, left to their own calculations they may produce awards of lesser amounts than may actually be warranted.

The present research involved a mock jury study designed to evaluate the impact of expert testimony on jurors' calculations of damage awards. Jurors were exposed to transcripts from an age discrimination case in which a midlevel manager had been terminated from his position and replaced by a younger person. Jurors were informed that the case was bifurcated, that liability had been previously determined in favor of the plaintiff, and that their task was to decide on an adequate damages award. One third of the jurors read testimony from an economist testifying on behalf of the plaintiff; one third read economic testimony from both sides; and one third were not exposed to any expert testimony. This design allowed us to test several hypotheses:

1. Jurors exposed to expert testimony from only one side will endorse the amount suggested by the expert.
2. Jurors exposed to conflicting expert testimony (i.e., by plaintiff *and* defense experts) will view the amounts suggested as constituting a range and compute a figure that falls near the middle of the range.
3. In the absence of expert testimony, jurors will fail to consider exponential growth factors and, as a consequence, will award less than jurors exposed to expert testimony.

METHOD

Participants

Participants were 156 jurors from El Paso County (Colorado Springs), Colorado. We recruited jurors from among those awaiting jury selection at the local courthouse.

All analyses were based on responses from 150 participants (6 jurors failed to follow instructions). The sample was predominantly female (65%) and ranged in age from 19 to 71 years (M = 39.85). Most had attended some college (M = 14.73 years of education). Their reported family income ranged from $1,258 to $200,000 annually (median = $35,000).

Materials

Juror questionnaire packets contained a consent form, instructions, summary of a trial transcript, special verdict form, and a questionnaire concerning their decision making.

Three versions of a civil age discrimination case were used. The suit involved the wrongful employment termination of the plaintiff. The essential features of the case were identical for each version. The cover page of the case contained a 150-word summary of the background to the case. Jurors were informed that the defendant, Wholesome Food Company, had previously been found liable and that their task was to determine compensation for the plaintiff. Further, they were informed that several facts were already on record. The plaintiff was 58 years old at the time of the trial, had a business degree, and had been employed by the company for 8 years prior to termination 4 years earlier. At that time he had been receiving an annual salary of $62,000. He continued to receive his health and retirement benefits and would continue to receive them in the future.

One version of the trial transcript was approximately 200 words long, consisting of the factual summary and opening and closing statements by the plaintiff and the defendant. The plaintiff claimed damages for lost back pay, lost future pay, and pain and suffering. The plaintiff claimed that he would have worked until age 65, that he had not worked since being terminated, that his future job prospects were not good, and that he had suffered extreme emotional distress. Wholesome Food Company contended that it was not liable for these damages. No specific dollar figures were suggested as an appropriate award.

The second version of the trial was approximately 400 words long. In addition to the factual summary and counsel's opening and closing statements, it included testimony from the plaintiff's expert witness, an economist, on direct and cross-examination. The economist testified that the present value of lost wages amounted to $719,354. He testified that his calculations were based on the plaintiff's age, past earnings, expected date of retirement, past salary increases, and inflation. On cross-examination, the expert conceded that the calculations were not discounted for any future income if the plaintiff obtained another job or died before age 65. Nor did the calculations reflect other uncertainties, for example, salary plateaus reached by senior employees. In this version of the transcript, the defendant's attorney simply argued in closing that the plaintiff's claim for damages should be reduced because of the uncertain assumptions upon which it was based and offered the figure of $321,000 as fair compensation.

The third version was approximately 800 words long. In addition to the factual summary, opening and closing statements, and expert testimony for the plaintiff, it included expert testimony by an economist for the defendant. The expert testified about a model he designed to forecast individual earnings and elaborated on several features of his model, including rates of growth for particular employment sectors, inflation and interest rates, average salaries and salary increases, and years of employment and average worklife expectancies for particular occupations. He related the model to the plaintiff's case by suggesting that the plaintiff had only a 60% chance of working to age 65 and testified that based on his calculations, the plaintiff was entitled to $321,000. The expert concluded that Wholesome Food Company should not be held responsible for the full damages that the plaintiff was claiming.

In summary, the three versions of the trial were a no expert condition (n = 50) wherein no specific damage figures were cited; a plaintiff's expert condition (n = 56) that contained the expert's calculated total award for lost salary ($719,354) and the defendant's counter offer ($321,000); and a "battle of the experts" condition (n = 44) that included the same suggested amounts as above with each amount calculated by opposing experts. Because they lack expertise in this area, the economists did not forecast future pain and suffering.

The trial summaries were followed by a set of commonly used jury instructions telling jurors that they should consider a reasonable value of lost salary, present value of the salary, and benefits reasonably certain to be lost. They were also told to consider both mental and physical pain and suffering experienced by the plaintiff now and in the future. (Jurors are typically given no further information concerning compensation for pain and suffering.) Further instructions stated that the burden of proof rested with the plaintiff and that awards had to be based upon evidence and not upon speculation, guess, or conjecture.

Jurors were asked to determine an award for lost wages and another for pain and suffering. They were then asked what factors came to mind while making their judgments. They selected factors from the following list: (a) the plaintiff's age; (b) salary; (c) the number of years he might have continued to work; (d) future raises and promotions; (e) a change of career; (f) the impact of inflation; (g) attorney's fees; and (h) other factors not listed. They were then asked to indicate the three factors they deemed most important. Finally, they were asked demographic questions.

Procedure

Jurors were approached while awaiting jury selection. They were told that participation was strictly voluntary and that they could withdraw at any time. A majority of those in attendance agreed to participate. The three versions of the trial transcript were then randomly distributed.

After signing the consent form, jurors were asked to read the transcript carefully at their own pace and not to discuss it with others. After reading the case they were directed to answer all questions completely. Written debriefing statements were distributed after the questionnaires were returned.

RESULTS

Summary of Monetary Awards

Three different awards were analyzed: (1) an award for lost salary, (2) an award for pain and suffering, and (3) the sum of these two awards (total award). Across the three conditions, awards ranged from \$1 to \$1,000,000 for lost salary, \$0 to \$500,000 for pain and suffering, and \$1 to \$1,219,354 for the total award. These data are shown in Table 1.

The modal award for lost salary was \$719,354. Recall that this was the exact figure mentioned by the plaintiff's expert to compensate the plaintiff for lost wages. This result suggests that many jurors wholeheartedly accepted the figures proffered by the expert for the plaintiff. Further evidence of endorsement of experts derives from the fact that the second most frequently occurring award was \$321,000, the figure put forth by the defendant's expert.

The Influence of Expert Testimony

To examine the influence of expert testimony on awards, a one-way ANOVA with three levels (no expert, plaintiff expert only, and two experts) was computed for each type of award. The alpha level was set at .05. All significant results exceeded that level.

The award for lost salary was significantly different across conditions, $F(2,149) = 6.14$. The plaintiff expert only condition resulted in the highest award ($M = 573{,}560$), the condition involving experts for both sides was next ($M = 544{,}729$), and the no expert condition resulted in the lowest award ($M = 429{,}582$). These data are shown in Table 2. Tukey's test indicated that both conditions involving expert testimony resulted in significantly higher awards than the condition involving no expert.

The total award also differed significantly across conditions, $F(2,149) = 4.9$.

Table 1. Awards for Lost Salary, Pain and Suffering, and Total Awards: All Conditions (in Dollars)

	Lost salary	Pain/suffering	Total award
Mean	517,110	75,739	592,344
Median	615,000	25,000	667,800
Mode	719,354	0	719,354
Range	1–1,000,000	0–500,000	1–1,219,354
$N = 150$			

Table 2. Measures of Central Tendency: Awards by Condition (in Dollars)

	Mean	Median	Mode
Lost salary			
No expert	429,582[a]	366,000	248,000
Plaintiff's expert	573,560[b]	700,000	719,354
Two experts	544,729[b]	630,000	719,354
Pain/suffering			
No expert	74,490	50,000	0
Plaintiff's expert	70,822	50,000	0
Two experts	83,388	10,000	0
Total award			
No expert	502,582[a]	498,000	*
Plaintiff's expert	644,382[b]	719,354	719,354
Two experts	628,116[b]	719,354	**

Note. Different superscripts *(a,b)* indicate significant differences ($p < .05$). $n = 50$, no expert; $n = 56$, plaintiff's expert; $n = 44$, two experts. *Three values tied for mode: 100,000, 248,000, 750,000. ** Two values tied for mode: 321,000, 719,354.

Further analysis (Tukey's) showed that the pattern of means for the total award was identical to the pattern for the lost salary award: The plaintiff expert only condition ($M = 644{,}382$) and the two experts condition ($M = 628{,}116$) each resulted in a significantly higher award than the no expert condition ($M = 502{,}582$). One-way analysis of variance of the awards for pain and suffering produced no significant differences. Thus, jurors who relied solely on their own calculations awarded significantly less compensation for lost salary and less compensation overall than jurors who were exposed to expert testimony. This was true even when jurors without expert testimony were compared to those exposed to expert testimony from an economist for the defense whose suggested figure was less than 50% of the plaintiff's figure.

To further evaluate jurors' tendencies to underestimate the value of an award when unaided, frequencies of "low" and "high" awards were analyzed. Recall that the plaintiff was earning $62,000 annually at age 54 when his job was terminated. A straight multiplication of worklife (assuming retirement at age 65) by salary results in $682,000 ($62,000 × 11) of lost salary. Low awards can be arbitrarily judged as those more than one standard deviation below this amount and high awards as those more than one standard deviation above. The standard deviation for the total award across all conditions was $254,783. Based on this figure, 66% of jurors (99 of 150) gave an award that was within one standard deviation of $682,000. Of the remaining 51 jurors, only 10 (7%) gave a high award and 41 (27%) gave a low award. What effect did expert testimony have on these low awards?

Examination of the total award by condition indicates that 54% of the low awards (22 of 41) occurred in the no expert condition, 22% occurred in the plaintiff's expert condition, and 24% occurred in the two experts condition. Stated otherwise, by this criterion 44% of jurors in the no expert condition gave a low award, as did only 16% in the plaintiff's expert condition and 23% in the two experts condition, $\chi^2(2, N = 41) = 21.95$. Without expert testimony, jurors tended to give lower awards.

Several analyses of modal awards clearly indicated that endorsement of the expert took place. The modal award for lost salary in the plaintiff's expert condition was the exact figure suggested by the expert, adapted by 37% of jurors in that condition. Likewise, in the two-experts condition, the exact amount suggested by the plaintiff's expert was given by 21% of jurors and the exact figure suggested by the defendant's expert was given by 20% of jurors. The modal award for total damages in each of the expert conditions was also the exact figure suggested by the plaintiff's expert. Interestingly, the modal award for pain and suffering was zero—consistent with the fact that no expert testimony supported these damages.

In summary, the analyses of monetary awards indicated that expert testimony influenced awards in an upward direction. Jurors unaided by expert testimony awarded significantly less than did those exposed to an expert. These analyses also supported the notion that jurors tended to match the values suggested by experts. The modal awards from the conditions involving expert witnesses reflected endorsement of the expert's figures. Finally, these data indicate that compromise awards in the condition involving a battle of experts were not common. On none of the three measures (lost salary, pain and suffering, and total award) was the mean award from the two-expert condition significantly different from the award when only the plaintiff's expert testified.

Analysis of Structured Question

Jurors were asked to indicate any and all factors about the case they considered important. After indicating the factors, jurors were asked to rank, in order, the three they considered most important. These factors are shown in Table 3.

Several noteworthy findings emerged. First, three factors dominated: the plaintiff's age, his salary, and his expected worklife. The plaintiff's age was rated as an important factor by 97% of all jurors. Not surprisingly, most jurors ranked age as the most important factor. The next two most important factors, salary and expected worklife, were indicated by 85% and 88% of jurors, respectively. Each

Table 3. Factors Jurors Said They Thought were Important: Percentages Overall and By Condition

Factors	Overall	No expert	Plaintiff expert	Two experts
Plaintiff's age at termination	96.7	94.0	98.2	97.7
Number of years to continue working	88.0	84.0	91.1	88.6
Plaintiff's salary at termination	84.7	92.0	82.1	79.6
Raises and promotions	36.7	28.0	42.9	38.6
Impact of inflation	28.0	24.0	33.9	25.0
Changing careers	25.3	26.0	23.2	27.3
Attorney's fees	25.3	26.0	32.1	15.9

Note. Totals add to more than 100% because jurors could indicate more than one factor.

of the remaining four factors (possible raises and promotions, inflation, possible career changes, and attorneys' fees) was mentioned by only 25%–37% of jurors. Finally, the factors jurors rated as important did not vary as a function of expert testimony. There were no significant differences across conditions in the factors jurors said they considered.

In general, the factors jurors reported attending to did not influence the amount of damages awarded. There were three exceptions to this generalization. Forty-two jurors said they considered the impact of inflation. When these 42 were compared to jurors who did not indicate that inflation was an important factor, analysis indicated that the former group awarded significantly larger amounts for both lost salary and the total award than did the latter group $t(148) = -2.55, p < .05$. Fifty-five jurors said they considered future raises and promotions the plaintiff might receive. These jurors also gave significantly larger awards than those who did not consider raises and promotions, $t(148) = -3.02, p < .05$. Finally, 38 jurors thought that a career change by the plaintiff was an important factor, and these jurors tended to award significantly *less* for pain and suffering $t(147) = 2.39, p < .05$. Perhaps these jurors felt that if the plaintiff changed careers he would find employment; thus they awarded him less.

DISCUSSION

Our results support the hypothesis that in determining damages, jurors match the figures suggested by an expert. In both of the expert testimony conditions, the modal awards were the exact amounts suggested by the expert. The most frequently occurring award for lost salary was the precise amount suggested by the plaintiff's expert, and the next most frequent award was the amount cited by the defense.

There is also evidence that jurors in the no expert condition may have "anchored" on a figure presented at trial. In the no expert condition, jurors relied on the plaintiff's annual salary figure at the time of termination. In this condition, the two most frequent awards were products of multiplying the salary at termination by either 4 (the number of years from termination to trial) or 11 (the number of years from termination to retirement at age 65).

Results confirmed that jurors in the no expert condition awarded less than jurors exposed to expert testimony, but there was equivocal support for the hypothesis that without expert testimony, jurors would fail to account for exponential growth factors. In fact, jurors in the no expert condition were as likely as jurors in the expert conditions to say they had *considered* exponential factors such as inflation, raises, and promotions. Of course, these jurors may have been responding to demand characteristics of the questionnaire and stated that they considered exponential factors, even if they had not actually done so. Perhaps jurors considered inflation and interest rates after calculating an initial award, but concluded that the initial sum was fair.

Only approximately one third of all jurors said they considered exponential factors, however. This finding is consistent with previous research which has examined damage computations (Goodman, Greene, & Loftus, 1989). Goodman et al. found that very few jurors intuitively used a strategy involving exponential computations. Although the evidence is indirect, it appears that the majority of jurors are not likely to spontaneously consider exponential components in their decision making.

There was little support for the hypothesis that the amounts suggested by opposing experts would serve as end points on a range of acceptable awards and that jurors would make a compromise award near the middle of the range. Instead of compromising, many jurors in the two-experts condition endorsed either the plaintiff's figures or the defense's figures. However, jurors who endorsed the defense's figures did show a slight tendency to compromise: They increased the defendant's suggested amount by approximately $100,000. Thus, although agreeing in principle with the defendant's figure, these jurors apparently considered the suggested amount to be too low. This finding is consistent with Zuehl (1982), who found that when the *ad damnum* was relatively low, jurors increased the award. Further research involving a manipulation in which the defendant's expert makes a *very* low request could confirm this finding.

It is possible that we failed to find evidence for compromise awards because jurors did not deliberate. In actual cases, in which individual jurors' sentiments about damages may differ radically, one likely resolution during deliberations would be a compromise verdict that satisfies both extremes on the jury. Data from posttrial interviews in actual cases suggest that such compromises do occur (Singer, 1988). The compromising process is apparently less likely to take place in the decision making of a given individual.

Expert testimony appears, then, to influence jurors' decisions. Relative to jurors without expert testimony, those exposed to an expert economist tended to give higher awards. There are several reasons why this may occur. Jurors may simply trust the experts and accept their testimony without question (Chaiken & Strangor, 1987). Higher awards may occur because there are no "going rates" for damages, and jurors may view the expert as someone who sets the rates. Interestingly, jurors were much more likely to endorse the defense figure if it came from an expert witness (two-expert condition), rather than from the defense attorney (one-expert condition).

Several caveats concerning the generalizability of these findings are in order. Jurors participating in this study knew that their decisions carried no real consequence and may have put less effort into the task than if the consequences were binding. This may have increased the likelihood of endorsing experts' assessments. In fact, reliance on the experts' figures may be an appropriate strategy for the task presented in this study but may not generalize to actual trials. Actual jurors also face moral and ethical obligations to carefully evaluate all of the evidence. Jurors who comply with that directive may not be content to simply "rubberstamp" experts' conclusions.

On the other hand, because judgmental heuristics serve to lighten the cognitive load, a real trial with its lengthy and complex testimony may also result in endorsement of expert testimony. This may be especially true when deliberations concerning the question of liability have been time-consuming. In this instance, jurors exposed to expert testimony may be especially prone to latch onto the figure suggested by an expert in an effort to lessen the complexity of their task, agree on damages, and complete their charge.

REFERENCES

Broeder, D. W. (1959). The University of Chicago jury project. *Nebraska Law Review, 38,* 744–760.

Cavoukian, A., & Heslegrave, R. J. (1980). The admissibility of polygraph evidence in court: some empirical findings. *Law and Human Behavior, 4,* 117–132.

Chaiken, S., & Stangor, C. (1987). Attitudes and attitude change. *Annual Review of Psychology, 38,* 575–630.

Eagly, A. H., & Chaiken, S. (1984). Cognitive theories of persuasion. In L. Berkowitz (Ed.), *Advances in experimental social psychology, 17.* New York: Academic Press.

Goodman, J. (1986). Probabilistic scientific evidence: Jurors' inferences. Unpublished manuscript, University of Washington.

Goodman, J., Greene, E., & Loftus, E. F. (1989). Runaway verdicts or reasoned determinations: Mock juror strategies in awarding damages. *Jurimetrics Journal, 29,* 285–309.

Kalven, H. (1958). The jury, the law, and the personal injury award. *Ohio State Law Journal, 19,* 158–178.

Keren, G. (1983). Cultural differences in the misperception of exponential growth. *Perception and Psychophysics, 34,* 289–293.

Samuelson, R. J. (1986). The litigation explosion: The wrong question. *Maryland Law Review, 46,* 78–85.

Singer, A. (1988). They didn't really blame the cigarette makers. *American Lawyer,* Sept., 31.

Thompson, W. C., & Britton, R. L. (1988). Communicating the results of paternity tests. Paper presented at American Psychology–Law Society, Miami.

Wagenaar, W. A., & Timmers, H. (1978). Extrapolation of exponential time series is not enhanced by having some more data points. *Perception and Psychophysics, 24,* 182–184.

Zuehl, J. J. (1982). The ad damnum, jury instructions, and personal injury damage awards. Unpublished manuscript, University of Chicago.

NOTES

JUDGES' NONVERBAL BEHAVIOR IN JURY TRIALS: A THREAT TO JUDICIAL IMPARTIALITY

The American Jury[1] by Kalven and Zeisel was one of the first attempts to study the jury's decision-making process empirically.[2] Among the more interesting of its conclusions is the assertion that in most cases the jury understands the evidence and instructions before it, a thesis at odds with much of the conventional wisdom[3] but later adopted by the Supreme Court in *Duncan v. Louisiana*.[4]

Looking at cases already decided by jurors, Kalven and Zeisel asked the presiding judge in each case how he would have decided it. They then compared the juries' actual decisions and the judges' hypothetical ones, finding concurrence about 75 percent of the time.[5] Because agreement occurred at a rate greater than chance, the authors concluded that the jury does in fact understand the case. To test this conclusion, they then divided the cases according to the difficulty of the evidence presented in each. They hypothesized that "if the jury has any propensity to misunderstand the case, it will be more likely to disagree with the judge in those cases it perceives as difficult."[6] However, the difficulty of the case was found to have no effect on the level of judge/jury agreement. The authors termed this result "a stunning refutation of the hypothesis that the jury does not understand."[7]

---

[1] H. Kalven & H. Zeisel, The American Jury (1966). This book represents the culmination of several years of study undertaken under the auspices of the University of Chicago Jury Project.

[2] Although it takes an empirical approach, the study suffers from severe methodological deficiencies which greatly weaken its conclusions, rendering it almost as non-empirical as those studies which preceded it. *See* Walsh, Book Review, 79 Yale L.J. 142, 144 (1969).

[3] For a sampling of those works concluding that jurors are incapable of understanding the factual and legal problems before them, see J. Frank, Courts on Trial 111-20 (1949); M. Gleisser, Juries and Justice 242-47 (1968); Broeder, *The Functions of the Jury: Facts or Fiction?*, 21 U. Chi. L. Rev. 386, 387-401 (1954); Hervey, *The Jurors Look at Our Judges*, 18 J. Okla. B. Ass'n 1508, 1511 (1947); Hoffman & Brodley, *Jurors on Trial*, 17 Mo. L. Rev. 235 (1952).

[4] 391 U.S. 145, 157 (1968) (citing the Kalven and Zeisel study). The *Duncan* Court ruled that the sixth amendment right to a *criminal* jury trial was incorporated in the fourteenth amendment's due process clause and therefore applicable to the states. There were thus a good many more social policy and constitutional arguments available to the Court in its support of the jury system, in addition to reliability, than there might have been in a *civil* case. In this respect, the Kalven and Zeisel hypothesis was perhaps not an essential part of the Court's ruling.

[5] H. Kalven & H. Zeisel, *supra* note 1, at 56, 63. This finding mirrors those of earlier studies. *Id.* at app. D.

[6] *Id.* at 157 (emphasis deleted).

[7] *Id.*

Since both factual and legal issues are often quite complex,[8] this finding is surprising indeed. It is hard to believe that a jury of laymen can understand every situation equally well regardless of its complexity. This note suggests an alternative explanation for the Kalven and Zeisel correlation. Judge/jury concurrence may result, at least in part, because the judge subtly and unintentionally conveys to the jury his feelings about the parties and participants in the case and because the jury is influenced by his cues. The note will first examine how a judge might influence a jury through these subtle and unintentional signals and then consider various methods to correct the difficulties presented by this communication process.

I. The Judge/Jury Influence Process

The legal community has long acknowledged that a special relationship exists between judge and jury. The Supreme Court recognized the susceptibility of jurors to judicial influence at least as early as 1893[9] and reaffirmed that recognition a year later in *Starr v. United States:*

> It is obvious that under any system of jury trials the influence of the trial judge on the jury is necessarily and properly of great weight, and that his lightest word or intimation is received with deference, and may prove controlling.[10]

This notion has become so strong in the federal courts that the "fact" that jurors are sensitive to the judge's behavior is now a matter for judicial notice.[11] This belief is also prevalent in the state courts with only slight dissent.[12] One lawyer has remarked that the jury always looks to the judge

---

[8] *See* note 3 *supra*.

[9] Hicks v. United States, 150 U.S. 442, 452 (1893).

[10] 153 U.S. 614, 626 (1894).

[11] Bursten v. United States, 395 F.2d 976, 983 (5th Cir. 1968). *See also* Moody v. United States, 377 F.2d 175, 179 (5th Cir. 1967). Not all federal judges, however, have felt that jurors are easily influenced by judicial behavior. Consider the following assertion of Judge Learned Hand, defending a trial judge's comments to the jury:

> The belief very commonly held by judges that a jury is excessively subject to the judge's influence, my own experience at least did not bear out. I found them generally quite robust enough to form their own opinions independently of any indications I might give them of mine.

United States v. Goldstein, 120 F.2d 485, 491 (2d Cir. 1941), *aff'd,* 316 U.S. 114 (1942). *See also* Statement of Judge A. Holtzoff, before Judicial Administration Section of the American Bar Association, in *The Right of a Judge to Comment on the Evidence in His Charge to the Jury,* 6 F.R.D. 317, 325 (1944) [hereinafter cited as *Right to Comment*].

[12] *See, e.g.,* Hernandez v. State, 87 Nev. 553, 557, 490 P.2d 1245, 1247 (1971); State v. Holden, 280 N.C. 426, 429, 185 S.E.2d 889, 892 (1972). *But see* Booren v. McWilliams, 26 N.D. 558, 586, 145 N.W. 410, 419 (1914) (dissenting opinion); Aaron v. Hampton Motors, Inc., 240 S.C. 26, 36, 124 S.E.2d 585, 590 (1962).

for guidance and "if he tells them what they are to do they are going to do just the thing he says."[13]

Although the recognition of a judge/jury influence process has developed largely through cases which focus upon the prejudicial content of a judge's instructions to the jury, comments upon the evidence, or admonitions to counsel, the judge may communicate his feelings about the case through unspoken behaviors as well.[14] In one case on appeal, the defendant alleged the following judicial conduct:

> [W]hen a brother of appellant testified that appellant was at home watching television on the night of the burglary, the trial judge "placed his hands flat to the sides of his head, shook his head negatively once, leaned back and swiveled his chair 180° around."[15]

Counsel for defendant may well have given up at this point, particularly if this evidence were crucial to his establishment of an alibi. Yet behavior need not be even this obvious to be communicative. As one juror suggests, because jurors are "highly sensitive to the demeanor of the [j]udge,"[16] the process of judicial influence may be quite subtle. She explains:

> During the testimony the attitude of the judge is very important. His movements and gestures, even his posture, affect the jury and they react accordingly.[17]

This note contends that such subtle behaviors do occur and that they can greatly influence the jury. Support for this assertion may be found in the results of current social science research conducted to study the problem of experimenter/subject interaction. As will be shown,[18] the judge/juror relationship in the courtroom is, in a variety of ways, similar to the experimenter/subject relationship in the experiment. By studying findings in this analogous situation, we can begin to see whether a judge/juror influence process takes place and, if so, through what medium and under what conditions.

---

[13] Statement of R. Polk, in *Right to Comment, supra* note 11, at 338-39.

[14] Legal writers have suggested that judge/jury influence may occur in subtle ways, including voice tone, stress, and inflection, *see* Statement of B. McKelway, in *Right to Comment, supra* note 11, at 335, and nonverbal behaviors, *see* Statement of L. Rover, in *id.* at 330; Conner, *The Trial Judge, His Facial Expressions, Gestures and General Demeanor—Their Effect on the Administration of Justice*, 9 TRIAL LAW. GUIDE, August 1965, at 61, 62. Generally, however, the legal literature has been concerned with less subtle behaviors.

[15] State v. Barron, 465 S.W.2d 523, 527 (Mo. 1971).

[16] Head, *Confessions of a Juror*, in PROCEEDINGS OF THE ANNUAL JUDICIAL CONFERENCE, TENTH JUDICIAL CIRCUIT OF THE UNITED STATES, 44 F.R.D. 330, 333 (1967).

[17] *Id.*

[18] *See* text accompanying notes 59-69 *infra*.

A. The Concept of Experimenter Bias

Social scientific experiments often differ from those of the physical sciences because their subjects — human beings — may behave differently in an experimental situation than they would in real life. The awareness and apprehension that subjects bring to the experiment are factors that the physical scientist does not face. Slightly more than a decade ago, experimental pyschologists became troubled by their methodology, suspecting that experimenter/subject relationships had a significant impact upon their data. They found that the experimenter would often unintentionally guide the subject in an effort to "come out right" and that he could succeed in doing so because the subject would unconsciously search for and respond to that guidance.[19] This influence process, known as the experimenter bias effect, is now one of the most well-established phenomena in social science.[20] An investigation by Rosenberg illustrates the process.[21] In this experiment subjects were asked to rate the "success" or "failure" level portrayed by individuals in each one of a set of photographs. The only contact between subject and experimenter occurred when the experimenter read a standardized set of instructions to his subjects. Rosenberg introduced two key variables into this scheme.

1. Experimenter's expectancy

The experimenters were divided into two groups. One group was led to believe that its subjects would perform in a particular manner; the other, that its subjects would perform in the opposite manner. Each experimenter thus had an illusion that there was a "correct" result to be expected from his subjects.

2. Subject's evaluation apprehension

The subjects were also divided into two groups. While both groups performed the same picture-rating task, they received different instructions

---

[19] Rosenthal, *Interpersonal Expectations: Effects of the Experimenter's Hypothesis*, in ARTIFACT IN BEHAVIORAL RESEARCH 181 (R. Rosenthal & R. Rosnow eds. 1969); Masling, *Differential Indoctrination of Examiners and Rorschach Responses*, 29 J. CONSULTING PSYCHOLOGY 198 (1965).

[20] Rosenthal, *Experimenter Expectancy and the Reassuring Nature of the Null Hypothesis Decision Procedure*, in THE SOCIAL PSYCHOLOGY OF PSYCHOLOGICAL RESEARCH 386, 392 (A. Miller ed. 1972). This is not to suggest, however, that its existence has been without challenge. *See* Barber, Forgione, Chaves, Calverley, McPeake, & Bowen, *Five Attempts to Replicate the Experimenter Bias Effect*, 33 J. CONSULTING & CLINICAL PSYCHOLOGY 1 (1969); Barber & Silver, *Fact, Fiction, and the Experimenter Bias Effect*, 70 PSYCHOLOGICAL BULL. 1 (1968 pt. 2).

[21] Rosenberg, *The Conditions and Consequences of Evaluation Apprehension*, in ARTIFACT AND BEHAVIORAL RESEARCH 279, 324-29 (R. Rosenthal & R. Rosnow eds. 1969).

at the outset. One received neutral instructions; the other, instructions designed to instill a fear that performance on the task could be used to evaluate their mental health. This provided an incentive to perform "correctly."

The results indicated that those subjects with a heightened fear of evaluation ("evaluation apprehension") performed in accordance with their experimenter's notion of proper performance ("expectancy") at a rate far greater than chance. The implication is thus that even with minimal interaction between experimenter and subject (here, the reading of a set of simple instructions), the experimenter will convey cues reflecting his hypothesis. Those subjects who are motivated to look for these cues will find them and alter their behavior accordingly.

B. *The Communication of the Experimenter Bias Effect*

Most theorists contend that this type of communication occurs in a subtle level beyond the conscious control of the parties involved,[22] through nonverbal[23] or paralinguistic[24] behaviors. As used in this note, nonverbal behavior refers to movements, positions, and postures of the head, trunk, and limbs or features of each. Paralinguistic behaviors are the noncontent parts of speech, such as loudness, pitch, tempo, emphasis, and hesitation.

1. *Nonverbal Communication*

Several general principles emerge from the many studies of nonverbal communication.[25] All individuals, including judges in the courtroom,

---

[22] *See* Duncan, Rosenberg, & Finkelstein, *The Paralanguage of Experimenter Bias,* 32 SOCIOMETRY 207, 218 (1969); Masling, *Role-Related Behavior of the Subject and Psychologist and Its Effects upon Psychological Data,* in 14 NEBRASKA SYMPOSIUM ON MOTIVATION 67, 68 (D. Levine ed. 1966); Riecken, *A Program for Research on Experiments in Social Psychology,* in 2 DECISIONS, VALUES AND GROUPS 25, 39 (N. Washburne ed. 1962); Rosenberg, *supra* note 21, at 304.

[23] Rosenberg, *supra* note 21, at 336; Rosenthal, *supra* note 19, at 253-54; Rosenthal, *Covert Communication in the Psychological Experiment,* 67 PSYCHOLOGICAL BULL. 356 (1967).

[24] Duncan, Rosenberg, & Finkelstein, *supra* note 22; Rosenberg, *supra* note 21, at 331-36; Rosenthal, *supra* note 19, at 250-53; Scherer, Rosenthal, & Koivumaki, *Mediating Interpersonal Expectancies via Vocal Cues: Differential Speech Intensity as a Means of Social Influence,* 2 EUR. J. SOCIAL PSYCHOLOGY 163 (1972).

[25] It is beyond the scope of this note to present an overview of the literature on nonverbal communication. R. BIRDWHISTELL, INTRODUCTION TO KINESICS (1952), the seminal work, is a good introduction to some of the more basic areas of nonverbal communication. Duncan, *Nonverbal Communication,* 72 PSYCHOLOGICAL BULL. 118 (1969), provides a general overview of the literature in the field. *See also* M. DAVIS, UNDERSTANDING BODY MOVEMENT (1972). Mehrabian is another major figure in the field. His work, A. MEHRABIAN, NONVERBAL COMMUNICATION (1972), brings together some of his more influential studies. The bibliography is also a helpful source for studies by other scholars. P. EKMAN, W. FRIESEN, & P. ELLSWORTH, EMOTION IN THE HUMAN FACE: GUIDELINES FOR RESEARCH AND AN INTEGRATION OF FINDINGS (1972)

manifest nonverbal behaviors.[26] These behaviors, which studies find account for approximately 60 to 65 percent of a person's total communicative output,[27] are particularly important in conveying attitudes and emotions,[28] either purposefully or unintentionally. They occur as inherent parts of normal communication,[29] largely beyond the sender's conscious control.[30] Even when an individual wishes to hide his feelings, research indicates that these feelings will escape through the nonverbal channel.[31]

[hereinafter cited as EKMAN], provides an exhaustive overview of literature devoted particularly to facial expressions.

[26] Nonverbal behavior is a broad term. Duncan, *supra* note 25, suggests that the term "nonverbal communication" has been used to describe body movements, paralanguage, proxemics (studies of distance). olfaction, skin sensitivity, and artifacts (like clothing). As explained in the text, the use of the term in this note will be more limited. *See also* note 28 *infra*.

[27] *See* J. Frahm, Verbal-Nonverbal Interaction Analysis: Exploring a New Methodology for Quantifying Dyadic Communication Systems 10, 1970 (unpublished Ph.D. dissertation at Michigan State University); H. Heger, Verbal and Nonverbal Classroom Communication: The Development of an Observational Instrument 26, 1969 (unpublished Ph.D. dissertation at Ohio State University).

[28] A. MEHRABIAN, SILENT MESSAGES 44, 111 (1971); Rosenfeld, *Instrumental Affiliative Functions of Facial and Gestural Expressions,* in INTERPERSONAL COMMUNICATION: SURVEY AND STUDIES 587-88 (D. Barnlund ed. 1968).

Nonverbal behaviors may serve additional functions as well. A. MEHRABIAN, *supra* note 25, at 3, suggests four, in addition to conveying attitudes:

(1) Emblem—a nonverbal act that can be accurately translated into words (*e.g.*, a handshake).

(2) Illustrator—really a part of speech serving the function of emphasis (*e.g.*, head and hand movements occur more frequently with primary-stressed words).

(3) Regulator—acts that help to initiate and terminate speech in a social situation (*e.g.*, eye contact is used to indicate when one is through talking so that another person will know when he may politely begin).

(4) Adaptor—acts relating to the satisfaction of bodily needs (*e.g.*, scratching).

[29] *See generally* A. MEHRABIAN, *supra* note 28.

[30] A. MEHRABIAN, *supra* note 28, at 46-47, 56; L. Greene, Effects of Field Independence, Physical Proximity and Evaluative Feedback on Affective Reactions and Compliance in a Dyadic Interaction 4, 1973 (unpublished Ph.D. dissertation at Yale University); J. Victoria, The Development of a Typology of Nonverbal Behavior and Observational Procedures for the Identification of Nonverbal Behavior of Student Teachers of Art 19-23, June 1970 (unpublished Ph.D. dissertation at Pennsylvania State University); Deutsch, *Analytic Posturology and Synesthesiology,* 50 PSYCHOANALYTIC REV. 40, 41 (1963); *cf.* E. GOFFMAN, THE PRESENTATION OF SELF IN EVERYDAY LIFE 7 (1959); Argyle, Salter, Nicholson, Williams, & Burgess, *The Communication of Inferior and Superior Attitudes by Verbal and Non-verbal Signals,* 9 BRIT. J. SOCIAL & CLINICAL PSYCHOLOGY 222, 230 (1970) [hereinafter cited as *Argyle*].

[31] A. MEHRABIAN, *supra* note 25, at 84-103; Ekman & Friesen, *Nonverbal Leakage and Clues to Deception,* 32 PSYCHIATRY 88 (1969). Mehrabian assumes that "the human organism cannot totally 'conceal' emotion." Therefore, "emotions denied expression [verbally] find another outlet" since they are "part of social life." A. MEHRABIAN, SILENT MESSAGES 46-47 (1971). This assumption bespeaks an inevitability which, if true, must be reckoned with in any attempt to remedy the problem of judicial nonverbal communication. Compare the following *de*

Among the most important nonverbal cues are those which reflect the sender's positive or negative evaluation of a particular reference object. Psychologists believe the following behaviors reflect a positive evaluation (the more frequently the behavior occurs, the more positive the effect): (1) smile, (2) gesticulations,[32] (3) positive head nods, (4) forward lean,[33] (5) eye contact, (6) shoulder orientation,[34] and (7) arm openness.[35] A negative evaluation is reflected by (1) low frequencies of the seven positive behaviors, (2) self-manipulation,[36] and (3) smile.[37]

---

minimis articulation in Allen v. State, 290 Ala. 339, 342-43, 276 So.2d 583, 586 (1973):

> The trial judge is a human being, not an automation or a robot. He is not required to be a Great Stone Face which shows no reaction to anything that happens in his courtroom. Testimony that is amusing may draw a smile or a laugh, shocking or distasteful evidence may cause a frown or scowl, without reversible error being committed thereby. We have not, and hopefully never will reach the stage in Alabama at which a stone-cold computer is draped in a black robe, set up behind the bench, and plugged in to begin service as Circuit Judge.

Cf. the discussion of training judges to mask their behavior in text accompanying notes 119-36 *infra*.

[32] "[A]ny noticeable movement of arm, hand, or finger, not in moving contact with another part of the body." Rosenfeld, *supra* note 28, at 590.

[33] "The number of degrees that a plane from the communicator's shoulders to his hips is away from the vertical plane. Angles are measured in units of 10 degrees; whereas reclining angles are scored as negative, forward-leaning angles are scored as positive." A. MEHRABIAN, *supra* note 25, at 192.

[34] "The number of degrees a plane perpendicular to the plane of the communicator's shoulders is turned away from the median plane of the addressee. This angle is estimated to the nearest 10 degrees, and cannot exceed 180 degrees." *Id.*

[35] V. Derlega, Social Penetration Processes: The Effects of Topic Intimacy and Support on Openness of Nonverbal Behavior, 1971 (unpublished Ph.D. dissertation at University of Maryland), measures arm openness by three distinct categories: (1) individual does not cross his arms and his hands do not touch, (2) individual crosses hands at wrist, and (3) individual crosses hands above wrist.

[36] Contact between parts of the body, either directly or mediated by instrument, such as scratching, rubbing, or tapping an arm or leg with a finger or pen. This gesture theoretically indicates discomfort and thus characterizes approval-avoiders. Rosenfeld, *supra* note 28, at 590.

[37] In contrast to most other nonverbal behaviors, the smile seems subject to conscious control. Consequently, it is often used to mask the individual's true feelings, particularly when they are "negative." In this context the smile actually serves as a cue reflecting negative evaluation and not, as indicated previously, positive affect. For a discussion of masking behavior, see text accompanying notes 119-36 *infra*.

Although the list of behaviors above is not exhaustive, it does contain those cues most generally recognized as related to positive or negative affect. *See* A. MEHRABIAN, *supra* note 25, at 2-7; V. Derlega, *supra* note 35; Brown & Parks, *Interpreting Nonverbal Behavior, A Key to More Effective Counseling: Review of Literature,* 15 REHABILITATION COUNSELING BULL. 176 (1972); ROSENFELD, *supra* note 28, at 590-91. Moreover, while these behaviors have consistently been associated with the communication of positive or negative feelings, this correlation does not suggest, for example, that whenever a person leans forward he is being friendly and whenever he leans back he is being aloof. Rather, the findings suggest that, if a behavior occurs *x* number of times, it will reflect the emotional state at a rate that is greater than chance.

Demonstrating that individuals emit nonverbal behaviors describes only half of the communication process. This finding is of limited value without a complementary finding that recipients can and do attend to and decode these messages. In an exhaustive overview of the literature on facial expressions, one group of psychologists finds substantial proof for the proposition that the sender's nonverbal cues can be accurately interpreted by untrained observers.[38] Johnson suggests that this decoding process occurs as a natural part of ongoing interactions.[39] For example, students in a classroom both seek and respond to the nonverbal behavior of their teacher.[40] And, just as senders emit cues unconsciously, recipients decode them unconsciously.[41]

A further qualification necessary here concerns definitions of the several behaviors listed above. The development of definitions for nonverbal behaviors and of systems for their observation has proceeded in a haphazard manner. For example, while many individuals report on the effects of smiling, there is no assurance that they are describing the same phenomenon, as each may define it in a slightly different way. Because of this lack of a common vocabulary, no one definition can be ascribed to the behaviors listed here, although those cited in notes 32-36 *supra* are examples of some attempted ones. For a general discussion of the problems caused by variations in the definition of behaviors and the methods for their scoring, see A. Greenbaum, The Systematic Observation of Nonverbal Behavior, Spring, 1973 (unpublished manuscript, Yale University) (on file at the offices of the Virginia Law Review).

[38] EKMAN, *supra* note 25, at 77-119, 176-77.

[39] E. Johnson, Pygmalion in the Testing Setting: Nonverbal Communication as a Mediator of Expectancy Fulfillment 38, 1970 (unpublished Ph.D. dissertation at the University of Michigan).

[40] *See* Galloway, *Teacher Nonverbal Communication*, 24 EDUCATIONAL LEADERSHIP 55, 59 (1966).

[41] It should be noted that individuals do differ in their ability to perceive and decode nonverbal stimuli. *Cf.* L. Reich, Nonverbal Communication of Emotions: A Study of the Relationship Between Training, Expression and Recognition of Emotions 53, Sept., 1970 (unpublished Ph.D. dissertation at Arizona State University) (based on a literature survey). But attempts to correlate these differences with particular personality types have often failed. *See* Davitz, *Personality, Perceptual, and Cognitive Correlates of Emotional Sensitivity*, in THE COMMUNICATION OF EMOTIONAL MEANING 57, 59 (J. Davitz ed. 1964). For example, the evidence concerning the relationship between sex and the ability to encode and decode nonverbal and paralinguistic behavior is contradictory. Davitz, *A Review of Research Concerned with Facial and Vocal Expressions of Emotion*, in *id.* 13, 20. Many of the early studies found no relationship. *See, e.g.*, Levy, *The Ability to Express and Perceive Vocal Communications of Feeling*, in *id.* 43, 54. More recent studies appear to indicate that women are better able to decode attitudes conveyed through these channels than are men. *See* A. MEHRABIAN, *supra* note 25, at 145; *Argyle, supra* note 30, at 230. If these later studies are correct, then one might conclude that the greater the number of women in the jury panel, the greater the possibility that the judge/jury influence process will occur. This fact, if true, might qualify as a rational reason for excluding women from jury service, if indeed a rational reason would be adequate to exclude them under the sixth amendment. Nevertheless, it would probably be outweighed by the policy behind the "fair cross section" requirement. *See* Taylor v. Louisiana, 419 U.S. 522, 533-35 (1975).

It is also important to ascertain whether individuals interpret only those cues directed toward themselves or also those directed toward others. This issue can be significant in the context of a trial, since most of the judge's nonverbal behaviors will be directed toward witnesses, parties, and attorneys rather than toward the jurors themselves. Mehrabian interviewed pairs of subjects and presented to each a series of pre-planned nonverbal cues conveying either positive or negative affect. He found that a subject's ratings of the interviewer's feelings toward himself and toward the other subject mirrored the planned nonverbal manipulation. Apparently, then, subjects are aware of nonverbal behavior directed both toward themselves and toward others and are also able to interpret it accurately.[42] In a similar study by Hicks,[43] leaders of discussion groups presented a series of pre-planned nonverbal cues to the members throughout the course of seemingly normal meetings. Hicks found that a member's rating of the leader's feelings about that member and about other members accurately reflected the messages contained in the nonverbal cues. Hicks concluded that the individuals were aware of the leader's nonverbally conveyed attitudes about themselves and others. He further asserted that individuals used these cues both to assess the worth of members of the group and also to evaluate the acceptability of ideas and suggestions submitted by individuals in the group.[44]

2. *Paralinguistic Communication*

Less data exists concerning paralinguistic communication,[45] but from the existing research a pattern paralleling that found for nonverbal communication emerges. Individuals can and do communicate feelings through paralinguistic cues,[46] and recipients can decode these cues and act upon them.[47] Moreover, the recipient will respond to paralinguistic cues even when he is unable to detect their existence. In one experiment[48] the researchers gave the subjects sets of tape-recorded instructions which varied in the vocal emphasis placed on different words. When asked to compare these sets of instructions, the subjects were unable to identify any

[42] Mehrabian, *Orientation Behaviors and Nonverbal Attitude Communication,* 17 J. Communication 324, 328 (1967).

[43] C. Hicks, An Experimental Approach to Determine the Effect of a Group Leader's Programmed Nonverbal Facial Behavior upon Group Members' Perception of the Leader 123, 1972 (unpublished Ph.D. dissertation at the University of Arkansas).

[44] *Id.* at 123-25.

[45] *Cf.* Duncan, *supra* note 25, at 209. It should be noted, however, that Rosenberg's leading study, *see* text accompanying note 21 *supra*, was a paralinguistic one.

[46] *See* A. Mehrabian, *supra* note 25, at 62-64, 105, 149, 156.

[47] *See* Duncan, Rosenberg, & Finkelstein, *supra* note 22; Scherer, Rosenthal, & Koivumaki, *supra* note 24.

[48] Scherer, Rosenthal, & Koivumaki, *supra* note 24.

variances in the tapes. However, even with manipulations this subtle, the recorded instructions produced the experimenter bias effect. Another study using other paralinguistic behaviors produced similar findings.[49]

In most instances the paralinguistic channel is less powerful than the nonverbal channel,[50] but this ordering is occasionally reversed for a particular emotion[51] or a particular individual.[52] Nevertheless, the paralinguistic channel has an independent potency[53] and may have a significant impact on the communication of a message.[54]

C. *Application of the Model to the Judge/Jury Relationship*

The nonverbal and paralinguistic communication process between experimenter and subject may provide a useful model to explain the judge's influence over jurors. The applicability of this model is grounded on the closely analogous nature of the experimenter/subject relationship in psychological research and the judge/juror relationship in jury trials.[55] The analogy may be seen at three points: (1) the context of the situation, (2) the juror/subject role, and (3) the judge/experimenter role.

1. *The Context*

Upon entering a courtroom or an experimental situation, both the juror and the subject, respectively, face a context which is dissimilar to and removed from their daily lives. For both, the novelty of the situation creates uncertainty about the appropriate way to behave.[56]

---

[49] Duncan, Rosenberg, & Finkelstein, *supra* note 22.

[50] Burns & Beier, *Significance of Vocal and Visual Channels in the Decoding of Emotional Meaning*, 23 J. COMMUNICATION 118, 127 (1973); Mehrabian & Ferris, *Inference of Attitudes from Nonverbal Communication in Two Channels*, 31 J. CONSULTING PSYCHOLOGY 248, 251 (1967).

[51] Burns & Beier, *supra* note 50, at 127.

[52] Mehrabian & Ferris, *supra* note 50, at 251.

[53] *See id.*

[54] *Id.*

[55] Generalizing from the social science literature appears quite proper. Rosenthal, *supra* note 19, asserts that research in experimenter/subject interaction has implications which reach into many other "social relationships," such as that between teachers and students. *Id.* at 269. For an application of this research to problems of police suggestion in lineup identifications, see Levine & Tapp, *The Psychology of Criminal Identification: The Gap from* Wade *to* Kirby, 121 U. PA. L. REV. 1079, 1114-15, 1119 (1973). There is no reason to believe that the phenomenon will not occur to some extent with judges and jurors as well.

[56] *See* Riecken, *supra* note 22, at 28-31, which alludes to this problem in the experimental situation. For a comment on the effect of the novelty of the trial situation on jurors, see Statement of Judge B. Laws, in *Right to Comment, supra* note 11, at 317; Hunter, *Law in the Jury Room*, 2 OHIO ST. L.J. 1, 5 (1935). Note, however, that if a member of a jury panel sits on more than one case during the course of his service, or if he has had previous jury experience in a different court, the novelty of the situation may decrease, with a resulting

Several factors coalesce to create the air of unfamiliarity in the courtroom. The first is the ceremony associated with the trial. Latin phrases, formal procedures, oaths, and judicial robes create an unaccustomed and austere atmosphere designed to accentuate the gravity of the task for those involved.[57] Coupled with this mystique is the actual likelihood that the trial itself may contain complicated rules of law and questions of fact beyond the comprehension of the juror.[58] Taken together, these factors present a novel, uncertain, and potentially anxiety-provoking context within which the juror, like the subject, may be unsure about how to act.

2. *The Juror/Subject Role*

The subject's behavior in the experimental situation is partly the product of two desires. Because participation in the experiment may be seen as an opportunity to contribute to the worthwhile goal of furthering

---

dissipation of the judge/juror influence. *Cf.* Broeder, *Previous Jury Trial Service Affecting Juror Behavior,* 506 INS. L.J. 138 (1965).

Psychological studies offer abundant support for the idea that, for whatever set of reasons, modern man seems incurably dependent upon being told what the "correct" way to perform is. The famous experiment by Milgram shows that in a strange context even objectively immoral behavior may be elicited by a legitimate authority figure. In his research, subjects gave what they were led to believe were increasingly painful and dangerous levels of electrical shock to other "subjects" under the guise of helping run a scientific experiment. Milgram, *Behavioral Study of Obedience,* 67 J. ABNORMAL & SOCIAL PSYCHOLOGY 371 (1963). The analogy to the judge, perhaps in his Solomonic role the most legitimate and authoritative of all legitimate authority figures, is clear. *See* text accompanying notes 66-69 *infra.*

[57] *See* ABA PROJECT ON STANDARDS FOR CRIMINAL JUSTICE, ADVISORY COMMITTEE ON THE JUDGE'S FUNCTION, STANDARDS RELATING TO THE FUNCTION OF THE TRIAL JUDGE 30 (Approved Draft, 1972) [hereinafter cited as *Trial Judge Standards*]; Head, *supra* note 16, at 331.

[58] *See* authorities cited in note 3 *supra. But cf.* H. KALVEN & H. ZEISEL, *supra* note 1, at 153-54, 157. Kalven and Zeisel sought to measure the difficulty of jury cases by asking the judges participating in the study the following question:

Compared to the average criminal case, was the evidence as a whole

	Results
easy to comprehend?	(86%)
somewhat difficult?	(12%)
very difficult to comprehend?	(2%)

Although they only obtained a measure of the *judge's* perception of the difficulty of the case in relation to the average case, the authors employed this finding as a measure of the *juror's* perception of difficulty. If this transformation is correct, then cases would seem seldom to present sufficient difficulty to create the degree of uncertainty in the juror's mind that would result in a subconscious reading of judicial cues.

However, Walsh, *supra* note 2, at 153, 154, severely criticizes the inferential process employed here. As he points out, there is no evidence to suggest that a judge's perception of the difficulty of a case mirrors that of a juror. In fact, Walsh's own research suggests that jurors find cases much more difficult than do judges. Further, no information is available concerning the difficulty that the "average" criminal (or, for that matter, civil) case presents for the juror. Hence, to say that a case is more or less difficult than the average case says little.

scientific knowledge, the subject will generally have a desire to be cooperative.[59] More importantly, the subject in a psychological experiment may be motivated by a desire to avoid disapproval,[60] fearing that "incorrect" behavior in the experiment will reflect upon the subject's competence or even his mental health.

The proposition that similar influences affect the juror in the courtroom may be open to some legitimate question. Both legal commentators[61] and lay journalists[62] suggest that citizens are discontented with the judicial process. If this is so, and if citizens carry such discontent into their jury service, a juror's desire to behave cooperatively and appropriately may be slight. This unwillingness to cooperate, however, is not borne out by available data. As Kalven reports,

> [T]here is much evidence that most people, once actually serving in a trial, become highly serious and responsible toward their task and toward the joint effort to deliberate through to a verdict. Whether they are good at the job may be open to question, but that they are serious about it and give it a real try is abundantly documentable.[63]

The comment of one juror appears typical:

> [The juryman] wants to serve and do his duty for society . . . . To be selected to judge his fellow man is indeed serious business, and he knows that he will likely be called upon for decisions that are much deeper than daily expressions of opinion.[64]

In addition to this desire to cooperate, several commentators suggest that the juror may also, like the subject, fear the negative evaluation which could accrue if he performs his task improperly. He may wish to avoid the sanction of the judge or the community for reaching an "improper" decision.[65] For whatever reason, then, the juror will probably have a general

---

[59] Orne, *Demand Characteristics and the Concept of Quasicontrols*, in ARTIFACT IN BEHAVIORAL RESEARCH 143, 145 (R. Rosenthal & R. Rosnow eds. 1969) [hereinafter cited as Orne I]; Orne, *On the Social Psychology of the Psychological Experiment*, 17 AM. PSYCHOLOGIST 776, 778 (1962) [hereinafter cited as Orne II]. *But see* Sigall, Aronson, & Van Hoose, *The Cooperative Subject: Myth or Reality?*, in THE SOCIAL PSYCHOLOGY OF PSYCHOLOGICAL RESEARCH 269 (A. Miller ed. 1972).

[60] Rosenberg, *supra* note 21, at 281.

[61] *Cf.* Miller, *Public Confidence in the Judiciary: Some Notes and Reflections*, 35 LAW & CONTEMP. PROB. 69 (1970); Stafford, *The Public's View of the Judicial Role*, 52 J. AM. JUD. SOC'Y 73 (1968).

[62] 75 U.S. NEWS & WORLD REP., Dec. 31, 1973, at 28.

[63] Kalven, *The Dignity of the Civil Jury*, 50 VA. L. REV. 1055, 1062 (1964); *cf.* M. BLOOMSTEIN, VERDICT: THE JURY SYSTEM 130-31 (1972), citing *inter alia* a finding by the Chicago Jury Project that 94 percent of jurors surveyed wanted to serve again.

[64] Brown, *A Juryman's View*, in SELECTED READINGS—THE JURY 102 (G. Winters ed. 1971).

[65] Coffin, *Jury Trial Tragic but Not Entirely Hopeless*, 25 J. AM. JUD. SOC'Y 13, 14 (1941);

fear of behaving improperly.

3. The Judge/Experimenter Role

When an individual desires to behave correctly but is in a novel context within which appropriate behaviors are often unclear, he may turn for guidance to an individual of higher status.[66] Because of his age, dress (white coat), education, and control over the situation, the experimenter is often perceived by the subject to be of higher status. As a result, the subject may rely on the experimenter for guidance, assuming that because of his higher status he also possesses special knowledge concerning the situation.[67] Similarly, because of the judge's dress (robe), education, and control over the situation, jurors may rely on him for the cues to proper behavior.[68]

In addition, both the judge and experimenter attempt to refrain from communicating information which might guide the behavior of those in the lower status positions. The experimenter attempts to remain neutral so that only the experimental manipulations will affect the subject's behavior. Similarly, the judge attempts to remain impartial so that only the cases of the opposing parties will affect the jurors.[69]

---

cf. Simon, *Trial by Jury: A Critical Assessment,* in APPLIED SOCIOLOGY: OPPORTUNITIES AND PROBLEMS 294, 304-05 (A. Gouldner & S. Miller eds. 1965). *See also* Statement of B. McKelway, in *Right to Comment, supra* note 11, at 335.

[66] *Cf.* Rosenthal, *On Not So Replicated Experiments and Not So Null Results,* 33 J. CONSULTING & CLINICAL PSYCHOLOGY 7, 8 (1969).

[67] *See* Riecken, *supra* note 22, at 28-31.

[68] *See* Statement of L. Rover, in *Right to Comment, supra* note 11 at 327; Conner, *supra* note 14, at 66-67. *But see* Miller, *supra* note 61; Stafford, *supra* note 61. These authors suggest that the image of the judiciary has declined in the eyes of the public. If respect for the judiciary as a whole has declined, it may well affect the respect that an individual juror gives an individual judge in a particular case. As a result, the jurors may ignore the judge and decide the facts on their own. They may even ignore instructions of law, as the whole concept of "jury nullification" admits. For a favorable historical and analytical account of this "community conscience" role of the jury, see Scheflin, *Jury Nullification: The Right to Say No,* 45 CALIF. L. REV. 168 (1972).

[69] *Cf.* ABA CANONS OF JUDICIAL ETHICS No. 34; *Trial Judge Standards, supra* note 57, § 6.4; Conner, *supra* note 14, at 76; *Assessment Conference—Developments in Law and Social Science Research,* 52 N.C.L. REV. 969, 1036-37 (1974).

Admittedly the roles of experimenter in the experiment and judge in the jury trial are not completely analogous. The experimenter is often the sole status figure to which the subject can turn for guidance, while the juror may turn to many figures other than the judge, including the attorneys, *see* Broeder, *The Impact of the Lawyers: An Informal Appraisal,* 1 VALPARAISO L. REV. 40 (1966), or the foreman, Bevan, Albert, Loiseaux, Mayfield, & Wright, *Jury Behavior as a Function of the Prestige of the Foreman and the Nature of His Leadership,* 7 J. PUB. L. 419 (1958). This may dilute the impact of the judge's behavior. Furthermore, the experimenter has an expected result in his experiments. As such he presents consistent cues to which subjects can respond. If a judge fails to evolve an opinion in a case or if he

D. Summary and Implications

Applying the findings concerning the experimenter/subject influence process to the analogous judge/juror relationship, one can refine the commonly-held view that the judge may exercise considerable influence over the jury to suggest that the following process takes place within the trial setting:

> (1) Any conscious or subconscious evaluative feelings a judge has toward the trial participants may be reflected in nonverbal and paralinguistic behaviors, despite his attempts to conceal such feelings.
> (2) Jurors can perceive these cues and interpret them accurately even when they consist of subtle behaviors directed toward others.
> (3) Jurors are likely to attend to, decode, and be influenced by these nonverbal and paralinguistic behaviors when the trial situation contains three factors: (a) a desire by the juror to behave correctly; (b) a context novel to the juror in which the the appropriate behaviors are perceived as unclear; and (c) a high status figure, the judge, emitting cues to proper performance.[70]

If such communication exists in the courtroom and influences jury decisions, judicial impartiality, a basic foundation of the adversary system,[71] becomes illusory.

This is ironic, in view of the extensive authority which regulates a judge's *verbal* communication under the guise of ensuring judicial impartiality. In the vast majority of states which have abolished the judge's common law right to comment on the evidence,[72] the citizen has what amounts to an

---

vacillates in his opinion as the trial progresses, he may fail to provide clear guidance for the jury.

[70] The social science literature suggests that the presence of all three factors may be necessary for this process to occur. In instances where one of these is absent, experiments fail to produce the experimenter/subject influence effect. *See* Minor, *Experimenter-Expectancy Effect as a Function of Evaluation Apprehension,* 15 J. PERSONALITY & SOCIAL PSYCHOLOGY 326, 331 (1970) (on the need for a desire among subjects to behave appropriately); Rosenberg, *supra* note 21, at 322-36; Orne I, *supra* note 59, at 148; Orne II, *supra* note 59, at 779-80 (on the need for sufficient ambiguity in the experimental situation). Moreover, if a situation is too ambiguous, it may also fail to foster the influence. *See* Rosenberg, *supra* note 21, at 319-21. *Cf.* Rosenthal, *supra* note 66, at 7-8 (on the required presence of an experimenter with high status).

[71] Both ABA CANONS OF JUDICIAL ETHICS No. 34 and ABA CODE OF JUDICIAL CONDUCT No. 2 mandate judicial impartiality. The ABA's standards for the trial judge contain three canons designed to assure his neutrality throughout the trial. *Trial Judge Standards, supra* note 57, at §§ 1.3, 5.6, 6.4.

[72] Note, *Judicial Intervention in Trials,* 1973 WASH. U.L.Q. 843, 846-47 & nn. 16, 20, provides a list of such jurisdictions.

absolute right to trial before an impartial judge.[73] In jurisdictions where the trial judge retains a right or duty to comment upon the evidence, on the other hand, the courts, legislatures, or citizens have effectively decided that the goal of evidentiary truth must override the contrasting danger posed to the integrity and independence of the jury. The principle underlying the right is that judicial comment may enhance the jury's understanding of the case before it.[74] Even in these jurisdictions, however, the courts have recognized that the protection of jury independence requires certain limitations upon the judge.[75]

No comparable series of controls regulates judges' nonverbal and paralinguistic behaviors. While some cases suggest that these behaviors fall within the judicial right to comment,[76] and, implicitly, that they can be controlled within its confines, focusing upon the principles which underlie this right will readily expose the weakness of this position. As has been

---

[73] *See, e.g.*, State v. McBryde, 270 N.C. 776, 778, 155 S.E.2d 266, 268 (1967).

[74] If the Kalven and Zeisel hypothesis that juries have few difficulties with the case, *see* notes 1-4, 58 *supra* and accompanying text, is correct, this rationale for the right to comment would of course be irrelevant. The right of verbal commentary would then seem to be too threatening to the jury's independent fact-finding role to justify its small contribution to clarity. Bearing in mind the Supreme Court's apparent adoption of the Kalven and Zeisel hypothesis in Duncan v. Louisiana, 391 U.S. 145, 157 (1968), it would seem that federal judges should curtail their more liberal comments upon the evidence.

[75] In general, the duty of the judge to remain impartial is of paramount importance. *See* United States v. Bukowski, 435 F.2d 1094, 1109 (7th Cir. 1970) (dictum); Moody v. United States, 377 F.2d 175, 180 (5th Cir. 1967); United States v. Carmel, 267 F.2d 345, 350 (7th Cir. 1959). The judge's comments should attempt (1) to order and simplify otherwise complicated issues of law and fact, Heron v. Heron, 393 F.2d 652, 656 (3d Cir. 1968); (2) to show the relationship between testimony and evidence, Quercia v. United States, 289 U.S. 466, 468-69 (1933); and (3) to show the weight of the evidence, *id.* at 469. While the judge may be permitted to give his opinion about the value of testimony and the credibility of witnesses, he is urged to use great care in doing so. *Id.* at 470. Such behavior was not part of the doctrine as originally conceived, Statement of Judge Curtis Bok, in *Right to Comment, supra* note 11, at 318, and even now is considered "close to the line which divides proper judicial action from the field which is exclusively the jury's." Billeci v. United States, 184 F.2d 394, 403 (D.C. Cir. 1950). If the judge does render an opinion, his instructions must "make it unequivocally clear to the jurors that conclusions upon such matters are theirs, not his, to make." *Id.* Only on the rarest of occasions may the judge suggest to the jury what their ultimate decision should be. 1 E. Devitt & C. Blackmar, Federal Jury Practice and Instructions § 8.04, at 179 (1970). *See also id.* § 7.05. Finally, the timing of the judge's comment is of great importance. The right to comment is usually confined to the judge's charge to the jury. Comment at the time of the introduction of evidence is considered an infringement on the jury's role. 4 B. Jones, Evidence § 24:8, at 89 (S. Gard ed. 1972).

See generally Note, *supra* note 73.

[76] *See* Billeci v. United States, 184 F.2d 394, 402-03 (D.C. Cir. 1950); Vinci v. United States, 159 F.2d 777, 778-79 (D.C. Cir. 1947).

noted,[77] the right is a carefully circumscribed one. Nonverbal and paralinguistic behaviors are not subject to the careful control necessary to bring them within this limited right. Because they are an uncontrolled reflection of the judge's own feelings about the case, it is difficult to conceive of them as helping to simplify complicated issues, to describe the relationship between testimony and evidence, or to weigh the evidence—those reasons given for the right to comment. While some cues might be considered an opinion on the evidence, their scope is clearly much broader than would be allowed under this concept. Further, the system's built-in protection to confine judicial comment, the instruction to the jury,[78] may not defuse the impact of nonverbal communication. Finally, it should be noted that these behaviors will occur throughout the trial, thus falling outside the appropriate timing for comment.

Because of their special propensity to affect the jury, and because of their resistance to regulation provided for verbal comments upon the evidence, nonverbal and paralinguistic cues present threats to impartiality which are necessary to control.[79] Eliminating these subtle threats, however, involves potential risks. The modern jury not only serves as the finder of fact in the courtroom but also performs several socially useful functions regardless of its accuracy. The jury is viewed as a dispenser of the law, as the democratic representative of the community, as a means of inducing public confidence in the law, and as an educating force in the community.[80] A critic of the jury system might suggest that these social functions do not outweigh the jury's deficiency as a fact-finding body.[81] Yet, if this note is correct, and jury decisions are often the product of judicial influence, then the jury's fact-finding deficiency may be nonexistent. One who requests a jury trial may actually receive a judge's decision clothed in a jury's verdict. In this fashion the present system arguably provides the competent resolution of legal and factual issues[82] as well as the perceived social benefits

---

[77] *See* note 75 *supra*.

[78] *See* note 75 *supra*.

[79] *See* Allen v. State, 290 Ala. 339, 342-43, 276 So.2d 583, 586 (1973) (asserting that ABA Canons of Judicial Ethics No. 34, which requires judicial impartiality, embraces nonverbal behavior); Conner, *supra* note 14, at 62. *See also* comment to *Trial Judge Standards, supra* note 57, § 1.3, at 30:

> The judge should be particularly careful by his demeanor not to convey unintended messages to the jury or to the participants in the trial process. Even the matter of facial expression may be misinterpreted. Jurors may read in the judge's face either belief or disbelief as he listens to witnesses' testimony or to arguments of counsel.

From this, one can infer that the organized bar recognizes the threat posed by the subtle communication of affect through nonverbal (and paralinguistic) channels to the proper exercise of the judicial function.

[80] *See generally* Broeder, *supra* note 3.

[81] *See* note 3 *supra*.

[82] This statement assumes that the judge is an accurate fact-finder. It also assumes that the judge is conveying to the jury his objective, correct theory of the case and not a

which result from the jury's incidental and extra-legal functions. The elimination of nonverbal and paralinguistic judicial cues would likely reduce the competency and reliability of the jury verdict, thereby decreasing the level of social and legal benefits accruing under the present system.

The answer to this argument must be that other more important social benefits arising from the jury system flow not from *perceived* but from *real* independence. For example, if the jury loses this quality, it would no longer perform the function of nullifying undesirable law[83] or checking arbitrary prosecution. Any deficiencies in competency or reliability that might result from the elimination of subtle judicial communications would thus be outweighed by the benefits of guaranteeing to the jury a position of independence.

II. Remedying the Experimenter Bias Effect in the Trial Setting

There are two possible approaches to eliminate the problem of subtle communications and their impact on the jury. One may either deal with the problem after it has occurred or seek to prevent it at its outset.

A. *Present Approaches: Remedying the Prejudicial Behavior After Occurrence*

When a judge violates his duty to remain impartial by imparting nonverbal or paralinguistic cues to the jury, his behavior is likely to prejudice one of the parties in the case before him. Solutions most commonly available in the judicial system, curative instructions and provisions for a new trial following either a motion for a new trial or an appeal, try to defuse the impact of this prejudicial behavior after it has occurred. These devices, however, may fail to deal adequately with prejudicial nonverbal and paralinguistic behaviors.

1. *The Curative Instruction*

Curative instructions during the trial allow judges to rectify the effect of prejudicial behavior directed toward the litigants, their witnesses, attorneys, or the subject matter of the litigation. The sufficiency of such instructions, often an issue on appeal, is determined on a case-by-case basis with the appellate court gauging the likelihood that the admonition was sufficient to erase the prejudicial impression from the jurors' minds. Instructions are often found insufficient when they are too general,[84] or

preconceived bias for or against one of the parties. The latter would be grounds for judicial recusal in any event. *See* 28 U.S.C. §§ 144, 455 (1970).

[83] *See* Scheflin, *supra* note 68.

[84] *See, e.g.*, Trupin v. New York City Interborough Ry., 237 App. Div. 515, 262 N.Y.S. 284 (1933).

appear insincere,[85] or involve prejudice too severe to be cured.[86]

For two reasons, curative instructions are unlikely to remedy the special prejudice created by nonverbal or paralinguistic communication. First, the communication often occurs without the conscious recognition of either the sender[87] or the receiver.[88] Thus, it is difficult to imagine how a standard instruction, one which directs the juror to disregard behavior that he does not realize occurred, would purge this influence process.[89] A second problem with the curative instruction is that individuals tend to resolve message conflicts between verbal and nonverbal channels in favor of the latter.[90] The judge's curative instruction to the jury may create such a message conflict. On the verbal level the judge asserts that he has no feelings about the matters before him or that those feelings which he does have should be disregarded. Yet throughout the trial, on the nonverbal and paralinguistic level, he may have indicated that he has definite feelings worthy of juror attention. Given the proclivity of individuals to rely more heavily on the nonverbal messages in such a situation, it is likely that the instruction will be ineffective.[91]

---

[85] *See, e.g.*, Crowder v. State, 77 Tex. Crim. 122, 126, 177 S.W. 501, 503 (1915).

[86] *See, e.g.*, United States v. Chibbaro, 361 F.2d 365, 379 (3d Cir. 1966).

[87] *See* notes 30-31 *supra*.

[88] *See* note 41 *supra*.

[89] Some instructions are couched in very general terms, without reference to any particular cue emitted. The following formbook example demonstrates this problem:

> You are instructed that I have not intended by anything I have said or done . . . to intimate or express in any way an opinion as to the existence or nonexistence of any facts in this case . . . . [Y]ou are the sole judges of the facts, and if . . . anything I have said or done has seemed to indicate to you that I believe any particular fact to be true or not true, then you must disregard such indication, and you and you alone must determine from the evidence the facts in this case.

23 Am. Jur. Pleading & Practice Forms Ann. *Trial* Form 249 (1973).

But even more immediate, specific instructions may also be ineffective. One judge tendered the following instruction, together with an apology, after chastising the defendent for interrupting him when the defendant was being cross-examined:

> You should not, by the tone of my voice, nor by any gesture on my part, interpret that as the court having any opinion on the guilt or innocence of this defendant. My sole venture, my sole mission here is to preside so that this defendant obtains a fair trial, and the government obtains a fair trial, and that is all. I have no interest whatsoever in the outcome of this lawsuit.

United States v. Demopoulos, 506 F.2d 1171, 1181 (7th Cir. 1974), *cert. denied*, 420 at U.S. 991 (1975). The Seventh Circuit held that the apology and instruction cured the defect. But even here one wonders how the juror can ignore something he never knew occurred, especially when the cure describes the gesticulations and tones with such generality. It is possible that the court recognized the irremediable prejudice engendered by these cues but, feeling powerless under the record as they saw it to determine the truth of the claim, hesitated to open the door to all comers.

[90] *See* A. Mehrabian, *supra* note 25, at 108; Galloway, *supra* note 40, at 59.

[91] Curative instructions, in sum, are powerless to remedy prejudice which the juror receives

2. *The Appellate Process*

To appeal a trial court's decision successfully on the basis of prejudice, the appellant must have (a) created an adequate record for appellate review, (b) made a timely objection during the trial, and (c) shown that the challenged behavior caused harmful error. Meeting these standards is difficult where prejudice is conveyed through subtle nonverbal and paralinguistic behaviors.

a. *Creating a Record*

The appellate court needs an adequate description of the trial judge's behavior if it is to review it. Failure to create such a record during the trial has impeded several appeals based upon a judge's allegedly prejudicial nonverbal or paralinguistic behavior, even when such behaviors were of some magnitude.[92]

In some cases the attorney established no record at trial.[93] In others, the record made was insufficient.[94] The problem lies in the inherent difficulty of describing nonverbal and paralinguistic behaviors with the written word.[95] Not surprisingly, appellate courts complain of their inability to visualize these behaviors from the "dry record."[96] A mere statement by

---

unconsciously. On the other hand, where the juror receives a more obvious cue and remembers it, a curative instruction may in some instances exacerbate the prejudice by reinforcing the cue in the juror's mind—a sort of unintentional "briarpatch" effect.

This raises the question, however, of those cues which while in the juror's subconscious mind might nevertheless be vulnerable to elicitation later on. In such cases, some jurors might be able to follow the judge's instruction to disregard his prior behavior. It may be, however, that the jurors would recall and then embody the prejudice in their decision, as in the "briarpatch" situation.

[92] *See, e.g.*, Hill v. State, 153 Tex. Crim. 105, 108, 217 S.W.2d 1009, 1011 (1948), where the defendant claimed the judge "indulged in facial expressions in the nature of scowls or frowns, and shook his head from side to side in a negative manner"; Loncar v. National Union Fire Ins. Co., 84 Mont. 141, 156, 274 P. 844, 849 (1929), the defendant asserting that the judge "exhibited a high degree of nervousness and by his actions appeared to be incensed against the defendant and its attorney and would at times shake his finger at counsel for defendant, loudly tap his desk with a pencil or other object, and talk in a loud and apparently angry manner."

Loncar was a civil case, unlike most every other case challenging the judge's nonverbal and paralinguistic behaviors. It is difficult to understand why so few challenges on the basis of judicial nonverbal and paralinguistic behavior have arisen in the civil context.

[93] *See, e.g.*, Coca Cola Bottling Works Inc. v. Hunter, 219 F.2d 765, 766 (D.C. Cir. 1955); State v. Barron, 465 S.W.2d 523, 527 (Mo. 1971).

[94] *See, e.g.*, Billeci v. United States, 184 F.2d 394, 402 (D.C. Cir. 1950); Allen v. State, 290 Ala. 339, 343, 276 So.2d 583, 586 (1973); People v. Walker, 150 Cal.App.2d 594, 605, 310 P.2d 110, 117 (1957).

[95] Conner, *supra* note 14, at 70; Annot., 62 A.L.R.2d 166, 195 (1958).

[96] State v. Christie, 91 N.J. Super. 420, 424, 221 A.2d 20, 22 (App. Div. 1966). *See also* United States v. Weiss, 491 F.2d 460, 468 (2d Cir. 1974); State v. Soriano, 107 N.J. Super.

counsel that the judge, through his facial expression, expressed his disbelief of the testimony of the defendant and his witnesses will be insufficient.[97] Attempts at more detailed description, although appreciated by the court, have also been found inadequate.[98] Some courts have tried to articulate guidelines for a sufficiently detailed record.[99] Nevertheless, no appellant, with the possible exception of the defendant in *State v. Barron*,[100] seems to have met these standards, and there the contention was dismissed because it was first raised in the appellate brief.[101]

If attorneys are unable to describe these incidents adequately in an objection, their ability to create a record concerning subtle, continuous nonverbal and paralinguistic behavior seems doubtful. Perhaps the only way of preserving an adequate record of such behavior is through film or videotape.[102] Its use would have advantages beyond the creation of a

---

286, 288, 258 A.2d 140, 142 (App. Div. 1968), *aff'd per curiam*, 54 N.J. 567, 258 A.2d 361 (1969). *Christie* overturned a jury verdict for the state on the basis of an accumulation of errors. The opinion is interesting in that it holds verbal commentary by the judge improper in light of possible (but unknowable) facial expressions that might have accompanied it. *Cf.* the more conventional, less daring approach of Hunter v. State, 314 So.2d 174, 175 (Fla. Dist. Ct. App. 1975) (per curiam), holding no reversible error evident from the record regarding the judge's remarks to or about counsel. The opinion then admits that any paralinguistic behaviors of the trial judge would remain undetected:

> We recognize that, perhaps, our remarks are more easily said than done; and that with respect to the instant proceeding our analysis of the "cold-typed transcript" may not accurately reflect the tone and tenor of the conduct and remarks of either the court, the jurors, counsel or witnesses.

[97] People v. Walker, 150 Cal.App.2d 594, 605, 310 P.2d 110, 117 (1957).

[98] Allen v. State, 290 Ala. 339, 343, 276 So.2d 583, 586 (1973).

[99] *See* Billeci v. United States, 184 F.2d 394, 402 (D.C. Cir. 1950); Allen v. State, 290 Ala. 339, 343, 287 So.2d 583, 586 (1973). Generally, the formulations hold that it is the duty of counsel to record the behaviors fully and accurately out of the jury's sight, including at what points during the trial they occurred. The court may then question the accuracy of the characterizations, resolving ultimate differences by the procedure regarding exceptions in existence prior to the use of court reporters. These guidelines have been incorporated into the general literature. *See* Conner, *supra* note 14, at 78; Annot., 49 A.L.R.3d 1186, 1194 (1973).

Other courts, however, appear either to ignore the issue completely or to give it limited consideration. *See, e.g.*, Cooper v. United States, 403 F.2d 71, 73 (10th Cir. 1968).

[100] 465 S.W.2d 523, 527 (Mo. 1971).

[101] *See also* the alternative holding in Veal v. State, 268 S.W.2d 345, 346 (Tenn. 1954), reversing a conviction where the trial judge, during the argument of the defense attorney, "shook his head in disagreement, without explaining to the jury what caused his action. The jury was so left to speculate whether his Honor's collar was too tight or whether he disbelieved what was being said for the defense." While the record below was not revealed in the appellate opinion in *Veal*, the success of the appeal indicates that some standards were met by the defendant.

[102] At least one case has suggested this possibility. United States v. Weiss, 491 F.2d 460, 468 n.2 (2d Cir. 1974). *Cf.* Annot., 62 A.L.R.2d 166, § 9 n.11 (1958). For a discussion of the use of videotaping to preserve a trial record, see Kennelly, *The Practical Uses of Trialvision and Depovision*, 16 TRIAL LAW. GUIDE 183 (1972). *See* text accompanying notes 146-54 *infra*

permanent record. Nonverbal and paralinguistic behaviors can be analyzed by trained observers,[103] and such analysis could isolate both the magnitude and the direction of the judge's evaluative communication.[104] This information could provide expert opinion upon which to base a claim before the appellate court that the behavior was prejudicial.

b. Timing the Objection

As a general rule, objections must be raised when the challengeable behavior occurs.[105] Raising the objection for the first time on appeal is usually insufficient.[106] But if the communication of bias through nonverbal and paralinguistic behavior occurs beyond the conscious awareness of the sender or receiver, the attorney will be unaware of the behavior when it occurs. How, then, can he raise a timely objection? Moreover, it may be a myriad of nonverbal and paralinguistic communications occurring throughout the trial which cumulatively create the prejudicial effect. In this situation an attorney might be unable to determine whether objectionable behavior has occurred until late in the testimony or even after the unfavorable verdict has been returned.[107]

---

for an expanded discussion of this possibility.

[103] See Trager, *Paralanguage: A First Approximation*, 13 STUDIES IN LINGUISTICS 1, 8-11 (1958), for a notational system for the recording of paralanguage. An example of its use is provided in Duncan, Rosenberg, & Finkelstein, *supra* note 22, at 211. A. MEHRABIAN, *supra* note 25, at 191 app. A., offers a system for scoring nonverbal and a limited number of paralinguistic behaviors.

[104] Through a scoring system observers could characterize the judge's behavior by recording the number of times particular behaviors occurred in particular contexts. From this one would develop a profile of the judge's behavior toward each party. Where the judge's behavior deviates both negatively and significantly from neutrality, the party would have cause to appeal.

[105] 4 B. JONES, *supra* note 75, § 28;1, at 274; 1 J. WIGMORE, EVIDENCE § 18, at 323 (3d ed. 1940).

[106] 1 J. WIGMORE, *supra* note 105, at 330.

[107] It is doubtful that a single subtle behavior will have prejudicial effect. It is the pattern of such behaviors that creates an unconscious influence on the receiver. *See* note 37 *supra*.

In this respect, one opinion by then Judge Bazelon, speaking to the timing issue, may have given in one hand by holding and taken away in the other by dictum. In Butler v. United States, 188 F.2d 24 (D.C. Cir. 1951), the lower court had refused to allow defense counsel to particularize a timely objection to the manner of delivery of the instructions, but six months later had offered defendant's counsel the chance to supplement the record. Counsel had alleged the use of certain "gesticulations" and "facial expressions," but the court had ruled these to be no basis for an objection. The D.C. Circuit remanded for a new trial, holding that since it is the duty of the attorney under Billeci v. United States, 184 F.2d 394 (D.C. Cir. 1950), to make a record for purposes of appeal, the trial court had erred:

> . . . retrospective description of matters so peculiarly ephemeral as a trial judge's "gesticulations or facial expression" furnishes a much less reliable basis for review than does a contemporaneous description. Similarly, the opportunity to cure, by means of precautionary instructions, whatever possible detrimental effect the judge's actions

A modification of the contemporaneous objection rule is necessary if the appellate process is to be responsive to this problem. The Supreme Court recognizes that the general rule may at times be inappropriate.[108] For example, in criminal cases it may be waived where failure to do so would be so prejudicial as to amount to a denial of due process.[109] As one state court writes,

> [I]f it appears . . . that the foregoing rule of procedure would defeat justice and bring about results not justified or intended by substantive law, the rule may be relaxed and subordinated to the primary purpose of the law to enforce constitutional rights in the interests of justice.[110]

Although such waivers are rare,[111] the special difficulties inherent in the challenge of nonverbal and paralinguistic bias may necessitate a waiver to preserve due process.[112]

c. *Showing Harmful Error*

Even if there is an adequate record of the challengeable behavior and a timely objection to it, an appealing party must still show that such behavior is prejudicial. The cases in this area suggest that the courts equate the visual magnitude of the behavior with the magnitude of its effect.[113] They seem to consider whether the jurors were *consciously* aware of and affected

> may have had upon the jury would be lost if the procedure adopted below were permitted.

188 F.2d at 27. Judge Bazelon's concerns about "ephemeral" cues may have been legitimate. However, his language here is such as to suggest no exception to the contemporaneous objection rule and thereby precludes treatment of the problems presented by accumulation.

[108] Henry v. Mississippi, 379 U.S. 443, 449 (1964) (suggesting in dictum the possibility that the Mississippi rule ought not to apply to a motion to suppress illegally obtained evidence where the attorney later made a similar motion for a directed verdict at the close of the state's evidence).

[109] *See* 4 B. JONES, *supra* note 75, § 28:1, at 275.

[110] Henry v. State, 253 Miss. 263, 287, 174 So.2d 348, 351 (1965), *on remand from* Henry v. Mississippi, 379 U.S. 443 (1964) (directing the trial court on further remand to consider the applicability of the suggestion of the United States Supreme Court).

[111] The contemporaneous objection rule is based upon a strong state policy. By requiring objections to be raised when objectionable behavior occurs, it provides the judge the opportunity to cure the error and thus avoid the delay and expense of a new trial. Henry v. Mississippi, 379 U.S. 443, 448 (1964). Because the rule serves a worthwhile purpose, a strong showing may be needed to induce its waiver.

[112] Chambers v. Mississippi, 410 U.S. 284, 290 n.3 (1973), suggests that where error is cumulative the contemporaneous objection rule does not apply. The Court left open the question whether other legitimate state interests might still bar consideration of objections raised in this fashion.

[113] *Cf.* Annot., 49 A.L.R.3d 1186, § 3, at 1190 (1973).

by the behavior[114] and whether the behaviors were *obviously* prejudicial.[115] Such standards inhibit the chances for successful appeal from error created by subtle nonverbal or paralinguistic cues.

The irony of this situation is that subtle cues are often more communicative and persuasive than more obvious behaviors. At the very least, research in experimenter/subject interaction indicates that subtle cues have a significant impact. In fact, those same studies suggest that when the experimenter's influence attempts become more obvious, their impact dissipates.[116] Some courts complement this finding by observing that when a judge's behavior becomes noticeably biased against a party, the jurors are likely to ignore his direction and come to the defense of the maligned.[117] In short, both scientific evidence and judicial wisdom suggest that there is an inverse relationship between the visual magnitude of the behavior and the magnitude of the harm.

B. *Methods for Preventing Prejudicial Behavior at the Outset*

Because of the difficulty of curing prejudice created by nonverbal and paralinguistic behavior once it has made its way to the jury, curtailing the behavior or its impact before it occurs may prove more effective. Solutions turn on regulating either the quality or the frequency of the interactions between judge and jury, or both. Three possible solutions considered here are (1) judicial training to control these subtle behaviors, (2) courtroom redesign, and (3) the use of videotape.[118]

---

[114] *See* Hill v. State, 153 Tex. Crim. 105, 111, 217 S.W.2d 1009, 1013 (1948).

[115] *Cf.* Vinci v. United States, 159 F.2d 777, 778 (D.C. Cir. 1949).

[116] *Cf.* Orne I, *supra* note 59, at 148; Orne II, *supra* note 59, at 780; Rosenberg, *supra* note 21, at 319-21.

[117] *See* Annot., 62 A.L.R.2d 166, 177 n.4 (1958). *See also* G. LEHMAN, WHAT YOU NEED TO KNOW FOR JURY DUTY 17 (1968).

[118] A fourth potential approach might be to rid the courtroom of the formalities which tend to elicit evaluation apprehension from the jurors. A similar approach has been suggested to deal with the problem of police suggestion in lineup situations: "[p]erhaps if witnesses had greater clarity regarding what to expect and more accurate information regarding the identification process, procedure and purpose, the influence of other actors in the lineup context would be substantially reduced." Levine & Tapp, *supra* note 55, at 1113. However, this approach has its problems when applied to the courtroom. Chief of these is that a certain amount of "cultism," *see* J. FRANK, COURTS ON TRIAL 254-61 (1949), is probably necessary to instill the civic duty required to ensure conscientious jury service. The ABA's *Trial Judge Standards, supra* note 57, § 1.3, urges the wearing of judicial robes to encourage public confidence in the administration of justice. *See also* Ferguson, *To Robe or Not to Robe?—A Judicial Dilemma,* 39 J. AM. JUD. SOC'Y 166 (1956); W. Kennedy, *The Cult of the Robe: A Dissent,* 14 FORDHAM L. REV. 192 (1945). A survey of Kentucky circuit judges some of whom wore robes and others of whom did not, found a consensus that the robe "was an important aspect of raising the level of respect for the judge and justice." J. Kennedy, *Judge-Jury-Counsel Relations in Kentucky,* 54 KY. L.J. 243, 245 (1966). *Cf.* J. FRAZER, THE GOLDEN BOUGH (1951).

1. Judicial Training to Control the Quality of Nonverbal and Paralinguistic Interaction

Professional gamblers, one psychologist has observed,[119] regularly defeat novices because they can guess the hand that the novice holds from how he holds his cards, how quickly he antes, where he antes, and how he looks. Recognizing the existence of such cues, the professionals take care that they themselves maintain a "poker face." Analogously, it may be possible to train judges to control their paralinguistic and nonverbal behavior in order that they might mask those feelings which arise during the trial and thus maintain an appearance of impartiality.

Foremost among several studies that suggest the theoretical feasibility of such training is a paper by Ekman and Friesen.[120] They hypothesize that although nonverbal and paralinguistic communication often occurs on an unconscious level, it is not completely beyond conscious control. When an individual receives feedback on his nonverbal behavior in a given situation, he begins to associate the particular behavior he manifests with the emotions he actually feels. Through this process he can learn to convey a particular emotion—whether genuine or not—by simulating the appropriate nonverbal or paralinguistic behavior.[121] The failure of most individuals to control their nonverbal and paralinguistic behavior stems from two factors: (1) often they are not provided with the feedback concerning their behavior essential for the learning process to occur,[122] and (2) naturally-occurring behavior cannot be masked without an effort,[123] an effort that most individuals fail to make.[124]

In testing this theoretical model, Ekman and Friesen took notice of the fact that one receives feedback on at least some of his nonverbal behavior in everyday interaction. Most feedback centers on facial expressions.[125] For example, comments from another about one's smile or glint in the eye are not uncommon. Body postures also evoke some comment,[126] but movements of the hands and feet[127] and subtler expressions of the face and posture rarely do.[128] Ekman and Friesen thus hypothesized that if one can in fact learn to control nonverbal behavior through feedback, he will be

---

[119] A. MEHRABIAN, *supra* note 28, at 1-2.

[120] Ekman & Friesen, *Nonverbal Leakage and Clues to Deception*, 32 PSYCHIATRY 88 (1969). *See also* EKMAN, *supra* note 25, at 23-25.

[121] *See generally* Ekman & Friesen, *supra* note 120 at 93-100.

[122] *Cf.* A. MEHRABIAN, *supra* note 25, at 178; Ekman & Freisen, *supra* note 120 at 96.

[123] *Cf.* Ekman & Freisen, *supra* note 120, at 96.

[124] *Cf.* E. GOFFMAN, THE PRESENTATION OF SELF IN EVERYDAY LIFE 7 (1959).

[125] Ekman & Freisen, *supra* note 120, at 94.

[126] *Id.* at 99.

[127] *Id.* at 95.

[128] *Cf. id.* at 97-99.

more successful in masking his facial behavior than that of his body.[129]

To test this hypothesis, they filmed 120 psychiatric interviews, from which they isolated three films in which the patients had attempted to convey one set of feelings while actually experiencing another. These films were presented without sound to two groups of untrained observers. One group saw films of the patients' heads; the other, films of their bodies. The groups were then asked to describe the behavior they had witnessed by checking appropriate adjectives from a checklist. Adjectives checked by the observers were placed in three clusters: (1) those recorded significantly more often by observers viewing only the patients' heads, (2) those recorded significantly more often by observers viewing only the patients' bodies, and (3) those recorded in comparable amounts by observers in both groups.

Analysis of adjectives from the first two categories lent support to the experimental hypothesis. Adjectives describing the facial behavior tended to reflect the emotion the patients were attempting to convey, and those describing the behavior of the body tended to reflect the patients' actual feelings. Of more interest, however, were those descriptive adjectives common to both sets of observers. For two of the three films the adjectives recorded by both groups of observers tended to reveal the patients' actual behavioral state. In sum, the experimental results indicate that those observing body cues received a relatively accurate portrayal of the patients' true feelings, and those decoding facial cues found elements of both actual feelings and those feelings the patients were attempting to convey.[130]

The import of these results is unclear.[131] Before one can estimate the probable success of any psychological training program for judges, three limitations on the applicability of this study must be considered. These limitations involve (a) the methodology of the study, (b) the implications of the study for the possibility of training people to mask their true feelings, and (c) the sufficiency of only a partial masking of true feelings.

a. The Impact of the Ekman and Friesen Methodology on the Validity of Their Findings

The Ekman and Friesen study dealt with the behavior of only two female mental patients; so any generalizations drawn from it are vulnerable to criticism. This is particularly true when one considers that the nonverbal communication of women differs significantly from that of men[132] and that

[129] *Cf. id.* at 100-02.

[130] *See* Ekman & Freisen, *supra* note 120, at 101-02. Mehrabian also tested this hypothesis and confirmed it. *See* A. MEHRABIAN, *supra* note 25, at 186.

[131] *Cf.* A. MEHRABIAN, *supra* note 25, at 85-87; A. Greenbaum, Cues to Deception: An Unobtrusive Exploration, Fall 1972 (unpublished manuscript at Yale University).

[132] A. MEHRABIAN, *supra* note 25, at 133-34.

the nonverbal communication of mental patients differs significantly from that of other individuals.[133]

Further, the three films used in the study were preselected as the ones most likely to contain deceptive communication. The researchers sought instances where the patient broke down after the interview, admitting her earlier behavior was a facade. One may question whether films of individuals who were "caught" in their deception are adequate representations of masking behavior. On the other hand, one might suggest that the partial masking found in this study represents a minimum capability and that others might accomplish the task more successfully.

Since another study has reported similar findings, however, the reliability of Ekman and Friesen's work increases. In his investigation of the nonverbal betrayal of feelings, Mehrabian measured the masking behavior of normal individuals in a controlled experimental setting.[134] He found that while most nonverbal behavior betrayed the subject's true feelings, the smile did not.[135] Taken together, these studies suggest that people can indeed mask feelings, through facial expressions.

b. *Implications of This Research for the Training of Individuals to Mask Their True Feelings*

These findings suggest that facial expressions are subject to some control. That this control is the product of learning is only a theoretical proposition. While the findings are consistent with the notion that one can learn to control nonverbal and paralinguistic behavior, they are not dispositive. At this time, data is unavailable from which to determine whether individuals can be trained to control their nonverbal and paralinguistic behavior, how much can be controlled, or how much training is required to accomplish sufficient masking.

c. *The Sufficiency of the Partial Masking of Behavior*

In the Ekman and Friesen study, the subjects achieved only a partial masking of their true feelings. Their faces conveyed information reflecting both their true and simulated feelings while their bodies reflected their true feelings alone. This partial masking of the sender's feelings presents a message conflict for the receiver. How he interprets these conflicting messages is unclear. Although research suggests that conflicts between verbal and nonverbal cues will be resolved in favor of the latter,[136] there is little information available to suggest how individuals resolve conflicting

---

[133] *See id.* at 134.

[134] *Id.* at 84-103.

[135] *Id.* at 99.

[136] A. MEHRABIAN, *supra* note 28, at 45.

messages presented in one body part (the face in this case) or between different body parts (here, the face and the body). This information may be important in determining whether all behavior need be trained or whether training will be sufficient if one masters only some level of partial masking.

At the very least, the Ekman and Friesen study and the questions it leaves unanswered argue for further investigation into the possibility of utilizing judicial training as a method of controlling the quality of nonverbal and paralinguistic communication in the courtroom. Ekman and Friesen found that even untrained individuals could partially mask their nonverbal behavior. Further investigation should explore whether the ability to mask could be increased to sufficient levels through training, and whether partial masking is sufficient to disrupt the unintended communication of influence between judge and jury.

2. *Courtroom Redesign to Control the Frequency of Interaction*

Although judicial training might neutralize the effect of a judge's nonverbal interaction with the jury, it would not reduce the frequency of that interaction. Courtroom redesign, however, may serve this function, thereby minimizing the opportunity for unintended influence to occur.

The location of the witness stand in most courtrooms, to the judge's side and adjacent to the jury box, maximizes the possibility that jurors will receive any unintentional cues about the trial participants conveyed by the judge. As one critic explains,

> Both the witness *and* the judge are within the jury's field of vision. In cinematography this is called a two-shot. The jurors simultaneously see the witness and the judge, and as the witness testifies they see the judge's reaction. These judicial reactions serve throughout the trial to orient the jury: to suggest belief or disbelief, sympathy or apathy, and so forth.
>
> This setup functions essentially as does a reaction shot. A reaction shot tells the audience how to feel about a piece of dialogue or a bit of business. It guides the audience, which is always uncertain about how to feel about the unfamiliar. The jury as audience is just as uncertain and just as susceptible to suggestion. And this is the great danger of having the witness stand "located at the judge's left and adjacent to the jury box."
>
> . . . It is impossible to make some people think or feel for themselves. But at least the judges' [*sic*] face [shouldn't] be thrust upon the entire jury like a countenance from Mt. Rushmore.[137]

[137] Harbinger, *Courtroom-in-the-Round*, in COURTHOUSES AND COURTROOMS 48, 49-50 (G. Winters ed. 1972). The traditional purpose behind this judge-witness proximity in the design of courtrooms is perhaps revealed in a recent ABA-AIA report on the modernization of courthouse facilities: "The witness also needs to be in close visual proximity to the judge so that he feels under the protection and, if necessary, the control of the judge." ABA-AIA JOINT

One suggestion to minimize this problem is a courtroom in the round.[138] The witness stand would be in the center of the chamber. The jury would sit directly in front of the witness, and the judge would sit facing the witness's profile and at a 90-degree angle to the jury. In this way the judge could be withdrawn from the juror's direct line of sight during the testimony of witnesses, thus reducing the juror's access to the judge's nonverbal behavior.[139]

This proposal is not without its limitations. The courtroom in the round would inhibit visual interaction between judge and jury during witness testimony but permit visual contact in other instances and paralinguistic contact in all instances. The sufficiency of such a partial restriction of interaction is unknown, because no information exists concerning the degree to which jury exposure to judicial behavior must be reduced before the chance for prejudicial communication is significantly minimized.[140] If a greater reduction in exposure is necessary, then so may be more radical alterations of the courtroom, perhaps even the complete removal of the judge.[141]

Even a proven solution might still be impeded by conservatism and cost. The American courtroom has changed little in the last two hundred years.[142] A movement toward courtroom redesign has recently begun, but the degree of its support is unclear.[143] Whether a drastic change in the

---

COMM. ON THE DESIGN OF COURTROOMS AND COURT FACILITIES, THE AMERICAN COURTHOUSE: PLANNING AND DESIGN FOR THE JUDICIAL PROCESS 26 (1973) [hereinafter cited as ABA-AIA JOINT COMM.]. This positioning is thus a response to the fear of witness intimidation and/or perjury.

In addition, the report emphasizes that of all figures in the courtroom, the judge is the most important, to be seen by all. *Id.* at 25. The concern is that above all else the judge must control the course of the trial, and that his central, elevated position is essential to this purpose. *See id.* at 27; Fort, *Facilities for the Administration of Justice,* in COURTHOUSES AND COURTROOMS 4, 7 (G. Winters ed. 1972). Interestingly, then, even the forces of modernized courtroom design are restricted implicitly by their traditional conception of the judge's role in the common law system. This may pose the most overwhelming barrier to the acceptance of a courtroom in the round. *See* text accompanying notes 142-45.

[138] Harbinger, *Courtroom-in-the-Round,* in COURTHOUSES AND COURTROOMS 48, 49-50 (G. Winters ed. 1972).

[139] *See id.* at 50.

[140] In the experimenter/subject interaction studies the experimenter's subtle cues were conveyed while he read a simple set of instructions to the subjects. *See, e.g.,* text following note 21 *supra.* Whether the greater complexity of the trial affects the amount of interaction necessary to create a biasing effect is unknown. If the same interaction is sufficient to influence the juror's behavior in a trial, then only the complete isolation of the judge from jury may be sufficient.

[141] Effective removal might entail televising the courtroom activity on a monitor for the judge outside the courtroom. Through a series of headsets the judge could communicate with the attorneys, thereby directing the trial without being overheard by the jury.

[142] Winters, *Preface* to COURTHOUSES AND COURTROOMS (G. Winters ed. 1972).

[143] *See* Stern, *In Pursuit of a Courthouse,* in *id.* 23. It should be noted, however, that this

courtroom would be acceptable either to jurists or to local officials is even more problematic. Moreover, with competing political constituencies vying for state and local funds, city councils and state legislatures are often reluctant to authorize spending for new court facilities.[144] A concerted effort by the local bar and judiciary would be essential to the adoption of any major change.[145]

3. Videotaped Trials to Control Both the Quality and Frequency of Nonverbal Interaction

More than thirty recent articles attest to the current interest in the use of videotapes in the trial process, especially for their economic and technical efficiencies.[146] A fully videotaped trial would film all witnesses, testimony, and rulings on motions without the presence of the jury. The judge could then delete extraneous material such as stricken testimony or motion rulings before presenting the tape to the jury. Except for judicial examination of witnesses and delivery of instructions, judicial behavior would be absent from the tape.[147] The jury would thus view only that information relevant to their weighing of the evidence and understanding of the law.

The idea of videotape is not without its disadvantages.[148] Principal among these is the loss of meaningful and often helpful interaction and confrontation between the jury and participants at the trial.[149] In addition, the use of videotape in criminal trials might pose constitutional questions regarding the abridgment of rights to due process, a public trial, a fair trial, a jury trial, and confrontation.[150] However, videotaped trials have for the most part been favorably received.[151] In Ohio five trials which were

movement proceeded not on the basis of any concern about nonverbal and paralinguistic communications by the judge but apparently from the perceived need for providing courtrooms with the conveniences of modern living. *See, e.g.*, The Washington Post, Aug. 27, 1975, § C, at 2, col. 1. In fact, one goal of the ABA-AIA report was to *improve* the visibility of all participants so that "facial expressions can be clearly seen, as the ability to observe a person's expression helps in understanding what he says." ABA-AIA COMM'N, *supra* note 137, at 25-26.

[144] *See* Stern, *supra* note 143, at 24.

[145] *Cf. id.* at 28.

[146] They are compiled in Doret, *Trial by Videotape—Can Justice Be Seen To Be Done?*, 47 TEMPLE L.Q. 228 n.1 (1974).

[147] One format of a videotape trial is described in more detail in *id.* at 232. *See generally* Note, *Videotape in the Courts: Its Use and Potential*, 3 RUTGERS J. COMPUTERS & L. 279, 295-300 (1974).

[148] *See, e.g.*, Note, *Videotape Trials: Legal and Practical Implications*, 9 COLUM. J. L. & SOC. PROB. 363 (1973). *See also* Doret, *supra* note 146, at 228 n.1.

[149] *See generally* Doret, *supra* note 146, at 248.

[150] *Id.* at 258.

[151] *Id.* at 230. In addition to citing the benefit of being able readily to excise prejudicial material, many point to the economies of videotape arising from its removal of time and space restrictions.

videotaped in their entirety and shown to the jury in taped form received the subsequent approval in commentaries of the participants themselves.[152] Indeed, the use of videotape in a growing number of trials seems probable.[153]

Because the use of videotape can eliminate unnecessary contact between the judge and the jury, the frequency of nonverbal interaction could be reduced. That interaction which remains, primarily delivery of instructions to the jury, could be controlled to ensure that it incorporates little reflection of the judge's feelings about the case. Scoring systems which exist to measure the content of both nonverbal and paralinguistic behaviors[154] could be employed to assay the judge's departure from impartiality. If necessary, the judge could retape his presentation until he has produced a neutral instruction, or a third party could read instructions prepared by the judge. Used in this way, videotaping could control not only the frequency but also the quality of the judge/jury nonverbal and paralinguistic interaction.

III. Conclusion

Psychological research seems to show that experimenters, through their nonverbal and paralinguistic behaviors, unconsciously convey to their subjects information which is received by them and influential in their behavior. Where the judge/juror relationship is analogous, there may exist a subtle threat to judicial impartiality that is far more serious than that imposed by the more obvious, and more controllable, verbal communications which are the subject of so much concern in the legal community today.

The experimenter bias effect is so complex that it would at this point be presumptuous to assert more than that, under certain conditions, the

---

[152] The enthusiasm of the two presiding judges at the first three of these trials has been well documented elsewhere. *See* Note, *supra* note 148, at 363 & n.2. *See also* McCrystal, *Ohio's First Video Tape Trial: The Judge's Critique,* 45 Ohio B. 1 (1972). The attorneys for both sides in the first case were also laudatory in their remarks. *See* Murray, *Comments on a Video Tape Trial — From Counsel for the Plaintiff,* 45 Ohio B. 25 (1972); Watts, *Comments on a Video Tape Trial — From Counsel for the Defense,* 45 Ohio B. 51 (1972).

According to one source, juror response so far has also been positive, in that "juries seem to be more motivated and interested" than they are in listening to conventional testimony. Shayne, *Question Box: Economics and the Law,* 173 N.Y.L.J., Mar. 25, 1975, at 1. It should be noted that the reference here was to a Michigan experiment not with fully videotaped trials but rather with videotaped portions of testimony. Three of the jurors in the second Ohio case echoed this view, however, *see* Note, *supra* note 148, at 374 n.67, although three more in the third case, a criminal trial, had difficulty maintaining interest, *see id.* at 388-89 n.161.

[153] *See* Note, *supra* note 147, at 280. Michigan may take the next step with its contemplated Project T.A.P.E. ("total application of prerecorded evidence"). *See* Brennan, *Videotape — The Michigan Experience,* 24 Hastings L.J. 1, 6-7 (1973).

[154] *See* note 103 *supra.*

average juror will probably be influenced by subtle judicial cues. The likelihood that this communication will occur is greatest in those trials where the analogy to the experimental context holds up in every way — ambiguous context, desire to behave correctly, and presence of a high status judicial figure with ideas of his own about outcome.[155]

For a variety of reasons, however, these qualities may be absent in a particular trial. In some cases, for example, either because the case itself is clear[156] or because of previous jury experience,[157] the juror may find the trial context unambiguous and thus be less likely to look to the judge for guidance in his decisionmaking.

Further, tempering of the judge/jury influence process will occur in cases where jurors lose their desire to behave correctly. Some may argue that jurors today, experiencing disillusionment with the judicial process, carry that disillusionment into their jury service and fail to attend to the reaching of a proper verdict. Others dispute this theory;[158] at any rate, it would seem that the cultism of the courtroom might divest citizens of such an attitude, at least temporarily.[159] A related but more difficult question, however, is whether jury nullification[160] or legislation may in some cases provide an effective preventative to the judge's cues, even assuming juror satisfaction with the judicial process in general. For example, it may be that the juror will ignore even instructions of law, so determined is he that a particular criminal statute under which the defendant is being prosecuted is unjust. Likewise, a juror may be quick to convict, no matter what cues the judge imparts to the contrary, if the defendant evokes inner prejudice in his mind.[161]

---

[155] *See* note 70 *supra*.

[156] *See* note 58 *supra*. *But cf.* authorities cited in note 3 *supra*.

[157] Broeder, *supra* note 56, suggests that jurors with prior service approach their task differently, being both more confident, at least in the deliberative process, *id.* at 143, and less concerned about proper performance after perceiving the minimal role of law in jury decisions, *id.* at 140. The use of longer juror terms in the federal system appears to be on the rise. FEDERAL JUDICIAL CENTER, GUIDELINES FOR IMPROVING JUROR UTILIZATION IN UNITED STATES DISTRICT COURTS 34 (1972).

[158] *See* Kalven, *supra* note 63.

[159] Further, juror disillusionment with the judicial process may not necessarily result in a loss of respect for the *judge*. It may well be that concerns about case backlogs and attorney practices provide the source for any popular disenchantment that might exist. Finally, attorney challenges and juror excuses may eliminate those potential jurors less likely to behave conscientiously.

[160] *See* Scheflin, *supra* note 68.

[161] Conversely, one might suggest that some other independent factor must first negate the experimenter bias effect before the juror's drive for nullification can manifest itself. Kalven and Zeisel's finding of a correlation between judge commentary on the evidence and "correct" jury verdict provides some support for this theory. *See* H. KALVEN & H. ZEISEL, *supra* note 1, at 425-27. The key to their argument is that any jury deviation from proper decisionmaking is a result not of any misunderstanding of fact but rather of a calculated decision to nullify

Finally, for two reasons the judge in a trial may in some cases provide insufficient guidance to jurors to influence their behavior. First, the juror in a trial, unlike the subject in most psychological experiments, has more than one authority figure to which he may turn for subtle suggestions. The advocates and even the jury foreman may exert considerable influence over a juror during the course of the trial.[162] The degree of this subsidiary influence in a particular case would no doubt dissipate the effect of judicial behavior. Second, even if the juror focuses on judicial behavior, the judge may not provide him with adequate guidance. In an experiment, the experimenter generally knows (or in fact hopes for) the correct outcome in advance.[163] Contrastingly, in a trial, the judge often has no theory of the case, or at least no strongly held one. In such situations, he will impart no consistent subconscious cues, thereby providing no direction to which the juror may turn. We therefore need to know how quickly the judge evolves a theory in particular cases to appreciate how serious the effect really is. It may well be that consistent nonverbal or paralinguistic cues are more likely in less complex cases, involving simple tort or criminal issues,[164] than in complex securities or patent cases tried to a jury.[165]

---

law. Assuming this theory to be correct, the correlation between judicial control through comment on the evidence and proper jury response would mean that judicial commentary inhibits the impulse to nullify. Similarly, one can argue that a judge's nonverbal and paralinguistic cues will override the nullification tendency unless they are otherwise defused.

The most probable explanation of the relation between nullification and nonverbal/paralinguistic influence is that the former occurs when the impulse to nullify is great (*e.g.*, in prosecutions under sumptuary laws) and the transmission of judicial cues is for some reason inhibited. Likewise, where there is no particular reason to nullify and the cues are widespread, the influence will probably predominate. The psychology behind the nullification impulse, however, is simply too complex an issue to be analyzed in detail here.

[162] *See* note 69 *supra*.

[163] At least in some experiments. Where experimenters use a double blind methodology — having a third person conduct the study with no prior intimation about outcome — the person actually conducting the study may more resemble the trial judge than he does the traditional experimenter. The problem he would present would thus be similar to that posed by the trial judge: after a certain point, the blind experimenter may begin to perceive a correct outcome and thereupon emit consistent cues to that end.

[164] Obviously, not all tort and criminal cases will be easy ones. For example, certain products liability cases will involve factual issues concerning product design that may tax even the most experienced judge. Likewise, criminal antitrust cases will involve factual questions the proper resolution of which requires mastery of the economic intricacies of the industry involved. *Cf.* Krause v. Rhodes, No. C70-544 (N.D. Ohio, verdict returned Aug. 27, 1975), a collection of constitutional tort cases involving the 1970 Kent State shootings, in which the judge's charge to the jury ran to 76 pages and included more than 100 variations of possible jury findings. The Washington Post, Aug. 23, 1975, § A, at 4, col. 5.

[165] Ironically, it may be the *most* complex cases —those that present unique factual issues even for the judge — that present the least dangers to jury integrity. Graphing jury influence as a function of case difficulty would result in a bell-shaped curve. The very easy and the very hard cases would present no problem of influence, in the former because they would

On all of these issues, more study is need to appreciate how susceptible jurors are in particular situations to any influence by the trial judge.[166] More fruitful inquiry may also be directed toward ways of preventing influential interaction from taking place. Because of a lack of basic information about the extent to which interaction must be altered or curtailed before its influence will be significantly dissipated, it is difficult to evaluate the merits of various proposals such as training, courtroom redesign, or videotaping. One difficulty must be admitted at the outset — the Anglo-American legal system's relative emphasis upon the active trial judge. This characteristic will likely impede any attempt to remedy the experimenter bias effect by downplaying the role or presence of the judge. While a practical solution to police suggestion in lineups might be to "minimize contact" with policemen,[167] the legal community is probably less likely to accept an analogous answer in the courtroom.[168] It is enough here, however, to alert that community to the probability that, at least in some situations, the experimenter bias effect threatens the integrity of the American jury so unqualifiedly praised by Kalven and Zeisel.

A.F.G.

create no ambiguity for the jurors and in the latter because they would result in no consistent nonverbal and paralinguistic cues from the judge. Only the cases which would be relatively difficult for the jury but relatively simple for the judge would be vulnerable to the experimenter bias effect. *Cf.* Walsh, *supra* notes 2, 58.

[166] Other such questions which might be explored concern the relationship between the demographic characteristics of jurors and their susceptibility to the judge's nonverbal or paralinguistic cues. *But see* note 41 *supra,* referring to the limitations upon jury composition imposed by the "fair cross section" requirement.

[167] *See* Levine & Tapp, *supra* note 55, at 1119.

[168] The practical probability of restructured courtrooms or videotaped trials used on a large-scale basis may therefore be questionable. *See* ABA-AIA Joint Comm., *supra* note 137. Part of this resistance is tied to the felt need for certain rituals, as described throughout this note. *Cf.* Doret, *supra* note 146, at 256.

Nevertheless, the movement in favor of videotaped trials is growing, *see* notes 151-53 *supra* and accompanying text. And the novel design of the District of Columbia Superior Court's new facility, which positions the judge, jury, and witness in a circular well so that "courtroom functions take place in a setting much like a threater [*sic*] in the round," has received the praise of the court's chief judge, among others. The Washington Post, Aug. 27, 1975, § C, at 1, col. 1. These trends indicate that the aforementioned proposals may indeed be viable.

NOTES

The Appearance of Justice: Judges' Verbal and Nonverbal Behavior in Criminal Jury Trials*

Due process requires that the trial judge conduct a fair, orderly, and impartial trial.[1] In a criminal trial, due process requires the absence of actual bias by the trial judge toward the defendant. But not only are trial judges required to be fair and impartial, they must also "satisfy the appearance of justice."[2] The trial judge's "appearance," or conduct and behavior, in a criminal jury trial must never indicate to the jury that the judge believes the accused to be guilty.[3] The appearance of bias alone

---

* Peter David Blanck, *Stanford Law Review*; Robert Rosenthal, Department of Psychology and Social Relations, Harvard University; and LaDoris Hazzard Cordell, Municipal Court Judge, Santa Clara County, California.

The authors gratefully acknowledge support from the National Science Foundation, and from the Irving H. Hellman, Jr. Memorial Fund Grant of the *Stanford Law Review*. We thank the trial judges, jurors, and lawyers who participated in this study. Professor Phoebe Ellsworth, Elizabeth DeAvila, Lizann Schloff, and Gary Alpert, all of Stanford University, provided invaluable assistance during the course of the study. We also thank Barbara Babcock, Miguel Mendez, and David Rosenhan for their helpful comments.

1. *In re* Murchinson, 349 U.S. 133, 136 (1955) ("A fair trial in a fair tribunal is a basic requirement of due process."); U.S. CONST. amends. V, VI, XIV; *see also* United States v. Robinson, 635 F.2d 981 (2d Cir. 1980), *cert. denied,* 451 U.S. 992 (1981).

2. Offutt v. United States, 348 U.S. 11, 14 (1954); *see also In re* Murchinson, 349 U.S. at 136 (quoting *Offutt*); Walker v. Lockhart, 726 F.2d 1238, 1244 (8th Cir.), *cert. denied,* 104 S. Ct. 2168, *cert. dismissed,* 105 S. Ct. 17 (1984); *id.* at 1251 (Arnold, J., concurring) ("If due process means anything, it means a trial before an unbiased judge and jury.").

3. United States v. Nazzaro, 472 F.2d 302, 310 (2d Cir. 1973), *cited with approval in Robinson,* 635 F.2d at 984; *see also* United States v. Beaty, 722 F.2d 1090, 1093 (3d Cir. 1983) (the judge must never "appear" to the jury to believe the accused guilty); United States v. Frazier, 584 F.2d 790, 794 (6th Cir. 1978) ("the basic requirement [of the trial judge] is one of impartiality in demeanor as well as in actions").

Professors Redish and Marshall have recently suggested that the appearance or "perception" of fairness is the most important value of procedural due process for the independent adjudicator. They write that "[f]ew perceptions more severely threaten trust in the democratic process than the perception that a litigant never had a chance because of the special favors that the decider owed the other side." Redish & Marshall, *Adjudicatory Independence and the Values of Procedural Due Process,* 95 YALE L.J. — (1986) (forthcoming).

is grounds for reversal even if the trial judge is, in fact, completely impartial.[4] Due process violations have been found when a trial judge's behavior created just the appearance of partiality, and courts have held such behavior sufficient to reverse criminal convictions.[5] Appellate courts recognize that the appearance of judicial bias or unfairness at the trial can be manifested by trial judges in explicit and subtle verbal and "nonverbal" ways that never show up on the "dry" appellate record.

Trial judges, like all human beings, develop beliefs about a defendant's guilt or innocence in a criminal jury trial and expectations for the verdict the jury will return.[6] Moreover, they may influence the trial process in ways that correspond to their expectations for trial outcome. During the jury trial, the judge may reveal these beliefs or expectations by trying to "engineer"[7] the trial in accordance with these expectations—for example, in comments on the evidence, in responses to witnesses, or in rulings on objections.[8]

4. Bollenbach v. United States, 326 U.S. 607 (1946); *see also* State v. Larmond, 244 N.W.2d 233, 236 (Iowa 1976) (the defendant is not required to show that the jurors were actually prejudiced by the judge's behavior but merely that the jurors could have inferred judicial bias).

5. *See* Johnson v. Metz, 609 F.2d 1052, 1057 (2d Cir. 1979) (Newman, J., concurring) (summarizing due process violations where trial judge appeared partial in jury trials). *But see, e.g.*, United States v. Poland, 659 F.2d 884, 894 (9th Cir.) ("an appearance of partisanship by the trial judge may affect the attitude of the jury toward the defendants," but even if the statements of the trial judge did constitute error, "the evidence of guilt of these appellants was far too strong to allow the verdict to be affected by any impatience, irritation, or sarcasm of the trial judge"), *cert. denied*, 454 U.S. 1059 (1981).

6. It is efficient to predict accurately other people's behavior as well as our own. In a legal sense, it may be important for trial judges to develop efficient means for deciding cases given their heavy caseloads. Enormous pressures are placed upon trial judges by an ever increasing criminal docket and by a demand for speedier trials of criminal defendants. *Nazzaro*, 472 F.2d at 304.

7. Williams v. United States, 228 A.2d 846, 848 (D.C. 1967) ("a trial judge has the responsibility of moving a trial along in an orderly and efficient manner; in short that he has the responsibility of managing the conduct of the trial").

8. Some of the principal ways in which trial judges can impermissibly influence the criminal trial process include:

> (1) Disparaging remarks or gestures concerning the defendant, the defense counsel, the prosecution counsel, or the witnesses. *See, e.g.*, People v. Franklin, 56 Cal. App. 3d 18, 128 Cal. Rptr. 94 (1976) (trial judge's unconscious facial expressions toward defense witness); *see also Beaty*, 722 F.2d at 1096 (trial judge's lengthy cross-examination of witness was "a frontal attack on her credibility," and the "jury could not have helped but conclude that the judge simply did not believe" the defendant); People v. Hefner, 127 Cal. App. 3d 88, 91–92, 179 Cal. Rptr. 336, 337–38 (1981) (trial judge prejudiced the jury by creating a "negative courtroom atmosphere" through numerous demeaning comments directed at defense counsel and by

It is possible that when judges expect or predict a certain trial outcome, they intentionally or unintentionally "appear" to behave toward jurors in a way that indicates what they think the outcome should be, thereby setting into motion behaviors and trial processes that increase the likelihood of the occurrence of a certain trial outcome. In other contexts, this predictive behavior has been called a "self-fulfilling prophecy" or an "interpersonal expectancy effect."[9] Thus, a trial judge's expectations for trial

---

accusing the attorney of using misleading vocal inflections while reading prior testimony before the jury); People v. Kenny, 20 A.D.2d 578, 246 N.Y.S.2d 92 (N.Y. App. Div. 1963) (trial judge cast doubt on defense witness's credibility during cross-examination); People v. Viscio, 241 A.D. 499, 272 N.Y.S. 213 (N.Y. App. Div. 1934) (trial judge cast doubt on defendant's credibility during cross-examination of defendant and charge to the jury).

(2) Bias in rulings, questions, or comments in favor of one party. *See, e.g.*, People v. Blackburn, 139 Cal. App. 3d 761, 765–66, 189 Cal. Rptr. 50, 52 (1982) (trial judge must allow defendants to fully present their case); People v. Ramirez, 113 Cal. App. 2d 842, 852–53, 249 P.2d 307 (1952) (trial judge continuously led prosecution witness, "pulling [witness] out of a hole every time"); People v. Frank, 71 Cal. App. 575, 236 P. 189 (1925) (trial judge joined with district attorney in high commendation of prosecution witness).

(3) Considering matters not in evidence. *See, e.g.*, People v. Handcock, 145 Cal. App. 3d Supp. 25, 193 Cal. Rptr. 397 (Cal. App. Dep't Super. Ct. 1983) (trial judge called witness to offer evidence derived from interrogation).

(4) Forming expectations for trial outcome before defense has presented its case. *See, e.g.*, People v. Barquera, 154 Cal. App. 2d 513, 517, 316 P.2d 641, 644 (1957) (trial judge stated to defense counsel, "I don't think you have got any defense . . . ."); *see also* Farley, *Instructions to Juries—Their Role in the Judicial Process*, 42 YALE L.J. 194, 212 (1932) (Professor Farley's classic analysis suggesting that "the federal judge usually has it in his power, if he so wills, to mold a verdict in accord with his own views").

(5) Statements to the jury that a mistake in convicting can be corrected by other authorities, *see* Annot., 5 A.L.R.3D 974 (1966), or statements to the jury that if the defendant is found guilty, his sentence will be suspended or appealed, *see, e.g.*, State v. Clark, 227 Or. 391, 392, 362 P.2d 335, 335 (1961) ("[The Supreme] Court can correct any mistakes which this court may make as to the law of the case . . . .") (emphasis omitted).

(6) Statements to the jury that "smart" jurors form rapid opinions. *See, e.g.*, People v. Kindelberger, 100 Cal. 367, 34 P. 852 (1893).

(7) Failing to control misconduct of counsel. *See, e.g.*, United States v. Young, 105 S. Ct. 1038, 1044 (1985) ("We emphasize that the trial judge has the responsibility to maintain decorum in keeping with the nature of the proceeding . . . ."); People v. Bain, 5 Cal. 3d 839, 489 P.2d 564, 97 Cal. Rptr. 684 (1971) (trial judge allowed the trial to be conducted at an emotional level that was destructive to a fair trial); *see also* D. DONOVAN, PROSECUTORIAL AND JUDICIAL MISCONDUCT (1979 & Supp. 1983); B.E. WITKIN, CALIFORNIA CRIMINAL PROCEDURE §§ 440–442, 528 (1963 & Supp. 1985) (reviewing California case law).

9. *See* Merton, *The Self-Fulfilling Prophecy*, 8 ANTIOCH REV. 193 (1948); R. ROSENTHAL, EXPERIMENTER EFFECTS IN BEHAVIORAL RESEARCH (1976). Merton and Rosenthal's concept of "the self-fulfilling prophecy" and "interpersonal expectancy effects" illustrates how a per-

outcome may prophesy, become related to, or improperly influence the actual outcome of the jury decisionmaking process.

This note empirically investigates how trial judges' expectations for trial outcome might predict both (a) the judges' unintended verbal and nonverbal behavior, and (b) the verdicts returned by juries. This note also describes how trial judges' unintended verbal and nonverbal behavior might predict the verdicts returned by juries. Part I describes the relationship between judicial behavior or influence and due process and describes the type of extreme and subtle influence judges may exert on jurors and perhaps on their decisionmaking process. The implication that this influence may have for a more complete description of procedural due process requirements for a fair and impartial trial, and for alerting appellate courts to the importance of the trial judge's behavior, is also discussed in light of present law.

Part II presents a preliminary model for the study of judicial influence and discusses several factors that may serve to increase or decrease judicial influence in the courtroom. Part III describes the research strategy used for testing aspects of this model, and part IV describes the findings of the research. The findings demonstrate how a trial judge's expectations for trial outcome can predict the manner in which the judge delivers instructions to the jury and how these expectations may predict and possibly influence the outcome of jury trials. Finally, part V discusses a potentially useful way to describe the transmission of judicial influence or beliefs through judges' subtle verbal and nonverbal behaviors and examines the implications of our findings for developing standards of appellate review for assessing whether judges' verbal and nonverbal behaviors exceeded the permissible limits of influence. This part also discusses ways of alerting trial judges, jurors, and lawyers to the importance of nonverbal behavior in the courtroom.

I. Judicial Behavior and Influence

While the trial judge in a criminal case is not required to be a mere moderator, there is a constitutional line across which he or she cannot go, in order to ensure that a defendant's guilt or inno-

son's prophecies or expectations for an event can change the behavior of the prophet in ways that make the event more likely.

cence is decided by twelve laypersons and not one judge.[10] This section introduces the legal concept of judicial influence, explores its relation to procedural due process, and discusses the permissible limits of judicial behavior. The section then discusses (a) instances where judicial influence occurred but was held not to be impermissible or reversible error, (b) instances where more blatant judicial influence occurred and was held to be reversible error, and (c) instances where subtle judicial influence occurred and was held to be reversible.

A. *Judicial Influence and Procedural Due Process: Defining the Role of the Trial Judge—Advocate, Arbitrator, or Automaton*

Procedural fairness during the course of a trial is due process in its primary sense.[11] But procedural fairness is not a fixed requirement unrelated to the circumstances and individuals involved in a particular trial.[12] Rather, it is an ongoing *process* of judgment conducted by the trial judge. Because procedural fairness is not determined by bright line legal rules, trial judges have considerable discretion in administering and applying the law. Thus, while a fair and impartial trial is always the goal, the role of the trial judge during the course of the trial may vary.

The trial judge deviates from the "model" of procedural due process and impartiality by becoming an *advocate* or partisan for one side.[13] In one case, for example, the defendant was con-

10. *See, e.g.*, Billeci v. United States, 184 F.2d 394, 401–02 (D.C. Cir. 1950) (where appellants alleged that trial judge, by subtle nonverbal cues, emphasized principles beneficial to prosecution and deemphasized principles beneficial to defendant, the court reversed the criminal conviction finding that a trial judge "may not coerce, or attempt to coerce, a jury by gesture any more than [the judge] may do so by words").

The research in this note focuses on criminal jury trials. The California Constitution provides that "[t]rial by jury is an inviolate right and shall be secured to all." CAL. CONST. art. I, § 16. This right to jury trials extends to all misdemeanors. (The sixth amendment to the United States Constitution provides for the federal right to trial by jury.) The California Constitution also allows a defendant to waive a trial by jury. *Id.* Trial judges' behavior in bench trials is not addressed by this note.

11. Joint Anti-Fascist Refugee Comm. v. McGrath, 341 U.S. 123, 161–64 (1951) (Frankfurter, J., concurring); *see also* Frank v. Mangum, 237 U.S. 309, 347 (1915) (Holmes, J., dissenting) ("Whatever disagreement there may be as to the scope of the phrase 'due process of law,' there can be no doubt that it embraces the fundamental conception of a fair trial, with opportunity to be heard.").

12. *Joint Anti-Fascist Refugee Comm.*, 341 U.S. at 162.

13. *See* note 8 *supra*. *See generally* Wyzanski, *A Trial Judge's Freedom and Responsibility*, 65 HARV. L. REV. 1281 (1952) (the duty to deliver evidential instructions to the jury is not equivalent to the rare occasion where a trial judge is prompted to examine a witness, and such interrogation by the court changes the role of the judge to advocate; while a judge may ques-

victed of the possession of an unregistered firearm by a felon based on testimony of the arresting officers that they actually saw the defendant with the sawed-off shotgun in his hands.[14] Yet the appellate court reversed this conviction on the grounds that the judge's active questioning of the defendant and witnesses prevented the defendant from receiving a fair trial. The judge "appeared" to take a prosecutorial role in the trial and the balance of procedural due process was therefore adversely tipped against the defendant. In effect, the judge's role lost its color of neutrality and tended to accentuate and emphasize the prosecutor's case.[15]

Certainly a judge's isolated questioning of witnesses to clarify ambiguities is not the same as the judge assuming the role of advocate and "taking over" an examination for one side.[16] But some appellate courts have concluded that even the slightest indication of partiality by the trial judge has an important effect on a jury.[17] For example, appellate courts have held that a judge should seldom intervene in the questioning of a witness, and then only to clarify isolated testimony or to prevent harassment of the witness by counsel.[18]

The appellate courts also recognize that a trial judge should

---

tion a witness to clarify a confusing response, he or she may not ask questions that indicate opinion as to the evidence or the outcome of the trial; voluntary interrogation is very different from the judicial duty to deliver instructions; the final jury instructions provide the trial judge with the last word on the case law of the trial, and this duty is not to be confused with commenting on the law).

14. United States v. Bland, 697 F.2d 262 (8th Cir. 1983).

15. *Id.* at 265–66 ("The trial judge's attitude may have unconsciously driven him to assume a prosecutorial role in the trial, a role which destroyed fair process for the accused."); *see also Beaty,* 722 F.2d at 1095 ("The court's vigorous participation in examining the defendant's witnesses, especially when contrasted with the complete freedom from hostile interruption of the prosecution's witnesses, must certainly have conveyed the judge's skepticism about [the defendant's] alibi to the jury."); United States v. Hill, 332 F.2d 105, 106 (7th Cir. 1964) ("the court should be careful to preserve an attitude of impartiality and guard against giving the jury any impression that the court was of the opinion that defendant was guilty"); Jackson v. United States, 329 F.2d 893 (D.C. Cir. 1964) ("claim of undue intervention in the trial by the judge in a manner prejudicial" is grounds for reversal); United States v. Hickman, 592 F.2d 931 (6th Cir. 1979) (where the trial judge interjected into the proceedings approximately 250 times, the appellate court noted the trial judge's "brilliant redirect examination that would have been entirely proper had it been done by the prosecutor."). *But see* United States v. Tilton, 714 F.2d 642 (6th Cir 1983) (a trial judge who interrupted counsel approximately 28 times, but whose conduct affected both the defendant and prosecution, did not prejudice the jury).

16. *Bland,* 697 F.2d at 265.

17. *Id.* at 265–66; *see also Billeci,* 184 F.2d at 402.

18. *See* note 15 *supra*; *see also* United States v. Singer, 710 F.2d 431 (8th Cir. 1983).

not be an *automaton*, as the judge has an affirmative duty to be an instrumentality of justice.[19] For example, to assist the jury in its deliberations, the judge may, within certain limits, comment on the evidence.[20] Over the years, the courts have struggled to define the role of the trial judge and the limits of comment or influence, noting on one hand that the judge must not unduly influence the jury's decision, thus denying a defendant the sixth amendment right to trial by jury, while on the other, that the judge has an affirmative duty to secure justice.[21] Indeed, one appellate court specifically noted that while the trial judge should not be an "automaton," he or she still must exercise care not to communicate bias to the jury by being overly reactive.[22] Another state appellate court writes:

> The trial judge is a human being, not an automaton or a robot. He is not required to be a Great Stone Face which shows no reaction to anything that happens in his courtroom. Testimony that is amusing may draw a smile or a laugh, shocking or distasteful evidence may cause a frown or scowl, without reversible error being committed thereby. We have not, and hopefully never will reach the stage in Alabama at which a stone-cold computer is draped in a black robe, set up behind the bench, and plugged in to begin service as Circuit Judge.[23]

Of course, there is no bright line standard for detecting impermissible judicial behavior and influence—for example, for separating a trial judge's remarks that are appropriate from remarks that may unduly influence a jury.[24] The appellate courts have attempted to balance a number of factors and have employed a "sliding scale" approach in assessing the propriety of a judge's behavior during the jury trial. Four factors which have been considered include (1) the materiality or relevance of the behavior or comment, (2) the emphatic or overbearing nature of

---

19. *See* note 23 *infra*; Gitelson & Gitelson, *A Trial Judge's Credo Must Include His Affirmative Duty to Be an Instrumentality of Justice*, 7 SANTA CLARA LAW. 7 (1966).

20. *See, e.g.*, Quercia v. United States, 289 U.S. 466, 469 (1933).

21. *See, e.g.*, United States v. Olgin, 745 F.2d 263, 268 (3d Cir. 1984), *cert. denied*, 105 S. Ct. 2321 (1985).

22. *See* Moody v. United States, 377 F.2d 175, 178 (5th Cir. 1967).

23. Allen v. State, 290 Ala. 339, 342–43, 276 So. 2d 583, 586 (1973); *see also* Fletcher v. State, 291 Ala. 67, 69, 277 So. 2d 882, 883 (1973) ("the trial judge is not required to be a robot without emotional reaction to happenings in his courtroom"); Oglen v. State, 440 So. 2d 1172, 1175 (Ala. Crim. App. 1983).

24. *See Beaty*, 722 F.2d at 1093 (" '[N]o absolute, rigid rule exists. Each case must be viewed in its own setting. The pattern of due process is picked out of the facts and circumstances of each case.' ") (quoting Riley v. Goodman, 315 F.2d 232, 234 (3d Cir. 1963)).

the behavior or comment, (3) the efficacy of any curative instruction used to correct the error, and (4) the prejudicial effect of the behavior or comment in light of the trial as a whole.[25] Our research suggests a more systematic method for assessing many of these "sliding scale" factors.

The sliding scale approach employed by the appellate courts also forces reviewing courts to balance the four considerations against other mitigating factors.[26] But appellate courts are not consistent in applying these factors and mitigating circumstances. For example, one appellate court concluded that it was proper to weigh the totality of these factors in determining whether the "quantum of harm" from a trial judge's behavior or statement amounts to reversible error.[27]

While the trial judge's role of advocate or automaton may vary during the trial, the duty of the judge to control or "arbitrate" the proceedings to ensure a fair trial is *continuous*. But the role of the judge at any given point in the trial process—advocate, arbitrator, or automaton—is determined by the circumstances necessary to ensure a fair trial. At times it requires the

---

25. The "factor approach" emphasizes:

(1) The materiality of the challenged comment as the preliminary focus of inquiry on appeal. The reviewing court is more concerned with a matter central to the defense than with a comment on a tangential issue. *Olgin,* 745 F.2d at 269–70; *see also* United States v. Anton, 597 F.2d 371, 374–75 (3d Cir. 1979) (the judge's comment on the defendant's credibility, an issue central to his defense, was one factor in the appellate court's reversal of the conviction).

(2) The emphatic or overbearing behavior or comments—both verbal and nonverbal—that a jury may accept as controlling. An example of an overly emphatic judicial statement is found in Stevens v. United States, 306 F.2d 834 (5th Cir. 1962). The appellate court held prejudicial the following statement by the trial judge: "All right. I don't believe I want to hear any more testimony from this witness. I want to certify in the record that the Court wouldn't believe him on oath, and I don't want to waste the jury's time taking any more testimony from him." *Id.* at 838.

(3) The efficacy of the curative instruction. For the instruction to be effective, the judge must clearly explain to the jury that it is free to disregard his or her behavior or remarks and must determine the facts of the case on its own. But such instructions do not always produce the desired effect. *See* text accompanying note 183 *infra.*

(4) The prejudicial effect of the comments in light of the jury instructions as a whole. While a potentially prejudicial comment cannot be evaluated in isolation, even the most minor remark can have a prejudicial effect. *Oglin,* 745 F.2d at 269.

26. *Id.*; *see also Nazzaro,* 472 F.2d at 304:

A claim of unfair judicial conduct, under these circumstances, requires a close scrutiny of each tile in the mosaic of the trial so that we can determine whether instances of improper behavior or bias, when considered individually or taken together as a whole, may have reached that point where we can make a safe judgment that the defendant was deprived of the fair trial to which he is entitled.

27. *Oglin,* 745 F.2d at 270.

judge to actively direct the proceedings in order to avoid error, misconduct, or possible prejudice by counsel.[28] As a result, there exists a basic tension among the several roles of the judge during the trial process. Although the judge has great discretion in being the instrumentality of justice, he or she often cannot intervene effectively in the adversarial discussion of the facts for fear of influencing the jury. One federal trial judge has described the result: "Without an investigative file, the American trial judge is a blind and blundering intruder, acting in spasms as sudden flashes of seeming light may lead or mislead him at odd times."[29] Because of the often intuitive or sporadic nature of these behaviors, any input by the judge during the trial, however subtle, may significantly influence the jury decisionmaking process.[30]

B. *The Limits of Permissible Behavior and Influence*

The possibility of undesirable judicial influence on jury verdicts was recognized by the Supreme Court early in our history.[31] Before the turn of the century, the Court noted that the *manner* in which a judge instructs and advises the jury can have an undesirable, although sometimes permissible, influence on the jury decisionmaking process.[32] The Court stated that jurors must remain

---

28. *See, e.g.*, City of Danville v. Frazier, 108 Ill. App. 2d 477, 248 N.E.2d 129 (1969) (the trial judge has a duty to control the proceedings to the extent necessary to ensure each litigant a fair trial); *see also* Gitelson & Gitelson, *supra* note 19.

29. Frankel, *The Search For Truth: An Umpireal View*, 123 U. PA. L. REV. 1031, 1042 (1975).

30. Judge Frankel writes:

> The jury is likely to discern hints, a point of view, a suggested direction, even if none is intended and quite without regard to the judge's efforts to modulate and minimize his role . . . .
>
> We should be candid, moreover, in recognizing that juries are probably correct most of the time if they glean a point of view from the judge's interpolations. Introspecting, I think I have usually put my penetrating questions to witnesses I thought were lying, exaggerating, or obscuring the facts. Less frequently, I have intruded to rescue a witness from questions that seemed unfairly to put the testimony in a bad light or to confuse its import.

Id. at 1043.

Judge Frankel believes our adversarial system poorly equips the trial judge for the position of advocate. The trial judge is best as a "relatively passive moderator" who can from time to time suggest lines of inquiry to counsel. *Id.* at 1043–44.

31. *See, e.g.*, Carver v. Jackson, 29 U.S. (4 Pet.) 1, 4 (1830).

32. *See, e.g.*, Starr v. United States, 153 U.S. 614 (1894). For reviews of judicial influence and the limits of judicial behavior, see Conner, *The Trial Judge, His Facial Expressions, Gestures and General Demeanor—Their Effect on the Administration of Justice*, 9 TRIAL LAW. GUIDE 251 (1965); Note, *Judges' Nonverbal Behavior in Jury Trials: A Threat to Judicial Impartiality*, 61 VA. L. REV. 1266 (1975); Annot., 49 A.L.R.3D 1186 (1973); Annot., 34 A.L.R.3D 1313 (1970). For a discussion of nonverbal behavior at the jury selection stage, see Suggs & Sales, *Using Communication Cues*

the triers of fact, and the trial judge's behavior must remain "guarded" so as to leave the jury free to exercise its own judgment.[33] No word, action, or behavior by the judge is allowed to indicate or transmit the judge's expectations for the defendant's guilt or innocence to the jury,[34] thus influencing impermissibly the jury decisionmaking process.[35]

The desirable behaviors of the trial judge include a duty to be thorough, courteous, patient, just, and impartial.[36] Overly reactive verbal and nonverbal communications—for example, facial expressions or gestures which tend to ridicule the defendant or counsel—are examples of undesirable judicial behavior. Yet such behavior has been held permissible when it does not destroy the fairness of a trial.[37] Thus, the courts have recognized that while certain behaviors of the judge have an undesirable effect on courtroom processes, they do not necessarily unduly influence

---

to Evaluate Prospective Jurors During the Voir Dire, 20 ARIZ. L. REV. 629 (1978) (describing methods that can be used to evaluate prospective jurors on the basis of their communicative abilities).

33. *Starr*, 153 U.S. at 625; *see also* Brown v. Walter, 62 F.2d 798, 799–800 (2d Cir. 1933) (Judge Learned Hand stated: "A judge . . . is more than a moderator . . . . Justice does not depend upon legal dialectics so much as upon the atmosphere of the courtroom, and that in the end depends primarily upon the judge."); *cf.* Judge Frankel's view in note 30 *supra*.

34. *See, e.g.*, State v. Barron, 465 S.W.2d 523, 527 (Mo. 1971) (prejudicial error by the trial judge resulted in reversal of a burglary conviction when the judge, hearing the defendant's brother testify that the defendant was at home watching television when the alleged burglary occurred, placed his hands to the sides of his head, shook his head negatively, and leaned back, swiveling his chair 180 degrees).

35. *See, e.g.*, United States v. Gaines, 450 F.2d 186, 189 (3d Cir. 1971), *cert. denied*, 405 U.S. 927 (1972) (if the trial judge exercises restraint in his comments to the jury and makes it clear in the charge to the jury that the jury remains the sole determiner of fact, the judge has not overstepped the permissible limits of comment); United States v. Meltzer, 100 F.2d 739, 746 (7th Cir. 1938) (jurors must be "left free" to determine the fact controversy). What is meant by "left free" is a question that this study examines empirically by assessing the degree to which both the intentional and unintentional behavior of the trial judge (a) can be predicted from a knowledge of the judge's belief about the defendant's guilt or innocence, and (b) can serve as a predictor of the jury's verdict. *See generally* Kline, *The Role of Suggestibility in Lawyer-Jury Relationships*, in SOCIAL PSYCHOLOGY AND DISCRETIONARY LAW 93 (L. Abt & I. Stuart eds. 1979).

36. Canon 3 of the California Code of Judicial Conduct states the fundamental principle that a judge should remain impartial at all times, CALIFORNIA CODE OF JUDICIAL CONDUCT Canon 3 (1974); Canon 34 of the ABA Canons of Judicial Ethics requires the judge to be thorough, courteous, patient, punctual, just, and impartial, ABA CANONS OF JUDICIAL ETHICS Canon 34 (1971). *See also* Etzel v. Rosenbloom, 83 Cal. App. 2d 758, 765, 189 P.2d 848, 852 (1948) (quoting Socrates: "Four things belong to a judge: to hear courteously, to answer wisely, to consider soberly, and to decide impartially.").

37. *Allen*, 276 So. 2d at 586.

the decisionmaking process of jurors and therefore do not automatically constitute impermissible influence.

Judicial influence that is extreme or prejudicial to the due process rights of the defendant requires a mistrial or reversal of conviction. But a judge's more subtle verbal and nonverbal expressions toward a defendant in the criminal jury trial are also enough to constitute reversible error.[38] The appellate courts recognize that the subtle communicative influence of the judge on the jury is "necessarily and properly of great weight [as] his slightest word or intimation is received with deference and may prove controlling."[39] One court commented that

> [i]t is well known, as a matter of judicial notice, that juries are highly sensitive to every utterance by the trial judge, the trial arbiter, and that some comments may be so highly prejudicial that even a strong admonition by the judge to the jury, that they are not bound by the judge's views, will not cure the error.[40]

Less blatant behavior by trial judges may also exceed the permissible limits of influence and violate a defendant's right to pro-

---

38. *Id.* ("We have little doubt that facial expressions, gestures, and nonverbal communications which tended to ridicule defendant and his counsel, could, standing alone, operate so as to destroy the fairness of a trial.").

39. *Quercia,* 289 U.S. at 470 (discussing judicial influence and the limitations on the trial judge's power to comment on the evidence). For a more recent discussion on the limits of the trial judge's power to comment on the evidence, see *Anton,* 597 F.2d at 375 (any comment by a trial judge concerning evidence or witnesses may influence the jury, thus depriving the defendant of his right to have the questions of fact and credibility determined by the jury); *see also* State v. Burton, 112 Wis. 2d 560, 334 N.W.2d 263 (1983). The *Burton* court cautioned:

> The judge is a figure of authority and respect during the trial; his or her intrusions into the sanctity of jury deliberations may affect those deliberations. Even a transcript of the judge's communication cannot reveal a judge's facial expressions or tone of voice. Defense counsel and defendant must be present to have the opportunity to observe the judge's demeanor first-hand, to object to statements or request curative statements in the event that the communication may be improper in any way.

Id. at 569, 334 N.W.2d at 267.

40. Bursten v. United States, 395 F.2d 976, 983 (5th Cir. 1968) (footnote omitted), *cert. denied,* 409 U.S. 843 (1972); *see also* State v. Wheat, 131 Kan. 562, 569, 292 P. 793, 797 (1930) (Jochems, J., dissenting). Jochems noted:

> The trial judge occupies a high position. He presides over the trial. The jury has great respect for him. They can be easily influenced by the slightest suggestion coming from the court, whether it be a nod of the head, a smile, a frown, or a spoken word. It is therefore imperative that the trial judge shall conduct himself with the utmost caution in order that the unusual power he possesses shall not be abused.

Id. at 569, 292 P. at 797; *see also* People v. Mahoney, 201 Cal. 618, 623, 258 P. 607, 608 (1927) (reversible error where trial judge made discourteous and disparaging remarks toward defense from which jury could plainly perceive extreme bias toward defendant— "[judges] cannot be too careful or cautious lest they by word, look, or inflection of the voice bring to bear upon the jury an influence not compatible with an unbiased verdict of the jury").

cedural due process.[41] Subtle judicial influence is more likely to be expressed through nonverbal messages, cues, or "channels" such as facial expressions or tone of voice, rather than through the actual words of the judge. In one case, an appellate court held that a defendant was deprived of his constitutional right to a fair trial when, during the testimony of the State's witnesses, the trial judge smiled favorably, nodded his head in agreement, and muttered "Uh-hum," while during the testimony of defense witnesses the judge expressed disapproval by a negative shaking of the head and negative mutterings such as "Hump," "Hu," and "No."[42] While appellate courts recognize that sometimes the judge's subtle verbal and nonverbal behavior intentionally or unintentionally influences jury verdicts in criminal jury trials, reversal is usually not allowed unless the judge's influence is either clearly prejudicial to the defendant or significantly affects the outcome of the trial.[43]

Appellate courts have in some cases attempted to assess the subtle influence of the judge's behavior on jury verdicts in criminal trials by questioning the jurors themselves.[44] For example, where a defendant claimed that he was deprived of a fair trial because the judge repeatedly expressed negative facial expressions, scowls, and head movements,[45] the court reviewed testimony from five jurors who stated that they saw these expressions but they had no effect on their decisionmaking process, and from

41. *See* People v. Jones, 94 Ill. 2d 275, 300–02, 447 N.E.2d 161, 173–74 (1982) (Simon, J., dissenting) (trial judges can unduly influence juries simply by a "slip of the tongue").

42. *See* State v. Larmond, 244 N.W.2d 233 (Iowa 1976).

43. *See* United States v. Hill, 526 F.2d 1019, 1025 (10th Cir. 1975), *cert. denied*, 425 U.S. 940 (1976) (appellate court, with the claim that "[a]ppellant was entitled to a fair trial but not a perfect one," held that where judge smiled or smirked at defendant's behavior in court, this conduct did not indicate to the jury that the judge believed the defendant guilty); Cantor v. State, 27 Ala. App. 40, 165 So. 597 (1936) (where trial judge merely smiled during part of the jury instructions relating to the defendant's alleged criminal conduct, the appellate court held this not to be reversible error). In *Cantor*, the appellate court noted that while the smile upon the benign face of a just judge would be preferable by far to a scowl, the appellate court would not interfere with the discretion of the trial judge when there is no clear influence on the jurors. The court did not address the legal standard for reversibility on the grounds of prejudicial error by the trial judge. For a related discussion, see notes 159–174 *infra* and accompanying text.

44. *See* People v. Lee, 38 Cal. App. 3d 749, 754, 113 Cal. Rptr. 641, 645 (1974) (jurors' affidavits are competent only to prove "objective facts" to impeach a verdict; objective facts are those open to sight, hearing, and other senses subject to corroboration). *But see* CAL. EVID. CODE § 1150 (West 1966) (jurors are usually not allowed to impeach their verdicts by appearing as witnesses).

45. Hill v. State, 153 Tex. Crim. 105, 217 S.W.2d 1009 (1948).

the other five jurors who stated they did not see the expressions at all. The appellate court dismissed the defendant's appeal and noted that it was at a loss to understand how it could rule on the expression on the face of a trial judge.[46]

Appellate courts remain reluctant to review a defendant's contention that a trial judge's nonverbal messages, demeanor, tone of voice, or facial expressions constituted an expression of opinion, reflecting the judge's bias against the defendant.[47] Only recently have appellate courts reversed longstanding rules that a trial judge's nonverbal messages are not reviewable on appeal. Claims of prejudicial verbal and nonverbal error by the trial judge are now reviewable in some courts if the appellant has completed a record that will enable an appellate court adequately to review the matter.[48] How a trial attorney might develop a "complete record" of the trial judge's subtle verbal and nonverbal behavior is discussed in the final section.

Judicial influence sometimes acts to deprive criminal defendants of their due process rights. The courts have recognized that judicial influence may be extreme or subtle, and may be transmitted to trial participants by the verbal and nonverbal behavior of the trial judge.[49] In extreme cases, judicial influence may constitute reversible error on the grounds that the defendant is denied the constitutionally protected right to a fair and impartial trial. Most appellate courts, however, continue to recognize only very limited grounds for appeal on the basis of undue judicial influence. This note analyzes actual judicial behavior in an attempt to help in the long-term understanding of the possible limits of judicial influence. The ultimate goal is to aid appellate courts in more effectively assessing judicial behavior, to help ensure the due process right to a constitutionally fair and impartial jury trial.

II. A Model for the Study of Judicial Influence

This section proposes a preliminary model for the study of the possible effects of judges' beliefs, expectations, and behavior on the verdicts returned by juries.[50] The model helps to identify

46. *Id.*

47. *See, e.g.*, Milhouse v. State, 254 Ga. 357, 329 S.E.2d 490 (1985) (trial judge's tone of voice or vocal emphasis is generally not reviewable on appeal).

48. *Id.* (Georgia Supreme Court noted that, in certain cases, a trial judge's tone of voice, vocal emphasis, facial expressions, or other demeanor can be prejudicial toward defendant).

49. *See* Note, *supra* note 32.

50. For a general model for the study of interpersonal expectancy effects, see Rosenthal,

the types of variables that need to be studied to better achieve a systematic understanding of judicial influence and the operation of expectancy effects in ongoing trial processes. The model is intended to serve as a theoretical guide for researchers, and not as a hard-and-fast working model for practitioners. The basic elements of the model are (A) background variables, (B) expectancy variables, (C) transmitting variables, and (D) outcome variables. The model is described in Figure 1 below:

Pavlov's Mice, Pfungst's Horse, and Pygmalion's PONS: Some Models for the Study of Interpersonal Expectancy Effects, in THE CLEVER HANS PHENOMENON 182 (T.A. Sebeok & R. Rosenthal eds. 1981).

FIGURE 1

Model for the Study of Judicial Influence

VARIABLE	Background	Expectancy	Transmitting	Outcome
EXAMPLE OF VARIABLE	Judge Sex Juror Education Lawyer Age Defendant Criminal History	Judge Belief (Defendant *Should* Be, or *Will* Be, Guilty)	Verbal Cues/ Nonverbal Cues (Content-Present: Normal Video and Audio, Audio Only; Content-Absent: Video Only, Content-Filtered Speech Only)	Jury Verdict (Trial Outcome)

CUMULATIVE EFFECT

A. Background Variables

Background variables refer to the more stable attributes of the trial participants—the trial judge, the jurors, the witnesses, the defendants, and the prosecution and defense lawyers. For example, background variables refer to sex, social status, education, ethnicity, intellectual ability, personality, and other personal history variables.

The model describes the relationship between the trial participants, their background variables, and the trial outcome (e.g., the A-D arrow of Figure 1). In *The American Jury*, Kalven and Zeisel noted, for example, that it is generally assumed that the background characteristics of defendants make no difference to the trial judge.[51] (This is an example of the defendant-trial judge relationship.) Our research questions this assumption.[52]

The background variables associated with the trial judge include, among others, age, sex, race, political ideology, and number of years on the bench. These variables have been shown to influence judicial behavior toward trial participants.[53] Researchers have also studied the effects of characteristics of the jurors themselves on trial outcome. For example, the political ideology, sex, race, occupation, income, and age of jurors have

---

51. H. KALVEN & H. ZEISEL, THE AMERICAN JURY 193 (1966) (examining the behavior of judges and jurors in criminal jury trials); *id.* at 497–98 ("The judge very often perceives the stimulus that moves the jury, but does not yield to it. Indeed it is interesting how often the judge describes with sensitivity a factor which he then excludes from his own considerations.").

52. For other examples of studies on the trial judge-defendant relationship, see Bell, *Racism in American Courts: Cause for Black Disruption or Despair?*, 61 CALIF. L. REV. 165 (1973); Champagne & Nagel, *The Psychology of Judging*, in THE PSYCHOLOGY OF THE COURTROOM 257 (N. Kerr & R. Bray eds. 1982); Dane & Wrightsman, *Effects of Defendants' and Victims' Characteristics on Juror's Verdicts*, in THE PSYCHOLOGY OF THE COURTROOM 83 (N. Kerr & R. Bray eds. 1982); *see also* Gross & Mauro, *Patterns of Death: An Analysis of Racial Disparities in Capital Sentencing and Homicide Victimization*, 37 STAN. L. REV. 27 (1985).

53. For example, in one exploratory study the researchers found (1) white judges gazed more at defendants than did black judges, (2) judges gazed more at defendant witnesses, as compared to civilian and police witnesses, and (3) a significant positive relationship (correlation = .48) existed between the rate of gaze at the defendant and the fine received if found guilty. *See* Dorch & Fontaine, *Rate of Judges' Gaze at Different Types of Witnesses*, 46 PERCEPTUAL MOTOR & SKILLS 1103 (1978).

Personality variables of the trial judge have also been employed as background variables. Early research in this area suggests that psychoanalysis may help to explain judicial influence by aiding in an understanding of the judge's self-concept and use of unconscious defense mechanisms (examples of background variables). *See* H. LASSWELL, POWER AND PERSONALITY (1976); Schroeder, *The Psychologic Study of Judicial Opinions*, 6 CALIF. L. REV. 89 (1918); Winnick, Gerver & Blumberg, *The Psychology of Judges*, in LEGAL AND CRIMINAL PSYCHOLOGY 121 (H. Toch ed. 1961).

been shown to influence jury decisionmaking processes.[54] Finally, research suggests that defendant characteristics indirectly affect judicial behavior. Studies in this area demonstrate the effects of the race of the defendant on sentencing in death penalty cases.[55] Similarly, researchers have found that juries are significantly more likely to convict a defendant who has a criminal record than one who does not.[56] The social psychological literature has generally supported the conclusion that the background characteristics of the defendant and his or her victim influence the decisions of simulated jurors.[57]

Although the background variables of the trial participants *have no direct legal bearing* on the guilt or innocence of the defendant in a criminal trial, these background variables influence judges and jurors in their decisionmaking process.[58] The model here includes the effects of trial participant background variables on judicial behavior in criminal jury trials. These background variables help predict the behaviors of trial participants and further the understanding of how these behaviors may influence trial outcomes.

---

54. *See* R. HASTIE, S.D. PENROD & N. PENNINGTON, INSIDE THE JURY (1983); Mills & Bohannon, *Juror Characteristics: To What Extent Are They Related to Jury Verdicts?*, 64 JUDICATURE 22 (1980); S.D. Penrod, D. Linz, L. Heuer & D. Coates, The Science of Advocacy (1985) (unpublished manuscript on file with the *Stanford Law Review*); *see also* Costantini, Mallery & Yapundich, *Gender and Juror Partiality: Are Women More Likely To Prejudge Guilt?*, 67 JUDICATURE 120 (1983) (finding females more likely than males to reveal partiality, as measured by belief in the defendant's guilt and by belief in one's own capacity to serve impartially as a juror at a particular defendant's trial).

55. *See, e.g.*, Zeisel, *Race Bias in the Administration of the Death Penalty: The Florida Experience*, 95 HARV. L. REV. 456 (1981); *see also* Dane & Wrightsman, *supra* note 52. *But see* Hagan, *Extra-legal Attributes and Criminal Sentencing: An Assessment of a Sociological Viewpoint*, 8 L. & SOC'Y REV. 357 (1974) (reviewing 20 studies on the relationship of criminal sentencing and defendant characteristics and finding a small nonsignificant positive relationship between these factors).

56. *See, e.g.*, S. KADISH, S. SCHULHOFER & M. PAULSEN, CRIMINAL LAW AND ITS PROCESSES 44–48 (4th ed. 1983); Brooks & Doob, *Justice and the Jury*, J. SOC. ISSUES, Summer 1975, at 171–77; Mendez, *California's New Law on Character Evidence: Evidence Code Section 352 and the Impact of Recent Psychological Studies*, 31 U.C.L.A. L. REV. 1003, 1047–49 (1984).

57. *See, e.g.*, Dion, Berscheid & Walster, *What Is Beautiful Is Good*, 24 J. PERSONALITY & SOC. PSYCHOLOGY 285 (1972); Jones & Aronson, *Attribution of Fault to a Rape Victim as a Function of Respectability of the Victim*, 26 J. PERSONALITY & SOC. PSYCHOLOGY 415 (1973); Landy & Aronson, *The Influence of the Character of the Criminal and His Victim on the Decisions of Simulated Jurors*, J. EXPERIMENTAL SOC. PSYCHOLOGY 141 (1969); Nemeth & Sosis, *A Simulated Jury Study: Characteristics of the Defendants and the Jurors*, 90 J. SOC. PSYCHOLOGY 221 (1973).

58. *See* Vinson, *Psychological Anchors: Influencing the Jury*, 8 LITIGATION 20 (1982); Wasserman & Robinson, *Extra-Legal Influences, Group Processes, and Jury Decision-making: A Psychological Perspective*, 12 N.C. CENTRAL L.J. 96 (1980).

B. *Expectancy Variables*

A judge's expectations for trial outcome and trial processes can influence the decisionmaking process of jurors and the actual trial outcome.[59] An "expectation" is a particular belief that an individual has for the outcome of some behavior. The relationship between a judge's particular "expectations" for trial outcome and the actual outcome of their trials would be an example of an "expectancy effect" if the expectation of the judge affected the behavior of the judge in such a way as to lead the jury to confirm the judge's expectations.[60] Our research assesses how a judge's expectations, as measured during the trial process *prior* to the jury verdict, relate to trial processes and actual trial outcome.[61] As described above, under some conditions, behavior flowing from a judge's expectancy might act to deprive a defendant of his or her right to a fair and impartial trial.

C. *Transmitting Variables: Verbal and Nonverbal Communications*

"Transmitting variables" or "transmitting behaviors" refers to the verbal and nonverbal processes by which expectations are communicated by the judge to the trial participants. In this study, trial judges' transmission variables were sampled when the

59. *See* texts accompanying notes 7–43 *supra,* 141–146 *infra.*

60. *See* note 50 *supra.* For a description of the assessment of trial judges' expectations, see Appendix B *infra* (Judge Questionnaire—Questions 9 and 10: "What should the verdict be?" and "What will the verdict be?"). In this study, we assessed judges' expectations for trial outcome for the first two major charges or counts against the defendant. *See* note 98 *infra.* What the judges thought the verdict *should* be and what the judges thought the verdict *would* be was significantly positively correlated ($r = .69, p < .001$ for count 1, and $r = .78, p < .001$ for count 2).

61. We measured the expectations (expectancy variables) in this study after the judges had become acquainted with a particular trial—near the close of the trial just before the judge gave instructions to the jury. Judges probably develop expectations about trial outcome throughout the entire trial process. These expectations, however, should be most clearly developed near the completion of the judge's role in the trial, after all the evidence has been heard. By examining expectations at the end of the trial, we related the effect of these attitudes on the judge's subsequent delivery of the jury instructions.

The expectancy variable can be induced experimentally or allowed to occur naturally. In field settings such as the courtroom, expectations are often measured as they occur naturally rather than varied experimentally. In studying naturally occurring expectations, some of the problems associated with experimental studies on courtroom processes are avoided, although some degree of experimental control is sacrificed. *See* notes 82–86 *infra* and accompanying text. The present study documents the operation and communication of naturally occurring expectations. *See generally* Blanck & Turner, *Gestalt Research: Clinical Field Research Approaches to Studying Organizations,* in THE HANDBOOK OF ORGANIZATIONAL BEHAVIOR (J. Lorsch ed. 1986) (forthcoming) (discussing the methodological issues of ecological validity and experimental control associated with studying naturally occurring versus experimentally induced effects).

judges gave final jury instructions. This is one time during the trial when the judge directly addresses the jury as to the law, and therefore may potentially have the greatest influence on the decisionmaking process of the jury.[62] All the judges in our study read pattern jury instructions. Thus, it was possible to isolate or "control" the effects of the judge's particular transmission variable—for example, verbal and nonverbal behaviors—from the content of the instructions themselves.[63] In short, we were afforded the rare opportunity in a real-life research setting to isolate some of the variables of interest.

Judges are aware of the problems associated with pattern jury instructions and have been reluctant to deviate from the "legally

---

62. *See* Andres v. United States, 333 U.S. 740, 765 (1948) (Frankfurter, J., concurring) ("Charging a jury is not a matter of abracadabra. No part of the conduct of a criminal trial lays a heavier task upon the presiding judge. The charge is that part of the whole trial which probably exercises the weightiest influence upon jurors.").

The jury's duty in a criminal trial is to reach a verdict by examining evidence presented during the trial. The jury is required to apply the law as described by the judge in the charge and in instructions given during the trial. The judge's instructions to the jury are meant to provide the jury with the legal standards for reaching a verdict. The appellate courts and legislatures have repeatedly charged the trial judge with this responsibility. For example, in 1908 the Supreme Court of Pennsylvania stated:

> [W]hen the trial judge has not succeeded in delivering instructions on the law in such a way that they will be understood by the jury, his charge is inadequate and justly open to objection by the defendant. As the very object of the instructions is to inform the jury as to the law applicable to the facts of the case, the charge fails of its purpose when the jury are ignorant of the law applicable to any material question in the case.

Commonwealth v. Smith, 221 Pa. 552, 553, 70 A. 850, 850 (1908).

But jurors sometimes reach a verdict that is inconsistent with the law by purposefully disregarding the judge's instructions or by unintentionally misunderstanding the judge's instructions and basing the verdict on an incorrect legal standard. *See* A.E. ELWORK, B.D. SALES & J.J. ALFINI, MAKING JURY INSTRUCTIONS UNDERSTANDABLE 4–5 (1982). Juror misunderstandings of the judge's instructions also arise from the syntax of the instructions, the manner of the judge's presentation, and the juror's unfamiliarity with legal terminology. *See* Charrow & Charrow, *Making Legal Language Understandable: A Psycholinguistic Study of Jury Instructions*, 79 COLUM. L. REV. 1306 (1979); Elwork, Sales & Alfini, *Making Jury Instructions Understandable: Jurors' Use of Judges' Instructions*, 11 SOC. METHODS & RESEARCH 501 (1983); Elwork, Sales & Alfini, *Juridic Decisions*, 1 LAW & HUM. BEHAV. 163 (1977); Forston, *Sense and Non-sense: Jury Trial Communication*, 1975 B.Y.U. L. REV. 601; Reed, *Jury Simulation: The Impact of Judge's Instructions and Attorney Tactics on Decisionmaking*, 71 J. CRIM. L. & CRIMINOLOGY 68 (1980); Schwarzer, *Communication with Juries: Problems and Remedies*, 69 CALIF. L. REV. 731 (1981); Severance & Loftus, *Improving the Ability of Jurors to Comprehend and Apply Criminal Jury Instructions*, 17 LAW & SOC'Y REV. 153, 154 (1982); Strawn & Buchanan, *Jury Confusion: A Threat to Justice*, 59 JUDICATURE 478 (1976).

63. *See* Channels, *The Methods of Social Science and their Use in Legal Proceedings*, 16 CONN. L. REV. 853, 862–64 (1984) (describing how control variables are held constant during the research process to isolate the cause and effect variables of interest and to refute rival hypotheses about other factors that could have caused the outcome of interest).

accurate" language that has been approved by higher courts. Trial judges are acutely aware that even minor changes in the wording of jury instructions have been the basis for reversals.[64] This awareness should make any deviations from the jury instructions, verbal and nonverbal, all the more unusual, more significant, and perhaps more influential. In the present research, all the participating judges read from the same set of California Pattern Criminal Jury Instructions,[65] allowing us to standardize the presentation of the judges' verbal content.

As described earlier, the courts have long acknowledged that *nonverbal* judicial behaviors, for example the facial expressions or tone of voice cues of the judge, can alone influence jury verdicts and sometimes do so in impermissible ways or to an impermissible extent.[66] More recently, social scientists have demonstrated that in analogous situations, experimenter, teacher, doctor, and therapist nonverbal behaviors significantly influence social inter-

---

64. In response, legislatures began to standardize jury instructions in the 1930s. Before then, instructions were typically generated by the suggestions of counsel submitted to the trial judge. Three problems with non-pattern jury instructions were: (1) The process was time consuming; (2) it often resulted in an inaccurate statement of the applicable law, therefore leading to reversals on appeal; and (3) trial judges ended up delivering legally accurate but often incomprehensible instructions to juries. *See* A.E. ELWORK, B.D. SALES & J.J. ALFINI, *supra* note 62; J. FRANK, LAW AND THE MODERN MIND 181 (1930) (summarizing the dilemma and stating that jury instructions "might as well be spoken in a foreign language").

Interestingly, one study found that pattern instructions have only marginally reduced the number of appeals based on erroneous jury instructions. *See* R.G. NIELAND, PATTERN JURY INSTRUCTIONS: A CRITICAL LOOK AT A MODERN MOVEMENT TO IMPROVE THE JURY SYSTEM (1979); Nieland, *Assessing the Impact of Pattern Jury Instructions,* 62 JUDICATURE 185 (1978). However, pattern instructions do seem to reduce the amount of time previously required to draft jury instructions and the chance of legal inaccuracies in jury instructions. *See* R. MCBRIDE, THE ART OF INSTRUCTING THE JURY §§ 9.06–9.14, at 342–53 (1969 & Supp. 1978). For a case discussing these issues, see People v. Garcia, 54 Cal. App. 3d 61, 126 Cal. Rptr. 275 (1975), *cert. denied,* 426 U.S. 911 (1976) (reviewing several erroneous variations in instructions concerning the meaning of "proof beyond a reasonable doubt" and reversing a conviction of murder on the grounds that the instructional errors of the trial court constituted harmful error).

65. *See* Appendix A.

66. *See* notes 37–48 *supra* and accompanying text. Nonverbal behavior, other than visual or auditory cues, has been defined to include the study of social distances and social artifacts. For example, in Milgram's famous studies of obedience to authority, a key variable related to the extent of "obedience" was social distance to the victim. As vocal cues, visual cues, and tactile cues were added, individuals became less likely to "shock" the victim. *See* S. MILGRAM, OBEDIENCE TO AUTHORITY (1974). For more detailed discussion and overview of this field, see R. BIRDWHISTELL, INTRODUCTION TO KINESICS (1952); R. BUCK, THE COMMUNICATION OF EMOTION (1985); A. MEHRABIAN, NONVERBAL COMMUNICATION (1972); Duncan, *Nonverbal Communication,* 72 PSYCHOLOGICAL BULL. 118 (1969).

action with subjects, pupils, patients, and clients.[67]

One of the earliest hints that nonverbal cues were involved in the transmission of expectancy effects came from the work of experimental social psychologists on the operation of "experimenter expectancy effects."[68] In these early experiments, college students were asked by other students designated as "experimenters" to judge whether a person pictured in a photograph had been experiencing success or failure in life. Despite the fact that all "experimenters" read the same instructions to their students—the use of "pattern instructions" to control for the verbal content of the experimenter's communications—students responded in accordance with the expectations that were experimentally induced in the minds of the "experimenters." In other words, the students thought the individuals in the photographs were more successful if the "experimenters" had been led to believe they were more successful.[69] Because all experimenters in these studies read the same verbal instructions, these results suggested that the nonverbal components of the interaction led the experimenters to *cause* the results that they had been led to expect—thus the term "experimenter expectancy effect."

In the present study, we videotaped judges delivering final jury instructions in order to study the type of nonverbal, as well as verbal, information that may transmit judicial influence and expectancy effects in the courtroom.[70] This design enabled us to

67. These investigations have studied the factors that increase or decrease expectancy effects and the processes of interpersonal communication that transmit the expectancy effects. *See, e.g,* R. ROSENTHAL, EXPERIMENTER EFFECTS IN BEHAVIORAL RESEARCH (1976); Blanck & Rosenthal, *The Mediation of Interpersonal Expectancy Effects: The Counselor's Tone of Voice,* 76 J. EDUC. PSYCHOLOGY 418 (1984).

68. *See, e.g.,* R. ROSENTHAL, *supra* note 67, at 196–210.

69. Later studies in which "experimenters" were filmed during the reading of the instructions confirmed that no serious deviations from the text had occurred in the reading of the written instructions. R. ROSENTHAL, *supra* note 67, at 259–80.

70. The videotapes of the judge's final instructions to the jury were modified in different ways to isolate the various communicative channels and channel combinations. The channels studied were:

(1) *Normal video and audio cues* (pattern transcript, visual cues, normal audio cues).

(2) *Audio only cues* (normal speech and content-present).

(3) *Video only cues* (facial and body cues only).

(4) *Tone of voice only cues* (content-filtered speech). For this channel, the master audio tapes are content-filtered, a process that removes from the tape the high frequencies on which word recognition depends but preserves sequence and rhythm.

See R. ROSENTHAL, J. HALL, R. DIMATTEO, P. ROGERS & D. ARCHER, SENSITIVITY TO NONVERBAL COMMUNICATION: THE PONS TEST 14–15 (1979); Rogers, Scherer & Rosenthal, *Content Filtering Human Speech: A Simple Electronic System,* 3 BEHAV. RESEARCH METHODS & INSTRUMENTATION

separate the verbal, video, and audio "channels." These different channels convey different amounts and types of information,[71] and individuals generally differ in the clarity of their communication through the various channels.[72]

The effect of auditory channel was measured in two ways: by studying the judges' normal speech only cues (content-present) and the judges' tone of voice only cues (content-absent). Considerable evidence shows that auditory cues alone may be sufficient to transmit expectancy effects.[73] In an interesting study bearing on the importance of auditory cues in the transmission of expectancy effects, experienced hypnotists read pattern instructions to two groups of people. The hypnotists believed one group to contain people of high susceptibility to hypnotic cues and one group to contain people of low susceptibility to hypnotic cues.[74] When the hypnotists were led to expect lower susceptibility scores, their voices were found to be significantly less convincing in their reading of the instructions to their subjects. These results were obtained despite the fact that the hypnotists were cautioned to treat their subjects identically, were told their performance would be tape recorded, and were aware of the

16 (1971). Although no norms exist for the proportion of words that can still be understood after content-filtering, recent studies have found that proportion to be between .11 and .17. *See* Blanck & Rosenthal, *supra* note 67, at 420. In the present study, 24 students (13 males and 11 females) listed the words they could understand after content-filtering for ten randomly selected segments across all the seven trials for one judge. For these few segments, the proportion of words correctly understood after content-filtering was .08.

71. For example, facial cues have been shown to convey a large percentage of emotional information. *See* R. ROSENTHAL, J. HALL, R. DIMATTEO, P. ROGERS & D. ARCHER, *supra* note 70.

72. *Id.*

73. *See* Rosenthal & Fode, *Psychology of the Scientist: V. Three Experiments in Experimenter Bias,* 12 PSYCHOLOGICAL REP. 491-511 (1963).

A two-stage study by Adair and Epstein further supports the idea that expectations might be communicated by an experimenter's tone of voice. Adair & Epstein, *Verbal Cues in the Mediation of Experimenter Bias,* 22 PSYCHOLOGICAL REP. 1045 (1968). In the first stage, experimenters were led to expect either high or low ratings of success from their research subjects. Consistent with earlier studies of this kind, experimenters did in fact obtain results significantly in the direction of their expectations. In the second stage of this experiment, subjects received tape-recorded instructions read by experimenters who had been given different expectations for how their subjects should rate the photos of faces. The results showed that the audio cues alone were sufficient to communicate to subjects the expectations of the experimenters. Other studies have shown that visual cues alone can transmit the effects of experimenter expectations, and have supported the general importance of nonverbal cues in the transmission of expectancy effects. *See* Blanck & Rosenthal, *supra* note 67; Harris & Rosenthal, *The Mediation of Interpersonal Expectancy Effects: 31 Meta-Analyses,* 97 PSYCHOLOGICAL BULL. 363 (1985).

74. *See* Troffer & Tart, *Experimenter Bias in Hypnotist Performance,* 145 SCI. 1330 (1964).

problem of experimenter expectancy effects. These conditions parallel those in this study in which trial participants received notice that the trials would be videotaped and judges were aware that the study examined judicial influence on juries.[75]

In many ways, the trial judge is analogous to the hypnotist, and the jury is analogous to the hypnotist's subject. When judges expect innocent verdicts, their voices, like that of the hypnotist, may be relatively warmer and less hostile when addressing the jury. When judges expect guilty verdicts, their voices may be relatively colder and more hostile when addressing the jury. Additionally, tone of voice cues alone may be sufficient to convey the judge's expectations for trial outcome to jurors in measurable ways.[76]

The second channel of interest is the visual or video channel.

---

75. *See* notes 118–119 *infra* and accompanying text (describing analogous results in the present study).

76. Two experiments have shown that the expectancy effect was approximately cut in half when subjects had access only to auditory cues from their experimenter. *See* Rosenthal & Fode, *supra* note 73 (showing 47 percent of the total expectancy effect when subjects had access only to experimenters' audio cues); Zoble & Lehman, *Interaction of Subject and Experimenter Expectancy Effects in a Tone Length Discrimination Task*, 14 BEHAVIORAL SCI. 357 (1969) (showing 53 percent of the total expectancy effect when subjects had access only to experimenters' audio cues).

It has also been possible to isolate particular aspects of vocal cues that are effective in influencing subjects' responses. For example, vocal emphasis— intensity or volume—is alone sufficient to function as a transmitting cue in the communication of expectancy effects. *See* Scherer, Rosenthal & Koivumaki, *Mediating Interpersonal Expectancies via Vocal Cues: Differential Speech Intensity as a Means of Social Influence*, 2 EUR. J. SOC. PSYCHOLOGY 163 (1972) (where subjects were exposed to audiotaped instructions giving relatively greater emphasis to "failure words," while other subjects were exposed to audiotaped instructions giving relatively greater emphasis to "success words," subjects tended to rate photographs of others in accordance with the words that the experimenters had emphasized in the audiotaped instructions).

Vocal emphasis is a commonly alleged ground for a trial judge's prejudicial error. *See, e.g.*, Walker v. Lockhart, 726 F.2d at 1243 (defendant asserted that the tone of voice and demeanor of the trial judge denied his constitutional right to a fair and impartial trial). Trial judges who emphasize the words "guilty" or "innocent," for example, when describing a defendant may affect the jury's perceptions of that defendant's guilt or innocence in significant ways.

Some pattern jury instructions committees have attempted to address these problems by drafting instructions that caution juries about the trial judge's vocal emphasis. For example, one judge uses a pattern instruction caution on the vocal emphasis of the trial judge in giving instructions:

> During my charge, I may emphasize words or sentences to eliminate monotony in my instructions. The purpose of this emphasis is to help you understand and remember the law a little better than if these instructions were delivered in a monotonous manner. Do not assume from my emphasis, gestures or manner that I am stating the law to the advantage of either (the State or the defendant) (party).

See R. MCBRIDE, *supra* note 64, § 15.06(a), at 175.

Several studies have shown that visual cues alone sometimes can be even more effective than auditory cues in the transmission of expectancy effects.[77] In one study, subjects who had access only to auditory cues were affected by their experimenter's expectancy only 53 percent as much as those who had access to both visual and auditory cues, while those subjects who had access only to visual cues were affected by their experimenter's expectancy 75 percent as much as those who had access to both information channels.[78] Thus, visual cues alone may be one of the most important factors in the transmission of expectancy effects and judicial influence.[79] For example, when judges expect an innocent verdict, their visual expressions (facial and body cues) may be rated as warmer, less hostile, and more open-minded in delivering instructions to juries.[80]

D. *Outcome Variables*

Outcome variables refer to the behavior of the "expectee" (e.g., the juror) after the interaction with the expecter (e.g., the judge) has occurred. In this study, outcome variables are measured by actual trial outcome. Outcome variables may them-

77. *See* Zoble & Lehman, *supra* note 76; A. Badini & R. Rosenthal, Visual Cues and Student Gender as Mediating Factors in Teacher Expectancy Effects (1982) (paper read at the Eastern Communication Convention, Hartford, Conn.) (students who had access to visual cues from their teachers were more affected by their teachers' expectations than were those students who had no access to visual cues from their teachers).

78. *See* Zoble & Lehman, *supra* note 76.

79. "Live" visual contact may not be a necessary condition for the transmission of expectancy effects. *See* J. Burnham, Experimenter Bias and Video Tape: A Methodological Step Forward (1971) (unpublished Ph.D. dissertation, Purdue Univ.). Additionally, when screens are placed between "experimenters" and their research subjects so that visual access is denied the participants, the size of the effect of experimenter expectations is cut approximately in half. This suggests that although expectancy effects can be transmitted by tone of voice alone, visual cues significantly contribute to their operation. *See* note 73 *supra* and accompanying text.

Finally, the use of video- or audiotape recorded jury instructions may reproduce and perhaps even reinforce any live expectancy effects that may have occurred during the actual trial. *See* note 185 *infra* and accompanying text. *See* Blanck, Rosenthal & Vannicelli, *Nonverbal Communication in the Clinical Context: The Therapist's Tone of Voice*, in NONVERBAL COMMUNICATION IN THE CLINICAL CONTEXT 99 (P.D. Blanck, R. Buck & R. Rosenthal eds. 1986); Blanck, Rosenthal, Vannicelli & Lee, *Therapist's Tone of Voice: Descriptive, Psychometric, Interactional, and Competence Analyses*, 4 J. SOC. & CLINICAL PSYCHOLOGY — (1986) (forthcoming); Ekman & Friesen, *Nonverbal Leakage and Clues to Deception*, 32 PSYCHIATRY 88 (1969); P. McLeod, R. Rosenthal, P.D. Blanck & S. Snodgrass, Micromomentary Movement and the Decoding of Face and Body Cues (1980) (presentation at the Am. Psychological Ass'n Meeting).

80. *See, e.g., Larmond*, 244 N.W.2d at 236 (noting the trial judge's "telegraphing" to the jury, by nonverbal behaviors and facial expressions, expectations for trial outcome).

selves be affected by other variables in the model. For example, defendants with a criminal history may be more likely to receive guilty verdicts.[81]

III. Research Strategy and Design

The generalizability of results to real-world social settings or across many social settings is called "external" or "ecological validity."[82] Our research sought to achieve the greater external validity of the observational and field-like studies in the courtroom, as well as the greater precision of the laboratory-like studies involving ratings of verbal and nonverbal behavior.[83] External validity describes whether the results obtained in a particular scientific study hold generally true in the real world. Laboratory simulation of courtroom processes often may not be generalizable to the actual courtroom context, and jury simulation research in particular has been criticized for a lack of external validity.[84]

Our research strategy and design attempted to maximize ex-

81. In this example, an alternative explanation is that defendants with a criminal history are actually more likely to be guilty. In studies involving naturally occurring, rather than experimentally induced interpersonal expectations, a high correlation among background variables, the trial judge's expectations for trial outcome, and actual trial outcome must be interpreted with caution. The presence of a high correlation of this sort makes it difficult to conclude, for example, that it is the judge's expectations alone, rather than the jurors' decisionmaking process or the selection characteristics of the defendant, that are "responsible" for subsequent verdicts. Covariance techniques, cross-lagged panel analyses, and related data analytic procedures are helpful in isolating such relationships. *See, e.g.*, Crano & Mellon, *Causal Influence of Teachers' Expectations on Children's Academic Performance: A Cross-Lagged Panel Analysis*, 70 J. Educ. Psychology 39 (1978).

When expectations are varied experimentally, the expected value of the background variable-trial judge expectancy correlation is zero; none of the attributes of any of the trial participants should be correlated with the judges' expectancies because subjects are randomly assigned to experimental conditions. Of course, experimentally varied expectations are not ethically possible in the actual courtroom context. *See* note 61 *supra*.

82. *See* T.D. Cook & D.T. Campbell, Quasi Experimentation: Design & Analysis Issues for Field Settings 37–39 (1979); Aronson, Brewer & Carlsmith, *Experimentation in Social Psychology*, in 1 The Handbook of Social Psychology 441 (G. Lindzey & E. Aronson eds. 3d ed. 1985).

83. *See* Blanck & Turner, *supra* note 61 (discussing field-based observational and experimental studies); Rosenthal, *Conducting Judgment Studies*, in Handbook on Methods in Nonverbal Communication Research 287 (K. Scherer & P. Ekman eds. 1982) (discussing studies involving ratings of nonverbal behavior).

84. *See* Ebbesen & Konecni, *On the External Validity of Decision-Making Research*, in Cognitive Processes in Choice and Decision Behavior (T.S. Wallsten ed. 1980); Weiten & Diamond, *A Critical Review of the Jury Simulation Paradigm*, 3 Law & Hum. Behav. 71 (1979); *see also* Experimentation in the Law: Report of the Federal Judicial Center Advisory Committee on Experimentation in the Law (1981); Bray & Kerr, *Methodological Considerations in the*

ternal validity and precision of the ratings of the judges' behavior by (1) collecting questionnaire data from actual trial participants concerning trial processes,[85] (2) videotaping actual trials,[86] and (3) employing independent groups of raters to assess the video- and audiotapes as to their communicative content.

A. *Description of the Trial Participants, Trials, and Ratings of the Judges' Behavior*

1. *Trial participants.*

Trial judges. In the first stage of the studies described in this note, five California Municipal Court judges (three males and two females) were videotaped delivering final jury instructions to jurors in actual criminal jury trials.[87] The judges ranged in age

---

Study of the Psychology of the Courtroom, in THE PSYCHOLOGY OF THE COURTROOM 287 (N. Kerr & R. Bray eds. 1982) (reviewing the methodological considerations in courtroom research).

85. The questionnaires completed by the trial judges, jurors, and lawyers in this study are presented in Appendix B. The directions to the trial participants explained the purpose of the study and the point during the trial at which the questionnaires were to be completed. The five trial judges completed one questionnaire before the verdict was announced in each of seven trials (one judge was videotaped in only six trials), during a short recess after the closing arguments and before delivering the final jury instructions. The judges completed an additional questionnaire after the verdict was announced.

The 61 participating lawyers (prosecution and defense) completed a questionnaire during the jury deliberation, before the verdict. Three hundred thirty-one jurors from the 34 trials completed a questionnaire after the verdict had been announced. All questionnaires took approximately five to ten minutes to complete, all the participants consented to participate in the study of their own volition, and all answers were completely anonymous.

86. Videotaping trials can also offer trial participants increased flexibility in arranging trial proceedings. *See* Barber, *The Problem of Prejudice: A New Approach to Assessing the Impact of Courtroom Cameras,* 66 JUDICATURE 248 (1983) (suggesting that news camera coverage has the potential to make trials more rather than less fair); McCrystal, *The Promise of Prerecorded Videotaped Trials,* 63 A.B.A. J. 977 (1977); McCrystal, *Videotape Trials: Relief for Our Congested Courts,* 49 DEN. L.J. 463 (1973).

Some commentators are concerned that videotaping trials may seriously affect juror or observer perceptions of the trial process. For example, researchers have found that while videotaping trials does not significantly affect perceptions and attitudes toward trial processes in general, black and white versus color videotape, editing techniques, and camera angle can affect viewer perceptions. *See* G. MILLER & N. FONTES, VIDEOTAPE ON TRIAL (1979); Bermant, *Critique—Data in Search of Theory in Search of Policy: Behavioral Response to Videotape in the Courtroom,* 1975 B.Y.U. L. REV. 467; Doret, *Trial By Videotape—Can Justice be Seen to be Done?,* 47 TEMP. L.Q. 228 (1974); Williams, Farmer, Lee, Cundick, Howell & Rooker, *Juror Perceptions of Trial Testimony as a Function of the Method of Presentation: A Comparison of Live, Color Video, Black-and-White Video, Audio, and Transcript Presentations,* 1975 B.Y.U. L. REV. 375.

87. We used color videotape and focused the camera on the trial judge with a straight-on camera shot. The camera was adjacent to the jury box so that the camera angle was almost identical to the jurors' view of the trial judge. The angle allowed a close-up view of the trial judge from the chest to the top of the head. *Cf.* note 86 *supra* (noting the effect of videotaping on juror and viewer perceptions).

from 34 to 51 years, with an average age of 44 years. The amount of time that the judges had been on the bench ranged from two months to five years. All judges but one were videotaped in seven different trials, the one exception was videotaped in six different trials, for a total of 34 trials observed.

Jurors. Three hundred thirty-one jurors, spread over the 34 trials, participated in this study, making 81 percent of all jurors participants in the research. In California, twelve jurors are required to sit for a criminal misdemeanor trial, and guilty and innocent verdicts must be unanimous.[88]

Forty-nine percent of the jurors were male, and 51 percent were female. The jurors had an average age of 42 years, with age ranging from 19 to 81 years. Eighteen percent of the jurors were unemployed, retired, students, or housewives; 26 percent were blue collar workers or service employees; and 56 percent were teachers, managers, or professionals. Two percent of the jurors had received less than a high school education, 26 percent had completed high school, 58 percent had graduated from a two- or a four-year college, and 14 percent had received some form of graduate education. Fifty-one percent of the jurors represented themselves as Democratic Party members, 37 percent as Republicans, and 12 percent as "other-affiliated," with most jurors ranking their political beliefs as moderate.[89] This was the first time that 69 percent of the jurors had served as jurors, 19 percent had served twice, 7 percent three times, and 5 percent four times or more.

Lawyers. Sixty-one attorneys (32 prosecution lawyers and 29 defense lawyers) participated in this study. The average age of counsel was 36 years. There were 39 male and 22 female attorneys. The average number of years of practice among all attorneys was 6 years, with the range of years of practice from 1 to 34 years. Seventy-five percent of all counsel rated themselves as Democrats, 10 percent as Republicans, and 15 percent as unaffili-

88. The California Constitution provides that in "cases of misdemeanor the jury may consist of twelve, or of any number less than twelve upon which the parties may agree [unanimously] in open court." CAL. CONST. art. I, § 16. Both guilty and innocent verdicts must be unanimous. *See* CALIFORNIA CONTINUING EDUCATION OF THE BAR, CALIFORNIA MISDEMEANOR PROCEDURE BENCHBOOK (REVISED) § 10.12, at 165 (K. Werdegar ed. 1975 & supp. Aug. 1984); *see also* note 10 *supra*.

89. Mean rating of juror political beliefs was 5.0, with a rating of 1 = very liberal and a rating of 9 = very conservative. *See* Juror Questionnaire, Appendix B.

ated. Most lawyers had slightly liberal political beliefs.[90]

Defendants. Eighty-two percent of the 34 defendants in these cases were male and 18 percent female.[91] The average age of the defendants was 34 years, with a range in age from 22 to 69 years. Seventy-eight percent of the defendants were white, 11 percent hispanic, and 11 percent of other races. Defendants' socioeconomic backgrounds ranged from 23 percent "low," to 58 percent "middle," to 19 percent "high." Seventeen percent of the defendants had less than a high school education, 25 percent had a high school education, 46 percent had attended either a two- or four-year college, and 12 percent had a graduate degree.

In terms of the background variable of criminal history, 18 percent of the defendants had a previous felony arrest, 9 percent had a previous felony conviction, 59 percent had a previous misdemeanor arrest, and 57 percent had a previous misdemeanor conviction.[92]

Trials. The 34 misdemeanor jury trials were conducted in California Municipal Court. The charges included, among others, vehicular manslaughter, drunk driving, carrying a concealed weapon, assaulting a police officer, child molestation, and prostitution. Each trial took approximately two days to complete, with the videotaping of the final jury charge conducted on the second day. Because the judges in our study regularly rotated assignments, all judges tended to have a mixed array of the charges listed above. The verdicts for this sample of trials were 60 percent guilty, 26 percent not guilty, and 14 percent hung for the first major charge, with 38 percent guilty, 62 percent not guilty, and 0 percent hung for the second major charge.[93]

---

90. Mean rating of lawyer political beliefs (defense and prosecution) was 4.1, with a rating of 1=very liberal and a rating of 9=very conservative. *See* Lawyer Questionnaire, Appendix B.

91. The defense lawyers provided questionnaire data about the background variables of the defendants. *See* Lawyer Questionnaire, Appendix B.

92. The median intercorrelation of the criminal history variables was .49, suggesting a positive predictive relationship between the criminal history variables. The basic intercorrelations among the criminal history variables were .74 for felony arrest and felony conviction, .45 for felony arrest and misdemeanor arrest, .53 for felony arrest and misdemeanor conviction, .39 for felony conviction and misdemeanor conviction, and .97 for misdemeanor arrest and misdemeanor conviction. For a discussion of the meaning of the correlation coefficient, see note 98 *infra*.

93. For a description of the coding of the first two major charges or counts, see note 98 *infra*.

2. *Ratings of the judges' behavior.*

Raters of the videotapes. Eighty individuals were hired to rate the video- and audiotapes on different verbal and nonverbal dimensions.[94] Raters were randomly assigned to rate all of the trials for one judge in one communicative channel. We explained to the raters that they were to assess the verbal and nonverbal behaviors or cues of the trial judge; for example, we explained that "warmth" in the judge's tone of voice would be a rating of the judge's nonverbal audio channel of behavior.[95]

Ratings of the segments of the jury instructions. Ten segments of the California Pattern Criminal Misdemeanor Jury Instructions were analyzed in the present study.[96] These segments were cho-

---

94. Eighty Stanford University undergraduates and law students were paid to rate the trials. Two male and two female raters were randomly assigned to rate all seven trials of one judge in one communicative channel condition (e.g., Judge A in the tone of voice only condition). Therefore, four individuals rated each of the five trial judges for the four channel conditions—two channels with content-present (normal video and audio, and audio only), and two channels with content-absent (visual only, and content-filtered speech only)—for a total of eighty raters. Raters were told that they would hear and/or see judges delivering instructions to juries. All raters rated all segments of the jury instructions on the form presented in Appendix C.

95. The rating variables were selected for several reasons. First, many of these variables have been employed in a variety of studies of verbal and nonverbal communication and interpersonal expectancy effects and are related to the transmission of these effects in laboratory contexts and to clinical processes in the clinician-patient relationship. *See, e.g.*, Blanck, Rosenthal & Vannicelli, *supra* note 79. Second, these variables also tend to describe accurately the emotional dimensions of the communication of affect. *Id.*

The analyses in this study aimed at describing the major communicative dimensions of the trial judge's behavior in delivering instructions to juries in criminal trials. Elsewhere, we have examined the therapist's interpersonal manner in the doctor-patient relationship employing similar variables. *See* Blanck, Rosenthal & Vannicelli, *supra* note 79 (interpersonal manner refers to the manner in which the psychotherapist relates to the patient); Blanck, Rosenthal, Vannicelli & Lee, *supra* note 79; *see also* Orlinsky & Howard, *The Relation of Process to Outcome in Psychotherapy*, in HANDBOOK OF PSYCHOTHERAPY AND BEHAVIOR CHANGE 283 (S. Garfield & A. Bergin eds. 2d. ed. 1978); Schaffer, *Multidimensional Measures of Therapist Behavior as Predictors of Outcome*, 92 PSYCHOLOGICAL BULL. 670 (1982).

Finally, judges, like therapists, communicate a wide range of affect and emotional meaning, and these communications may influence courtroom processes. For descriptions of warmth, empathy, and genuineness by therapists in relating to patients, see Gomes-Schwartz, *Effective Ingredients in Psychotherapy: Prediction of Outcome from Process Variables*, 46 J. CONSULTING & CLINICAL PSYCHOLOGY 1023 (1978); Gomes-Schwartz & Schwartz, *Psychotherapy Process Variables: Distinguishing the "Inherently Helpful" Person from the Professional Psychotherapist*, 46 J. CONSULTING & CLINICAL PSYCHOLOGY 196 (1978); Mintz, Luborsky & Auerbach, *Dimensions of Psychotherapy: A Factor-Analytic Study of Ratings of Psychotherapy Sessions*, 36 J. CONSULTING & CLINICAL PSYCHOLOGY 106 (1971); Rogers, *The Necessary and Sufficient Conditions of Therapeutic Personality Change*, 21 J. CONSULTING PSYCHOLOGY 95 (1957).

96. Sections I, II, III, IV, XII (two parts), XV, XVI, XVII, and XVIII of the California Pattern Criminal Misdemeanor Jury Instructions. *See* Appendix A.

sen to reflect the beginning, middle, and ending portions of the instructions, and all of these segments were rated for all 34 trials.[97] No raters had any difficulty in understanding or performing the task.

---

97. Segments varied in length from 7 seconds to 565 seconds (approximately 9.5 minutes), with an average length of 51 seconds. This research approach compares to the recent trend in the area of psychotherapeutic research to sample approximately one to five minutes of the therapist's speech. *See* R.E. PITTENGER, C.F. HOCKETT & J.J. DANEHY, THE FIRST FIVE MINUTES (1960) (demonstrating the verbal and nonverbal richness of the first five minutes of the therapeutic interview); Bachrach, Curtis, Escoll, Graff, Huxster, Ottenberg & Pulver, *Units of Observation and Perspectives on the Psychoanalytic Process,* 54 BRIT. J. MED. PSYCHOLOGY 25 (1981); Blanck, Rosenthal & Vannicelli, *supra* note 79 (demonstrating that important information could be communicated even in segments lasting only a few seconds).

Future analyses of our data will address the methodological and psychometric factors to be considered in "live" courtroom research. There is a growing concern about the reliability, validity, and consistency of the units or segments of observation of the trial process. One question concerns how much of the trial judge's behavior during the trial process needs to be studied in order to generalize to the trial judge's behavior in the entire trial.

In studying brief segments of judges' behavior and then extrapolating to behavior in entire trials, it may be reasonable for researchers to first study judges' video only cues because visual cues, unlike audio cues, are always available to jurors. *See, e.g.*, Blanck, Rosenthal, Vannicelli & Lee, *supra* note 79 (demonstrating the reliability and validity of ratings of brief nonverbal behaviors); Mintz & Luborsky, *Segments Versus Whole Sessions: Which is the Better Unit for Psychotherapy Process Research?*, 78 J. ABNORMAL PSYCHOLOGY 180 (1971) (suggesting that brief segments—four minutes—of the therapeutic hour can be a useful research unit for many of the communicative variables of psychotherapy).

Future analyses will also assess the consistency of the judge's behavior across the segments of the jury instructions themselves. For an example of such an analysis in the psychotherapeutic context, see Gurman, *Instability of Therapeutic Conditions in Psychotherapy*, 20 J. COUNSELING PSYCHOLOGY 16 (1973) (therapists varied considerably in their level of facilitative therapeutic functioning both across and within sessions with the same patients); *see also* Blanck, Rosenthal & Vannicelli, *supra* note 79 (suggesting that brief segments of therapeutic sessions cannot be substituted naively for entire session assessments but claiming that the stylistic variables associated with therapists' behavior in talking with patients may be estimated reliably from very brief segments of therapeutic sessions).

A final set of analyses will address what parts of the trial process are most likely to convey unintended judicial influence. A related analysis is found in Karl & Ables, *Psychotherapy Process as a Function of the Time Segment Sampled,* 33 J. CONSULTING & CLINICAL PSYCHOLOGY 207 (1969) (demonstrating a marked tendency for certain segment lengths of the therapeutic process to be categorized by some content categories more than others); *see also* Schaffer, *supra* note 95 (suggesting that the length of the segment sample or scoring unit be defined by the type of behavior). Future research should address the critical points in the trial process where judicial influence is most likely to occur and should seek to establish the point when cumulative influence is likely to constitute prejudicial error. This research needs to be conducted before any conclusive statements can be made about the validity and reliability of our "segment analyses."

IV. Testing the Model for the Study of Judicial Influence

A. *The Results*

We have discussed how trial judges may engage in highly effective and influential communication while delivering instructions to juries in criminal trials. We now examine systematically the arrows or relationships of the model for the study of judicial behavior and influence, shown in Figure 1.[98]

A-B. Our first interest was in examining the relationship between the background variables of the trial participants and the

---

98. For "statistical significance testing" the sample size or "*n*" is diminished by 2 (n–2) to obtain the "degrees of freedom" required. In our study, the degrees of freedom are 32 for trials, 32 for defendants, 59 for attorneys (30 for prosecution and 29 for defense), and 329 for jurors. *See* R. Rosenthal & R. Rosnow, Essentials of Behavioral Research 458 (1984) (Table 6 gives significance levels of correlations for different sample sizes).

In the presentation of our results, we have used "*r*," the standard abbreviation for the Pearson product-moment correlation coefficient. A correlation can take on values between –1.00 and +1.00. A value of –1.00 means that there is a perfect negative linear relationship between the two variables (i.e., as one increases linearly the other decreases linearly). A value of +1.00 means that there is a perfect positive linear relationship between two variables (i.e., as one increases linearly the other increases linearly), and a value of .00 means that there is no linear relationship between the two variables. Correlational analyses describe predictive relationships between two variables and do not isolate the "causes" and "effects" of that relationship. *See* Appendix B (listing the raw values and scales assigned to the particular variables used in the correlational analyses).

The abbreviation "*ns*" indicates that the correlation was "not significant" at the $p \leq .10$ level (two-tailed test). A two-tailed test of significance in this context is one in which the null hypothesis is rejected because it is unlikely to be true either because the correlation deviates too far above zero or too far below zero.

Statistical significance can be indexed by a probability value that an observed correlation would have been found if, in the population from which we had sampled, the true correlation were zero. Social scientists generally consider that findings are "significant" if they could have occurred by chance one time in twenty or less, thus having a "*p*-value" of .05 or smaller. We have presented both significant and nonsignificant results for all tests having a *p*-value of .10 or smaller. Social scientists realize that even small correlations can suggest important trends, and almost any level of significance can be achieved arbitrarily simply by increasing sample size, given a true non-zero relationship in the population. *Id.* at 231.

P-values of .10 or smaller have been found useful in assessing the types of variables in the research here. *See* Kerr, *Trial Participants' Behaviors and Jury Verdicts: An Exploratory Field Study*, in The Criminal Justice System: A Social-Psychological Analysis 271 (V.J. Konecni & E.B. Ebbesen eds. 1982) (discussing the use of *p*-values of .10 as a cut-off point in exploratory research on the jury decisionmaking process); *see also* Rosenthal & Gaito, *Further Evidence for the Cliff Effect in the Interpretation of Levels of Significance*, 15 Psychological Rep. 570 (1964) (discussing the use of *p*-values of .10 as a cut off point in social science research); N. Nelson, R. Rosnow & R. Rosenthal, Interpretation of Significance Levels and Effect Sizes by Psychological Researchers (1985) (unpublished manuscript) (also discussing the use of *p*-values of .10 as a cut off point). Finally, the use of *p*-values of .10, or even of .50, has been suggested to meet the Federal Rules of Evidence test that all "evidence having any tendency to make the existence of any fact that is of consequence to the determination of the action more probable or

judge's expectancy variable. This relationship describes how a judge's expectations for trial outcome may be predicted from the background variables of the trial participants.

Judges' expectations for trial outcome tended to be related to defendants' background variables in predictable ways. For example, there was a tendency for judges to expect a guilty verdict when defendants had a more serious criminal history and to expect an innocent verdict when defendants had a relatively less serious criminal history.[99] This was particularly true for defend-

---

less probable than it would be without the evidence." FED. R. EVID. 401; *see* Lempert, *Statistics in the Courtroom: Building on Rubinfeld,* 85 COLUM. L. REV. 1099 (1985).

The *n* (sample size) for count 1 and count 2 differed. Every defendant had at least one charge and one count—"count 1." Fifteen of the 34 defendants had two or more charges or counts—"count 2." (In five of the 34 trials, count 2 refers to the second count of the first charge, and in ten of the 34 trials, count 2 refers to the first count of the second charge.) The degrees of freedom therefore are 32 for count 1 and 13 for count 2. The degrees of freedom for juror responses to variables involving the second count are 137.

Typically, the first charge and the second charge did not differ substantively. In one trial, for example, charge 1 and charge 2 were identical. In another trial, charge 1 was "unlawfully attempting to commit a violent injury on the person of another" and charge 2 was "unlawfully using force and violence on the person of another." In only two trials did the charges seem substantially different. Therefore, we included both charges in our analyses, as the first two charges seemed to capture the most general information about the alleged crimes. For analyses involving judges' expectations (a "B" variable in Figure 1) or trial outcome (a "D" variable), correlations are presented for both charges or counts. For a similar methodology, see Kerr, *Trial Participants' Behaviors and Jury Verdicts: An Exploratory Field Study,* in THE CRIMINAL JUSTICE SYSTEM: A SOCIAL-PSYCHOLOGICAL ANALYSIS 269 (V.J. Konecni & E.B. Ebbesen eds. 1982) (discussing the jury verdict criteria in social science research).

Future analyses of our data will address the extent to which the judge or other trial participants may perceive the subset of defendants who had two or more charges differently than defendants who had just one charge. In the present study, all significance testing on count 2 was based on an *n* of 15.

99. When the judges believed the verdict *should be* guilty, defendants tended to have (1) a previous felony arrest ($r = -.15$, *ns* for count 1; $r = -.34$, *ns* for count 2); (2) a previous felony conviction ($r = -.11$, *ns* for count 1; $r = -.19$, *ns* for count 2); (3) a previous misdemeanor arrest ($r = -.32$, $p = .07$ for count 1; $r = -.39$, *ns* for count 2); or (4) a previous misdemeanor conviction ($r = -.32$, $p = .07$ for count 1, $r = -.41$, *ns* for count 2).

When the judges believed the verdict *would be* guilty, defendants tended to have (1) a previous felony arrest ($r = -.01$, *ns* for count 1; $r = -.12$, *ns* for count 2); (2) a previous felony conviction ($r = -.19$, *ns* for count 1; $r = -.51$, $p = .05$ for count 2); (3) a previous misdemeanor arrest ($r = -.44$, $p < .01$ for count 1; $r = -.48$, $p < .07$ for count 2); or (4) a previous misdemeanor conviction ($r = -.41$, $p < .01$ for count 1; $r = -.18$, *ns* for count 2).

The trend in these results is consistent with (but does not firmly establish) Kalven and Zeisel's findings that the judge is sometimes not able to avoid being influenced by the defendant's criminal history—what we have termed a background variable of the defendant. *See* H. KALVEN & H. ZEISEL, *supra* note 51, at 124. In support of this suggestion, Kalven and Zeisel noted:

> [In addition to the judge's] wide experience with the likelihood that the defendant before him is guilty, the judge is exposed to prejudicial information which the law, in its regard for the right of the defendant, aims to screen out of the evaluation of his

ants with a previous misdemeanor arrest or conviction.[100] Judges also tended to infer guilt when defendants were of a lower socioeconomic status.[101] These results suggest that although the background characteristics of defendants have no legal bearing on guilt or innocence, they do seem to relate to, and perhaps influence, how judges perceive the guilt or innocence of defendants.[102]

Our results also indicated that the background characteristics of jurors relate to, and perhaps influence, judges' expectations for trial outcome. For example, this sample of judges showed a tendency to expect that the verdict *should be* guilty on count 1 in trials with more educated jurors,[103] and a tendency to expect that the verdict *should be* guilty on count 2 with relatively younger jurors.[104]

A-C. We next examined the relationship between trial participants' background variables and judges' verbal and nonverbal behavior. We were particularly interested in the extent to which information about defendants' criminal histories (an "A" variable) could be inferred solely from judges' verbal and nonverbal behavior (a "C" variable). The presence or absence of a previous felony arrest or conviction, or of a previous misdemeanor arrest or conviction, defined a defendant's "composite criminal history."[105] The measure of composite criminal history is a summary statistic computed by incorporating all the information about defendants' previous felony and misdemeanor criminal histories.[106]

---

guilt or innocence. The law's ideal in these situations may be something of a libertarian luxury.

Id. at 127.

100. *See* note 99 *supra.*

101. When judges believed the verdict *should be* guilty, defendants tended to be of a lower socioeconomic background ($r = .28$, *ns* for count 1; $r = .52, p < .05$ for count 2); when the judges believed that the verdict *would be* guilty, defendants did not tend to be of a lower socioeconomic background ($r = -.09$, ns for count 1; $r = -.31$, *ns* for count 2).

102. *See* notes 57–58 *supra* and accompanying text.

103. When judges believed the verdict *should be* guilty, jurors tended to be more educated ($r = -.19, p < .001$ for count 1; $r = -.03$, *ns* for count 2); when the judges believed the verdict *would be* guilty, jurors were not more educated ($r = -.08$, *ns* for count 1; $r = -.05$, *ns* for count 2).

104. When judges believed the verdict *should be* guilty, jurors tended to be younger ($r = .02$, *ns* for count 1; $r = .19, p < .05$ for count 2); when the judges believed the verdict *would be* guilty, the jurors were not younger ($r = .00$, *ns* for count 1; $r = -.02$, *ns* for count 2).

105. *See* Appendix B (Lawyer Questionnaire noting defendant's criminal history).

106. The measure of composite criminal history provides a single estimate of previous criminal history. The composite score is computed by combining the results for previous

Table 1 presents the correlations between the defendants' composite criminal history and ratings of the judges' communicative behavior across the various channels of communication. A positive correlation indicates that the judges were rated higher on the relevant communicative dimension in delivering instructions to juries when the defendant had a more serious composite criminal history. A negative correlation indicates that judges were rated lower on the relevant dimension when the defendant had a more serious composite criminal history.

The pattern of correlations in Table 1 suggests, for this sample of 34 trials, that all judges "appeared" in the normal content-present conditions (i.e., either the normal video and audio, and/or audio only conditions) to be substantially warmer, more open-minded, more dominant, more competent, more dogmatic, wiser, and less hostile in delivering jury instructions for defendants with more serious composite criminal histories. As Table 1 shows, the mean correlation for the content-present condition with composite criminal history was .21. In short, these judges *appeared* to be acting as wise, impartial, and fair arbitrators during the trial process when delivering instructions to juries where the defendants had more serious composite criminal histories.

Quite remarkably, however, judges were actually rated as substantially less professional, less open-minded, less honest, less competent, less dogmatic, less wise, more hostile, and more anxious in either or both of the *purely nonverbal conditions* (content-absent: video only, and content-filtered speech only) in delivering instructions to juries where defendants had more serious composite criminal histories. Table 1 shows that the mean correlation for the content-absent condition with composite criminal history was –.22. In short, ratings of the judges' *purely nonverbal channels* seem to suggest a partial, and perhaps subtly unfair, communicative style when delivering instructions to juries where the defendants had more serious composite criminal histories.

These results are consistent with a series of studies which sug-

felony arrest, felony conviction, misdemeanor arrest, and misdemeanor conviction, while considering the interrelationships between the variables—for example, the median intercorrelation among these variables was .49. *See* note 92 *supra* (noting individual correlations among the criminal history variables). For a complete discussion of the calculation and use of the composite measure, see Rosenthal & Rubin, *Meta-Analytic Procedures for Combining Studies with Multiple Effect Sizes*, — PSYCHOLOGICAL BULL. — (1986) (forthcoming) (the computations associated with equations 1–5 describe how to combine the multiple results of a single study and test the composite measure for significance).

TABLE 1

Correlations Between Defendants' Composite Criminal History and Judge Communicative Behavior in Four Channels of Communication

	CHANNEL			
	CONTENT-PRESENT		CONTENT-ABSENT (NONVERBAL CUES ONLY)	
	Normal Video and Audio	Audio Only	Video Only	Content-Filtered Speech Only
COMMUNICATIVE BEHAVIOR				
Professional	0.07	0.02	−0.52***	−0.22
Warm	0.48***	−0.05	0.29*	0.17
Open-minded	0.28	0.17	−0.38**	−0.18
Honest	0.02	0.22	−0.40**	−0.29*
Dominant	0.37**	0.43***	−0.00	0.30*
Competent	0.41**	0.35**	−0.45***	−0.28
Dogmatic	0.26	0.45***	−0.45***	0.16
Wise	0.46***	0.10	−0.42**	−0.51***
Not Hostile	−0.17	0.33**	−0.15	−0.39**
Not Anxious	−0.01	0.02	−0.20	−0.50***
Mean Correlation	0.22	0.20	−0.27	−0.17
Mean Correlation[a]	0.21		−0.22	
Difference Between Mean Correlations[b]	0.43			

Note: * = $p < .10$; ** = $p < .05$; *** = $p < .01$; **** = $p < .001$.

All tests of significance are two-tailed.

A positive correlation means that when the defendant had a more serious composite criminal history, the judge was rated higher on the relevant dimension.
A negative correlation means that when the defendant had a more serious composite criminal history, the judge was rated lower on the relevant dimension.

[a]Mean correlations for Content-Present and Content-Absent conditions
[b]Difference between mean correlations for Content-Present and Content-Absent conditions

gest that individuals might "leak" or send their true underlying feelings, beliefs, or expectations about other people through nonverbal channels.[107] The findings suggest that the subtle nonverbal cues of the judge might "leak" the judge's expectations for trial outcome, expectations perhaps (but not necessarily) formed from the judge's knowledge of the defendant's criminal history. As Table 1 shows, these findings are particularly dramatic when considering the difference between the mean correlation for the content-present condition and the mean correlation for the content-absent condition (difference = .43). Taken together, the findings support our suggestion that judges may convey subtly their expectations for trial outcome to jurors through nonverbal cues, and as our questionnaire data revealed, jurors may *not* always be aware of these subtle influences.[108]

Other background variables were related to judges' verbal and nonverbal behavior. For example, these five judges' verbal and nonverbal behavior was related to judges' age and sex, defendants' socioeconomic status, and jurors' age and level of education.[109] Table 2 shows that for this sample of 34 trials and for this sample of five judges, older as compared to younger judges tended to be rated in the normal condition as relatively warmer, more open-minded, more dominant, more dogmatic, and wiser, but less honest, more hostile, and more anxious in delivering the jury instructions.[110]

Interestingly, although raters tended to perceive older judges as warmer, more open-minded, more dominant, more competent, more dogmatic, and wiser than younger judges in the content-present conditions (e.g., mean correlation in Table 2 for the normal video and audio condition, and the audio only condition was .22), older judges were rated as substantially less profes-

107. *See* Blanck & Rosenthal, *Developing Strategies for Decoding "Leaky" Messages: On Learning How and When to Decode Discrepant and Consistent Social Communications*, in DEVELOPMENT OF NONVERBAL BEHAVIOR IN CHILDREN (R. Feldman ed. 1982); Ekman & Friesen, *supra* note 79, at 88.

108. *Cf.* notes 122–123 *infra*.

109. For this set of analyses, the correlations involving judge age and sex must be viewed with caution as the results are based only on a sample of five judges in seven trials each. Although we can probably generalize from these results to how these judges would behave in other trials, we cannot generalize with confidence to how other judges (older and younger, male and female) would behave in other trials. For a discussion of issues of generalizability, see notes 139–140 *infra* and accompanying text.

110. *See* notes 141–158 *infra* and accompanying text (discussing the climate factor in the transmission of judicial influence).

TABLE 2

Correlations Between Judge Age and Judge Communicative Behavior in Four Channels of Communication

	CHANNEL			
	CONTENT-PRESENT		CONTENT-ABSENT (NONVERBAL CUES ONLY)	
COMMUNICATIVE BEHAVIOR	Normal Video and Audio	Audio Only	Video Only	Content-Filtered Speech Only
Professional	−0.27	−0.24	−0.94****	−0.25
Warm	0.74****	0.09	0.35**	0.44***
Open-minded	0.34**	0.06	−0.83****	0.06
Honest	−0.33**	0.13	−0.86****	0.14
Dominant	0.72****	0.83****	0.21	0.42**
Competent	0.12	0.51***	−0.95****	0.07
Dogmatic	0.72****	0.88****	−0.60****	0.28
Wise	0.72****	0.09	−0.95****	−0.46***
Not Hostile	−0.64****	0.47***	−0.85****	−0.46***
Not Anxious	−0.39**	−0.08	−0.87****	−0.71****
Mean Correlation	0.17	0.27	−0.63	−0.05
Mean Correlation[a]	0.22		−0.34	
Difference Between Mean Correlations[b]	0.56			

Note: * = $p < .10$; ** = $p < .05$; *** = $p < .01$; **** = $p < .001$.

All tests of significance are two-tailed.

A positive correlation means that when the judge was older, the judge was rated higher on the relevant dimension.
A negative correlation means that when the judge was older, the judge was rated lower on the relevant dimension.

[a]Mean correlations for Content-Present and Content-Absent conditions
[b]Difference between mean correlations for Content-Present and Content-Absent conditions

sional, less open-minded, less competent, less dogmatic, less wise, more hostile, and more anxious than younger judges in the purely nonverbal (content-absent) conditions, especially in the video only condition (e.g., mean correlation in Table 2 for the video only condition, and the content-filtered speech only condition was –.34).

This pattern of results suggests that while older judges may appear to jurors as "judicially competent," they may be perceived as substantially less judicially competent, compared to younger judges, in the purely nonverbal channels. This pattern is further demonstrated by the difference between the mean correlation of the content-present condition and the mean correlation of the content-absent condition displayed in Table 2 (difference = .56).

We next were interested in predicting information about judge behavior from judge sex. Table 3 shows that raters generally perceived (across all four channels) our male judges to be relatively more professional, while perceiving our female judges to be more hostile and more anxious (what our raters typically described as "nervous") in delivering instructions. It is interesting to note that although female judges tended to be rated as more open-minded and warm than males in the normal content-present conditions, they were rated as substantially less open-minded and warm than males in the purely nonverbal conditions.

The pattern of correlations between our judges' communicative behaviors and judge sex replicates the results of earlier research on the relationship between the psychotherapists' sex and transmission of nonverbal behavior, and is consistent with a socialization hypothesis of the development of sex differences in nonverbal communication skills and styles.[111] Despite the consis-

111. Various explanations for these sex differences in verbal and nonverbal skills have been set forth and have ranged from socioemotional hypotheses (e.g., varying levels of empathy in males and females) to biological hypotheses (e.g., brain functioning differences between males and females). *See* J.A. HALL, NONVERBAL SEX DIFFERENCES (1984); Blanck & Rosenthal, *supra* note 107, at 203 (showing that women, as compared to men, tend to grow more polite or "accommodating" in their decoding of both verbal and nonverbal messages); Blanck, Rosenthal, Snodgrass, DePaulo & Zuckerman, *Longitudinal and Cross-sectional Age Effects in Nonverbal Decoding Skill and Style*, 18 DEVELOPMENTAL PSYCHOLOGY 491 (1982) ("although older children performed better than younger children at most nonverbal decoding tasks, the advantages of age were especially great for the decoding of the more discrepant or leakier channels"); Blanck, Rosenthal, Snodgrass, DePaulo & Zuckerman, *Sex Differences in Eavesdropping on Nonverbal Cues: Developmental Changes*, 41 J. PERSONALITY & SOC. PSYCHOLOGY 391 (1981) ("[R]esults [were] consistent with a socialization interpretation that as females grow older,

TABLE 3

Correlations Between Judge Sex and Judge Communicative Behavior in Four Channels of Communication

	CHANNEL			
	CONTENT-PRESENT		CONTENT-ABSENT (NONVERBAL CUES ONLY)	
COMMUNICATIVE BEHAVIOR	Normal Video and Audio	Audio Only	Video Only	Content-Filtered Speech Only
Professional	−0.52***	−0.08	−0.68****	−0.38**
Warm	0.57***	0.36**	−0.17	−0.12
Open-minded	0.28	0.32*	−0.60****	−0.32*
Honest	−0.49***	0.28	−0.45***	0.17
Dominant	−0.17	0.46***	−0.37**	0.53***
Competent	−0.25	0.08	−0.58****	0.14
Dogmatic	−0.12	0.10	0.12	0.43***
Wise	−0.09	−0.14	−0.58****	−0.56****
Not Hostile	−0.51***	−0.05	−0.85****	−0.04
Not Anxious	−0.26	−0.61****	−0.68****	−0.32*
Mean Correlation	−0.16	0.07	−0.48	−0.05
Mean Correlation[a]	−0.04		−0.26	
Difference Between Mean Correlations[b]	0.22			

Note: * = $p < .10$; ** = $p < .05$; *** = $p < .01$; **** = $p < .001$.

All tests of significance are two-tailed.

A positive correlation means that when the judge was female, the judge was rated higher on the relevant dimension.
A negative correlation means that when the judge was female, the judge was rated lower on the relevant dimension.

[a]Mean correlations for Content-Present and Content-Absent conditions
[b]Difference between mean correlations for Content-Present and Content-Absent conditions

tency of our findings with previous work, it is important to point out that our results could reflect the sex role socialization of our raters (that is, when a female judge was rated, certain "feminine" qualities were ascribed, and the reverse was true for males) or perhaps the fundamental differences in the communicative behaviors of males and females.

As described above, Table 3 also shows that the raters perceived our female judges as relatively more open-minded and warm in the content-present conditions, but as relatively less open-minded and warm in purely nonverbal (content-absent) conditions. This result is consistent with the general tendency for the female judges in our sample to be rated as more "nervous" (hostile and anxious) than males in delivering jury instructions. The findings also may support our earlier suggestion that females, as compared to males, better "mask" their overt feelings in socially uncomfortable situations; for example, while all judges believed that the majority of verdicts in these trials *should be* guilty,[112] females as compared to males, tended to *appear* open-minded but "leaked" their true feelings through the purely nonverbal channels.[113] The difference between the mean correlation for the content-present condition and the mean correlation for the content-absent condition tends to support this suggestion (displayed in Table 3, this difference = .22).

Finally, there was a tendency for our raters to perceive judges' *purely nonverbal behavior* to be more professional and more competent in delivering jury instructions when defendants were of a higher socioeconomic status.[114] These findings are consistent with our suggestions that judges may "leak" their beliefs about defendants, beliefs perhaps related to perceptions of defendants'

they may learn to be more nonverbally accommodating."); Blanck, Rosenthal & Vannicelli, *supra* note 79; Blanck, Rosenthal, Vannicelli & Lee, *supra* note 79; Steckler & Rosenthal, *Sex Differences in Nonverbal and Verbal Communication with Bosses, Peers, and Subordinates,* 70(1) J. Applied Psychology 157 (1985); S. Snodgrass, S. Krasner & R. Rosenthal, Is the Executive Woman an Oxymoron?: Tone of Voice and the Evaluation of Executive Competence (Sept. 1985) (unpublished manuscript on file with the *Stanford Law Review*) (showing that male voices were rated as more professionally competent than female voices).

112. *See* note 130 *infra* (judges reported that in 89% of the trials defendant *should be* guilty on count 1, and in 75% of the trials defendant *should be* guilty on count 2).

113. *See* note 111 *supra.*

114. The correlations between defendants' socioeconomic status and judges' communicative behavior were (1) for the professional dimension: $r = .39$, $p < .05$ for the video only condition; $r = .40$, $p < .05$ for the content-filtered speech condition; and (2) for the competent dimension: $r = .42$, $p < .05$ for the video only condition.

background characteristics. Across all conditions, raters also tended to perceive judges in this study as warmer, more professional, more open-minded, and less dominant in the presence of older, and more educated jurors.[115] These results suggest that judges may be subtly respectful of defendants and jurors they perceive to be of higher social status or intelligence. Whether this difference in behavior indicates an intentional or unintentional attempt to influence jurors, or simply reflects general social beliefs, is difficult to evaluate on the basis of our results.

Our results thus suggest that certain background variables of trial participants, and in particular of defendants, may be related to, and perhaps influence, the communicative behaviors of trial judges. These variables may provide a valuable additional avenue to the study of courtroom processes that can help address the logistical and ethical problems sometimes encountered in the study of interactions between judges and trial participants. Careful analysis of even brief segments of judges' verbal and nonverbal behavior, in this case the final jury instructions from a two-day trial, increases substantially the ability to predict the type of person (for example, a defendant with a criminal history) about whom the judge is speaking. Future analysis must address the extent to which these behaviors actually affect the due process rights of defendants.

A-D. Background variables were also found to be related to trial outcome. Our results showed some relationship between juries' verdicts and the background characteristics of the defendants. For example, defendants who had a previous felony arrest were more likely to be found guilty, while those who had no previous felony arrest were more likely to be acquitted.[116] Granted,

---

115. The correlations between juror age and judges' communicative behavior were $r = .18$, $p < .001$ for the warm dimension in the normal condition; $r = .11$, $p < .01$ for the professional dimension in the content-filtered condition; and $r = .17$, $p < .01$ for the open-minded dimension in the normal condition.

The correlations between juror level of education and judges' communicative behavior were $r = .13$, $p < .05$ for the warm dimension in the normal condition; $r = .17$, $p < .01$ for the professional dimension in the normal condition and $r = .19$, $p < .001$ in the audio only condition; $r = .21$, $p < .001$ for the open-minded dimension in the normal condition; and $r = -.14$, $p < .01$ for the dominant dimension in the audio only condition and $r = -.14$, $p < .01$ in the content-filtered condition.

116. The correlations between guilty verdict and (a) previous felony arrest ($r = .30$, $p < .10$ for count 1; $r = .45$, $p < .10$ for count 2); (b) previous felony conviction ($r = .05$, *ns* for count 1; $r = .25$, *ns* for count 2); (c) previous misdemeanor arrest ($r = -.20$, *ns* for count 1; $r = -.21$, *ns* for count 2); and (d) previous misdemeanor conviction ($r = -.08$, *ns* for count 1; $r = -.07$, *ns* for count 2). These results must be interpreted with caution as the relationship of

defendants with a criminal history may be more likely to be guilty. Nonetheless, viewed in combination with our results on judge "leakage" of criminal history (i.e., the A-C results), this finding indicates that the criminal history of the defendant, a legally irrelevant factor, might influence juries more than heretofore assumed.[117]

B-C. This aspect of the model describes how judges' expectations for trial outcome relate to judges' verbal and nonverbal behavior. When judges expected the verdict *would be* guilty, raters in the normal condition perceived the judges to be somewhat warmer and substantially more open-minded in delivering the jury instructions.[118] In the *purely nonverbal channels*, however, raters tended to perceive judges who expected a guilty verdict to be less warm, less competent, less wise, and more anxious in delivering instructions.[119] These findings again tend to support our hypothesis that judges may "leak" their true underlying beliefs or expectations about defendants' guilt or innocence through subtle nonverbal cues. Intentional or unintentional, leakage may influence trial outcome, although the judge may "appear" to the jurors to be impartial.

We finally sought to explore how judges' expectations for trial outcome (a "B" variable) predict, and perhaps may influence, jurors' and lawyers' perceptions of the judges' behavior (a

---

guilty verdict to previous criminal history varies with type of criminal history (e.g., felony or misdemeanor history).

117. We also found that defendants of higher socioeconomic status received relatively more guilty verdicts than defendants of lower socioeconomic status, especially for the first count. The correlations between guilty verdict and defendant socioeconomic status were $r = -.34$, $p < .05$ for count 1; $r = -.33$, *ns* for count 2. Future analyses must address the extent to which the type of charge (e.g., drunk driving) influences whether defendants of a higher or lower socioeconomic background are likely to receive certain verdicts in certain courts (e.g., municipal court). *See* notes 52, 55 *supra* (examples of studies on the background variables of defendants).

118. The correlations between judges' behavior in the normal condition and judges' belief that the verdict *would be* guilty were (1) $r = -.21$, *ns* for count 1; $r = -.43$, *ns* for count 2 for the warm dimension; and (2) $r = -.20$, *ns* for count 1; $r = -.49$, $p < .10$ for count 2 for the open-minded dimension.

119. The correlations between judges' behavior in the content-filtered speech only condition and judges' belief that the verdict *should be* guilty were $r = .24$, *ns* for count 1; $r = .53$, $p < .05$ for count 2 for the warm dimension.

The correlations between judges' behavior in the video only condition and judges' belief that the verdict *would be* guilty were (1) $r = .35$, $p < .05$ for count 1; $r = .39$, *ns* for count 2 for the competent dimension; (2) $r = .33$, $p < .05$ for count 1; $r = .44$, *ns* for count 2 for the wise dimension; and (3) $r = -.33$, $p < .05$ for count 1; $r = -.50$, $p < .07$ for count 2 for the anxious dimension.

"C" variable).[120] For example, especially for the first count, when judges expected the defendant to be guilty, jurors tended to perceive the judge as speaking *less* clearly during the trial and during the jury instructions.[121] However, across both counts, the jurors did not generally report on the questionnaires that the judges' nonverbal behaviors, facial expressions, and gestures revealed what the judge thought the verdict *should be*,[122] nor did they accurately report the judges' expectations for what trial outcome *should be*.[123]

Finally, judges' expectations for trial outcome tended to relate to prosecution and defense lawyers' perceptions of the trial process. The relationship between judges' expectations for trial outcome and lawyers' perceptions of the trial process varied for prosecution and defense lawyers. When the judge expected a guilty verdict, the prosecution tended to perceive the judge as holding more order during the trial,[124] as being more interested

---

120. Jurors' and lawyers' perceptions of trial processes provide an additional view of the transmitting behaviors of judges (a "C" variable), a view complemented by our independent raters' perceptions of the judges' behavior in the four channels of communication.

121. When judges believed the verdict *should be* guilty, jurors tended to perceive judges as speaking less clearly during (a) the entire trial ($r = .15, p < .01$ for count 1; $r = .07$, *ns* for count 2), and (b) the jury instructions ($r = .10, p < .10$ for count 1; $r = .04$, *ns* for count 2); when judges believed the verdict *would be* guilty, jurors tended to perceive the judge as speaking less clearly during (a) the entire trial ($r = .11, p < .05$ for count 1; $r = -.01$, *ns* for count 2), but not in (b) the jury instructions ($r = .08$, *ns* for count 1; $r = -.06$, *ns* for count 2).

122. When judges believed the verdict *should be* guilty, jurors did not perceive that judges' nonverbal behavior during the entire trial gave them clues as to what the judges thought the verdict should be ($r = -.03$, *ns* for count 1; $r = .03$, *ns* for count 2); when judges believed that the verdict *would be* guilty, jurors tended to perceive that judges' nonverbal behavior during the entire trial gave them clues as to what the judges thought the verdict should be ($r = -.02$, *ns* for count 1; $r = .16, p < .05$ for count 2).

123. When judges believed the verdict *should be* guilty, jurors did not perceive that judges thought the prosecution should win ($r = .01$, *ns* for count 1; $r = -.02$, *ns* for count 2); when judges believed that the verdict *would be* guilty, jurors tended to perceive that judges thought the prosecution should win ($r = -.15, p < .01$ for count 1; $r = -.08$, *ns* for count 2).

These results must be interpreted with caution as the jurors completed their questionnaires *after* the verdict was given. The jurors' generally inaccurate reporting of judges' expectancies for trial outcome might reflect jurors' beliefs that they acted in accordance with the law and that they were not influenced in their decisionmaking process. But as the above results show, when judges believed the verdict *would be* guilty, jurors reported accurately that the judges thought the prosecution should win the case. For a related discussion that might help to explain these findings, see Vinson, *supra* note 58, at 58 ("The basic dynamic of jury deliberation is the resolution of cognitive dissonance.").

124. When judges believed the verdict *should be* guilty, the prosecution tended to perceive that judges kept more order ($r = -.31, p < .07$ for count 1; $r = -.51, p < .05$ for count 2); when judges believed the verdict *would be* guilty, the prosecution did not perceive that judges kept more order ($r = -.12$, *ns* for count 1; $r = -.13$, *ns* for count 2).

in the case,[125] and as believing that the prosecution should win the case.[126] When the judge believed the verdict *would be* guilty, defense counsel tended to perceive the judge to have relatively less respect for all the trial participants, especially for the second count.[127] Defense counsel also tended to perceive the judge to speak less clearly throughout the trial, and less clearly in his or her delivery of the final jury instructions in particular, when the judge believed the verdict *should be* guilty.[128] Finally, when the judge believed the verdict *would be* guilty, defense counsel tended to perceive that the judge thought the prosecution should prevail, especially for the first count.[129] Overall, the prosecution and defense lawyers' opinions of judges seem to relate in predictable ways to their perceptions of judges' expectations for trial outcome.

B-D. This relationship describes how judges' expectations for trial outcome are related to the verdicts returned by juries. Importantly, our results showed that judges' expectations for trial outcome tended to be negatively related, or not related at all, to actual trial outcome.[130] The "pencil and paper" response format

125. When judges believed the verdict *should be* guilty, the prosecution tended to perceive judges as more interested in the trial ($r = -.38$, $p < .05$ for count 1; $r = -.42$, *ns* for count 2); when judges believed the verdict *would be* guilty, the prosecution tended to perceive judges as more interested in the trial ($r = -.30$, $p < .10$ for count 1; $r = -.46$, $p < .10$ for count 2).

126. When judges believed the verdict *should be* guilty, the prosecution tended to perceive that judges thought the prosecution should win the case ($r = -.34$, $p < .05$ for count 1; $r = -.39$, *ns* for count 2); when judges believed that the verdict *would be* guilty, the prosecution tended to perceive that judges thought the prosecution should win the case ($r = -.30$, $p < .10$ for count 1; $r = -.57$, $p < .05$ for count 2).

127. When judges believed the verdict *should be* guilty, defense counsel did not perceive judges as having less respect for trial participants ($r = .15$, *ns* for count 1; $r = .05$, *ns* for count 2); when judges believed that the verdict *would be* guilty, defense counsel tended to perceive judges as having less respect for trial participants ($r = .28$, *ns* for count 1; $r = .51$, $p = .05$ for count 2).

128. When judges believed the verdict *should be* guilty, defense counsel tended to perceive judges as (a) less clear during the trial ($r = .29$, $p < .10$ for count 1; $r = .36$, *ns* for count 2), and (b) less clear in the instructions to the jury ($r = .30$, $p < .10$ for count 1; $r = .35$, *ns* for count 2); when judges believed that the verdict *would be* guilty, defense counsel did not perceive judges as (a) less clear during the trial ($r = .17$, *ns* for count 1; $r = -.00$, *ns* for count 2), or (b) less clear in the instructions to the jury ($r = .12$, *ns* for count 1; $r = .04$, *ns* for count 2).

129. When judges believed the verdict *should be* guilty, defense counsel did not perceive that judges thought the prosecution should win ($r = -.27$, *ns* for count 1; $r = .24$, *ns* for count 2); when judges believed the verdict *would be* guilty, defense counsel tended to perceive that judges thought the prosecution should win ($r = -.54$, $p < .001$ for count 1; $r = -.40$, *ns* for count 2).

130. The correlations between judges' beliefs that the verdict *should be* guilty and actual trial outcome were $r = -.29$, $p < .10$ for count 1; $r = -.22$, *ns* for count 2); the correlations

used by the judges in our study was a poor predictor of jury verdicts. These findings are consistent with the judges' own reports that they often disagreed with trial outcome.[131] The tendency for judges' expectations for trial outcome *not* to be related to actual trial outcome runs counter to our basic hypothesis that jurors' decisionmaking processes may be importantly influenced by, and consistent with, judges' expectations for trial outcome.

As Kalven and Zeisel argue in *The American Jury*, however, the judge and the jury might not be "deciding the same case."[132] Exclusionary rules of evidence keep some information about the case from the jury which is only available to the judge.[133] This is why the "appearance of justice" may not always equal actual justice: Our results suggested that judges tend to "leak" through subtle nonverbal channels their beliefs or expectations regarding information not available to the jury. In particular, our results seem to support Kalven and Zeisel's suggestion that the extra information most frequently available to the judge, and perhaps most often "leaked" by the judge to the jury, is the defendant's criminal history.[134] Our present analyses do not address the extent to which jurors' perceptions of judges' leaky cues influence the jury decisionmaking process. A complete analysis of the A-B-C-D chain of Figure 1 is required to address this question.

C-D. This relationship describes how judges' unintended verbal and nonverbal behaviors alone may predict the verdicts returned by juries.[135] Table 4 shows that when the verdict was

---

between judges' beliefs that the verdict *would be* guilty and actual trial outcome were $r = .06$, *ns* for count 1; $r = .17$, *ns* for count 2.

As the B-D correlations show, the judges' expectation of what the verdict *would be* was a somewhat better predictor of actual trial outcome than the judges' expectation of what the verdict *should be*. The response rates for this sample of judges were (a) for verdict *should be* on count 1: 89% guilty and 11% not guilty; for verdict *should be* on count 2: 75% guilty and 25% not guilty; (b) for verdict *would be* on count 1: 43% guilty, 23% not guilty, and 34% hung; for verdict *would be* on count 2: 38% guilty, 31% not guilty, and 31% hung. For the rates of the actual verdicts for this sample of trials, see text accompanying note 92 *supra*. Note that we did not include the "hung" response opportunity for the judges' question "what do you think the verdict should be?" because this question aimed at assessing the judges' own expectations for trial outcome, not what they believed the jury "would" do.

131. In fact, our judges *disagreed* significantly with their juries' verdicts (correlation of judges' agreement with verdict and actual verdict: $r = -.66, p < .001$ for count 1; $r = -.75, p < .01$ for count 2).

132. H. KALVEN & H. ZEISEL, *supra* note 51, at 121.

133. *Id.*

134. *Id.* at 127, 147. *See* results described in Table 1 *supra* and accompanying text.

135. Several analogous studies have examined the relationship between therapist behavior and therapeutic outcome (i.e., the C-D relationship of Figure 1). *See, e.g.*, Parloff, Waskow

TABLE 4

Correlations Between Verdict and Judge Communicative Behavior in Four Channels of Communication

	CHANNEL							
	CONTENT-PRESENT				CONTENT-ABSENT (Nonverbal Cues Only)			
	Normal Video and Audio		Audio Only		Video Only		Content-Filtered Speech Only	
COMMUNICATIVE BEHAVIOR	Count 1	Count 2	Count 1	Count 2	Count 1	Count 2	Count 1	Count 2
Professional	0.24	0.58**	0.15	0.04	0.00	0.00	−0.08	−0.09
Warm	−0.18	−0.05	−0.01	−0.02	−0.04	0.32	−0.10	0.11
Open-minded	−0.18	0.02	0.05	−0.03	0.00	0.17	−0.17	−0.10
Honest	0.12	0.31	0.10	0.03	−0.02	0.04	−0.44***	−0.57**
Dominant	0.21	0.46*	−0.05	−0.04	0.34***	0.42	−0.03	−0.19
Competent	0.19	0.61**	0.16	0.18	−0.03	−0.06	−0.24	−0.34
Dogmatic	0.28	0.54**	0.04	0.14	−0.07	−0.29	0.03	−0.06
Wise	0.08	0.45*	0.23	0.19	0.02	0.03	−0.16	−0.22
Not Hostile	0.09	0.15	0.13	0.24	0.16	0.38	−0.23	−0.19
Not Anxious	0.08	0.06	0.22	0.41	0.15	0.31	−0.18	−0.05
Mean Correlation	0.09	0.31	0.10	0.11	0.05	0.13	−0.16	−0.17
Mean Correlation[a]	0.15				−0.04			
Difference Between Mean Correlations[b]	0.19							

Note: * = $p < .10$; ** = $p < .05$; *** = $p < .01$; **** = $p < .001$.

All tests of significance are two-tailed.

A positive correlation means that when the verdict was guilty, the judge was rated lower on the relevant dimension.
A negative correlation means that when the verdict was guilty, the judge was rated higher on the relevant dimension.

[a]Mean correlations for Content-Present and Content-Absent conditions
[b]Difference between mean correlations for Content-Present and Content-Absent conditions

guilty, raters perceived judges' verbal and nonverbal behavior in the normal condition to be less professional, less dominant, less competent, less dogmatic, and less wise, particularly when the verdict was guilty on the second count.

There is also a trend in Table 4 suggesting that when the verdict was guilty, the *purely nonverbal channels* were perceived as less dominant (in the video only condition), but *more* honest (in the content-filtered speech only condition). These perceptions of judges' "leaky honesty" and their relationship to actual trial outcome are consistent with our findings demonstrating that in fact these judges believed most verdicts *should be* guilty[136] and our suggestions that these beliefs are likely to be conveyed by nonverbal messages.[137]

Taken together, these results suggest that certain dimensions of judges' verbal and nonverbal behaviors better predict juries' verdicts.[138] But this "C-D" relationship was not consistent across the various channels of the judges' behavior or across count 1 and count 2. For example, when a guilty verdict was later reached, judges tended to be rated as particularly honest in the purely nonverbal channel content-filtered speech, but not in the more overt content-present channels. The findings may suggest that while the communicative behavior of the judge in talking to juries may predict trial outcome, this result may vary with the type and "leakiness" of the communicative channel researchers are studying.

The results, however, are particularly encouraging given that our raters were completely blind to trial outcome and to all trial processes. Perhaps the most compelling conclusions to be drawn from these findings are that judges' behavior alone can predict

& Wolfe, *Research on Therapist Variables in Relationship to Process and Outcome,* in HANDBOOK OF PSYCHOTHERAPY AND BEHAVIOR CHANGE: AN EMPIRICAL ANALYSIS 233 (S. Garfield & A. Bergin eds. 2d ed. 1978); Pope, *Research on Therapeutic Style,* in EFFECTIVE PSYCHOTHERAPY: A HANDBOOK OF RESEARCH 356 (A. Gurman & A. Razin eds. 1978) (research review); Schaffer, *supra* note 95 (research review).

136. *See* note 130 *supra* (judges reported that in 89% of the trials verdict *should be* guilty for count 1, and in 75% of the trials verdict *should be* guilty for count 2).

137. *See* notes 37–49 *supra* and accompanying text.

138. Subsequent juror perceptions of trial processes were found to be related to actual trial outcome as well (e.g., a "C-D" relationship). *See* note 120 *supra.* For example, when the actual verdict was guilty, jurors tended to report *subsequently* that judges thought the prosecution should win the case, and when the verdict was innocent that judges thought the defense should prevail ($r = -.15, p < .01$ for count 1; $r = -.12$, *ns* for count 2). These post-verdict perceptions may simply reflect jurors' rationalization, justification, or "cognitive dissonance" processes for verdict choice. *See* Vinson, *supra* note 58.

the verdicts returned by juries, and perhaps juries' decisionmaking processes. Future researchers will need systematically to assess more detailed samples of judges' communicative behavior during trials in different channels of communication.

B. *Issues for Future Consideration*

1. *Research on cumulative effects in the model.*

The present study was designed to aid in understanding how judicial behavior may predict, and perhaps influence, jury verdicts and trial processes. For this set of trials it was possible to predict aspects of the trial process and outcome from the judges' unintended verbal and nonverbal behavior alone.

Future research will need to focus on the more complex *cumulative effects* in the model of judicial influence. The model presented here may enable researchers to analyze chains of variables that together may better predict juries' verdicts and jurors' decisionmaking processes. One example of such a chain might include the background variable of the trial judge's susceptibility to biasing information (an "A" variable), perhaps as indicated by other presiding judges' ratings of a particular trial judge's open-mindedness. The trial judge's expectations for trial outcome could be assessed (a "B" variable), and the verbal and nonverbal transmissions of these expectations measured (a "C" variable). Finally, jury verdict would be included as the outcome variable (a "D" variable).

For this chain (A-B-C-D), we might hypothesize that more biased and less open-minded trial judges would be more prone to expectancy effects, perhaps treating defendants of perceived guilt more negatively and defendants of perceived innocence more positively. "Unbiased" trial judges, on the other hand, might treat defendants of perceived high and low expectancy more equally. This pattern of behavior might influence trial outcome in measurable ways.

2. *Issues of generalizability.*

As described earlier, external validity refers to the extent to which a particular result or relationship can be generalized to other real world settings.[139] Our goal was to maximize the external validity of our research by studying judges' behavior in actual

139. *See* notes 82–84 *supra* and accompanying text.

trials. Even when studying a sample of actual trials, however, questions concerning the generalizability of any given set of results obtained from any particular study must be raised.

The first issue regarding the generalizability of our results relates to the extent to which our results would hold true *across the population of trial judges*. It was not logistically or economically possible to randomly select a large sample of trial judges from the population. Although there is no reason to believe that the judges in our study were not representative of the population of trial judges, generalizations to other judges and to populations of judges in other settings or with other court procedures must remain cautious.

A second issue of generalizability relates to the extent to which our results would hold true *within this sample of judges, but over many trials*. We observed only seven jury trials for each judge, and therefore must be alert to the possibility that our sampling of trials for each judge might not be representative of the judge's behavior in other trials. In fact, a sample of trials for these judges as large or even larger than the sample of trials we employed, would be necessary to generalize with confidence to the larger population of judges and trials.[140] However, for all the judges in our study, the trials sampled did seem to be representative of the types of trials that these judges would see over longer periods of time (e.g., types of charges and defendants).

Questions about the generalizability of our results do not deny the fact that for this sample of trials conducted by these judges a predictive relationship was hypothesized and documented between the judges' behavior and other aspects of the trial process. Our results provide only a first attempt at examining these relationships. Future researchers will need to replicate and isolate many of our preliminary findings and hopefully employ them as a foundation for the analysis of the more complex interactions that are part of the trial process.

V. Implications

Our research has explored the longstanding observation that subtle, and perhaps unintentional, judicial behavior might predict trial processes. By implication, our results suggest that ex-

140. *See* R. Rosenthal & R. Rosnow, *supra* note 98, at 308 (discussing generalizations in terms of "fixed" and "random" models of statistical analysis).

tremely prejudicial judicial behavior might act to deny defendants their constitutionally protected right to a fair and impartial trial. In this closing section, we discuss a framework that may be helpful in summarizing the transmission of judicial influence. The documentation of judges' nonverbal behavior in ways that assist appellate courts in more effectively reviewing judges' verbal and nonverbal behavior is also examined. Finally, the implications of our findings for extra-legal concerns such as the study of judges and jurors are discussed.

A. *The Transmission of Judicial Influence*

Many studies demonstrate that subtle verbal and nonverbal cues can transmit expectancy effects even in nonlaboratory settings.[141] In an early study testing expectancy effects in the classroom, Rosenthal and Jacobson demonstrated that when school teachers were led to expect better performance from their pupils, they were significantly more likely to receive such improved performance.[142] The teacher-student relationship Rosenthal and Jacobson studied is analogous to our study of the judge-jury relationship.[143] Unlike the results with teachers, we found that trial judges' beliefs, as measured by our questionnaire, did not predict accurately the verdicts returned by juries. The judges' beliefs or expectations for trial outcome, however, seemed to be conveyed more subtly—"leaked" to jurors by the judges' verbal and nonverbal behaviors.[144] For example, our results suggest that the ex-

141. *See generally* R. ROSENTHAL, ON THE SOCIAL PSYCHOLOGY OF THE SELF-FULFILLING PROPHECY: FURTHER EVIDENCE FOR PYGMALION EFFECTS AND THEIR MEDIATING MECHANISMS (1974) (Module 53, MSS Modular Publications) (discussing mediating or transmitting mechanisms of interpersonal expectancy effects).

142. R. ROSENTHAL & L. JACOBSON, PYGMALION IN THE CLASSROOM (1968).

143. *Cf.* Note, *supra* note 32, at 1275–78 (discussing the analogy between the trial judge-jury relationship and the experimenter-subject relationship). One problem with the analogy of judges to teachers is that, unlike judges, teachers' expectations seem to relate to a specific performance outcome for a student (for example, a high expectancy student would be expected to "perform better" on a test). Judges' expectations for trial outcome may not be related to a specific performance outcome (for example, expectations of innocence may not reflect a judge's belief that the defendant should or will perform better during the trial process).

144. Our results suggest that trial judges' expectations might "directly" or "indirectly" influence jurors' perceptions of defendants. Direct judicial influence could occur when addressing specific comments or beliefs about the case to the jury. Judicial influence could occur indirectly when addressing comments to counsel, defendants, or other trial participants. *See* note 8 *supra*. Both direct and indirect influence might affect jurors' decisionmaking process.

tent to which judges' behavior "leaks" to juries may be related to defendants' criminal history.

Many studies in nonlegal contexts support the view that beliefs or expectations can be transmitted through subtle verbal and nonverbal cues. A quantitative review of 345 studies of expectancy effects has estimated, for example, that the effect of experimenter and teacher expectations on research tasks and intellectual performance can be substantial.[145] These studies suggest that experimenters, teachers, managers, and psychotherapists who have been led to expect superior performance from particular subjects, students, employees, or clients, treat these "special" or high expectancy persons differently than "less special" or low expectancy persons. These "special" individuals tend to receive different treatment in a variety of ways: (1) interpersonal climate, (2) feedback patterns of behavior, (3) input patterns of behavior, and (4) output opportunities.[146] The study of these factors can help to generate a more general understanding of how judges may transmit influence to juries.

The first factor, "interpersonal climate," refers to the different social and emotional environments that expecters provide individuals for whom they hold high or low expectations. These climate variables, for example, "warmth" in tone of voice when talking to high expectancy individuals as compared to "hostility" in tone of voice when talking to low expectancy individuals, are often nonverbal.[147]

In the courtroom context, we predicted and found that trial

145. Rosenthal & Rubin, *Interpersonal Expectancy Effects: The First 345 Studies*, 3 BEHAVIORAL & BRAIN SCI. 377 (1978) (estimating the average size of the expectancy effect to be equivalent to ten IQ points in terms of most IQ tests—the mean IQ score = 100, and the standard deviation = 15); *see also* Harris & Rosenthal, *supra* note 73.

146. R. ROSENTHAL, *supra* note 141, at 14–24; Rosenthal & Rubin, *supra* note 145, at 377.

147. *See* Blanck & Rosenthal, *supra* note 67, at 424 (demonstrating that human beings engage in highly influential nonverbal communication when talking to others; for example, camp counselors' tones of voice were rated as significantly warmer and less hostile when counselors were talking about children for whom they held high rather than low expectations); *see also* Babad, Inbar & Rosenthal, *Pygmalion, Galatea and the Golem: Investigations of Biased and Unbiased Teachers*, 74 J. EDUC. PSYCHOLOGY 459, 468 (1982); Babad, Inbar & Rosenthal, *Teachers' Judgment of Students' Potential as a Function of Teachers' Susceptibility to Biasing Information*, 42 J. PERSONALITY & SOC. PSYCHOLOGY 541 (1982) (a similar line of study examining climate variables and finding that biased teachers treated low expectancy pupils in a substantially less friendly manner, while less biased teachers treated all students more equally); Eden & Shani, *Pygmalion Goes to Boot Camp: Expectancy, Leadership, and Trainee Performance*, 67 J. APPLIED PSYCHOLOGY 194 (1982) (climate study in which military boot camp trainees whose instructors had been led to expect high performance, not only performed better on a test of military performance, but also felt more support from their instructors).

judges' more leaky nonverbal behavior, demeanor, or "climate" in delivering jury instructions were less warm, less competent, less wise, and more anxious when the judge expected a guilty verdict than when the judge expected an innocent verdict.[148] A similar study has indirectly tested the judges' behavior in terms of climate variables in the courtroom context: Students rated trial judges' verbal "respect" for various participants in trials. Judge favoritism toward the contesting attorneys related significantly to less severe jury verdicts.[149] Our results, and those of other studies, suggest that judges may create a relatively more favorable courtroom climate for defendants they believe are innocent as compared to those they believe are guilty.

The second factor, "feedback," concerns patterns of behavior by the judge relating to actual responses by a trial participant, for example, the behavior of the defendant on the stand. In the classroom, teachers often give their "special" students more helpful verbal and nonverbal feedback on performance.[150] In the courtroom, a judge may be generally more supportive of defense counsel when the judge holds expectations for the defendant's innocence, and less supportive when holding expectations for guilt. Another example is the case where the judge, expecting the verdict to be guilty, responds to prosecution counsel's incorrect objection by correcting the objection or asking for further elaboration.[151] But the operation of the feedback factor in the courtroom can be even more subtle. For example, trial judges

---

148. *See* notes 118–119 *supra* and accompanying text; *see also* note 33 *supra* (Learned Hand's description of the "atmosphere" of the courtroom).

149. *See* Kerr, *supra* note 98, at 261, 276, 282. Interestingly, Kerr also found that trial judges were perceived as (1) more respectful toward the prosecution than the defense, and (2) less impartial and displaying more responsive motor mannerisms (nonverbal behavior) toward the prosecution. Also, judges who were more respectful were perceived to be more courteous and impartial; and all judges were more respectful toward older attorneys—both defense and prosecution—relative to younger attorneys. Finally, when judges were respectful and courteous, all other trial participants were perceived as being respectful as well. It seems the judge importantly sets the "tone" or atmosphere of the trial for all the participants. *Id.*

150. *See* Rothbart, Dalfen & Barrett, *Effects of Teacher's Expectancy on Student-Teacher Interaction*, 62 J. EDUC. PSYCHOLOGY 49 (1971); S.W. Kester, The Communication of Teacher Expectations and their Effects on the Achievement and Attitudes of Secondary School Pupils (1969) (unpublished doctoral dissertation, University of Oklahoma).

151. These are examples of the trial judge's indirect influence on the jury decisionmaking process. *See* note 144 *supra.*

It may be, however, that providing the defendant extra "feedback" does not violate due process rights. It is possible that all that is constitutionally required from a trial judge is a minimum level of support, or "feedback," below which the judge would be acting prejudicially against the defendant.

may read the jury instructions more slowly if they believe the defendant to be innocent.[152]

The third factor, "input," may also be useful in understanding the subtle transmission of judges' beliefs to juries. This factor suggests that judges not only may provide more feedback, but actually may become more "involved" in the trial process on the side they believe should prevail. An extreme case would be the judge who effectively becomes an advocate for one side, thereby exceeding the constitutional limits of judicial influence.[153] The input factor in the transmission of the judge's beliefs for a defendant's guilt or innocence thus translates into how much the judge actually departs from judicial impartiality by taking an active interest in one side over the other.[154] Thus, in the same way that a teacher may show more interest in "special" pupils by teaching them more difficult material, judges may show more interest in defendants they believe are innocent; for example, by asking more difficult and probing questions of the defendant taking the stand to testify, in order to clear up any previous misunderstandings which might work in the prosecution's favor.[155]

Finally, special or high expectancy individuals also seem to be given greater opportunities for "output." For example, teachers allow pupils they believe are brighter more time in which to answer questions.[156] In the courtroom, judges may provide more opportunities to those defendants whom they believe are innocent, and discourage "output" from defendants they believe are guilty. Such encouragement may not only involve asking more questions, but also may entail allowing a defendant more time to respond when on the stand, prompting or partially shaping responses to questions so that they become more correct, or perhaps even recalling a defendant to the stand to discuss matters

152. We are presently conducting analyses of our videotapes on variables such as the judges' reading pace, eye contact with jury, and head nods, smiles, and self-touching behavior. P.D. Blanck & R. Rosenthal, Judges' Nonverbal Behavior (January 1986) (unpublished data and manuscript).

153. *See* text accompanying notes 13–15 *supra.*

154. *See* text accompanying notes 11–18 *supra.* Due process requirements are not fixed, however, and what remains determinative is whether the appearance of justice (or injustice) resulted in actual unfairness toward the defendant.

155. Future research is needed to address this issue, for an argument could be made that judges put more difficult questions to defendants whom they believe are guilty, perhaps to make a more complete case against such defendants when they take the stand to testify. *Cf.* Judge Frankel's view in note 30 *supra.*

156. *See* Rosenthal & Rubin, *supra* note 145.

not covered by counsel.[157]

The four factors are not independent of each other. They are merely presented as factors that, when taken together, may be a useful way for judges, lawyers, or jurors to group and recognize the often subtle verbal and nonverbal transmission of judicial influence. The output factor, for example, may operate in conjunction with the feedback factor. Judges who allow lawyers for one side more opportunity to respond to questions are also likely to give more feedback on the accuracy or appropriateness of those responses. Future research is needed to assess whether lawyers for defendants whom judges perceive as innocent receive different opportunities to demonstrate their client's innocence.[158] These preliminary factors provide a general starting point for analysis of the transmission of judicial influence.

B. *Appellate Review and the Limits of Judicial Behavior*

As early as 1892, the Kentucky Court of Appeals recognized the problem of appellate review of judicial behavior: "[T]here are many ways that a partial or prejudicial judge may knife a party that he is trying, without it appearing from the record . . . ."[159] The appellate record often does not accurately reflect the behavior of the trial judge toward the jury or other trial participants.[160] Although alerting judges, jurors, and lawyers to the verbal and nonverbal components of the judges' behavior might reduce the unintended influence of judges in criminal jury trials,[161] trial lawyers still must actively and clearly document the impact of the

---

157. It is improper for the judge to recall a defendant to interrogate him regarding matters not covered in his original examination. *See, e.g.,* People v. Farrell, 7 A.D.2d 642, 643, 179 N.Y.S.2d 540, 541 (1958) ("[E]xpressions of the views of the court as to the evidence and the recalling of the appellant to stand to interrogate her on matters, theretofore left untouched, deprived appellant of her constitutional right to a fair and impartial trial and . . . the interests of justice require a new trial."). We cannot conclude, however, that judges know the "correct" answer. We only mean to suggest that judges may sometimes engineer the trial process so as to receive the answer that they believe to be correct. *See* notes 6–8 *supra* and accompanying text.

158. This research would address an important tactical issue for defense counsel. Deciding whether to permit a client to testify may depend, in part, on a rough assessment of the judge's expectations for trial outcome. *See* H. KALVEN & H. ZEISEL, *supra* note 51, at 127–28.

159. Massie v. Commonwealth, 93 Ky. 588, 591, 20 S.W. 704, 704 (1892).

160. *See* notes 5–6 *supra* and accompanying text. The problem is illustrated in State v. Soriano, 107 N.J. Super. 286, 288, 258 A.2d 140, 142 (1968), *aff'd,* 54 N.J. 567, 258 A.2d 361 (1969) (acknowledging that the "dry record" did not enable visualization of challenged facial expressions).

161. *See* notes 179–181 *infra.*

judge's behavior in ways that enable appellate courts to determine whether the behavior constitutes reversible error.

Judges' nonverbal behaviors generally do not appear on the "dry" or "cold" appellate record, making it difficult for counsel to preserve properly these subtle, or sometimes not-so-subtle, influences. Even where the judge's reaction to defense testimony is clearly prejudicial—for example, placing his hands on the side of his head, shaking his head negatively, and leaning back and swiveling 180 degrees in his chair—appellate courts have held the record insufficient to require a new trial due to the lack of a reliable record of the allegedly prejudicial behavior.[162] In a case where the judge charged the jury while rapping on the bench each time he spoke about the defendant, the appellate court refused to review the trial in the absence of an objection by counsel to these behaviors.[163]

Documentation of the judges' nonverbal behavior for the trial record is a difficult task for trial counsel for other reasons as well. Although trial attorneys must object to and document the alleged prejudicial behavior of the judge for that behavior to be reviewed on appeal,[164] counsel must be careful not to be overly zealous or he or she may lose credibility in the eyes of the jurors, who view the judge with great respect.[165] Objections by trial counsel to every nonverbal communication and behavior of the judge would soon antagonize the judge as well.[166]

---

162. State v. Barron, 465 S.W.2d 523, 527–28 (Mo. 1971).

163. State v. Grant, 295 So. 2d 168, 173–74 (La. 1973) (if the alleged conduct were substantiated by the record and was the subject of a contemporaneous objection or motion for a mistrial, the conduct would be improper and possible grounds for a mistrial), *overruled on other grounds*, 339 So. 2d 1194 (La. 1976); *see also* United States v. Oglin, 745 F.2d 263 (3d Cir. 1984), *cert. denied*, 105 S. Ct. 2321 (1985). The *Olgin* Court noted that the defense failed to object to the effectiveness of the judge's curative instructions and that

> it was incumbent upon defense counsel to request a further curative instruction or to register an objection to the efficacy of the one already presented to the jury before the jury retired to consider its verdict . . . .
>
> Thus counsel's lack of a timely challenge to the efficacy of the judge's curative instruction . . . forecloses assigning as error that portion of the charge.

Id. at 271.

164. *See* Milhouse v. State, 264 Ga. 357, 329 S.E.2d 490 (1985); *see also* 4A C.J.S. *Appeal and Error* § 714 (1955).

165. *See* notes 39–40 *supra* and accompanying text.

166. One trial attorney has suggested that counsel may attempt to neutralize any antagonism between judge and lawyer by delivering a set speech thanking the judge for his or her patience. F. Bailey & H. Rothblatt, Successful Techniques for Criminal Trials § 29.2, at 780 (2d ed. 1985). *See generally* Note, *supra* note 32, at 1286–87 (suggesting modification of the contemporaneous objection rule for objections to nonverbal behavior of trial judge).

The appellate courts have suggested general guidelines to help counsel effectively document the "cold" record. Several courts have suggested that if the intonations and gestures of a judge are thought to be prejudicial to a defendant in a criminal case, defense counsel must (1) make timely objections and record these objections before the jury leaves the room,[167] (2) record what transpired descriptively, fully, accurately, and on the record, (3) record any disagreement between judge and lawyer as to what happened, and, most important, (4) show that the behaviors actually denied the defendant his or her right to a fair and impartial trial.[168]

Several appellate courts have noted, however, that even with these suggested guidelines it is difficult to assess claims that the judge indicated partiality by his nonverbal behavior in the absence of video- and audiotape recordings of trials.[169] A few appellate courts have required the defense attorney to present an affidavit by the defendant or by anyone who has personal knowledge of the judge's behavior, or to present a brief on appeal specifying the details of the alleged prejudicial behaviors and noting where the record did not substantiate any of the defendant's allegations.[170]

Unfortunately, "[t]here is simply no handy tool" with which to gauge a claim that a trial judge's behavior or conduct biased a

167. One attorney has suggested an appropriate objection at trial to the allegedly prejudicial nonverbal cues of a trial judge:

> Your Honor, the defendant respectfully excepts to the tone and inflection in which Your Honor is putting questions to this witness. They suggest to the jury that his testimony is unworthy of belief. He respectfully suggests that the question is improper as the jury must remain the sole judge of the credibility of witnesses.

F. Bailey & H. Rothblatt, *supra* note 166, § 29.5, at 785. A similar objection might be appropriate if prejudice to the defendant occurs when the trial judge emphasizes the prosecution case over the defense case. *Id.* § 29.10, at 791.

168. *See* Billeci v. United States, 184 F.2d 394, 402 (D.C. Cir. 1950); Curtin, *Objections*, 8 Litigation 37, 39 (1982) (proposing ways of raising objections in order to preserve alleged judicial error); Note, *supra* note 32 (discussing methods of preserving the trial record).

169. *See* United States v. Robinson, 635 F.2d 981, 984 n.2 (2d Cir. 1980), *cert. denied*, 451 U.S. 992 (1981); United States v. Weiss, 491 F.2d 460, 468 n.2 (2d Cir.), *cert. denied*, 419 U.S. 833 (1974); *see also* Note, *supra* note 32, at 1285 (suggesting that perhaps the only way to preserve an adequate record of such behavior is through the use of film or videotape).

170. *See, e.g.*, Petro v. State, 270 Ind. 86, 87–88, 383 N.E.2d 323, 324 (1978) (affidavit of appellant's attorney inadequate in itself to establish abuse of trial court discretion or prejudice to appellant since it did not set forth specific details of the alleged improprieties and since the record did not substantiate the allegations). *But see* note 44 *supra* (jurors not allowed to impeach their own verdicts).

trial against the defendant.[171] Appellate courts continue to approach the problem on a case-by-case basis by studying and reading the record and paying particular attention to every comment of the judge. Appellate courts remain reluctant to question the discretion of the trial judge[172] and have only recently begun to qualify longstanding rules that judges' nonverbal behavior is not reviewable on appeal.[173] To have any chance for reversal, defense counsel must carefully document at trial the alleged prejudicial behavior of the judge in a way that will allow an appellate court to determine that the judge's behavior contributed to the conviction.[174]

Future research must address the extent to which it is practically and administratively feasible for counsel to document for an appellate court the judge's behavior in terms of (1) the major communicative channel—visual, audio, or verbal cues, (2) the overall affect or emotion expressed in a particular channel—warmth, open-mindedness, or hostility, (3) the focus of the behavior—for example, to whom the behavior is directed, (4) any

---

171. United States v. Nazzaro, 472 F.2d 302 (2d Cir. 1973). The court noted:

> The special quandary we face in such cases [involving the prejudicial behavior of the trial judge] stems from the fact that "we are not given the benefit of witnessing the juxtaposition of personalities which may help prevent reading too much into 'the cold black and white of a printed record.' "

Id. at 304 (quoting United States v. Grunberger, 431 F.2d 1062, 1067 (2d Cir. 1970)).

172. *See, e.g.*, Oglen v. State, 440 So.2d 1172, 1175 (Ala. Crim. App. 1983) (concluding that the trial judge, while showing some impatience, "was attempting to exercise his rightful control over the proceeding"). Another appellate court reacted to alleged examples of misconduct by stating that the allegations "represent an exaggeration and a too thin-skinned reaction to a perfectly normal inquiry by the court." United States v. Poland, 659 F.2d 884, 893 (9th Cir.), *cert. denied*, 454 U.S. 1059 (1981).

Article VI of the California Constitution specifically gives the trial judge great discretion during the trial process: "The court may make such comment on the evidence and the testimony and credibility of any witness as in its opinion is necessary for the proper determination of the cause." CAL. CONST. art. VI, § 10; *see also* People v. Cook, 33 Cal. 3d 400, 408, 658 P.2d 86, 91, 189 Cal. Rptr. 159, 164 (1983) (it "is difficult to draw a precise line of demarcation between those comments on the evidence which are authorized by article VI, section 10 and those which are not").

173. *Milhouse*, 329 S.E.2d at 490 (qualifying a longstanding appellate policy in Georgia that a trial judge's vocal emphasis and nonverbal behavior is not reviewable on appeal). Earlier cases in Georgia had held that the tone of voice of the trial judge in instructing the jury was not reviewable. Wilson v. State, 229 Ga. 224, 225, 190 S.E.2d 78, 79 (1972), *overruled on other grounds*, 230 Ga. 525, 198 S.E.2d 180 (1973); Williams v. State, 170 Ga. 886, 890, 154 S.E. 363, 365 (1930); Whiddon v. State, 160 Ga. App. 777, 779, 287 S.E.2d 114, 117 (1982); Perdue v. State, 147 Ga. App. 648, 652, 249 S.E.2d 657, 661 (1978).

174. *Cf.* Chapman v. California, 386 U.S. 18, 24 (1967) (before a constitutional error can be held to be harmless, the court must be able to declare its belief that it was harmless beyond a reasonable doubt).

inconsistencies or "leakage" in the verbal and nonverbal behavior of the judge, such as a nervous smile or sarcastic behavior that may transmit expectancy effects, (5) the duration, frequency, and consistency of the behavior, (6) the four factors described earlier—climate, feedback, input, and output—that might be useful in summarizing the verbal and nonverbal transmission of the judge's expectations, attitudes, and beliefs for trial outcome, (7) the post-verdict reactions of jurors to the judge's behavior during the trial,[175] and (8) any other reactions to the judge's behavior gained by calling and questioning as witnesses people who were in the courtroom at the time of the alleged prejudicial behavior.[176] This general strategy, when replicated and qualified by future researchers, may eventually aid appellate courts in understanding more thoroughly what behavior occurred, and whether it had a measurable and documented effect on the defendant's right to a fair and impartial trial.[177] Trial lawyers and judges may decide that the videotaping of courtroom proceedings should play an increasingly important role in this process.[178] But it remains for the state legislatures to decide the future role of videotaping in the courtroom.

C. *Extra-Legal Concerns*

1. *Studying trial judges.*

There were important differences among the judges participating in our study in the clarity and force of communication through different verbal and nonverbal channels. Future researchers should address the question of what kind of judges, in terms of communicative skills and perhaps other personality variables, are prone to influence prejudicially what kind of jurors and

175. Post-verdict juror questionnaires, however, will probably be "contaminated" or biased by the jurors' actual decision. A better strategy would be to survey jurors before they retire to the jury room. *See* note 123 *supra*. Unfortunately, such data may be difficult to collect without prejudicing the jury decisionmaking process.

176. *Milhouse*, 329 S.E.2d at 490.

177. Appellate courts have not been persuaded by allegations that the "general attitude" of the trial judge toward the defendant's case influences or creates an atmosphere in which the defendant may not have a fair trial. *See, e.g.*, State v. Larmond, 244 N.W.2d 233 (Iowa 1976) (when a trial judge "telegraphs" to a jury purposeful exclamations, gestures, or facial expressions reflecting his or her beliefs concerning the guilt or innocence of a defendant, the proper procedure is for counsel to promptly make a record in chambers of the offending conduct, coupled with an objection, or to enter an objection supported by a bill of exceptions); State v. Barnholtz, 287 S.W.2d 808, 812 (Mo. 1956).

178. *See* note 86 *supra*.

other trial participants.[179] This type of information may aid in understanding communication processes during the trial and may help to alert judges and other trial participants to recognize biasing or prejudicial behaviors in the trial process that could act to deprive defendants of their due process right to a fair and impartial trial.[180]

More systematic investigations of judges' communicative behavior are possible and are needed. Trial judges' behavior could be examined in terms of (1) the emotions and information expressed in various channels of communication (e.g., verbal versus nonverbal channels), (2) the potential impact on the jury of various channels of judges' behavior (e.g., tone of voice versus facial expressions), (3) the extent to which especially "leaky" verbal and nonverbal cues convey judges' expectations for trial outcome to jurors, and (4) the cumulative effects of judge communicative style on trial processes and trial outcome. This general line of study might also help to describe better the limits of judicial influence and to aid in a more systematic understanding of how judges' behavior influences trial processes.

---

179. *See* Givens, *The Way Others See Us*, 19 JUDGES J. 20 (1980). Eventually, it may be possible to "match" judicial competencies with the type of case before the court. *See* Shapiro, *Can We Match the Skills of Our Judges to the Needs of Our Courts?*, 62 JUDICATURE 164 (1978) (discussing the possibility of matching judicial knowledge and information with the type of case).

It has been possible to specify the accuracy of senders and receivers of verbal and nonverbal cues in social interaction and to develop instruments designed to measure sensitivity to various channels of social communication. *See* Blanck & Rosenthal, *supra* note 107. Many special groups have been tested with standardized tests, and those scoring best have been actors and students of nonverbal communication. Interestingly, clinical psychologists, psychiatrists, and other clinicians scored no higher than college students, but clinicians rated as more effective by their supervisors scored significantly higher than did clinicians rated as less effective by their supervisors. R. ROSENTHAL, J. HALL, R. DIMATTEO, P. ROGERS & D. ARCHER, *supra* note 70, at 295–97. The communicative skills of judges, jurors, and lawyers have yet to be assessed.

180. Judicial training centers already exist across the country, teaching judges in ways consistent with the modifications suggested here. For example, the California Center for Judicial Education and Research (CJER) is the California judiciary's program for improving the administration of justice by furthering the education and broadening the experiences of trial judges. CJER offers a course on effective courtroom communication. Each judge in this course has an opportunity to conduct a judicial proceeding before a video camera. At later seminars, the recording of the judge is played back to other judges and to the teaching faculty for general comments about the strengths and weaknesses of the judge's communicative skills. For a description of the CJER study program, see Bancroft, Avakian, Gyemant, Levie, Mills & Kaplan, California Center for Judicial Education and Research, Courtroom Fairness (Winter 1984) (unpublished collection of course materials on file with the *Stanford Law Review*); *see also* FEDERAL JUDICIAL CENTER, ANNUAL REPORT (1983); Middleton, *Courtroom Kinesics: What Judges Don't Say*, 67 JUDICATURE 699 (1981) (discussing the training of trial judges and the use of videotaping in the courtroom).

2. *Studying jurors.*

It is also important that jurors are made aware of the verbal and nonverbal behaviors of the judge that may influence the trial process. Because judges' verbal and nonverbal behavior may leak to jurors the judges' beliefs for trial outcome, jurors who are especially sensitive or attentive to verbal and nonverbal signals may also be more susceptible to judicial influence in their decisionmaking process.[181] The extent to which jurors' accurate perceptions of leaky behaviors influence their decisionmaking processes is a question for future research.

More research is needed to assess the susceptibility of jurors to biasing information in order to aid in the understanding of the effects of judge behavior on jury decisionmaking processes. Perhaps improving the receiving skills of potential jurors so as to make them more aware of how leaky nonverbal channels transmit expectations would make them less susceptible to judicial influence.[182] Future researchers might attempt to alert jurors to the verbal and nonverbal components of judges' behavior and then assess the extent to which these strategies help to ensure that judges' unintended behavior does not influence juries' verdicts. These research strategies could eventually merge into a general educational program administered by the state, perhaps in conjunction with standard jury selection procedures already in place. A comprehensive approach for understanding judicial behavior and influence on jurors may be more effective than merely relying on the pattern curative instruction warning to jurors that they are not to be influenced by anything the judge has "said or done."[183]

---

181. An "expectancy" experiment exploring a related hypothesis found that children who were more adept at decoding tone of voice were more affected by their teacher's expectations than children who were less accurate in decoding tone of voice. Better senders or encoders of nonverbal cues are also more effective in producing expectancy effects. *See* Conn, Edwards, Rosenthal & Crowne, *Perception of Emotion and Response to Teachers' Expectancy by Elementary School Children,* 22 PSYCHOLOGICAL REP. 27 (1968). *But see* Christensen & Rosenthal, *Gender and Nonverbal Decoding Skill as Determinants of Interpersonal Expectancy Effects,* 42 J. PERSONALITY & SOC. PSYCHOLOGY 75 (1982) (finding no systematic relationship between subjects' nonverbal decoding ability and their susceptibility to expectancy effects).

182. *But see* note 181 *supra* (it is possible that improved receiving skills could make jurors *more* susceptible to judicial influence). Future research must address the effects of training receivers (jurors) to be more accurate at interpreting more and less leaky messages and the effect such training has on susceptibility to influence.

183. *See* Appendix A, Section XV. The general effectiveness of such curative instructions needs attention from future researchers. Curative instructions to the jury allow trial judges the opportunity to correct any prejudicial behavior by the judge that may impermissi-

Another interesting issue for future research relates to whether trial judges should provide jurors with an audiotaped version of the jury instructions to take into deliberations. The Eleventh Circuit has permitted judges to provide the jury with a tape recording of the jury instructions for use during its deliberations and has rejected a defendant's claim that the audiotaped instructions in the jury room were per se reversible error because they prejudiced the jury to overemphasize certain parts of the instructions.[184] Our results suggest that the Eleventh Circuit's ruling may be incorrect. Indeed, judges' expectations for trial outcome, and other beliefs and attitudes, may be subtly transmitted by judges' tone of voice alone. Although providing the jury with a written transcript of the particular jury instructions might

---

bly influence the jury decisionmaking process. Appellate courts have allowed judges broad discretion in utilizing curative instructions. *See, e.g.*, State v. O'Connor, 42 N.J. 502, 201 A.2d 705, *cert. denied*, 379 U.S. 916 (1964) (where the defendant was convicted of murder and appealed on the grounds that the trial judge's facial expressions showed disgust, amusement, disbelief, and annoyance toward the defendant during the trial, the trial judge stated that he was not aware of these facial expressions; in affirming the judgment, the appellate court noted that during the jury instructions the judge cautioned the jury that they should not be influenced by any outward reactions of the judge toward the defendant); *see also* People v. Franklin, 56 Cal. App. 3d 18, 24, 128 Cal. Rptr. 94, 98 (1976) ("Even where conduct by a trial judge may approach the boundaries of improper discretion, an admonition to disregard his conduct can be deemed curative, and it must be assumed that the jury was possessed of ordinary intelligence and followed such instructions.").

Appellate courts consider on a case-by-case basis whether a curative instruction had the desired effect of removing prejudicial influence. But the extent to which these instructions actually "cure" the verbal and nonverbal errors of the trial judge is not known. Psychologists have begun to study systematically the efficacy of curative instructions. *See* Thompson, Fong & Rosenhan, *Inadmissible Evidence and Juror Verdicts*, 40 J. PERSONALITY & SOC. PSYCHOLOGY 453, 461 (1981) (demonstrating that jurors tend to ignore judges' instructions to disregard inadmissible evidence); Brooks & Doob, *supra* note 56, at 176–77 (showing that jurors are likely to ignore judges' instructions limiting the use of the defendant's previous convictions to impeach credibility); Tanford & Penrod, *Social Inference Processes in Juror Judgments of Multiple Offense Trials*, 47 J. PERSONALITY & SOC. PSYCHOLOGY 749 (1984) (indicating that joining several charges within a realistic trial setting increases the likelihood that a defendant will be convicted on a particular charge regardless of the similarities of the charges or the evidence; the use of the judges' instructions did not effectively reduce the tendencies toward conviction).

Skepticism about the effectiveness of curative and evidential instructions is not new. In 1697, Lord Holt denied that the jury had an "absolute despotick [sic] power" to disregard the judge's instructions. *Quoted in* J. FRANK, LAW AND THE MODERN MIND 307 (1930). Judge Learned Hand also described the customary instruction to disregard as a mental gymnastic beyond anyone's power. Nash v. United States, 54 F.2d 1006, 1007 (2d Cir. 1932).

184. *See* United States v. Watson, 669 F.2d 1374, 1385–86 (11th Cir. 1982) (the presentation of an audiotaped or written charge to the jury could aid juror comprehension, as well as expedite proceedings). *But see* Table 4 *supra* and accompanying text (displaying the significant relationship between the judge's verbal and nonverbal behaviors in delivering jury instructions and the trial outcome).

prevent the communication of unintended nonverbal behaviors of the judge,[185] such a transcript might be less effective in improving juror comprehension of the instructions.[186] Future research must address this question while remaining aware of the extra-legal information conveyed to jurors by the judge in the way he or she delivers the instructions.[187] Video- and audiotape techniques are well suited for the study of these problems because they enable researchers to vary systematically the verbal and nonverbal information in the instructions, as well as their legal accuracy.

Finally, future researchers need to examine how the jury's overall comprehension of the jury instructions relates to the behavior of the judge. It may be that the *less* jurors actually understand the instructions, the *more* their decisionmaking process is influenced by subtle verbal and nonverbal behaviors of the judge. Although jurors' inability to understand instructions will almost never show up on the "dry" appellate record, juries' decisionmaking processes could be significantly influenced by subtle judicial behavior in predictable ways. Courts and legislatures should not assume that jurors, for the most part, are "free" to understand and faithfully follow instructions.[188]

CONCLUSION[189]

The behavior of the trial judge can sometimes influence jury

185. *See, e.g.*, Wagner v. State, 76 Wis. 2d 30, 39, 250 N.W.2d 331, 341–42 (1977) (court discouraged the jury's unrestricted use of taped jury instructions in part because the instructions would reproduce the tonal inflections of the trial judge).

186. *See* Charrow & Charrow, *supra* note 62, the first empirical linguistic study of the comprehensibility of standard jury instructions. The study isolated those linguistic features of standard jury instructions—grammar, semantics, vocabulary, and structure—that cause comprehension problems. The researchers recorded fourteen California standard civil jury instructions on audio cassettes and played the instructions to prospective jurors. The results suggested that subjects have difficulty comprehending jury instructions. When the same instructions were modified—eliminating passive verbs and replacing them with active verbs, eliminating multiple negatives, and improving the organization of the instructions—the results showed that the modifications yielded improved comprehension.

187. An interesting future study could examine the possibility of presenting "pattern video and audiotaped instructions" to juries at the close of the trial. The use of pattern video and audiotaped instructions might prove to increase jurors' comprehension of the instructions while minimizing the possible influence of the judges' unintended behavior.

188. R. TRAYNOR, THE RIDDLE OF HARMLESS ERROR 73–74 (1970).

189. In closing, this note has focused on the trial judge's behavior, often from a critical viewpoint. We would be remiss not to point out that the spirit of this note, and of the investigation as a whole, was to describe and improve the already exceptional performance of many of the trial judges in our criminal jury system. Indeed, discussion with the judges who

verdicts so as to deny a defendant's constitutionally protected right to a fair and impartial trial. Our study proposed and empirically employed a general model for the study of predicting juries' verdicts from judges' verbal and nonverbal behavior. The variables in the model included: (A) the background variables of the trial participants, (B) the expectancy variable of the trial judge, (C) the verbal and nonverbal transmission of the judge's expectancy, and (D) the trial outcome. We found that judges' expectations for trial outcome predict judges' verbal and nonverbal behavior and that this behavior also relates to the verdicts returned by juries. The findings have implications for understanding whether judges' beliefs for trial outcome "leak" to juries and, if so, how. They may also aid in the development of standards of appellate review that would enable courts to evaluate more systematically the permissible limits of judicial behavior and to give guidance for the future study of trial judges, jurors, and trial counsel with respect to the effects of communicative behavior in the courtroom.

---

participated in this study clarified many of our hypotheses and analyses. Such a high level of ecological validity is rare in the social sciences. As we stated at the outset, our goal was to study judges in their natural environment, the courtroom.

APPENDIX A

California Pattern Jury Instructions—Criminal
Fourth Revised Edition—1979 MISDEMEANOR INSTRUCTIONS
PART 16

Below are the composite basic instructions for misdemeanor trials in California:

Section I: Duties of thc Judge and Jury

Ladies and Gentlemen of the Jury: Now we come to that part of the trial where you will be instructed on the law.

Whether a defendant is to be found guilty or not guilty depends upon both the facts and the law.

As jurors you have two duties to perform in order to reach a verdict. One duty is to determine the facts of the case from the evidence received in the trial and not from any other source. The word "fact" means something that is proved directly or circumstantially by the evidence.

Your other duty is to apply the law to the facts as you determine them and in this way to reach your verdict.

It is my duty in these instructions to explain to you the law that applies in this case. You must accept and follow the law as I state it to you.

You must not be influenced by pity for a defendant or by prejudice against him.

You must not be biased against the defendant because he has been arrested; charged with a crime or brought to trial. These facts are not evidence of his guilt.

You must not be swayed by mere sentiment, conjecture, sympathy, passion, public opinion or public feeling.

Section II: Composition of Instructions

The instructions are to be construed as a whole and each individual instruction is to be considered in light of all the others.

The order in which the instructions are given has no significance as to their relative importance.

For simplicity, the masculine form of pronoun as used in the instructions applies equally to all persons.

Section III: Statements of Counsel, etc.

You must not consider any statement by either attorney as evidence. If the attorneys have agreed to any fact or if any fact has been admitted, that fact is proved.

You must not consider as evidence any offer of proof that was rejected or any evidence that was stricken out.

As to any question to which an objection has been sustained you must not guess what the answer might have been.

You must not assume to be true any insinuation suggested by a question asked a witness.

Section IV: Direct and Circumstantial Evidence

Evidence consists of testimony of witnesses, writings, material objects, or anything presented to the senses and offered to prove the existence or nonexistence of a fact.

Evidence is either direct or circumstantial.

Direct evidence is evidence that directly proves a fact.

Circumstantial evidence is evidence that proves a fact from which an inference of the existence of another fact may be drawn.

An inference is a deduction of fact that may logically and reasonably be drawn from another fact or group of facts established by the evidence.

Both direct evidence and circumstantial evidence are acceptable as means of proof. Neither is entitled to any greater weight than the other.

Section V: Sufficiency of Circumstantial Evidence

A finding of guilt as to any crime may not be based on circumstantial evidence unless the proved circumstances are not only (1) consistent with the theory that the defendant is guilty of the crime, but (2) cannot be reconciled with any other rational conclusion.

Further, each fact which is essential to complete a set of circumstances necessary to establish the defendant's guilt must be proved beyond a reasonable doubt. In other words, before an inference essential to establish guilt may be found to have been proved beyond a reasonable doubt, each fact or circumstance upon which such inference necessarily rests must be proved beyond a reasonable doubt.

Also if the circumstantial evidence [as to any particular count] is susceptible to two reasonable interpretations, one of which points to the defendant's guilt and the other to his innocence, it is your duty to adopt the interpretation which points to the defendant's innocence, and reject that interpretation which points to his guilt.

If, on the other hand, one interpretation of such evidence appears to you to be reasonable and the other interpretation to be unreasonable, it would be your duty to accept the reasonable interpretation and to reject the unreasonable.

Section VI: Admissions and Confessions

A statement made by the defendant other than at his trial may be either an admission or confession.

An admission is a statement by a defendant, which by itself is not sufficient to warrant an inference of guilt, but which tends to prove guilt when considered with the rest of the evidence.

A confession is a statement by a defendant which discloses his intentional participation in the criminal act for which he is on trial and which discloses his guilt of that crime.

You are the exclusive judges as to whether an admission or a confession was made by the defendant and if the statement is true in whole or in part. If you should find that such statement is entirely untrue, you must reject it. If you find it is true in part, you may consider that part which you find to be true.

Evidence of an oral admission or an oral confession of the defendant ought to be viewed with caution.

[No person may be convicted of an offense unless there is some proof of each element of the offense independent of any admission made by him outside the trial.

However, the identity of the person who committed the offense may be established by an admission.]

Section VII: Credibility of Witness

Every person who testifies under oath [or affirmation] is a witness. You are the sole judges of the believability of a witness and the weight to be given to his testimony.

In determining the believability of a witness, you may consider anything which tends in reason to prove or disprove the truthfulness of his testimony, such as: his conduct, attitude and manner while testifying; his capacity to hear or see that about which he testified and his ability to recollect or to relate such matters; whether or not there was any bias, interest or other motive for him not to tell the truth; [any statement previously made by him that was consistent with his testimony] [or,] [any statement previously made by him that was inconsistent with his testimony;] [his character for honesty or veracity or for dishonesty or untruthfulness;] [any admission by him that he did not tell the truth;] [his prior conviction of a felony].

If you believe that a witness willfully testified falsely as to a material fact, you should distrust the rest of his testimony and you may disregard all of his testimony.

However, you should bear in mind that discrepancies in a witness's testimony and that of others, if there were any, do not necessarily mean that you should disbelieve the witness, because forgetting is common and innocent mistakes are not unusual. Two persons witnessing the same incident often see or hear it differently.

You also should consider whether any such discrepancy concerns an important fact or only a trivial detail.

Section VIII: Weighing Conflicting Testimony.

You should not decide any issue merely by counting the number of witnesses who have testified on the opposing sides.

The final test is not in the relative number of witnesses, but in the relative convincing force of the evidence.

Section IX: Sufficiency of Testimony of One Witness

[Testimony which you believe given by one witness is sufficient for the proof of any fact. However, before finding any fact required to be established by the prosecution to be proved solely by the testimony of such a single witness, you should carefully review all the testimony upon which the proof of such fact depends.]

Section X: Expert Testimony

[In determining the weight to be given to the opinion of any expert who has testified in this case, you should consider the qualifications and credibility of such expert and the reasons given for his opinion.

You are not bound to accept an expert opinion as conclusive, but should give to it the weight, if any, to which you find it to be entitled.]

[If there was any conflict in the testimony of expert witnesses, you should consider their relative qualifications and credibility in weighing the opinion of one expert against that of another as well as the reasons given for each opinion and the facts upon which it was based.]

Section XI: Presumption of Innocence and Burden of Proof

A defendant in a criminal action is presumed to be innocent until the contrary is proved, and in case of a reasonable doubt whether his guilt is satisfactorily shown, he is entitled to a verdict of not guilty. This presumption places upon the State the burden of proving him guilty beyond a reasonable doubt. Reasonable doubt is defined as follows: It is not a mere possible doubt; because everything relating to human affairs, and depending on moral evidence, is open to some possible or imaginary doubt. It is that state of the case which, after the entire comparison and consideration of all the evidence, leaves the minds of the jurors in that condition that they cannot say they feel an abiding conviction, to a moral certainty, of the truth of the charge.

Section XII: [Here give the Particular Instructions as to the Offense Charged.]

Section XIII: General Intent

[In the offense with which the defendant is charged [in Count—,] there must be a joint operation of act or conduct and criminal intent.

When a person intentionally does that which the law declares to be an offense, he is acting with criminal intent, even though he may not know that his conduct is unlawful, or even though he may not intend to violate the law.]

Section XIV: Specific Intent

[In the offense with which the defendant is charged [in Count —,] there must be a joint operation of act or conduct and the required specific intent and unless such specific intent so exists that offense is not committed.]

Section XV: Take No Cue from Judge

I have not intended by anything I have said or done or by any question I may have asked to suggest what you should find the facts to be or that I believe or disbelieve any witness.

If anything I have said or done has seemed to suggest my opinion as to the facts, you will disregard it and form your own opinion.

Section XVI: Duty to Deliberate

When you start your deliberations, it is important that you avoid expressing a fixed opinion or a determination to hold out for a certain verdict.

Each of you must decide the case for yourself but should do so only after an open-minded discussion of the evidence and instructions with the other jurors.

Once you have reached a conclusion, you should not change it merely because other jurors disagree with you. However, if you become convinced you have reached a wrong conclusion, you should not hesitate to change it.

You should remember in deciding this case, that you are not advocates or partisans for either side but that you are the impartial judges of the facts.

Section XVII: Avoid Considering a Penalty

In your deliberations, or in arriving at a verdict, you must not discuss or consider the subject of penalty or punishment. That is a matter which must not in any way affect your decision.

Section XVIII: Concluding Instruction

You shall now retire and select one of your number to act as foreman, who will preside over your deliberations. In order to reach a verdict, all twelve jurors must agree to the decision [and to any finding you have been instructed to include in your verdict]. As soon as all of you have agreed upon a verdict, you shall have it dated and signed by your foreman and then shall return with it to this courtroom.

Appendix B

Courtroom Questionnaires

All the trial judges, jurors, and lawyers were asked to complete the following questionnaires about the trial process—the directions to the trial participants explained the purpose of the study and the time when the questionnaires were to be filled out:

Judge Questionnaire (Before instructions to the jury)

Name ________________ Date ________________
Age ________________ Name of Case ________________
Sex ________________ Date Appointed to Bench ____________
List offenses for which defendant is being tried (code sections).

____

1. How interesting was this trial?

1	2	3	4	5	6	7	8	9
not at all interesting				somewhat interesting				very interesting

2. How complex were the legal issues in this case?

1	2	3	4	5	6	7	8	9
not at all complex				somewhat complex				very complex

3. How complex were the factual issues in this case?

1	2	3	4	5	6	7	8	9
not at all complex				somewhat complex				very complex

4. In this trial, how attentive was the jury?

1	2	3	4	5	6	7	8	9
not at all attentive				somewhat attentive				very attentive

5. In this trial, how sophisticated was the jury?

1	2	3	4	5	6	7	8	9
not at all sophisticated				somewhat sophisticated				very sophisticated

6. In this trial, how open-minded was the jury?

1	2	3	4	5	6	7	8	9
not at all open-minded				somewhat open-minded				very open-minded

7. In this trial, how competent was the defendant's lawyer(s)?

1	2	3	4	5	6	7	8	9
not at all competent				somewhat competent				very competent

8. In this trial, how competent was the prosecutor?

1	2	3	4	5	6	7	8	9
not at all competent				somewhat competent				very competent

9a. What do you think the verdict should be (circle)?

Not Guilty Guilty

(Indicate for each count if necessary and label below.)

9b. Why?

10a. What do you think the verdict will be (Circle)?

Not Guilty Guilty Hung Jury

(Repeat for each count if necessary and label below.)

10b. Why?

11. Additional comments regarding jury and/or lawyer's behavior?

ANSWER FOLLOWING QUESTIONS AFTER VERDICT

12. What was the verdict? (Code sections—and repeat for each count if necessary and label below.)

13. Do you agree with the jury verdict?

1	2	3	4	5	6	7	8	9
not at all				somewhat				very much

14. Additional comments on any aspect of your performance during the trial?

JUROR QUESTIONNAIRE (AFTER VERDICT)

Name ________________ Date ________________
Age ________________ Name of Case ________________
Sex ________________ Occupation ________________
Highest level of education ________________
How many times have you served on a jury? ________________

1. In this trial, did the judge keep order in the courtroom?

1	2	3	4	5	6	7	8	9
not at all				somewhat				very much

2a. In this trial, did the judge speak clearly?

1	2	3	4	5	6	7	8	9
not at all clearly				somewhat clearly				very clearly

2b. In the jury instructions in particular, did the judge speak clearly?

1	2	3	4	5	6	7	8	9
not at all clearly				somewhat clearly				very clearly

3. In this trial, did the judge treat the lawyers and jurors with respect and concern?

1	2	3	4	5	6	7	8	9
not at all				somewhat				very much

4. Overall, how competent was the judge in this trial?

1	2	3	4	5	6	7	8	9
not at all competent				somewhat competent				very competent

5. In this trial, how interested did the judge seem?

1	2	3	4	5	6	7	8	9
not at all interested				somewhat interested				very interested

6. In this trial, how open-minded was the judge? lawyer(s)?

1	2	3	4	5	6	7	8	9
not at all open-minded				somewhat open-minded				very open-minded

7a. In this trial, which side do you think the judge thought should win?

1	2	3	4	5	6	7	8	9
very much for the defendant				split				very much for the prosecution

7b. How could you tell this?

8. In this trial, to what extent did the judge's facial expressions, gestures, tone of voice, etc., give you a clue as to what the judge was thinking?

1	2	3	4	5	6	7	8	9
not at all				somewhat				very much

9. In the jury instructions in particular, did you feel that the judge, by tone of voice, facial expressions, or any type of behavior other than his or her actual words, let you know what he or she thought the verdict should be?

1	2	3	4	5	6	7	8	9
not at all				somewhat				very much

10. Additional comments about how the judge handled the trial?

11a. In general, what are your political beliefs?

1	2	3	4	5	6	7	8	9
very liberal				middle				very conservative

11b. What is your political party? (circle)

Democrat Republican Other

12. In general, how open-minded are you?

1	2	3	4	5	6	7	8	9
not at all open-minded				somewhat				very open-minded

Lawyer Questionnaire (before verdict)

Name ________________ Date ________________
Age ________________ Name of Case ________________
Sex ________________ Defense or Prosecution (circle one)
Number of years in practice ____________________________

1. In this trial, did the judge keep order in the courtroom?

1	2	3	4	5	6	7	8	9
not at all				somewhat				very much

2a. In this trial, did the judge speak clearly?

1	2	3	4	5	6	7	8	9
not at all clearly				somewhat clearly				very clearly

2b. In the jury instructions in particular, did the judge speak clearly?

1	2	3	4	5	6	7	8	9
not at all clearly				somewhat clearly				very clearly

3. In this trial, did the judge treat the lawyers and jurors with respect and concern?

1	2	3	4	5	6	7	8	9
not at all				somewhat				very much

4. Overall, how competent was the judge in this trial?

1	2	3	4	5	6	7	8	9
not at all competent				somewhat competent				very competent

5. In this trial, how interested did the judge seem?

1	2	3	4	5	6	7	8	9
not at all interested				somewhat interested				very interested

6. In this trial, how open-minded was the judge? lawyer(s)?

1	2	3	4	5	6	7	8	9
not at all open-minded				somewhat open-minded				very open-minded

7a. In this trial, which side do you think the judge thought should win?

1	2	3	4	5	6	7	8	9
very much for the defendant				split				very much for the prosecution

7b. How could you tell this?

8. In this trial, to what extent did the judge's facial expressions, gestures, tone of voice, etc., give you a clue as to what the judge was thinking?

1	2	3	4	5	6	7	8	9
not at all				somewhat				very much

9. In the jury instructions in particular, did you feel that the judge, by tone of voice, facial expressions, or any type of behavior other than his or her actual words, let you know what he or she thought the verdict should be?

1	2	3	4	5	6	7	8	9
not at all				somewhat				very much

10. In this trial, how competent was the jury?

1	2	3	4	5	6	7	8	9
not at all competent				somewhat competent				very competent

11. How often have you appeared in the judge's court for matters other than arraignments? (approximate number of appearances) ___________

If you were the defense attorney, please answer question 12.

12a. Defendant's sex _________ race _________ age _________
Highest level of education ___________
Socioeconomic background (circle one)
low medium high

12b. Defendant's prior criminal history (circle).

Felony arrests	yes	no
Felony convictions	yes	no
Misdemeanor arrests	yes	no
Misdemeanor convictions	yes	no

13. Additional comments about the judge's behavior in this trial?

14a. In general, what are your political beliefs?

1	2	3	4	5	6	7	8	9
very liberal				middle				very conservative

14b. What is your political party? (circle)

Democrat Republican Other

15. In general, how open-minded are you?

1	2	3	4	5	6	7	8	9
not at all open-minded				somewhat				very open-minded

APPENDIX C

RATING QUESTIONNAIRE OF THE JUDGES' BEHAVIOR

Name ____________________ Trial ____________________
Sex ____________________ Trial Date ____________________
Date ____________________ Judge ____________________

SEGMENT NUMBER ___

not at all Warm	1 2 3 4 5 6 7 8 9	very Warm
not at all Hostile	1 2 3 4 5 6 7 8 9	very Hostile
not at all Anxious	1 2 3 4 5 6 7 8 9	very Anxious
not at all Dominant	1 2 3 4 5 6 7 8 9	very Dominant
not at all Competent	1 2 3 4 5 6 7 8 9	very Competent
not at all Professional	1 2 3 4 5 6 7 8 9	very Professional
not at all Wise	1 2 3 4 5 6 7 8 9	very Wise
not at all Open-minded	1 2 3 4 5 6 7 8 9	very Open-minded
not at all Dogmatic	1 2 3 4 5 6 7 8 9	very Dogmatic
not at all Honest	1 2 3 4 5 6 7 8 9	very Honest

Based on this segment, the judge believes the jury should find the defendant:

1	2	3	4	5	6	7	8	9
Definitely Guilty		Probably Guilty		Not Sure		Probably Innocent		Definitely Innocent

Acknowledgments

Kassin, Saul M. and Lawrence S. Wrightsman. "On the Requirements of Proof: The Timing of Judicial Instruction and Mock Juror Verdicts." *Journal of Personality and Social Psychology* 37 (1979): 1877–87. Copyright 1979 by the American Psychological Association, Inc. Reprinted by permission. Courtesy of Yale University Sterling Memorial Library.

Severance, Laurence J., Edith Greene, and Elizabeth F. Loftus. "Toward Criminal Jury Instructions that Jurors Can Understand." *Journal of Criminal Law & Criminology* 75 (1984): 198–233. Reprinted with the permission of Northwestern University School of Law. Courtesy of Yale University Law Library.

Wissler, Roselle L. and Michael J. Saks. "On the Inefficacy of Limiting Instructions: When Jurors Use Prior Conviction Evidence to Decide on Guilt." *Law and Human Behavior* 9 (1985): 37–48. Reprinted with the permission of Plenum Press. Courtesy of Yale University Law Library.

Imwinkelried, Edward J. and Lloyd R. Schwed. "Guidelines for Drafting Understandable Jury Instructions: An Introduction to the Use of Psycholinguistics." *Criminal Law Bulletin* 23 (1987): 135–50. Reprinted with the permission of Warren, Gorham and Lamont, Inc. Courtesy of Yale University Law Library.

Hoffheimer, Michael H. "Effect of Particularized Instructions on Evaluation of Eyewitness Identification Evidence." *Law & Psychology Review* 13 (1989): 43–58. Reprinted with the permission of the University of Alabama, School of Law. Courtesy of Yale University Law Library.

Kramer, Geoffrey P. and Dorean M. Koenig. "Do Jurors Understand Criminal Jury Instructions? Analyzing the Results of the Michigan Juror Comprehension Project." *University of Michigan Journal of Law Reform* 23 (1990): 401–37. Reprinted with the permission of the University of Michigan Law School. Courtesy of Yale University Law Library.

Horowitz, Irwin A., Kenneth S. Bordens, and Marc S. Feldman. "A Comparison of Verdicts Obtained in Severed and Joined Criminal Trials." *Journal of Applied Social Psychology* 10 (1980): 444–56. Reprinted with the permission of V.H. Winston & Son, Inc. Courtesy of Yale University Sterling Memorial Library.

Davis, James H., Robert W. Holt, Craig E. Spitzer, and Garold Stasser. "The Effects of Consensus Requirements and Multiple Decisions on Mock Juror Verdict Preferences." *Journal of Experimental Social Psychology* 17 (1981): 1–15. Reprinted with the permission of Academic Press Inc. Courtesy of Yale University Sterling Memorial Library.

Tanford, Sarah and Steven Penrod. "Biases in Trials Involving Defendants Charged with Multiple Offenses." *Journal of Applied Social Psychology* 12 (1982): 453–80. Reprinted with the permission of V.H. Winston & Son, Inc. Courtesy of Yale University Sterling Memorial Library.

Goodman, Jane, Edith Greene, and Elizabeth F. Loftus. "Runaway Verdicts or Reasoned Determinations: Mock Juror Strategies in Awarding Damages." *Jurimetics Journal* 29 (1989): 285–309. Reprinted with the permission of the American Bar Association. Courtesy of Yale University Law Library.

Loftus, Elizabeth F. and Willem A. Wagenaar. "Lawyers' Predictions of Success." *Jurimetics Journal* 28 (1988): 437–53. Reprinted with the permission of the American Bar Association. Courtesy of Yale University Law Library.

Raitz, Allan, Edith Greene, Jane Goodman, and Elizabeth F. Loftus. "Determining Damages: The Influence of Expert Testimony on Jurors' Decision Making." *Law and Human Behavior* 14 (1990): 385–95. Reprinted with the permission of Plenum Press. Courtesy of Yale University Law Library.

Notes. "Judges' Nonverbal Behavior in Jury Trials: A Threat to Judicial Impartiality." *Virginia Law Review* 61 (1975): 1266–98. Reprinted with the permission of the University of Virginia, School of Law. Courtesy of Yale University Law Library.

Blanck, Peter David, Robert Rosenthal, LaDoris Hazzard Cordell. "The Appearance of Justice: Judges' Verbal and Nonverbal Behavior in Criminal Jury Trials." *Stanford Law Review* 38 (1985): 89–164. Reprinted with the permission of the Board of Trustees of the Leland Stanford Junior University. Copyright 1985. Courtesy of Yale University Law Library.

For Product Safety Concerns and Information please contact our EU representative GPSR@taylorandfrancis.com
Taylor & Francis Verlag GmbH, Kaufingerstraße 24, 80331 München, Germany

www.ingramcontent.com/pod-product-compliance
Ingram Content Group UK Ltd.
Pitfield, Milton Keynes, MK11 3LW, UK
UKHW022206190926
475702UK00003B/235
9780815314226